STATE TERRORISM
AND THE UNITED STATES

STATE TERRORISM
AND THE UNITED STATES

From Counterinsurgency to the War on Terrorism

Frederick H. Gareau

Clarity Press, Inc.

Atlanta

Zed Books

London

In-house editor: Diana G. Collier

*State Terrorism and the United States: From Counterinsurgency to the
War on Terrorism* was first published in the United States
by Clarity Press, Inc.

Published outside North America by Zed Books Ltd.

Library of Congress Cataloging-in-Publication Data

Gareau, Frederick H. (Frederick Henry)
State terrorism and the United States : from counterinsurgency to the
war on terrorism / by   Frederick H. Gareau.
    p. cm.
Includes bibliographical references and index.
 ISBN 0-932863-39-6
 1. State-sponsored terrorism. 2. United States—Foreign
relations—20th century. 3. United States—Foreign relations—2001- 4.
Victims of state-sponsored terrorism. 5. War on Terrorism, 2001- 6.
Human rights. 7. Counterinsurgency. 8. United States—Military
relations. 9. Intervention (International law) I. Title.
 HV6432.G373 2004
 303.6'25—dc22

                       2003017816

A catalogue record for this book is available from the British Library

Zed ISBN: 1 84277 535 9

Cover design by Impact Graphics
Photo Credit: AP/Wide World Photos

CLARITY PRESS, INC.   ZED BOOKS
Ste. 469, 3277 Roswell Rd. NE   7 Cynthia Street
Atlanta, GA. 30305   London N1 9JF

http://www.claritypress.com   http://www.zedbooks.demon.co.uk

Acknowledgments

As I read and reread the manuscript that has now become this book, I was struck by the improvements in it suggested by Diana Collier, my Editor at Clarity Press. During its preparation, Diana sent a steady stream of emails my way that arrived on weekdays, weekends, and holidays. She had little time left over to go to the beach. Their acceptance improved both the form and the substance of the pages that follow. Even before its acceptance by the editorial board, she encouraged me to go ahead with the project. Edna, my *esposa fiel,* left her imprint on the book as well. She was ever ready to help, and did so when requested. She did not complain as the grass in the front yard grew higher and higher, and the neighbors scowled more and more. We did not go to the beach. When the computer, a vital tool in the preparation of the manuscript, was disobedient, I called upon my good friend Koichi to bring it into line. He did so cheerfully, expertly, and expeditiously.

My debt is broader and deeper than this. It is owed above all to my gang, my support group—an extended family of relatives and friends that make my life bearable and enjoyable. Without Mom and Pop, there would be no gang. They were the best of all parents and my first and best teachers. They taught me to hate war, and Pop taught me that I was a member of the working class. Their love is ever present, as is the love of my son, Karl. He has passed away also. Maggie's love and voice are members. We talk on the phone, and love each other as only father and daughter can. Edna's love is always there, and it was in her Brazil that I learned to be critical of the establishment. Florence is the matriarch of the group, a fiercely loyal and generous sister. She became a nurse to help people and rose to the rank of a navy captain in the public health service. Hers is the success story of the gang, but she also makes great cookies. Anna and Fred are valued friends and gang members, ever ready to help with their time, their cars, and their house. With his photographic memory, Fred provides the database for the gang's history. Anna is our linguist, but she also is a good cook. Mother and daughter, niece and grandniece, Julie and Donna are members. Julie took care of Mom when she was sick. Donna, the beauty of the group, returns faithfully each month from central Florida, and the gang eats together at Anna's. A former student of mine left over from the seventies, Ed is a member by telephone. He calls nearly every day, and we exchange men's talk, coarse discourse meant to disguise that we care for each other.

Table of Contents

Introduction

This entire book is written in blood and
with much love for our country.*

TERRORISM STRIKES HOME

Shortly after nine in the morning on September 11th, 2001 my sister Florence phoned to tell me that two airplanes had crashed into the twin towers of the World Trade Center in New York City and set them on fire. I turned on the television, watching intermittently as I continued to work on this book on terrorism. I was working on the chapter on Chile and had just finished reading the *Report of the Chilean National Commission on Truth and Reconciliation*, a 907-page report on the "forced disappearances" that occurred during the previous 17 year administration of General Pinochet. Based on thousands of interviews, the two-volume account indicated that it had identified the names but not the remains of 2,279 "disappeared" persons, though many more still remained unnamed. These unfortunates were secretly killed, their bodies burned or thrown into the ocean. This was done to add to the torment of the surviving families by denying them closure and the comfort that comes from a proper burial. Sometimes the victims' stomachs had been cut open before they were thrown into the ocean so that their bodies would not wash ashore.

As I sat before the computer, similarities between the United States and Chile came to mind. One such convergence is the belief of the country's citizens in its "exceptionalism"—their country does not act like other countries—although the North American belief seems to be more encompassing and enduring. Chile has not had a long history of coups and of the military governments that result from them. Its citizens have insisted that Chile is not a "banana republic". At least, this was their belief before the 1973 coup.

Later, I would discover another similarity. Many of the families of the victims of the September 11th disaster would also be denied closure—though this likely had not been part of the perpetrators' intent. This, because many of the victims of the twin towers disaster were burned beyond recognition and beyond identification by DNA matching. New York policemen and firemen, lucky enough because of their former positions to be allowed to come to ground zero, were coming every morning to search for, and remain close to, their departed sons. They picked through the debris looking for clues—a ring, a piece of familiar clothing, or a body part to rush off to the DNA laboratory. A 63-year-old retired fireman found the remains of one son, but not the other. He continued to exercise his visiting privileges, searching the debris, and telling his missing son that he loved him.

As I sat before the computer, suddenly a startling coincidence came to mind: the coup that deposed the President of Chile, Salvador Allende, and introduced the dictatorship of General Pinochet had also occurred on September

---

*These words were first written by Cardinal Arns, Archbishop of Sao Paulo, concerning a Archdiocese report on torture in Brazil[1] and I echo them here in this book on state terrorism, with great love for my own country, the United States.

11th! The terrorist attacks on the World Trade Center and on the Pentagon took place on the twenty-eighth anniversary of the coup in Chile. General Pinochet, the newly installed dictator, declared September 11th to be a national holiday. The terrorists crashed their planes into the twin towers of the trade center at 8:48 A.M. and 15 minutes later at 9:03, creating an inferno that burned thousands of innocent victims alive. The Chilean putschists started their conventional bombing runs on the presidential palace La Moneda at 11:52 A.M. The palace was set on fire, President Allende committed suicide, and the military took over. A further striking coincidence: the twin towers of the World Trade Center were dedicated in April of 1973—five months before the Chilean coup.

The series of terrorist acts committed on September 11th constituted private terrorism, but they were unusual insofar as they were of such a large dimension as to rival state terrorism. Because of its relatively low mortality rates prior to this date, private terrorism has been labeled "retail terrorism" whereas state terrorism has been called "wholesale terrorism". The three acts of private terrorism committed on American soil on that date, however, cost the lives of an estimated 3,119 victims who died or were missing and presumed dead.[2] This did not count the 19 terrorists who perpetrated the crimes. Two thousand eight hundred and ninety-five met this fate at the World Trade Center, 184 at the Pentagon, and 40 in Pennsylvania. Coverage of the tragedies committed at the trade center received the most attention, and rightfully so. However, I was personally most affected and outraged by the attack on the Pentagon, where I might have worked during my five-year stint with Air Force Intelligence, had the Pentagon had room to house it.

DEFINING TERRORISM: PROBLEMS AND PERSPECTIVES

This volume focuses on terrorism—actually state terrorism—even if a good deal of its content is given over to the related subjects of human rights and torture. My first inclination was to lay aside all definitions and let the acts of terror, torture, and violations of human rights portrayed in the volume speak for themselves without labels. But I was made aware while doing the research for a textbook on the United Nations of the extent to which diplomats formulate definitions to satisfy their particular political agendas.[3] As indicated in Chapter 5, the South African government passed an anti-terrorist law in 1967 which viewed the phenomenon in such a manner that virtually any political or social act came under its purview. Cooperating with UNICEF to reduce infant mortality or revealing the misconduct of a state official could have been construed as "terrorism" by the white South African government of that time. P.W. Botha, the head of the apartheid government, characterized Nelson Mandela, the head of the African National Congress, as a "communist terrorist." On the other hand, the American Democratic Party's 1998 platform referred to South Africa itself as a "terrorist state." Clearly, some definitions are required if the observer is to escape being the victim of any particular state's agenda.

The United Nations has never been able to define terrorism, though several times the world organization has condemned it in the abstract or specific acts of it. The explanation for this should not be sought in the predisposition of diplomats for meticulous precision. They are forced to operate in that murky realm that mixes semantics with politics, and politics has dominion. Diplomats on any given side of an issue are forced to promote certain political agendas, and, to reiterate the well-known saying: one man's terrorist is another man's freedom fighter. The anti-colonial third world exempted guerrillas fighting for independence from this denomination. The United Nations did recognize the legitimacy of liberation movements fighting for independence, but that still leaves open the question of how the fight was carried on. Washington either excused infractions committed by those third world governments it supported, or labeled them "violations of human rights" rather than the more abusive term, terrorism.

A definition of terrorism has become critical since Washington has become engaged in "the war on terrorism." The question has become: just what is it that we are fighting against? The General Assembly and the Security Council dutifully condemned the attacks of September 11th, and this time the Security Council ordered the members of the world organization to report on the actions they are taking to combat terrorism. One hundred and seventeen responses were received, and the chairperson of the Council's counter terrorism committee stated that "an extremely good start" had been made. However, human rights groups warned of the dangers of a battle where there is no definition of the enemy.[4] Mary Robinson, the United Nations High Commissioner for Human Rights, charged that what has been done in some countries is to use the international duty to act against terrorism as an excuse to suppress the legitimate expression of grievances and to justify the oppression of minorities. The government of Zimbabwe labels as "terrorists" journalists who report on political violence. Human Rights Watch charges that both China and Russia use the preoccupation with terrorism to deal with their minority problems. China does this in dealing with Muslims in Xinjiang province who seek independence, and Russia applies it in Chechnya. Uzbekistan has arrested thousands of members of the Islamic Movement of Uzbekistan, a group linked to al Qaeda by Washington. Human Rights Watch also noted that Israel uses the issue of terrorism to justify its oppressive actions against the Palestinians.

The Post 9-11 Rush to Pin the Terrorist Label

George Bush's post 9-11 declaration of "war on terrorism" was followed by a rash of similar labeling worldwide, as states jumped on the bandwagon, and sought to tar their enemies with the terrorist brush. On July 16, 2002 the Indian government renewed its demand that Washington declare Pakistan a terrorist state.[5] This was just four days after an attack by Kashmiri terrorists wounded at least 13 in Anantnag, Kashmir. An Indian spokesman declared that Washington could put an end to the terrorist structure in Kashmir supported by Pakistan by declaring Pakistan to be a terrorist state. Of course, Washington did not do this, nor did it declare Pakistan to be a supporter of Kashmiri terrorists despite the existence of substantial evidence that the latter was the case. This is an example of the non-use of the term, when its use was justified. To use it would have been contrary to Washington's then current attempts to befriend the government of Pakistan.

That the definition of terrorism is not only political, but also unusually malleable and negotiable is suggested by Washington's treatment of the East Turkestan Islamic Movement. In late August 2002 a visiting American diplomat in Beijing disclosed that Washington had acted to freeze the financial assets of this Islamic group because it had indiscriminately killed civilians. Deputy Secretary of State Richard L. Armitage stated, "after careful study we judged that it was a terrorist group, that it committed acts of violence against unarmed civilians without any regard for who was hurt."[6] Early the next month Washington joined China in persuading the United Nations to add the organization to the global watch list of rld institution. A Chinese spokesman characterized this as "an encouraging re from China's cooperation with the United States and other countries in fighting terrorism."[7] On September 12th, a State Department spokesman charged that the Islamic organization "is a violent group believed responsible for committing numerous acts of terrorism in China, including bombings of buses, movie theaters, department stores, markets and motels; assassination; and arson." The charge has been greeted with skepticism by many scholars and Western diplomats. The State Department did not provide specific evidence to substantiate its charge. Rather it rehashed old Chinese allegations, but with one big difference. Beijing attributed its list of atrocities to some nine violent organizations operating in Xinjiang province, whereas State attributed what appeared to be the same list to the East Turkestan Islamic Movement. In any case, Beijing scored a diplomatic victory in its offensive against this movement in a campaign that it initiated in January 2002.

A self-serving brand of politics rather than semantics or logic was again uppermost as President Bush prepared to attend the Asia-Pacific Economic Forum held in Shanghai in October 2001. Bush's aids were reported "scrambling to find a middle ground at the summit meeting with a declaration against terrorism that leaves every country free to define how it pursues that mission."[8] Already the Bush administration was carefully avoiding the term "dissidents" to describe the Muslim separatists in the far western region of Xinjiang, China and in Tibet. The Chinese government for its part has claimed that "these terrorists" have been trained and financed by Osama bin Laden and the Taliban.[9] Since September 11th, Beijing has justified its suppression of these separatists as being part of the international war on terrorism. It has seized upon this war as an excuse to curtail religious freedom in Xinjiang and to suppress ethnic separatism there. As will be revealed in the following chapters, Beijing's behavior is typical of that of state terrorists during the Cold War. They pinned the label "terrorist" on the leftist opposition, whether it was violent or not. Chapter 4 reveals that state terrorism in Argentina had an anti-Semitic side to it, and Chapter 2 indicates that state terrorism in Guatemala was charged with being anti-Catholic, while the suppression of the Mayas in Guatemala reached such a level that it was branded "genocide".

The serpentine nature of the term "terrorists" was revealed when former Yugoslav leader Slobodan Milosevic based his defense on it before the International Criminal Court for the Former Yugoslavia at The Hague, claiming that he was protecting the Serbian population from terrorists.[10] This is the standard claim made by state terrorists, despite the fact that state terrorism is far more lethal than private terrorism. Milosevic's government killed thousands of ethnic Albanians and ethnic-cleansed hundreds of thousands more. The ethnic Albanian separatists produced far fewer victims.

A Definition of Terrorism

Terrorism consists of deliberate acts of a physical and/or psychological nature perpetrated on select groups of victims. Its intent is to mold the thinking and behavior not only of these targeted groups, but more importantly, of larger sections of society that identify or share the views and aspirations of the targeted groups or who might easily be led to do so. The intent of the terrorists is to intimidate or coerce both groups by causing them intense fear, anxiety, apprehension, panic, dread, and/or horror. Obviously, the groups that have been directly targeted experience these emotions to a much higher degree than the larger sections of society that the terrorism is also intended to intimidate and coerce. The overall purpose of terrorism is to intimidate and coerce, not to eliminate a group physically or socially. The latter is called genocide. The classic example is the Holocaust, in which the Nazis tried to kill all the Jews. That the two concepts terrorism and genocide can overlap, however, is illustrated in Chapter 2, which indicates that the government of Guatemala tried to eliminate, either physically or culturally, at least one Mayan group, the Ixil.

Human rights are those rights that every human being possesses by virtue of his or her being human. Terrorism is a violation of human rights, but the converse is not always true. Burning people alive by kamikaze-type crashes is both an act of terror and a violation of human rights, but denying one the right of freedom of speech is not an act of terrorism. Terrorism is inflicted by the use of torture, which also can be physical or psychological. But torture can also be used to punish the victim, or to obtain information or a confession from him or her.[11]

The definition of terrorism adopted here is broad, including that practiced by states (state or government terrorism) and individuals (private terrorism), during peace or war. This study concentrates on the state terrorism of rightwing dictatorships, but it also discusses the private terrorism of guerrillas and those who committed the September 11th attack. The terrorism of the rightwing dictatorships was directed at those who challenged or sought to change the status quo, while the terrorism of those who would change or overturn the status quo was directed at the government and at those who supported both it and the status quo. While the definition of terrorism used in this study is broad, including that practiced by individuals and states, during wars or peace, this volume's special focus is its systematic application by the state for political ends.

Monitoring Terrorism

Washington publishes an annual list of governments that it alleges aid terrorists. Typically, this list contains a majority of governments of Arab states plus Iran, Cuba, and North Korea. This highlights the importance of how terrorism is defined. If state terrorism were included in the definition, Washington would have to include itself on the list! In 1974, amendments to a foreign assistance act built the foundation for a system of monitoring and reporting on the human rights situation in countries receiving U.S. aid. The amendments required the president "except in extraordinary circumstances" substantially to reduce or to terminate aid to any government "which engages in a consistent pattern of gross violations of internationally recognized human rights."[12] The president was obliged to advise Congress of the extraordinary circumstances concerned.

The legislation was later broadened and toughened. "No assistance" was decreed, as well as presidential certification, and other provisions. The Carter administration upgraded the official in the State Department responsible for human rights from a coordinator to the Assistant Secretary for Human Rights and Humanitarian Affairs. The Clinton administration produced further reforms. Since 1977 the State Department has been publishing the annual, *Country Reports on Human Rights Practices*. This publication started small with only 137 pages and contained an assessment of the human rights situation in only those countries which received aid from the United States. By the year 2000 the publication had grown to a total of 6,000 pages of typescript, setting forth the State Department's estimate of the fate of human rights in 194 countries. Within a week of its publication, 150,000 people either read or downloaded at least part of the report.

Congress, for its part, has decreed that the executive cut off aid to any country that by its actions reveals a consistent pattern of violating human rights. No matter the restrictions, administrations determined to provide aid to governments practicing terrorism or in other ways violating human rights have usually succeeded. Moreover, the restrictions and the reporting give the impression that Washington is a firm upholder of human rights and a foe of terrorism.

A guide to terrorism published in 1988 asserted that proving "state terrorism is usually more difficult than proving insurgent (private) terrorism."[13] The guide went on to explain that except in unusual circumstances such as the Nuremburg and Tokyo trials there are no courts collecting evidence that prove that a regime is guilty of state terror. But the situation has changed. International criminal courts have been set up for Rwanda and the former Yugoslavia, and one with general jurisdiction, the International Criminal Court, has been established as well. More significantly, this evidentiary deficiency has been filled by truth commission reports--extensive studies, each based on thousands of interviews conducted under the auspices of post-terrorist governments, the United Nations, or the Catholic Church.

At least one of these reports has been completed for each of the following countries: El Salvador, Guatemala, Chile, Argentina, and South Africa. This study used these reports as the evidentiary base for analyzing the situation in these countries and may be the first to draw on an aggregation of their findings. Most typical were the studies used for El Salvador and Guatemala. The United Nations sponsored one study for each of these countries after it had helped negotiate settlements of what were generally referred to as guerrilla wars. The studies were published in 1993 and 1999. The one on El Salvador was based on the interviews of 22,000 people. The findings of the study on Guatemala were generally in accord with the findings of a later but similar study sponsored by the Catholic Archdiocese of Guatemala City. This study was notable in that most of the interviews were carried on in Mayan languages. Two days after the Archdiocese of Guatemala issued its report, Bishop Juan Gerardi, the head of the project that produced it, was beaten to death with a cement block. He had also served as the director of the Human Rights Office of Guatemala City's Archdiocese. In its own ugly way, his murder testified to the authenticity of the report. Based on 7,380 interviews, the original report of the commission on Argentina came to 50,000 pages. The report published by the truth commission for South Africa was packaged in five volumes and came to 2,759 pages. It was based on over 21,296 statements of victims and 7,000 amnesty applications filed by the guilty.

THE CONTENTS OF THIS BOOK

The data generated by the above-mentioned studies are used as the evidentiary backbone for the five chapters that follow this introductory one. These countries in order are El Salvador, Guatemala, Chile, Argentina, and South Africa. Each one of these five chapters focuses on the study of one country, except that the first chapter also includes a portrayal of the School of the Americas. Thus the search for validity, the attempt to convince the critical, is a main ingredient in determining the contents of this study. The strong representation of Latin America is explained by the existence of truth commission reports there, by the quality of the evidence available for these countries. Indonesia is added so that Asia would be represented in the sample, and South Africa also expands the geographical base of the study. There is no truth commission for Indonesia, but there is evidence that serves in its place. Examples are provided by the Secretary-General of the United Nations, the head of the Human Rights Commission of the United Nations, the foreign minister of the Vatican, and a local bishop in East Timor who was co-winner of the Nobel Peace Prize in 1996.

Other reliable sources are called upon to enhance the credibility of the conclusions reached in the study. One such source is that offered by Father Falla, a Jesuit priest and an anthropologist who interviewed hundreds of surviving Indians fleeing the Guatemalan highlands to seek refuge in Mexico. Another is a CIA study that focuses on the agency's relations with Chile during, and especially before, the Pinochet years. A systematic study of the recorded votes cast in the United Nations General Assembly is included in chapter 3 to mark the relative relationship of Washington with the Pinochet regime. Another United Nations source used was the task force set up by the world organization to determine the devastation caused by the repression in southern Africa. The six countries chosen for detailed exposure are all from the third world, but they are diverse in size and in population, and to some extent in location.

Chapter 7 adds both geographic width and historic depth to the study. It expands its geographic and historical reach to include many cases and many administrations. It examines the relations of administrations from Harding through Clinton to a diverse set of administrations and situations in Africa and Latin America, but also in Europe and Asia. Washington not only aided the Contras in their terrorist activities against the Sandanista government, but it also engaged in terrorism itself. Most of the terrorist governments supported by Washington were rightwing dictatorships, but the chapter includes its support for the Khmer Rouge, usually regarded as an extreme leftist government, which occurred because of Khmer Rouge opposition to the Soviet Union.

Chapter 8 examines Washington's policies in the Middle East in an effort to comprehend the roots of the terrorist response. While it inevitably addresses Washington's long and almost solitary support for Israel, it also investigates what many would consider to be the incredible charges that for years Washington supported Saddam Hussein in Iraq. The ideologies and the political interests involved in these scenarios are not those common to the other cases examined in the first chapters of this study. However, these charges deserve to be investigated for the light they shed upon the conclusions of the study. The investigation of support for Saddam Hussein is the more interesting, because the ideologies and the political interests involved then are also present in Washington's support for dictators in the war against terrorism. The reason the Iraqi dictator was given support was that he was fighting an Iranian government dominated by an Islamic clergy that subscribed to an extreme form of their religion. The fear was and remains that they would spread this form of Islam throughout the Middle East to the detriment of Western interests. Chapter 9 examines the war on terrorism. It discusses the new Bush doctrine of preemption, and examines both how and with what success that doctrine has been applied in Afghanistan and Iraq. It also briefly addresses the emergence of counterterrorism, reflected in Washington's support for it in Russia, Algeria and Colombia. Chapter 10 sets forth the major findings of the study and presents further corroborative materials relevant to the validity of these findings: quantitative studies on the export of arms, especially to those countries that violate human rights. Washington's resistance to the establishment of the International Criminal Court is examined. Suggestions for an appropriate response to terrorism are put forward, with a view to modifying and recasting the war on terrorism so that it does not result in the creation of more terrorists. The establishment of a truth commission to investigate Washington's support for state terrorism is called for, so that the American public will find out what has been done in its name.

The Central Questions of This Research

Archbishop Tutu's views are rich in allusions having a bearing on the purpose, contents, and perspective of the current study. Winner of the Nobel Prize for Peace in 1984 and Chair of the Truth and Reconciliation Commission in South Africa, Tutu had no difficulty in distinguishing between the moral and legal position of the apartheid regime that ruled South Africa and those who fought against it: those who fought against this unjust apartheid regime clearly were fighting for a just cause while the government was "an illegal, oppressive, and inhuman system imposed on the majority without their consent."[14] This moral and legal superiority was interpreted to mean that in principle the state terrorism and other acts of oppression committed by the government were immoral and illegal, whereas the bellicose acts by the guerrillas were not. I agree with the archbishop, and I apply the same judgment generally to the cases of state terrorism supported by Washington discussed in this study. Like the other truth commissions, the one for South Africa applied the "two devil theory" to the conflict. Regardless of whether the goal was just or unjust, the means applied to attain it had to meet certain standards, one being that of not targeting "soft targets". The targeting of civilians was off limits. This is in accord with international law that regards this practice as a war crime, and with just war theory that condemns it as immoral. I apply this principle both to the Cold War and to the current war on terrorism, to the governments and to the private forces involved in these struggles.

This principle is applied not only to those who commit terrorism, but also to those who give support to terrorists. This study concentrates on Washington's support of state terrorists during these "two wars," acting as an accomplice to governments that terrorize groups seeking to improve society and that target civilians to accomplish their aims, or who join the war on terrorism. Archbishop Tutu observed that the communist threat was taken seriously by Pretoria and by many other governments. The government of South Africa was far from being alone in its crusade against communism. Nations defined themselves in terms of the Cold War, and it acted as the determinant in identifying allies and surrogates and in determining the size of defense budgets. As a result, Tutu pointed out, prominent democracies such as the United States were led to support "some of the world's worst dictatorships, such as Pinochet's government in Chile." They did not seem to care about the human rights records of their "surrogates." The reader is reminded that the "human rights violations" to which Tutu usually referred—those with which this study is concerned—are in fact instances of terrorism practiced by the state, and perpetrated on its own citizens, and that this type of violation is the one featured in this study.

The main reason for my writing, and for encouraging you to read, this volume is to have you examine the evidence that I have gathered that indicates that Washington was, and continues to be, an accomplice to state terrorism. This venture is a moral and a legal one, offered in the face of the knowledge that, while many realists look askance at international law and look upon the welfare of other people and other nations as political currency available to be spent freely in the promotion of selfish and national interests, others rightly find that such behavior demands a heavy price, one that they refuse to pay, and seek to resist. It is true that the Cold War was won without a nuclear holocaust, a tribute to both Washington and Moscow and that Washington has the right to defend the United States against terrorism. But Washington's victory was paid for by the blood and horror of the victims of state terrorism in the many dictatorships that Washington supported, and Washington is repeating this practice. The injustice is the more egregious in that state terrorists enjoyed, and continue to enjoy, a general impunity, despite the fact that their crimes are more reprehensible and numerous than those of the private terrorists.

The evidence presented on the six principal countries examined in the study responds to these three central questions:

1) Did the government being studied actually commit state terrorism? Other forms of government repression such as torture and violations of human rights will be looked for as well.

2) Given that each of the governments examined was engaged in combating a guerrilla war, to what extent was the terror committed by states, and to what extent was it private terror committed by the guerrillas? The answer to this question is facilitated by the fact that the truth commissions operated on the basis of the "two-devil theory." They investigated the terror and atrocities committed both by the government and by the guerrillas. An auxiliary issue addressed by the study is the extent to which the perpetrators got away with it.

3) Was the country that perpetrated the terror upon its own citizens actually supported by Washington? In what ways was this support provided? For example, did Washington train the forces in counterinsurgency so that later they could commit the terror? Did it provide weapons for these forces, or cover up for them after the terror had been committed? Details of this support will also be investigated and documented.

This study also addresses state terrorism subsequent to September 11th, 2001. It will ask: has Washington's call for a war on terrorism impacted other states in such a manner as to support their commission of state terrorism, and has direct American action in Afghanistan and Iraq itself entailed acts of state terrorism? A critique of the way that the war on terrorism is being conducted, especially the wars in Iraq and Afghanistan, is included.

A "Practical" Reason for Examining the Charge Against Washington

Morality and legality aside, there exists a quite "practical" reason for examining the charge that Washington has supported "some of the world's worst dictatorships." This reason should appeal to the realist. The support took the form of a tripartite pattern in which Washington supported rightwing dictators against what was advertised as an internal communist threat. The victims of the resulting government repression and terror were often insurgent guerrillas, but they included a wide spectrum of society—teachers, union leaders, priests, nuns, workers, and peasants. This is the dark side of the Cold War, which could engender—perhaps it already has—hatred and antipathy in the victims and their survivors, possibly providing the basis for the cultivation of new crops of terrorists. A review of the Cold War period provides the opportunity to be forewarned of the pitfalls of such a policy in waging the war on terrorism. This opportunity is based on the widely held assumption that the policies implemented in Washington have impacts on other countries and groups, including their policies toward the United States. This assumption is more logical than the romantic notion floated by President Bush that the attacks of September 11th were based on the jealousy harbored by the terrorists as they viewed the freedom that Americans enjoy. Mr. Hamid Mir, the one journalist who has interviewed bin Laden after the September 11th attacks, recognized this when he declared that bin Laden is not a hero in much of the third world because of his ideas. He is a hero by default. The Pakistani journalist insisted that "Osama bin Laden's real strength is bad American policies."[15] The tripartite pattern of the Cold War could follow the same pattern as that of the Arab-Israeli dispute and produce similar results.

The tripartite pattern found in the Arab-Israeli struggle is one of the major causes of the anger and hatred of the Arabs and the Muslims directed not only against Israel, but also against the United States. The Arab and Muslim worlds often hold guilty not only Israel, but also the United States. In their eyes, the principal is guilty, but also those whom they regard as the accomplice who provided the support and aid that has allowed and continues to allow the principal to behave in the way it does. As one observer stated with respect to the Arab-Israeli conflict, the anger and outrage felt by madrasa students, those attending Quranic schools, is overwhelming and pervasive. After Friday prayer in a mosque in Islamabad, a group of these students shouted: "Israel engages in terrorism every day! Why doesn't America do something about that."[16]

Assigning Guilt for the Support of Terrorism

My first reaction is to assign the guilt resulting from supporting rightwing terrorist regimes during the Cold War and terrorist regimes during the war on terrorism to the American elites, not to the American public. These elites manipulate this public, which is generally oblivious to its government's support of those rulers who practiced and are practicing terrorism. So it appears not to be morally responsible. However, the reader is asked to visit Chapter 5 on South Africa for a thoughtful analysis of the guilt of sectors of that society. Some of the points made there might be applicable to American society. American society does have the duty as well as the right to know what Washington does and has done in its name. Democracy asks for no less. This serves as a second justification for this research. A means to increase the public's knowledge of what happened is proposed in the concluding chapter. This volume marks the distinction between the elite and the public by referring to the former as "Washington" or by indicating the specific president or administration in power. The term "United States" has been given broader meaning and includes the American public.

STATE TERRORISM AND SILENCE: HAMBURG

The plot to crash the planes on American targets on September 11th was hatched in Hamburg, the large port city in northern Germany where some of the plotters attended engineering school. Having already received an engineering degree in Cairo, the chief plotter Mohammed Atta studied city planning in the German city. Evidently with this in mind, the Hamburg Chamber of Commerce plus local churches and other organizations there took out a full-page ad in the *New York Times* two weeks after the September 11th attacks.[17] The ad declared in bold letters "America Hamburg stands by you." It went on to say that the victims of the attack "are in our deepest thoughts" and that Hamburg will never forget "your help and support in rebuilding our city after World War II." Kind words, the more so because it left unsaid the fact that during that war 60 percent of Hamburg's port facilities and 55 percent of its residential area were destroyed and 55,000 of its inhabitants were killed.[18] This was done by British "carpet bombing" in which the bomb pattern covered the target as snugly as a carpet covers a floor, mixing highly explosive weapons with incendiaries so as to cause a "fire storm" that burned out the entire target area. For ten nights as many as 700 bombers dropped a shower of bombs on the city. "Great conflagrations leap up almost simultaneously through the entire area of the attack," Martin Caidin wrote, in *The Night Hamburg Died*.[19] Hamburg's fire defenses were completely overwhelmed. Thousands of individual fires within the target area burned up the oxygen, and the resultant vacuum sucked up the individual fires and joined them in a sea of flame one and a quarter miles in diameter. This was by no means the first, nor would it be the last, such tragedy to befall a city. In fact, it was Germany, Nazi Germany, that is usually singled out and given the blame for initiating terror bombing. The first instance occurred when German planes bombed Guernica during the Spanish Civil War, the horror of which is immortalized in the painting by Picasso.

Hamburg serves here to illustrate that the definition of terror should include the phenomenon as it occurs in wars between states and also as an example of terrorism kept quiet. The 55,000 carpet-bombing victims killed in Hamburg represent somewhat more than ten percent of the half million German civilians estimated to have been killed by Allied bombing during the last years of World War II. But it was only after fifty years, at the turn of the 21st century, that *German* historians and writers finally began to write about this series of tragedies, this terror bombing.[20] It was only then that the Germans experienced a delayed collective recall, the recollection of a devastating experience that had left little trace in the written chronicles of the nation.

Why the prolonged silence, the sustained effort not to write down what happened? The answer is found in the fact that the victims of the bombing were the "generation of the perpetrators." No matter that they were soft targets: they were charged with carrying out the evil plans of Hitler, or looking the other way while others did so. This story is recounted here to highlight the overall goal of the current volume, which seeks to help break the silence that surrounds Washington's support for state terrorists during the Cold War, a support which continues during the present war on terrorism. My intention is to inform my fellow citizens as well as others of what Washington has done in our name.

I realize that I might have a hard sell, and you the reader might have an uncomfortable read, when I explore with you Washington's support for rightwing dictators, particularly when the evidence reveals that Washington supported them even though they violated the human rights of their people or worse. A hard sell and an uncomfortable read, because the American socialization process leads to the opposite conclusion, and this is now re-enforced by the patriotic feelings spurred on by the events of September 11th. But Washington, which poses as the world's ombudsman on terrorism and human rights, has invaded Iraq without United Nations support, remains there as an occupying power, and is now engaged in what it calls a war on terrorism that has an open perimeter.

CHAPTER 1

The School of the Americas and Terror in El Salvador

THE SCHOOL OF THE AMERICAS

In 1983 Father Bourgeois and two companions climbed a tree near Fort Benning, Georgia in front of the School of the Americas.[1] Once perched in this strategic location, they used a microphone to broadcast the message of Archbishop Romero, the martyred prelate who had been assassinated March 24, 1980 while celebrating mass in the Chapel of the Hospital de la Divina Providencia in El Salvador. The message called upon the soldiers in the name of God and in the name of his suffering people to stop the repression. Father Bourgeois and his two companions were forced down from the tree, stripped, beaten, and handcuffed. Bourgeois received the longest sentence, 18 months in a federal prison. It was not to be the last time that this militant priest would be sent to prison. By the year 2002, 71 demonstrators had served a total of 40 years of jail time for protesting in front of the school.[2] In 2002 alone, 29 activists were sentenced to from three to six months plus fines for trespassing. Among the group were three priests, one nun, and two Presbyterian ministers. The previous year 23 were sent to prison on the same charge. This included two nuns who are sisters, one 69 years old, the other 88 years old.[3] The latter refused "motherhouse arrest," so that she could serve her sentence with the rest of the group. One month into her sentence, however, she was transferred to a "residential facility" for health reasons. Her sister was transferred with her. The arrests have led Father Bourgeois to comment, "Those who speak out for justice are facing harsh prison sentences while School of the Americas (SOA) torturers and assassins are operating with impunity."

> By the year 2002, 71 demonstrators had served a total of 40 years of jail time for protesting in front of the School of the Americas.

These incidents—and the School of the Americas itself—provide a succinct introduction to the third central question investigated in each case study: whether the country that perpetrated the terror upon its own citizens was actually supported by Washington? In what ways was this support given? Father Bourgeois is convinced that the training of military personnel at the School of the Americas, personnel who later commit terror, makes Washington an accessory. He argues that this school is responsible for what its alumni do, a thesis explored in greater detail below, and has devoted his life to closing down the school.

Earlier in his career, Father Bourgeois antagonized the authorities in Bolivia by visiting the jails of La Paz. He found them to be filled with political prisoners. Some had obviously been tortured. Others were held incommunicado. This was during the dictatorship of General Hugo Banzar Suarez, one of the graduates of the School of the Americas. A portrait of the general hangs in the school's Hall of Fame, on the stairwell leading to the Commandant's office. A later investigation revealed that during the dictatorship of General Banzar from 1971 to 1978 his government had murdered 468 Bolivians, imprisoned or held incommunicado 4,318 for their political beliefs and activities, deported 663, and tortured 100 who had survived their ordeal.[4] During his dictatorship, the general arranged several massacres, and his main targets were peasants and labor unions, both Catholic and non-Catholic. The militant priest lays part of the blame for this at the School of the Americas. He has been denied re-entry to Bolivia.

Father Bourgeois' latest mission is located just outside the school. There the former naval officer and Vietnam veteran heads a grassroots movement called SOA Watch, one of whose purposes is to monitor and to expose the abuses committed by the school's alumni. Each year Father Bourgeois leads a demonstration against the institution, hoping that the school will soon be closed. As he puts it, "this is where the killing starts." On another occasion he remarked, "What got to me more than anything was that the killing was being done by the military we were arming and training." Exposing this became his mission because, at least at first, most Americans did not know about this U.S. taxpayer-supported institution. Their knowledge of it was certainly broadened by the Congressional hearings in 1989 into the murder of six Jesuit priests of the University of Central America, along with their cook, and her sixteen-year-old daughter. This university is located in San Salvador. The only crime of the Jesuits "was that they spoke out against the policies of the government and were perceived as FMLN (guerrilla) sympathizers."[5] An examination of the list of graduates of the School of the Americas put out by the SOA Watch indicates that no less than nineteen of the school's graduates were involved in the planning, execution, and cover-up of these murders. Actually, the orders were to kill Father Ignacio Ellacuria, Rector of the University, but to leave no witnesses, hence the execution of the other six. Two hundred SOA Watch groups have been established throughout the United States.

The School of the Americas was opened in 1946 under the name of the Latin American Training Center-Ground Division. It assumed its most persistent name in 1963, and it moved from the Canal Zone to its present location in Fort Benning, Georgia in 1984. The school officially closed on December 15, 2000— perhaps solely in an effort to escape its widely-circulated epithet as the School of Assassins—for it swiftly reopened the next January 17 with a new name: the Western Hemisphere Institute of Security Cooperation. It is located on the same premises and—according to its critics—teaches essentially the same courses to the same clientele.[6] Its original purpose was to promote closer ties with the militaries of Latin America and to assist the military and police forces in the region better to maintain control of their environment. Over time the main focus of the training became counterinsurgency and low intensity warfare, and its graduates, and others similarly trained, became notorious for their suppression of human rights and worse. More recently, the school has introduced a course in human rights, but the impact of the course is problematical. Indeed, its critics question the motive for its introduction. The school is the most famous of more than 150 facilities in **Ten of the graduates of the school became the president/dictators of their countries, 23 became ministers of defense.** the United States and abroad used to train foreign soldiers. The school has trained upward of 59,000 Latin American military personnel, policemen, and civilians. Ten of the graduates of the school became the president/dictators of their countries, 23 became ministers of defense, and 15 ministers of other departments.[7]

Serving as the head of Guatemalan Intelligence, General Manuel Antonio Callejas y Callejas was responsible for the disappearances and deaths of thousands of Guatemalans. He was not only a graduate of the school, but his

UN Report: The School of the Americas has graduated over 500 of the worst human rights abusers in the hemisphere.

portrait hangs on the wall at the school's headquarters along with that of General Banzar and other distinguished alumni who have been selected for the Hall of Fame. Over two-thirds of the more than sixty officers cited for the worst human rights abuses in

the United Nations report on the repression in El Salvador graduated from the school. It "has graduated over 500 of the worst human rights abusers in the hemisphere, who are implicated in the murder and torture of countless Latin Americans."[8] General Hector Gramajo Morales, a graduate of the school and formerly Guatemalan Defense Minister, has been honored in a different way. His term as Defense Minister was up in 1989, and the following year he became a Fellow of the Edward Mason Program at the Kennedy School of Government of Harvard University. In 1993 he delivered the commencement address to the graduating class of the officers of the Command and General Staff College of the School of the Americas.[9]

What made these events of particular interest was that in 1991, just two years before this, a civil court in the United States ruled that the general was responsible for the rape and torture of Sister Diana Ortiz, an American Ursuline nun. The general maintained that the more than one hundred burn marks on the nun's body were the result of a failed lesbian love affair. Sister Ortiz told a quite different story of what happened, a very moving and graphic account, part of the "encyclopedia of horror" recounted in this volume. It is a story of gang rape and torture, physical and psychological. But its telling has beauty, truth beauty. She was abducted from the backyard of the Posada de Belem retreat center in Antigua by the Guatemalan security forces.[10] They took her to a secret prison where she was tortured and raped repeatedly. Her chest and back were burned more than 111 times with cigarettes. And then she was lowered into an open pit packed with human bodies—the bodies of children, men and women, some decapitated, some lying face up and caked with blood. Some were dead, some were alive. All were swarming with rats.

After hours of torture, Sister Ortiz was returned to the room of rape and interrogation where her ordeal continued. As her torturers began to rape her again, they said " Alejandro, join us and have some fun." Alejandro was a tall, light complexioned man, who spoke broken Spanish, but perfect North American English. They usually referred to him as "boss". He cursed, and ordered them to stop, because their victim was a North American nun, and her disappearance had become public. Several times Alejandro said that he was sorry about what happened. Sister Ortiz asked what would happen to the other people she saw being tortured. He told her not to be concerned about them. Then he threatened her, stating that he had photographs that would incriminate her of crimes.

Sister Ortiz continued:

> The memories of what I experienced that November day haunt me even now. I can smell the decomposing bodies, disposed of in an open pit. I can see the blood gushing out of the woman's body as I thrust the small machete into her. For you see, I was handed a machete. Thinking it would be used against me, and

at that point in my torture wanting to die, I did not resist. But my torturers put their hands onto the handle, on top of mine. And I had no choice. I was forced to use it against another human being. What I remember is blood gushing—spurting like a water fountain—and my screams lost in the cries of the woman. In spite of the memories of humiliation, I stand with the people of Guatemala. I demand the right to heal and to know the truth. I demand the right to a resurrection.[11]

When Frank R. LaRue, formerly a labor lawyer in Guatemala, appeared before the House Subcommittee on Western Hemisphere Affairs in July 1990, he referred to the case of Sister Ortiz. He said that he knew her personally. He added that she testified that she was driven to the torture house in a police car. The driver was a policeman in uniform and the siren of the police car was on. He used the case of the sister to exemplify his position that repression still existed in the country. General Gramajo was at the same hearing, an amazing twist of fate. He had volunteered to appear before the subcommittee, and from what one gathers from reading the report of this body, he never lost his composure or self-confidence. Mr. La Rue continued by affirming that when the general was still Minister of Defense he claimed that Sister Ortiz "had self-abducted herself." He went on to say that according to the Guatemalan government the victims tend to victimize themselves.[12] This led the chairman of the committee to face the general and to ask: "Do you share that view, General Gramajo, about the Sister from Kentucky? Do you share the view that she abducted herself?"

According to the Guatemalan government, the victims tend to victimize themselves.

The general responded: "I said that before. Because of the information I had. I believe it was so."

The chairman pressed the general: "You believe she abducted herself?"

The general responded: "Yes."

The chairman went on: "And the cigarette burns that were on her body?"

The general countered: "I have not seen these burns. She was not willing to testify immediately. She was not willing to present her case. As all I know, [*sic*] she did not let the U.S. Ambassador in Guatemala see her."

The chairman. "There is a medical record. She was examined by a physician."

The general: "I have not seen it."

Sister Ortiz revealed that for nearly a year before her abduction and torture she had been receiving death threats. When she emerged from the secret prison 24 hours later, she never wanted to see the Bible again. After leaving Guatemala, Sister Ortiz settled in Chicago, and the people she stayed with at first were all survivors of torture. They were victims who had lost their ability to speak, whose wives and husbands had been forcibly disappeared, and those who nearly died under torture. She got to know them and to love them. She could offer them a smile or a hug, but she felt helpless and hopeless. She was still angry. There was nothing to do to heal them, to undo their past, to heal their suffering. When she looked at her life, she thought:

> When looked at objectively, my life was nothing and no one was capable of putting it back together again. What I had lost was

25

lost. The same went for the other survivors. If all of us had been entirely logical, we would have killed ourselves. ... As time passed, I forgave God for not working some dramatic miracle, undoing my past. I learned that God was working a quiet, unobtrusive miracle, healing me through other people.

These small hugs, smiles, and kind words, which were all we had to offer each other in that house in Chicago, had begun to counteract the power of the torturers' smirks and punches. I still had the horrible past with me—I carried it in my memory and in my skin and always will—-but laid over it, like new skin over a wound, is a newer past, a past of caring and love.

Those who doubt that the world can ever be torture free or free of violence, those are the realists... the ones who can only think in terms of the math. We who have faith in the unexpected, the miraculous, the power of ourselves and of God working through us, we don't stop. We offer what we have and believe that it will be enough. We are the miracle workers.

On July 30, 2000, Sister Ortiz received the Pope Paul VI Teacher of Peace Award.[13]

EL SALVADOR: THE SEMINAL REVOLT AND MASSACRE

El Salvador is a postage stamp size country, the area of Massachusetts. It is a country in which the demand for land greatly outstrips what nature has supplied. Nonetheless, El Salvador has been large enough to house and to witness a massacre in 1932 and a 12 year guerrilla war which began in 1980 and repression by the Salvadoran government. Typical of Latin America, and further facilitated by its size, El Salvador is run by and for a landowning oligarchy that has close ties with the higher ranks of the armed forces. It is usually said that the country is run by forty families, a statement essentially true, even though the number should not be taken literally. The power of the oligarchy is based upon the ownership of large haciendas which produce coffee, introduced to the country in the mid-nineteenth century, mainly for export. The oligarchs consolidated their control of the haciendas in the 1880's. Communal lands were eliminated, and vagrancy laws allowed the state to force peasants to work on the haciendas for low wages.

The peasants paid a high price as the country shifted from the production of staple crops such as corn and beans on small farms to the production of coffee on haciendas for export. Tens of thousands of them were displaced from the small farms they had worked.[14] In the 1920's the amount of land devoted to coffee increased by one-third, and food had to be imported from the United States. The price of corn and beans skyrocketed. The price of coffee dropped dramatically during the depression, as did the wages of the peasant turned farm worker. This provided the fuel for the peasant revolt which was ignited on January 22,1932. While the leader of the revolt was a communist (Augustin Farabundo Marti), as were a few participants, the vast majority were simply disgruntled peasants and, to a lesser extent, Indians. The communists did try to organize the discontent and control the revolt. But they failed as shown by the fact that the party's last minute attempt to call off the revolt failed. The revolt failed as well. Armed with machetes, the peasants attacked army posts in the western part of the country, and they even managed to control a few towns. But they were quickly put down by government forces.

The insurrection cost the lives of 100 people. This contrasts with the 30,000 killed in the subsequent *matanza* (massacre) committed by government security forces. What happened in 1932 was more government terror than guerrilla or private terror. The death ratio between the two events was 300 to one. Being suspected of being a leftist, wearing Indian dress, or merely running from the security forces made one eligible for extermination. The government forces raided hotels, and those with blond hair were seized and executed as suspected Russians. Captured men were tied thumb to thumb and then thrown into mass graves that they were first forced to dig. Political organizations and labor unions were abolished. The *matanza* fits the definition of terrorism given in the first chapter. It consisted of deliberately slaughtering peasants so as to intimidate and coerce those who worked for social change by causing them intense fear, anxiety, apprehension, panic, dread, and/or horror.

The insurrection cost the lives of 100 people. This contrasts with the 30,000 killed by government forces in the subsequent massacre.

The massacre occurred during the dictatorship of General Martinez, who had come to power the previous December in a coup d'état engineered by the army. A dedicated theosophist and an eccentric, the general sold patent medicines. He was called *el brujo* (the sorcerer), evidently not in his presence. His belief in reincarnation led him to defend the *matanza* by stating that it is more of a crime to kill an ant than a man because a man is born again at death, whereas an ant dies forever. The general was more than eccentric; he was pro-Fascist and pro-Nazi as well. By 1936 Germany and Italy were the most frequent destinations for the military officers trained abroad.[15] In 1938 a German colonel was appointed the director of the Salvadoran Military Academy. Later the general removed the German colonel because of pressure from the United States.

Martinez replaced Arturo Araujo, the first president in El Salvador's history to come to office in a free election. But the oligarchy and the army opposed Araujo, because of his reformist and "socialist" policies. Washington did not at first recognize the Martinez government. This was not in protest to the *matanza*. It was rather to uphold and promote the spirit of a treaty concluded in Washington in 1923 which pledged that the signatories would not recognize regimes that came to power by coups d'état. Although Washington itself did not sign this treaty, it supported it as a means to bring stability to the region. It wanted to recognize the Martinez regime, but it also wanted to abide by the spirit of the Washington treaty. Its chance came after Nicaragua, Honduras, and Guatemala recognized this regime. The Roosevelt administration granted recognition on January 26, 1934.

Schmitz concludes that far from hurting his standing with Washington, the *matanza* bolstered Martinez's position.[16] The massacre brought forth no protest or condemnation from that quarter. The day after the rebellion, McCafferty, a special American envoy to El Salvador, urged the State Department to aid the Martinez government in every way to prevent the establishment of a communist state. His advice to send a fleet was honored. Three warships carrying marines were dispatched to El Salvador from the Special Service squadron in Panama in case they were needed. Secretary of State Simpson hoped that they would not be needed, "for it would make a bad impression in Latin America"[17] But their dispatch was thought necessary should the government lose control of the situation.

Thus, despite its delayed recognition of the Martinez government, Washington did support the *matanza*. It provided armed protection for those committing state terrorism. The Division of Latin American Affairs in the State Department drew up a five-page memorandum on the existence of communism in the Central American country. It linked all of the then current unrest in El Salvador to the infiltration of communists from Mexico. The memorandum found no connection between the unrest and local social conditions, even though it did grant that a large percentage of the population was extremely poor and that both good land and wealth were concentrated in a few hands.

The State Department's report to the press was in the same vein. State labeled the revolt a genuinely communist one, not a popular one. Warning that the situation was serious, it lauded the Martinez government for taking energetic steps to suppress the rebellion. Washington did grant that this suppression involved the utmost severity, but it was over in a short time. And order was restored. It called the suppression "a display of efficiency," and it asserted that it had strengthened Martinez's position in El Salvador. The *matanza* was ignored, and the "communist revolt" was blamed for the atrocities. Washington again rendered support to the Salvadoran state terrorists, this time by ignoring their deeds and placing the blame on communist insurgency.

WASHINGTON TEACHES AND UNDERWRITES COUNTERINSURGENCY

By the mid-1950s, mutual defense assistance agreements linked the U.S. Army with the armies of every Latin American country with the exception of Argentina and Mexico. Washington enjoyed a virtual monopoly on the provision of military equipment and supplies to the region. Until the 1960s, however, Congress prohibited military assistance in the region for internal security purposes, although these were ill-defined. After 1960, counterinsurgency doctrine and U.S. security assistance induced changes both in the strategies and structures of the region's security systems. Counterinsurgency doctrine gave spirit to the new structures. In El Salvador, Guatemala and Chile, this doctrine was applied in bitter conflicts between ruling elites and peasant or urban majorities. And in each it was applied in a somewhat different way, varying with specific circumstances.

Reacting to the success of Castro in Cuba, President Kennedy became intensely interested in counterinsurgency, a doctrine that later was taught by the American military to the military forces in many third world countries. His interest and fascination extended to the choice of the uniform for a new military elite which he created, going so far as to prevail over the military brass in choosing its hallmark green beret. By January 1961 Kennedy called upon the armed forces to add a counterinsurgency dimension to the national military capability. By 1963, 5,600 special forces (later called the Green Berets) had been trained who taught counterinsurgency to foreign troops in Latin America during the Cold War. By the time of the war on terrorism, the Navy and the Air Force had added their own versions of this type of warrior and warfare, known as "special ops."

The U.S. Army's regional Latin American center for counterinsurgency was the School of the Americas, formerly located at Fort Gulick in the Canal Zone. From here, it sent mobile training teams to teach Latin American armies counterinsurgency techniques. Included were El Salvador, Guatemala, Chile, Argentina, and Brazil—-the first four of which are included in this study. The doctrine was also taught by American intelligence agencies, and to other third world countries as well. It must be emphasized that counterinsurgency was not thought applicable to the internal situation of the United States, nor as an appropriate subject to be taught to regular U.S. armed forces. The teaching of the doctrine in foreign settings was accompanied by technical assistance and the provision of the economic resources required to build the infrastructure necessary to apply the doctrine.

Washington's involvement in the counterinsurgencies of El Salvador and Guatemala divides logically into two periods. The first is the preparatory one of technical assistance, in which the doctrine was taught, and its practical adaptation to local conditions applied. This first period involved what in retrospect appear to be moderate amounts of economic and military aid. Local intelligence and communications capabilities were strengthened as a necessary complement of the counterinsurgency capability. The second period witnessed the geometric growth of this capability, spurred on by massive infusions of military and economic aid from Washington. At least this was the case for El Salvador.

Counterinsurgency Ideology

The basic tenet of the counterinsurgency doctrine was the identification of communism as the threat and the enemy as its agents.[1] To find the enemy one must look inward, not outward. A similar focus is needed for the mission of the armed forces: to protect against internal enemies, not external ones. The army is to be aided in this endeavor by the police and by paramilitary organizations. After the Cuban revolution, U.S. military doctrine took the very broadest definition of the enemy and its agents, as well as of subversion. It tended to lump together all opposition to the status quo as either actual or incipient insurgency. The U.S. Joint Chiefs of Staff in 1962 defined insurgency as "illegal opposition to any existing government"——the scope of subversive activities ranging from passive resistance, illegal strikes, and demonstrations, to large-scale guerrilla operations. The communist enemy was pictured as being pernicious, powerful, and perverted, something that must be annihilated. By extension, opposition to the status quo was put in the same bag to be crushed as well. But in reality, much of the opposition was by no means either communist or armed and violent.

It tended to lump together all opposition to the status quo as either actual or incipient insurgency.

The world of counterinsurgency thus is a stark bipolar one, much too simplistic to reflect reality, with no neutral middle ground to stand on. This paradigm has been resurrected by the Bush administration in its war on terrorism. One side in both counterinsurgency and the war on terrorism is the free world; on the other dark side is the world of communist treachery and slavery—or in contemporary terms, of terrorism, depicted as baseless irrational hatred. There is no place for any mediating conceptualization designed to meet the needs of the poor, especially if such a force, even for tactical reasons, works together with the communists or to produce social change. The counterinsurgency doctrine served to target as enemies the progressive wing of the Catholic Church, as well as other non-communist leftists. In his own speeches and interviews President Kennedy stopped short of declaring that Americans should "fight dirty". Rather he posed the matter as a dilemma. In an interview in April 1961, he asked how "an open, non-conspiratorial society... can compete with a secret, conspiratorial society using all the instruments of subversion."[2] Others and other sources have been less discrete. A 1960 Special Forces manual entitled *Counterinsurgency*

Operations eschewed ethical limits in counter-guerrilla warfare and reserved the use of terror as a legitimate tactical tool of unconventional warfare.

McClintock, a senior staff member of Amnesty International, spent several years investigating Washington's support for the regimes in El Salvador and Guatemala. He devoted an entire chapter to the question of terror as taught in American military schools, first under the guise of psychological warfare and then under the counterinsurgency label. Weapons were evaluated for their terror effects, as were methods of interrogation, abduction, and assassination. He concluded that the prescription of terror for American counterinsurgency and unconventional warriors remained a feature of American doctrine in the 1960s and afterwards. Usually the phenomenon was described by the oblique term "counter-terror," but it would assume the same forms as terror: assassinations, "disappearances," mass executions, and the like. And it was an item for export. A 1962 Special Warfare school text entitled *Concepts for U.S. Army Counterinsurgency Activities* outlined the training curriculum for overseas allies. Included were: guerrilla warfare, propaganda, subversion, intelligence and counterintelligence, terrorist activities, civic action, and conventional combat operations.[3]

Counterinsurgency Manuals Prescribe the Use of Terrorism

The terrorism committed by the Contras in Nicaragua has been traced to U.S. government training manuals. One such manual was *Psychological Operations in Guerrilla Warfare* published in Spanish in 1983. "The 1983 manual provided a documentary link to prior U.S. army field manuals that explicitly prescribe the use of terrorism."[4] A reference to terror operations as a "phantom image" which appeared in a 1965 U.S. *Psychological Operations* manual (FM 33-1) appeared at about the same time in the journal of El Salvador's School of Command and General Staff in the context of counterinsurgency.[5] The article argued that terror and counter-terror are actions designed to create uncertainty and fear, "creating a kind of phantom presence." A 1966 *Military Review* article outlining the theoretical framework of counter-terror was reprinted in the *Revista Militar de Guatemala* of the Guatemalan army.[6] The reprinting occurred just as the government declared a state of siege and proceeded to engage in a campaign of mass terror.

Washington taught the counterinsurgency doctrine to the security forces of El Salvador and provided its government with the intelligence and communications resources to implement it. The evidence provides the groundwork for accusing Washington of being an accessory to any acts committed in accordance with the counterinsurgency doctrine. The case is strengthened by the fact that Washington taught this doctrine and provided these resources in the Salvadoran setting where those wielding power divided society along rigid lines into the ins and the outs, the haves and the have-nots, who shared a belief in the dichotomy as well. Both sides had this division inscribed in their historic memories by the events of 1932.

COUNTERINSURGENCY OPERATIONALIZED IN EL SALVADOR

Washington's teaching and aid resulted in a dramatic change in the Salvadoran military, shifting it from a narrow view of the purpose of the military to a much broader view, including the sharing of the military function with other agencies. This was followed by U.S. programs to upgrade the local police departments, military communications and intelligence capabilities—improvements necessary if the counterinsurgency doctrine was to be implemented. A heavily politicized paramilitary organization, the Organisacion Democratica Nacionalista (ORDEN), was formed. It became a large governmental and semi-governmental terrorist institution, a source of death squads. The new dispensation was reflected organizationally in ORDEN, and also in Salvadoran military journals.[7] This came none too soon for the cold warriors of the time. A U.S. embassy's threat assessment in early 1961 implied that El Salvador was perilously close to succumbing to Castro, or more particularly, to the influence of communism.

By the beginning of 1980 El Salvador's security system was a reflection of 20 years of Washington's security assistance provided in accordance with the precepts of the doctrine of counterinsurgency.[8] This system consisted of the traditional security forces—a regular army of 9,000, an air force, and a minuscule navy. But there existed in addition a vast body of paramilitaries and irregulars (ORDEN), and a sophisticated intelligence apparatus. This system was under the control of the officer corps of the army; it also maintained effective control over the rest of the government through its influence in the junta and with the minister of defense. The size of the army increased to 19,000 by June 1980 and to 22,400 by March 1983. At this latter date the army was backed by 11,000 members from the National Guard, the Treasury Police, the National Police, and some 50,000 from ORDEN. By 1992 the army alone had reached 60,000, at a time when the guerrillas could claim only 6,800.

By 1979 several separate guerrilla organizations were operating in the country. Two years later they united to form a single organization, the Farabundo Marti National Liberation Front (FMLN), named after the communist leader of the uprising of 1932. If 30,000 were killed in the earlier *matanza*, over 75,000 lost their lives in the one that followed, and one-fourth of the population was displaced. The FMLN received aid from Nicaragua and Cuba, but U.S. aid was of a different order of magnitude. Between 1979 and 1992 this aid amounted to 6 billion dollars.[9] This aid correlates with the increases in the army's strength and that of the paramilitary forces, and with the degree of state repression and the number of governmental murders. By 1983 the CIA had some 150 agents operating in the country. By 1983 almost all Salvadoran officers had been trained by the United States. In 1984 it was revealed that top members of the army, the police forces, and the paramilitary forces were being paid retainer fees by the CIA.[10] The conclusion is warranted that Washington trained the army in El Salvador for the repression it committed and subsidized the government while it was engaged in the repression.

The government repression reached its zenith in the 1980s against the background of a number of coups d'état that saw a reformist government replaced by a traditional one determined to preserve the status quo. In 1981 the FMLN announced "the final offensive". It fizzled and failed. Greatly outnumbered, the guerrilla organization could do little against governmental forces and their North American sponsor. The five Central American powers were the prod that led to the termination in 1992 of the fighting between the government and the FMLN. The cease-fire was actually initiated on November 14, 1991 when the FMLN unilaterally announced a cessation of all offensive operations.[11] This initiative followed the defeat of the Sandinistas who, due to the unremitting warfare conducted against Nicaragua by U.S. surrogate forces, the Contras, from Honduras, lost the elections in Nicaragua in 1989, thereby depriving the FMLN of a source of support and supplies. The FMLN announcement was followed by a similar government announcement and still later by an official cease-fire agreement that took place February 1992. This was in turn followed by phased reductions under international supervision of the armed forces and the FMLN, a partial amnesty, land reform and settlement, and many other actions that addressed complicated issues. The United Nations was the major vehicle used in the process, while the Organization of American States was relegated to a minor role. The world organization gave priority to human rights in the "peace progress," thus emphasizing a major thesis of this chapter. It also called for a truth commission, whose report came to be called *From Madness to Hope: the Twelve-Year War in El Salvador*

THE UN TRUTH COMMISSION ON EL SALVADOR

The Reception of the UN Report

The report of the commission was presented to the Secretary General of the United Nations on March 15, 1993. This gave Boutros Boutros-Ghali the opportunity to express his view of the document, a view vigorously contested by those found to be the chief perpetrators of the crimes described in the report. He declared that in order to put the war behind them, the Salvadorans would have to go through the catharsis of facing the truth.[12] He went on to assert that bringing the truth to light is part and parcel of the process of reconciling Salvadoran society. There can be no reconciliation without the public knowing the truth. Since the armed conflict left no one untouched, all citizens must be made aware of the truth contained in the report. It should become a part of their culture and their history, so that they can better face the future. He concluded that once the truth came to light, they could contemplate forgiveness.

These lofty and noble terms contrast with what another United Nations report characterized as an "outcry" sparked by the release of the report of the truth commission. Immediately after the publication of the report, the Christiani government rushed through the Salvadoran legislature an across the board amnesty for all charged with serious acts of violence. The outcry originated with the High Command of the Armed Forces, the President of the Supreme Court, and other highly placed government officials. Indeed, tension mounted as these political figures, joined by segments of the media, rejected the commission's findings and recommendations. They charged that the commission had exceeded its terms of reference and had arrogated to itself the judicial function. Heightened criticism of the world organization followed, as did threats to the United Nations personnel stationed in the country. In contrast to this, the FMLN, the guerrilla organization, accepted the report, including its recommendations to reform the government.

That the armed forces, the supreme court, and much of the government reacted this way is understandable in view of their indictment by the report. The indictment of the judicial system was such that the commission did not recommend that those found guilty be prosecuted. It found the judicial system compromised beyond the point at which it could conduct fair trials. The commission put the blame for most of the crimes at the door of the armed forces, including those committed by the death squads. Governmental officials were often found to have participated in the work of these squads and their structure was found to be still in place. Indeed, the three members of the Ad Hoc Commission that had drawn up

The Salvadoran judicial system was found to be compromised beyond the point at which it could conduct fair trials.

a report critical of the officer corps "delivered their report in New York and, fearing for their lives, remained outside El Salvador for some time."[13] The sub-committee report charged over 100 officers, including the Minister of Defense and the Chief of the General Staff, with serious violations of human rights and called for their dismissal. This report of the sub-committee was intended to be secret, but was leaked to the press before the publication of the committee's report, *From Madness to Hope.*

Another outcry, but this for a vastly different reason, came from the Honorable Robert G. Torricelli, Chairman of the House Subcommittee on Western Hemisphere Affairs. The chairman began the hearings on the report of the truth commission in the standard and traditional way, this time by echoing some of the noble and upbeat sentiments voiced by the Secretary General indicated above. He congratulated the parties to the dispute and the peacemakers for having successfully concluded a peace agreement. But then he added that the report of the truth commission was of concern not only to El Salvador, nor would his comments be limited to that country only. Nor would his comments be limited and mild, the usual characteristics of the opening remarks of the chairman of a committee. Mr. Torricelli's "outcry" began with the affirmation that rarely as a member of "this institution" had he been more "personally offended or betrayed" than when he learned of the findings of the truth commission.[14] This was the case because for years he had listened to the testimony of so many witnesses of different administrations informing the committee about what they reputably knew about the crimes committed in El Salvador. He next turned to the process established by the Congress, whereby President Reagan would periodically certify that El Salvador was making progress in respect to human rights. As a reaction to positive certifications, Congress provided military assistance to the government to fight the war there. The chairman gave an example of this, Presidential Determination 82-4, dated January 28, 1982. It was worded as follows:

> I hereby determine that the government of El Salvador is making a concerted and significant effort to comply with internationally recognized human rights. I hereby determine that the government of El Salvador is achieving substantial control over all elements of its own armed forces. I hereby determine that the government of El Salvador has made a good-faith effort to investigate the murders of the six U.S. citizens in El Salvador in December 1980 and January 1981.[15]

Mr. Torricelli commented by charging that:

> It is now abundantly clear that Ronald Reagan made these certifications not only in disregard of the truth but in defiance of it. Members of his administration came forward to this Congress and swore that they had no knowledge of acts of violence. Peace was being restored and rights respected. It was a lie.

He continued his indictment by arguing that the process of certification "has been poisoned" and concluded that based on what was then known about the credibility of certification, no future Congress could ever establish

Deceit and betrayal induced Congress to invest the nation's fortune and honor in a conflict in the blind belief that it was being told the truth.

such a process again. On this point he has not proved to be an accurate fore-caster of Congressional behavior. He was back on track when he referred to the "deceit and betrayal" that induced the Congress to invest the nation's fortune and honor in a conflict "in the blind belief that we were being told the truth." This he found to be "a shameful chapter in American foreign policy."

Congress was not as innocent as Torircelli's remarks suggest, but it did set up a system that ostensibly was designed to restrain the executive from aiding governments engaged in a consistent pattern of gross violations of inter-nationally recognized human rights. Presidential certification was required under certain conditions. None of this, however, seemed to deter either Reagan or subsequent executives from continuing to aid governments they were determined to help.

Mr. Torricelli aimed his barbs not only in the direction of the Reagan administration, but also at the FMLN. Four representatives of the guerrilla organization were present at the hearings. The chairman asked rhetorically if they understood the difficulty "for us" to sit across from people whose organization participated in the murder of American servicemen? The head of the FMLN delegation responded that during the period of the war the administration of the United States was dedicated to the complete destruction "of us," the FMLN. One of his colleagues added that if the chairman wished to pursue this subject "you must realize how we feel sitting here before representatives of a government who financed, armed, fully supported, and trained the Salvadoran military which was responsible for murdering thousands of Salvadorans."[16] This ended the exchange, though the representatives of the guerrillas did admit that their organization had therefore regarded all American military personnel as fair targets to be eliminated.

The Organization of the Truth Commission

The commission was selected by the Secretary General of the United Nations, and consisted of Reinaldo Figueredo Planchart, former Foreign Minister of Venezuela, Belisario Betancourt, former President of Colombia, and Professor Thomas Buergenthal, former President of the Inter-American Court for Human Rights.[17] It was aided by a staff whose numbers ranged from twenty to thirty. They were lawyers, sociologists, social workers, and forensic anthropologists recruited from Latin America, the United States, and Europe. Understandably, the commis-sion used graphic terms to describe the massacre that claimed 75,000 lives. It spoke of the violence as a fire that swept across the fields of El Salvador, bursting into villages, cutting off roads and destroying highways and bridges, entering homes, sacred areas, and educational centers, and singling out as an enemy anyone who was not a friend. It spoke of institutionalized impunity for repeated human rights violations committed by members of the armed forces. It addressed "the warped psychology" that had been engendered by the conflict and that led to "a compulsion of violence." The civilian population in guerrilla controlled areas as well as political opponents in general were automatically assumed by govern-mental forces to be subversive and to be the enemy. Counterinsurgency practice found its classic expression in cutting the guerrillas' lifeline. In turn, the guerrillas assumed that all mayors and all American troops were their enemies. The report exemplified how far the position of the military leadership had hardened by refer-ring to the assassinations of Archbishop Romero and the Jesuit priests of the Central American University. It accused this leadership of perverse sentiments and of the most absurd obfuscation in covering up the truth as to who had given the orders to kill.

The commission was mandated to investigate "serious acts of violence that have occurred since 1980 and whose impact on society urgently demands that the public should know the truth." The commission interpreted this to mean that it should take into account the particular importance of each act, its repercussions, and the social unrest to which it gave rise. Based on these instructions, the commission investigated individual acts but also acts with similar characteristics revealing a systematic pattern of violence or ill treatment that, taken together, outraged Salvadoran society. No attempt was made to establish Washington's role as accessory or that of any other country. To publicize its presence, the commission advertised in newspapers and bought time on radio and TV. Offices were opened in San Salvador and other cities. At first, Salvadorans were deathly afraid to appear and to talk, and initially the military had built a protective wall around itself. But soon this changed. "The three commissioners were shocked to find that the terror, brutality, and suffering inflicted on the people of El Salvador between 1980 and 1991 was much worse and more persuasive than we had imagined."[18]

The commission registered more than 22,000 complaints of serious acts of violence that had occurred in El Salvador during this period.[19] Over 7,000 of these complaints were received at the commission's offices in various locations. The remainder came through governmental and non-governmental institutions. Over 60 percent complained of extra-judicial executions, over 25 percent of disappearances, and over 20 percent included complaints of torture. Those giving testimony attributed almost 85 percent of the cases to agents of the state, paramilitary groups allied to them, and the death squads. Members of the armed forces were accused in almost 60 percent of the complaints, members of the security forces in some 25 percent of the cases, members of military escorts and civil defense units in some 20 percent, and members of the death squads in more than 10 percent. In contrast to these complaints against governmental and semi-governmental institutions, only five percent of the total were registered against the guerrilla organization, the FMLN. The conclusion is warranted that what happened in this tiny Central American country from 1980 to 1991 was more state terror committed by the government and semi-governmental institutions than private terror committed by the guerrillas. This answers one of the central questions posed by this study.

Truth Commission Findings: Government Terrorism and Repression, Not Guerrilla Warfare

Professor Buergenthal verified this when he confessed that the commissioners "assumed and hoped that we would find a more or less equal number of serious acts of violence attributable to each side to the conflict. That would have made our task politically easier and given us the credibility that derives from the public perception of evenhandedness."[20] The assumption that the commissioners would find an even split on serious acts of violence was due to what Buergenthal calls the "massive wartime propaganda" on the part of the government. The professor went on to say that given the findings, this hope could not be realized, because the success of the commission and the integrity of its members depended upon the writing of a completely

Ten of the twelve officers responsible for the El Mazote massacre were graduates of the School of the Americas.

honest and impartial report. The activities of the guerrillas were given space in the report, but most of the space was reserved for the major actors. The commission charged the guerrillas with killing several U.S. Marines while they were enjoying themselves in a local tavern. They were guards at the U.S. embassy. This killing was in accord with the general policy of the FMLN of treating all U.S. military personnel as the enemy, and thus as appropriate targets. The guerrillas also targeted local mayors.

Much more lethal were the actions of the Salvadoran military in general, and particularly their attacks on villages. The massacre of the village of El Mozote in the department of Morozan that occurred on December 11,1981 provided one of several examples. After a night spent locked in their homes, the peasants were deliberately and systematically executed in groups: first the men, then the women, and lastly the children. The men were first interrogated and tortured before they were killed. After exterminating the entire population, the soldiers set fire to the houses and other structures in the village. The number of bodies later identified was over 200, higher if unidentified victims are taken into account. Forensic experts determined that a majority of the victims were minors. The authorities did not order an investigation of this or the other massacres that occurred in the area. When questioned by the commission, the Minister of Defense and the Chief of the Armed Forces Joint Staff denied that they had any information that would make it possible to identify the units and the officers that had participated in the operation. No less than ten of the twelve officers cited in the United Nations report as being responsible for the El Mozote massacre were graduates of the School of the Americas.[21]

Another noteworthy aspect of this episode is that the Atlacatl Battalion took part in it. This was a rapid deployment infantry battalion, the first of such units specially trained for counterinsurgency warfare, which had completed its training under the supervision of United States military advisers at the beginning of 1981.[22] Washington restored military aid to El Salvador on January 14 of that year after it had been briefly interrupted because of the bad publicity that followed the murder of the American nuns. This type of aid as well as economic assistance had then increased at a rapid pace, the increasing flow intended to train, modernize, and expand the armed forces.[23] The chief victims of the resulting military operations were the non-combatant civilian population. In 1981 the number of displaced persons in this tiny Central American country reached 164,000. The number of their deaths skyrocketed, and they were subjected to a new type of repression. This repression took the form of terror, mass, indiscriminate slaughter, mutilation, and gang rape. It was personified by Captain Juan Grande of the Atlacatl Battalion, better known as "Cuchillo Grande" (Big Knife). He received journalists in a t-shirt emblazoned with the slogan, in English, "Kill them all, let God sort them out later."[24]

"Kill them all, let God sort them out later."

Death Squads

The commission revealed that it had received a great many complaints of serious acts of violence perpetrated by death squads. The commission charged that between 1980 and 1991 these squads violated human rights wholesale, and in a systematic and organized manner. The members of such groups wore civilian clothing, were heavily armed, operated secretly, and hid their affiliation and identity. They abducted members of the civilian population and rebel groups. They tortured their hostages, were responsible for their disappearance, and often killed them. Military and civilian government personnel were active members in many such groups, and even organized and led them. The government turned a blind eye to their operations. The commission found that these squads were not an isolated or marginal phenomenon. They developed into an instrument of terror used systematically for the suppression, and too often the physical elimination, of political opponents of the elites. Many civilian and military authorities, especially during the 1980s, participated in, encouraged, and tolerated the activities of these groups. The commission offered the startling prediction that they could be reactivated again, if high government circles so desired, and this could trigger the resumption of massive repression in the future.

The commission traced the history of the death squads to the violence committed by groups in the past, groups that were neither part of the government nor ordinary criminals. This history involved complicity between business and landowners who entered into a close relationship with the army and intelligence and security forces. The commission alleged that these shadowy relations persist to the present. A milestone in the history of these squads was the founding of the National Guard in 1910. Indeed, it was this institution that became the main source of training for ORDEN (the Democratic Nationalist Organization). This occurred after 1967, the year that General Jose Alberto Medrano was appointed as head of the guard. At birth, ORDEN was a nation wide, paramilitary network of informants that extended intelligence gathering to the grass roots level. As it matured, it provided personnel for death squads, and it engaged in irregular warfare. If its training after 1967 came from the National Guard, its recruits came mainly from the military reserves. By 1967 its name had come into the public domain, and it announced its mission as being the promotion of patriotism and all-out opposition to communism.[25]

After the coup d'état of 1979, Major Roberto D'Aubuisson emerged as what the landed and business elites regarded as the indispensable leader. These elites considered the junta formed after this coup to be infiltrated by Marxist officers. The major acted as a leader and as a useful connection, joining the intelligence services and other security forces with the business and landed elites. He thereby combined in a strategic relationship money and weapons, together with the information gathered by intelligence agencies necessary to target violence where it would produce the most damage to the enemy. Indeed, he had come from the intelligence services, and he not only took some of the files with him when he left intelligence, but he also maintained relations with these services. After the assassination of Archbishop Romero, an act that in very close circles he took credit for having planned, his prestige and influence grew among those groups that wielded economic power. They placed more resources at his disposal. He planned and directed the activities of numerous death squads while in El Salvador, and for a short time, in Guatemala as well. The commission also discussed the death squads sponsored by the intelligence section of the National Guard. Again, it charged that local business and landed elites were involved. Furthermore, it charged that the United States government tolerated, and apparently paid little official notice to, the activities of Salvadoran exiles living in Miami, especially between 1979 in 1983. According to testimony received by the commission these exiles "directly financed and indirectly ran certain death squads."[26]

The truth commission presented the assassination of Archbishop Romero as an example of the work of the death squads. On March 24, 1980 the archbishop was shot with a single 22 high velocity bullet while celebrating mass in the chapel of the Hospital da la Divina Providencia. He bled to death. The commission found that Major Roberto D'Aubuisson gave the fatal orders to the death squad, along with the precise instructions to his lieutenants on how it should be carried out. Two of the three officers cited in the death of the archbishop, including D'Aubuisson, were graduates of the School of the Americas.[27] The conspirators hired a professional assassin to do the job. The archbishop had posed a threat to the regime, not only as an upholder of human rights, but also by seeking to interfere with army discipline and with aid from the United States.[28] His sermons deeply irritated rightwing civilian and military circles, and newspapers charged that he preached terrorism from the cathedral.[29] He wrote a letter to President Carter charging that the escalation of government violence in the first weeks of 1980 was directly related to foreign military assistance. He called upon Carter on Christian principles to stop additional military aid to El Salvador.[30] Perhaps more significant, certainly more dangerous, was his appeal to the members of the armed forces to disobey orders when those orders were commands to torture and to kill. He pleaded for this in his last broadcast sermon, reminding the lower ranks that they were from the same social background as most of their victims. Asserting the principle that in the face of the order by man to kill, the law of God must prevail, he argued that it was past time for the soldiers and the paramilitary forces to obey their consciences and not orders which would compel them to sin. He seemed to have been legitimizing the revolt of the guerrillas when he argued that the church regards insurrectional violence as legitimate when a dictatorship attacks human rights and human welfare, and when all avenues of rationality and understanding are closed. In this message, he foretold that "my hour approaches." It did, the very next day. Four days after his death nearly 100,000 mourners gathered in Cathedral Square for his funeral service. True to form, Salvadoran troops with machine guns fired into the crowd killing at least 40 mourners.[31]

The Rape and Killing of Nuns

Shortly after 7 P.M. on December 2,1980 members of the National Guard of El Salvador arrested three American nuns and one American lay missionary as they were leaving the Comalapa International Airport. Two of the nuns, members of the Maryknoll Order, were returning from Nicaragua, and the other two women were picking them up at the airport. The four women were beaten, raped, and murdered. Their bodies were thrown in a ditch. The truth commission concluded that this atrocity was planned ahead of time, that the sergeant in charge of the actual executions was acting on orders from higher up, that the head of the National Guard, then Colonel Carlos Eugenio Vides Casanova, among others, had facilitated the cover up of the crime, and that General Jose Guillermo Garcia, the Minister of Defense, made no serious effort to determine who was responsible for the murders.[32] General Garcia had taken the counterinsurgency course at the School of the Americas in 1962, and Colonel Vides Casanova (later promoted to general) was a guest speaker there five years after the rape and assassination of the religious women.

The report contains several incidents that suggest cover-ups. These included judicial instances of cover-ups and the refusal of a group of forensic doctors to perform autopsies, because they said they had no surgical masks. In this instance, indicative of what would indeed be possible if Washington were to seriously desire to prevent state terrorism or the cover-up in its aftermath, the day after the murders, the Carter administration suspended aid to El Salvador. On April 26 of the following year embassy officials met with Generals Garcia and Vides Casanova to inform them that the failure to investigate the murders was jeopardizing American aid. Just three days after the meeting five enlisted members of the National Guard were arrested, and the following day $25 million in aid was approved.[33]

And then something unique in the history of the country occurred. For the first time, members of the armed forces were convicted by a judge. To be sure, they were enlisted personnel. The higher ups who had ordered the murders were not made to face judicial proceedings, despite the fact that four of the convicted enlisted men later admitted that they were acting under orders. Three have since been freed from custody. The day after the convictions, the U.S. Congress approved $62 million of emergency aid for El Salvador.

Two weeks after the murders, Jeanne Kirkpatrick, who was to serve as the Reagan Administration's Ambassador to the United Nations, offered her opinion about the murders. She exclaimed:

> I don't think the government (of El Salvador) was responsible. The nuns were not just nuns; the nuns were political activists. We ought to be a little more clear-cut about this than we usually are. They were political activists on behalf of the Frente (the guerrillas) and somebody who is using violence to oppose the Frente killed them.[34]

Sometime later Secretary of State Alexander Haig declared before the House Foreign Affairs Committee:

> I would like to suggest to you that some of the investigations would lead one to believe that perhaps the vehicle that the nuns were riding in had tried to run a road block or may have accidentally been perceived to have been doing so, and there may have been an exchange of fire.[35]

Congressman Torricelli questioned Professor Buergenthal, the American member of the truth commission, about these statements. After having read these statements to him, Torricelli asked if he had received any testimony from anyone suggesting how Haig had come to this conclusion.

Buergenthal answered "no."

Torricelli persisted, "Among the hundreds of people you talked to, no one suggested that this was a possibility?"

Buergenthal insisted, "No. The statement is outrageous."[36] With respect to Kirkpatrick's statement, he advised that one might have concluded that the nuns and the lay missionary were sympathetic to the FMLN, but not that they were involved in the conflict. He went on to say that there was no doubt that there was no basis for Kirkpatrick's statement as a justification for the killing of the churchwomen. They may have been sympathetic to the FMLN, but to Buergenthal and to the commission, this was totally irrelevant. They were unarmed, and they were not members of the FMLN and there was therefore was no justification for killing them.

THE AFTERMATH

Rewards and Punishments

In October 2000 those who read the inside pages of the *New York Times* were able to keep up with the lives of Generals Vides Casanova and Garcia. They had retired, and they lived in South Florida. They had been living there since 1989, and as the lawyers for the plaintiff alleged in a lawsuit soon to be described, they lived there "surrounded by relatives." They had been granted "green cards," permanent residence, by the United States government. In addition, they received awards from the United States military, as well as the United States Legion of Merit award from President Ronald Reagan in 1984.[37]

The relatives of the murdered churchwomen interrupted their peaceful retirement, but only temporarily. The relatives brought a civil, wrongful death suit against the generals under the 1992 Torture Victim Protection Act. It was only the twelfth of such suits, the first to test the military command structure. The relatives initiated the proceedings after they had discovered that the generals had been living in Florida. The new law allows victims or their surviving relatives to sue those who knew of crimes or the probability of their occurring but took no action to stop them. The generals alleged that they knew that some killings were taking place, but their subordinates told them that the killings were caused by legitimate military action. They swore that they had not covered up anything. They were acquitted,[38] to return to their retirement homes in Florida "surrounded by their relatives." One member of the jury revealed that he and his cohorts did not find a direct link between the generals and the crimes committed in the confusion of the time. The truth commission was convinced that such a link existed, but it did not pretend to be a judicial body. Unfortunately, the judicial bodies in El Salvador that were in a position to make such a determination were forbidden to do so by President Christiani's general amnesty. Moreover, the truth commission found these bodies so corrupt that it did not advise that they try the likes of the generals.

A year and a half later the retirement of Generals Garcia and Vides Casanova was again interrupted, this time by a suit brought under the same law by three Salvadoran citizens who accused their government of the time of torturing them. The plaintiffs gave graphic testimony of beatings, gang rape, and other forms of torture. They and other witnesses described how the army hunted down civilians suspected of being guerrilla sympathizers.[39] Bloodied bodies littered the streets each day, and entire villages were eliminated by government troops. One plaintiff testified that she was eight months pregnant at the time. Her torturers placed a metal bed frame over her pregnant belly and seesawed on top of her.[40] They gang raped her every night. Her infant son was born prematurely and died of his injuries. Soldiers wrapped iron wires around the fingers of another plaintiff, a surgeon, thus cutting off the circulation He could no longer practice his profession. The surgeon testified that he was tortured in San Salvador's National Guard Headquarters, 100 feet from Vides Casanova's office. Vides Casanova visited the cell where he was tortured.

The generals used the same defense in the second trial that they did in the first, and their lawyer compared them to Thomas Jefferson and John Adams in that they tried to bring democracy to their country. He pointed out, quite correctly, that the generals had received honors from the United States government. Robert E. White, US envoy to El Salvador at the time, testified that the generals did know about the crimes and actually seemed to encourage them.[41] The jury agreed that the generals did know and that they did nothing to prevent the crimes from happening. It awarded $54.6 million to the plaintiffs. The lawyer for the plaintiffs explained that a big difference between the two trials was in having live torture victims tell their stories to the jury. The executive director of the Center for Justice and Accountability said that the verdict was one of very few since World War II in which a civilian jury held military commanders responsible for torture. She added that the verdict was particularly significant for El Salvador where none of the military were court-martialled for human rights abuses committed during the rule of the generals and where a broad amnesty was given to all combatants after the peace accords.

CONCLUSION

As is usually the case with truth commissions, the one for El Salvador did not focus on Washington's support for the government. Despite this, the chapter provides sufficient evidence to prove this support for San Salvador along with the other two central questions that the evidence is asked to resolve. That terror was committed in El Salvador is not disputed. Those who doubt this should reread the above and realize that an estimated 75,000 were killed in this small country in the period 1980 to 1991. The truth commission found that the terrorism that was committed in the country was overwhelmingly governmental terrorism, committed by the Salvadoran army, the National Guard, and their death squads and affiliated agencies. They were responsible for 95 percent of the deaths, the guerrillas for only five percent.

These were the same institutions that were the concern and the favorites of Washington—receiving its indoctrination and training and profiting from its largess. El Salvador received six billion dollars in aid from Washington in the period 1979 to 1992. This subsidy to the tiny country during the government repression and terrorism came to average out at $100,000 for each member of its armed forces. This subsidy allowed the government to pay for the terrorist activities committed by the security forces. By virtue of this largess and the military training, notably in counterinsurgency warfare, Washington emerges in this chapter as an accessory before and during the fact. By covering up for San Salvador after it had committed terror, Washington was an accessory after the fact. It gave diplomatic support to state terrorism. By training and equipping the Salvadoran security forces in, and for, counterinsurgency warfare, Washington served as an accessory before and during the fact. This may sound like blaming the teacher for what the student does. Or, as McClintock phrased it, Washington's activity was programmatic and open ended, not distinct and episodic.[42] The doctrine was taught to foreign troops to be implemented by these troops at some future time and perhaps over a sizeable period of time, and even with local innovations and variations. The fact that its implementation was in the hands of a foreign army created obvious problems for oversight—but also obvious advantages for the avoidance of direct responsibility.

> **Washington's subsidy to the tiny country during the government repression and terrorism came to average out at $100,000 for each member of its armed forces.**

In the case of El Salvador, however, Washington taught counterinsurgency "with malice aforethought," in the face of what it and the elites in El Salvador considered to be the communist threat. Given the memory of the 1932 *matanza*, this was, at minimum, a dangerous doctrine to teach to government forces that were greatly influenced by, if not ultimately under the control of, the plutocracy determined to hold on to its land and its privileges. The case against Washington is stronger than this. The subsidy and the training were provided with the intent that they be used in general in the way they were used. Certainly Washington's culpability exceeds that required by the Torture Victim Protection Act of 1992, which allows victims or their surviving relatives to sue those who knew of crimes or the probability of their occurring but took no action to stop them. Washington knew of the crimes committed in El Salvador and provided the means and the training to commit them.

The Clinton administration offered some praise for the report of the commission when it first appeared. When asked if the Reagan and Bush administrations had failed to protect human rights in El Salvador, Mr. Boucher, the State Department spokesperson, finessed the issue in a way that paid tribute to his chosen profession, diplomacy. He replied: "That's something that the analysts and the historians can try to judge. I'm not going to make that judgment at this point."[43] He went on to say that "we feel" that the report is important in terms of its revealing the truth, and this is a key element in a national reconciliation.

The situation existing in El Salvador in 1980 has now been re-established, complete with massive social injustice and a considerable amount of violence. ARENA won the runoff elections in 1994 and also the 1999 elections. It implemented none of the reforms recommended by the truth commission, nor has it advertised its findings. The government is under the control of ARENA, a party founded by D'Aubuisson, who was supported by the elites, founded many death squads, and was charged by the truth commission with many atrocities, including ordering and planning the assassination of Archbishop Romero. With only 40 percent of the vote, Francisco Flores was victorious in the 1999 election. A strange and contradictory ideological mix and the heir to a cattle ranch, he praises D'Aubuisson, the founder of his party. But he is said to follow a guru who teaches non-violence.[44] The present situation in El Salvador is grim, providing more of the same, perhaps moderated, internal violence without social justice. The future does seem brighter because of the recent electoral gains of the FMLN, now reconstituted as a legitimate political party.

In this chapter, the central questions posed in this volume have been answered affirmatively. To summarize the findings:
1. The government of El Salvador did commit state terrorism.
2. The terrorism that occurred in El Salvador was overwhelmingly state terrorism, with only some five percent committed by the guerrillas.
3. Washington rendered support for this government's terrorism before, during, and after it was committed.

The data presented in the next chapter are asked to answer these questions for Guatemala, the subject of the second case study.

CHAPTER 2

Guatemala:
A Country Incommunicado

WHY GUATEMALA?

Guatemala is a Central American country the size of Ohio. To the newly arrived tourist, it appears to be a tropical paradise—tropical, but also mountainous, resulting in an ideal climate. It has not been a paradise. Guatemala was chosen as a case study for analysis principally because of the quality of the sources available for answering the central research questions of the volume. These sources include two truth commissions, one conducted under the auspices of the United Nations, the other sponsored and carried out by the archdiocese of Guatemala City. The third is the work of Father Falla, a Jesuit priest and anthropologist who interviewed hundreds of Mayan Indians as they fled from the highlands of Guatemala to seek refuge in Mexico.

Guatemala is a poor Central American country, with a very unequal distribution of wealth and income common to Latin America, but aggravated by the prejudice that the Ladinos (the Mestizos) hold toward the majority of the population who are Mayan Indians. The Maya live in grinding poverty. To the delight of tourists, they wear their traditional colorful clothing—at least this was the case in the past. In this the land of the former Mayan empire, the rich have disproportionate wealth and income, while the poor are forced to get along on very little. President Arbenz and the predecessor regime of Juan Arevelo, a liberal who was elected to office after over a century of rule by despotic caudillos, tried to do something about poverty. For the first time in Guatemalan history a labor code was promulgated, forced labor was abolished, and land reform was instituted. Arevelo undertook to narrow the gap between those who have and those who have not and to improve the lot of the majority Indian population through a series of measures which antagonized the latifundia, foreign investors, and military officers. Arbenz continued with these reforms, pushing through parliament a far-reaching program of agrarian reform, and announcing his intention of expropriating the unused land of the United Fruit Company. The U.S. State Department announced on May 17, 1954 that Guatemala had received a shipment of arms from Czechoslovakia.[1]

The CIA proceeded to train and to supply an invasion force in neighboring Honduras under the command of a Guatemalan colonel, Carlos Castillo Armas. The force's main function was to serve as a psychological rallying point for Washington's pre-invasion propaganda campaign. A "liberation-army" radio campaign was inaugurated, and every effort was made to ensure that the Guatemalan government and army were aware of its presence just across the border in Honduras. Armas was a graduate of the U.S. Army Command and General Staff College at Fort Leavenworth, Kansas. According to E. Howard Hunt, then a CIA operative and later a "plumber," Armas had been chosen because "our paramilitary people... were impressed with Castillo's qualities as a leader."[2] John Peurifoy, newly appointed United States Ambassador, was put in charge of the operation in Guatemala. The general headquarters for the project was sited in Opa Locka, Florida. It involved some 100 CIA agents, and enjoyed its own infrastructure, communications system, and a budget of between five and seven million dollars. It was given the code name Project PB SUCCESS.

It was the army that in 1954 turned the invasion into the coup that deposed Arbenz. The "liberation army" of Armas was not an impressive force. Totalling only 300 troops, it was composed of Guatemalans, as well as mercenaries from Nicaragua, Honduras, and Panama. It was stopped just 20 miles from the Honduran border by the regular Guatemalan army.[3] More important were the bombing and strafing of CIA and Air Force planes flying out of Nicaragua.[4] Targets were chosen mainly for their psychological impact: ammunition dumps, military drill fields, and oil storage facilities. Other significant developments were taking place at army headquarters and at the national palace.

President Arbenz ordered that the workers and campesinos be armed so as to oppose the invaders. His chief of staff carried out his orders, but he had to report back that army officers under him refused to do so. Nine days after the invasion, on June 27, representatives of the officer corps confronted the president to demand his resignation, a more decisive action than the invasion in bringing an end to the regime. In any case, both were part of a scenario planned and orchestrated by the CIA. Colonel Armas arrived at the Guatemalan capital not as the commander of a victorious invasion force, but in the airplane of the American ambassador! The colonel was assassinated three years later. The coup that toppled the Arbenz regime in 1954 was a watershed in the history of the Central American country. It was the last effort before the bloody repression that followed to bring a measure of justice to the Guatemalan underclass.

The factual basis for portraying this repression is the reports of two truth commissions and a study conducted by Father Falla, the Jesuit priest and anthropologist who interviewed 773 refugees in Mexico who had escaped the horror of Guatemala. The first of the truth commission reports was published in April 1998 by the Catholic Archdiocese of Guatemala City, the second by the United Nations. The result of three years of effort, the report of the archdiocese came to four volumes, and was entitled *Recovery of Historical Memory.* Eight hundred parish workers were trained to interview the 5,465 witnesses who provided the informational base for the project. Thirty-nine percent of the interviews were held in Spanish, the remaining and thus the great majority, in indigenous languages. Most of those interviewed were either the victims of oppression or survivors of victims. A few were perpetrators. If members of the army, they were subject to retaliation for breaking the code of silence of the organization. Since the publication, *Recovery of His-*

Two days after the publication of the report, Bishop Gerardi, the director of the project that produced it, was beaten to death with a cement block.

torical Memory, was not available to the author; use was made of a summary of it, entitled *Guatemala Never Again.*[5] Two days after the publication of the larger work, Bishop Gerardi, the director of the project that produced it, was beaten to death with a cement block. The elucidation of this tragedy awaits its turn.

The second truth commission report was mandated by the peace accord of Oslo, an agreement negotiated by the United Nations. It was a nine volume work, released to the public on February 25, 1999, and entitled *Guatemala:*

Memory of Silence. The work was based on an eight months investigation headed by the Historical Clarification Commission, the leg work being done by a staff of 272. It also is based upon thousands of interviews. It cost ten million dollars to produce. The Commission consisted of a German jurist, Christian Tomuschat, who acted as the chairperson and two Guatemalans, one a lawyer, the other a prominent educator. The agreement at Oslo brought to a close what was touted to be the longest guerrilla war in Latin America. What is generally referred to as the guerrilla war in Guatemala was of thirty-five years standing. However, the findings of this report plus those of the report of the Archdiocese require that this long period of violence be denominated as a period of government repression and terror rather than of guerrilla warfare. Both reports point to the Guatemalan government and its allies and collaborators as responsible for more than 95 percent of the crimes committed. This conclusion is consonant with that regarding El Salvador, and it provides an answer to one of the three principal questions posed in this study. The conclusions and the recommendations of the United Nations report were published in 1999 by the Science and Human Rights Program of the American Association for the Advancement of Science. This source was used by the author in the preparation of this chapter.

ASSIGNING BLAME FOR VIOLENCE IN GUATEMALA

The UN commission recorded 42,275 victims of acts of violence and human rights violations that occurred in the period between 1962 and 1996.[6] This number represents some of the unfortunate victims successfully and directly targeted by the government and the guerrillas. Of these, 23,671 were executions and 6,159 were victims of forced disappearance. This means that 56 percent of the reported human rights violations and acts of violence were executions and over 14 percent were forced disappearances. Since those forcibly disappeared were usually killed, both the absolute number killed and ratio of those killed to human rights violations in Guatemala were very high. The commission estimated that the total number of victims in the two categories in actuality had exceeded 200,000. No matter how viewed or arranged, the repression in this Central American state was very lethal. The majority of the victims recorded by the commission were civilians, not guerrillas or members of the armed forces. One fourth were women, who were often raped before they were tortured or killed, and many were children, who were also sometimes raped before they were tortured or killed. Eighty-three percent of the victims were Mayan, the remaining seventeen percent Ladino (mestizo). Ninety-one percent of the violations recorded by the commission occurred during the period 1978 to 1984 (during the Carter and Reagan administrations). Similarly, nearly 80 percent of the violations documented by the report of the Archdiocese occurred between 1980 and 1983 (mostly during the Reagan administration).[7] These facts are consonant with the fact that this period was the one in which the state was carrying out its policy of massacring Maya in rural areas.

The UN commission found that in Guatemala the problem was government repression much more than guerrilla warfare. Ninety-three percent of the violations recorded by the commission, including 92 percent of the executions

The majority of the victims recorded by the commission were civilians, not guerrillas or members of the armed forces.

and 91 percent of the forced disappearances, were committed by the state and related paramilitary groups. Only three percent of the executions, forced disappearances, and tortures were laid at the door of the guerrillas.[8] This included five percent of the executions and two percent of the forced disappearances. The remaining four percent of the executions, forced disappearances, and tortures were labeled "private." These crimes were committed by unidentified armed groups, civil elements, and public officials. The investigation revealed that the groups other than the guerrillas often worked together in committing the offenses. The commission also attributed many more massacres to the state than to the guerrillas. The state committed 626 of them, the guerrillas 32.

Similarly, the report of the Archdiocese blamed the guerrillas for 16 massacres of a total of 422.[9] It defined a massacre as an incident in which three or more were killed. It added that as a matter of general policy the guerrillas were more selective in the use of collective murders than the army, inspired as it was by counterinsurgency doctrine. The army was found to be implicated in 90.52 percent of the massacres, acting alone in 55 percent of the cases and in collaboration with military commissioners and civil patrols in the rest. The latter were involved in 35.54 percent of the massacres, but only in 4.5 percent acting alone. The commissioners who wrote the United Nations report used the term "massacre" to include, in the case of the guerrillas, the collective killing of a defenseless population, including women and children[10] whereas the massacres attributed to the state were scorched earth operations resulting in the complete extermination of many Mayan communities, along with their homes, cattle, crops, and other resources essential to their survival.[11]

In a majority of the massacres committed by the state, especially by the army, the counterinsurgency strategy led to multiple acts of savagery, such as the killing of defenseless children, often by beating them against walls or throwing them alive into pits where the corpses of adults were later thrown; impaling the victims, amputating their limbs; burning them alive; extracting their viscera while still alive and in the presence of others; confining those who had been mortally tortured, thus making them agonize for days; and opening the wombs of pregnant women.[12] The portrayal of the situation that existed in Guatemala took on the dimensions of an encyclopedia of horror, and the picture portrayed is at minimum, state terrorism. Some have labeled it genocide, a charge examined below. Furthermore, both truth commissions found that the terrorism, if that is the label to be used, was overwhelmingly governmental terrorism, not private terrorism.

> **The counterinsurgency strategy led to multiple acts of savagery, such as the killing of defenseless children.**

For several months, Father Falla interviewed Guatemalan refugees from across the Guatemalan border in southern Mexico. Given limitations of space, his contribution to the present encyclopedia of horror is brief. He documented the cases of 773 civilian victims of the government's counterinsurgency operations in Ixcan province (in neighboring Guatemala) from 1975 to 1982.[13] He found an ebb and flow in the army's activity, from massive to selective terror and repression. But whatever the level, systematic torture was always an integral part of the process. Army torture at times proceeded by well known, traditional methods: burning by fire brands, submerging in water, and asphyxiation. But burning people alive was a favorite method. The victim was first stabbed, and his or her wounded body was thrown into a pit. Soldiers (or paramilitaries) next threw in firewood, doused it with gasoline, and ignited it with a match. A small explosion followed, the fire burned brightly, but the firewood moved because the stabbed victim was still alive. More gasoline, more fire, and the pit was calm.

The Silence of the Terrorized

The report of the United Nations was given the suggestive name *Guatemala: Memory of Silence*. The report itself concluded that the cost of the repression was high in terms of lives lost, "but also because Guatemala became a country silenced, a country incommunicado."[14] Free speech was a victim along with other human rights. "To write about political and social realities, events, or ideas meant running the risk of threats, disappearances, and torture." The large news agencies in general went along with the government and engaged in self-censorship and distortion of the facts. This is the same phenomenon that occurred in El Salvador, a social malady common to our case studies. Government repression produced not only silence among the masses of people, but passivity and a dehumanizing effect as well.

The large news agencies in general went along with the government and engaged in self-censorship and distortion of the facts.

The huge increase in military spending diverted funds from education and other social programs. The increases in military spending were also facilitated by the large amount of economic aid provided by Washington. This aid allowed the Guatemalan government to pay for the non-military services it considered to be essential. The commission estimated that the total economic loss to the country of the government repression was equivalent to 121 percent of the 1990 gross domestic product of the country. This loss included the total destruction of the possessions of families, especially Mayan families. The fear is that the repression might have the same degrading impact on Mayan culture that the *matanza* of 1932 in El Salvador had on Indian culture in that country.

As indicated above, the state, especially the army, committed numerous acts of savagery against the Maya, including the destruction of their homes, cattle, crops, and other elements essential to survival. The cultural rights of the Mayan were also violated. The army destroyed their ceremonial centers, their sacred places, and their cultural symbols.[15] It killed their elders and destroyed their corn, which has a special significance in their culture. It targeted for repression their language, their dress, and other types of cultural identification. Often the women lost their traditional clothing in the general destruction of a massacre, or they switched to different dress, or given their poverty, to rags to prevent identification and its attendant repression.[16] To Maya, female dress is an object experienced with particular intensity. It provides a sense of identity and is full of symbolism. Its loss was more than material, and must be understood in terms of personal dignity. The army broke the traditional authority structure of communities by militarizing them, and it prevented the use of traditional norms and procedures to regulate social life. In place of them, it substituted authoritarian practices and the arbitrary use of power. It degraded Mayan culture by using Mayan names and symbols for military structures and task forces. It obstructed and prevented the exercise of either Mayan spirituality or the Catholic religion.

The above litany of army crimes did not go unchallenged by some brave souls, but Mayan resistance will not be discussed here, due to its relative insignificance. Government massacres "led to the flight en masse of a diverse population, the majority of which was Mayan, but which also included a considerable number of Ladino families, especially in the newly settled areas close to the Mexican border."[17] The United Nations report asserted that estimates of the number of internally and externally displaced persons during the period 1981 to 1983 vary from one-half million to a million and a half. The divergence in the estimates reflects the intrinsic difficulties in making them plus the changing nature of the displacement. Some 150,000 sought safety in Mexico. One-third of this number were settled in camps and were accorded refugee status by the United Nations High Commission for Refugees. Another third went to Chiapas, and the last third to other locations in Mexico. Far fewer went to Honduras, Belize, and the United States. The report of the Archdiocese puts the total number of those displaced somewhat higher, and adds that it reached "massive proportions" during the early eighties.[18] This report asserts that one million were internally displaced, an estimate that evidently refers to the early eighties.

Whether internally or externally displaced, all shared common experiences—the loss of relatives and property and the jarring experience of suddenly being uprooted from the security of their normal lives. In addition, all those who fled had to remain constantly on the move while in Guatemala, so as to avoid being hunted down by the army. "Military persecution, being constantly on the move, and the threat of death made their existence extremely difficult. Living exposed to the elements, malnutrition, and the severe emotional traumas that resulted from having witnessed numerous atrocities, left people vulnerable, especially children and the elderly, a great number of whom died during the flight and displacement."[19]

COUNTERINSURGENCY TRAINING

Targeting Women and Children

The authors of the report of the Archdiocese emphasized the violence perpetrated by the army against women and children, particularly Mayan women and children. At times women were successful in resisting their oppressors, a subject not explored here. Children were less able to resist. They had more difficulty in fleeing, and often their families went down before them, and could not help them. Nor did they grasp the mechanics of violence. "Half of the massacres recorded included the collective murder of children."[20] The accounts of their deaths often included references to atrocities: incineration, machete wounds, drawing and quartering, and, most frequently, severe head trauma. Many young girls were raped. The examples included in the report of the archdiocese are often explicit and graphic. A few are recounted here to indicate the horror and terror of the government repression in Guatemala, a message that statistics are unable to provide. Collective testimony about an incident which occurred in 1982 illustrates the brutality of the suppression of children:

> A 13-year-old girl was handed over to me, the poor girl crying bitterly. "What's wrong with you, girl?"
> "Only God knows where they will take me," the child said.
> I took out my handkerchief and gave it to her. "Clean yourself instead." So a certain military instructor, Basilio Velasquez, comes over.
> "What's up, and what's with her? She should be vaccinated,

no? She's good."

"That vile individual raped her, and after raping her, sent her to the well. How was it that they executed those poor people? Look, they blindfolded her and clubbed her on the head all the way to the well."[21]

Another testimony describes the murder of children, this time the killing of three year olds, arguably the most precious of God's creations:

"They buried the ones that the army killed. They were decapitated with a tourniquet around the throat. They crumpled them up, they handled them like little balls. They were three-year-old children. We went to see. We saw them, three kids, they were hanging there without any heads. Their little dolls were behind them."[22]

The children were sometimes eliminated so that later they would not seek out those who killed their parents to get even. Or they were tortured or threatened so as to get information from their parents. The murder of these children was also consistent with the military training and instructions given to soldiers. The murder of children was adopted by the army as terrorism—as a counterinsurgency tactic, part of a scorched earth operation. The carefully designed strategy included the elimination of entire communities including the children. It had the potential for success, because of its tremendous impact upon survivors, particularly upon the Maya. To them, violence against children is an assault to the community that includes not merely the living, but the ancestors and the descendants. Together with the living, children are a bridge between the two. This is apparent in the language. For example, among the Achi Maya the word "Mam" serves equally to denote ancestors and grandparents as well as newborn grandchildren.

The children were sometimes eliminated so that later they would not seek out those who killed their parents to get even. Or they were tortured or threatened so as to get information from their parents.

Women gave half of the testimonies compiled for the report of the Archdiocese, and they constituted some twenty-five percent of the victims. Special types of violence were perpetrated against them by the army, especially during massacres. The report of the Archdiocese stated that although there "may not have been an explicit counterinsurgency objective that targeted women, there was a deliberate attempt to destroy the community social fabric, a fabric woven and sustained primarily by women. Women were also the ones to repair broken social ties, preserving family cohesion even under the most adverse conditions. They were the ones to preserve the essential ingredients for re-establishing ties among groups of survivors."[23] The army used them as a source of ridicule, and as a way by which the soldiers would entertain themselves. There were several variations of rape. Gang rape served the purpose of entertaining the soldiers. A variation of this was to have the uninfected soldiers go first, with those infected with gonorrhea and syphilis going last.

One testimony asserted that the villagers heard the soldiers laughing, and they went to see what was going on.[24] The soldiers made the male prisoners grab the women and have sex with them. "And that's what they were laughing at." The male "lovers" had not eaten or slept and had been beaten. One of the most powerful genre of ways used to crush the psyches and terrorize mothers was to use their children to these ends. The example given revealed that in that massacre the children saw everything that the soldiers did to their mothers, their sisters, and other members of their family, "and afterwards they killed them (the children) too." The atrocities were committed against pregnant women as well. "One of them was in her eighth month, and they cut her belly, and they took out the little one, and they tossed it around like a ball. Then they cut off one breast, and they left it hanging in a tree." Still another testimony spoke of fetuses being left hanging by their umbilical cords from trees.

During massacres women experienced atrocities and violations in the guise of their daily routines. One such atrocity occurred when the soldiers demanded that each of twelve women cook a hen for them for lunch. "Maybe we aren't going to kill you." After they brought the hens from their houses, the killing began:

> "If the son was carrying out his patrol duty, and the father was not, then the son had to kill the father; if the son was the one who wasn't complying, then the father had to stain his hands by killing his son. After that, the clay pots with the twelve hens inside were put on the fire, and the women themselves began to cook. The army ordered them to make sure the food was well prepared after they (the soldiers) had killed the twelve men. They killed them and tortured them, and they went to get gasoline. When they were all burned up, they applauded and they started eating."

The figures collected by the writers of the report of the Archdiocese found that rapes were most common during acts of collective violence.[25] The testimonies of victims indicated that these acts occurred in 16 percent of the massacres in which the army and their allies sought to destroy communities. In addition, 149 individual rapes were reported. For every ten women raped, one girl was raped. The writers of the report warned that because of the shame suffered by the victim, her family, and sometimes even by the community, the incidence of this crime is probably grossly under reported. This report characterized rape as a terror tactic, the ultimate humiliation for the victims and their families, a tactic used to signal male dominance, victory over adversaries, and contempt for its victims. It was often combined with counterinsurgency violence, *i.e.* accusations that the victims were guerrillas was often used as an excuse for the crime. It was presented to the soldiers as a "perk" and as a compensation for the inconvenience of their military service. The female body was seen as one more possession available for use by the victors.

One example of rape and two examples of extreme forms of sexual abuse and torture follow.[26] The first is from an accomplice to the crime.

> "We found a woman, I called the soldiers and I told them: take charge of the woman, she is a present from the second lieutenant.
>
> 'Understood, corporal,' he answered, and he called the boys and said: 'there's meat, guys.'
>
> So they came and grabbed the girl. They took her little boy from her and they all raped her. It was a gang rape. Afterwards,

I told them to kill the woman first so she wouldn't feel so bad about the death of her son."

Collective testimony from a Mayan village after a massacre indicated that:

"There are women hanging. Well, the stick goes into her private parts and then the stick comes out of her mouth. They had her hanging there like a snake."

Another testimony in a different Mayan village told this story:

"Before murdering her, they nailed her to a cross they had made. They stuck huge nails into her hands and chest, then they put her inside the house to burn her up. They found her burned, still on the cross; her son was beside her, also burned—badly burned."

The publication of the Archdiocese provides an illustration of a rape committed by some part of the government or perhaps a death squad associated with the government. The incident occurred in Guatemala City, and was not associated with a massacre. The horror was experienced by Yolanda Aguilar Urizar, the daughter of a prominent Christian Democrat.[27] Her father and her brother had died four years before in a deliberately managed car accident. That attack was actually intended for her mother who worked for the National Workers Central. Years later her mother was forcibly disappeared. The victim was led to a room, stripped, and the volume of the radio was turned up. For the first time she realized that she would be tortured. Next there appeared a nineteen or twenty-year-old man, with blond hair and blue eyes, who could have come out of any private school in Guatemala. He played the role of the "good cop." He said that he really wanted to help her, but that his companions were really bad. "So I want to be friends, I want you to tell me everything you know."

But then the "bad cops" arrived, and the rape began. "And I can remember clearly that about 20 men raped me." While one was doing it, the others were masturbating and grabbing her breasts. She lost consciousness several times. "That was when they hit me. They slapped my face, and others put cigarettes on my breasts, and each time I started to come around, I saw a different man on top of me. And I remember when I could no longer feel that someone was with me. I was in the pool of urine, semen, and, I guess, blood too. It was truly humiliating, incredibly humiliating."

They took her to a sink full of filth, covered with fungus and mold. There was a horrible smell. They put her head in it once or twice. "The feeling of suffocation is one of the most terrible things, you know. Every time you want to breathe, you fill up with shit, so you do everything possible not to breathe, but you can't." They took her to another room where there were planks on top of the doorway. "Have you seen the crucifixion? Well here, very nearly, was Jesus Christ; there was a man, there was half a man—the most horrendous thing I have ever seen— a man totally disfigured. He already had worms, he had no teeth, no hair, his face was disfigured, he was hanging, I mean, by his hands."

Then someone from the judiciary arrived. He was carrying a tiny scythe. It was red hot, and he grabbed the penis of the hanging man and cut it off. "That guy let out a scream that I have never forgotten, a terrible scream, so horrifying that for many years I remembered that scream. He died. Later there was a cassette of Spanish music that had a scream almost like it, and I guess I fainted."

After having had her traveling papers prepared, Yolanda Aguilar Urizar left for Mexico, Cuba, and Nicaragua. She completed her recovery in Cuba, where she found the medical system "fabulous" and where the peace and security helped her a lot. She then went back to Nicaragua.

If anything, the decision to characterize government repression in Guatemala as state terrorism is overdue.

Training for Terror and Massacres

The question arises as to how the army and its allied agencies could commit such atrocities, especially since most of the perpetrators were enlisted personnel from the same class and the same ethnic group as the great majority of the victims. Part of the answer is provided by the counterinsurgency training that army personnel received from Washington. The truth commission reports, however, did not dwell upon this, just as their general focus was on what institutions within Guatemala did, not on how these institutions were affected by outside forces, The authors of the Archdiocesan report rejected the explanation that human nature was responsible or that the perpetrators were demented. Rather they sought a structural explanation—in the training of the Guatemalan army. The report of the archdiocese found that the army developed a military training system based on forcible recruitment, absolute obedience, strict control over groups, and "complicity in atrocities".[28] The inner two characteristics are common to armies, the outer two are not. The army did have volunteers as well. Those of military age in the villages were sometimes spared torture or worse, but then forced to fill the ranks of the army. If they objected, they were accused of being guerrillas and were threatened with death.

Once in training, whether volunteers or not, they entered a system designed to suppress their individuality, one whose premise was an absolute submission to orders and isolation from their customary social surroundings. Failure to obey orders was met with harsh punishment, isolation in small cells, or even death. The entire group was often punished for the disobedience of one member, actions that encouraged monitoring by the group itself. The army fostered a sense of group loyalty and a frame of reference that justified their actions. The recruits were taught the code of silence, not to inform on each other. They were shown news clippings and videos from Argentina, in which solders engaged in this "disloyal and criminal conduct." They were fed an ideology that pinned the ills of the country, including poverty, upon the communists and their local representatives, the guerrillas.

The army used the "foot in the door approach"—gradually, deliberately, and systematically inducing the recruit to accept his role as a perpetrator of repression. One recruit told the story this way:

"They put you through tests that gradually eliminate people. They stain your hands with blood. This is important to make you loyal, since then you can't back out. Or, if you want out, they kill you. They order you to kill to implicate you, to test you. They give you a target."[29]

Learning the Step of Death

Besides implicating the recruits, the training was designed to inure them to the suffering of others, to foster contempt for their life. One soldier's period of training coincided with the widespread atrocities of the late seventies and earlier eighties. He evidently had been sent to the field for some practical training. While searching for the officer to whom he had been ordered to report, he heard the voices of soldiers. They yelled to him, "hurry or you are going to miss out on something good." But by the time he got there he was too late. Only one of the boys was left, and they were cutting off his head.

"Okay today we are going to learn how to kill people."[30] These were the opening words to one session in a series in which the recruits learned different methods of killing, how to organize massacres, and how to conceal corpses. They were taught "the step of death." For this they practiced on a fellow recruit. It was practice killing at short range, that typical of murdering civilians, perhaps in a massacre. How calmly to shoot the victim in the chest or the head, perhaps after he had dug his own grave. The trainees would learn torture techniques for three days, followed by a period of rest. It was the second section chief, an intelligence officer, who gave the orders actually to kill. "He specifically gave orders even to the point of killing someone, finishing someone off." Evidently, the reference here is to a surplus prisoner that the army had on hand.

The commissioners who wrote the United Nations report were impressed with "the degrading contents of the training of the Army's special counterinsurgency force, known as Kaibiles."[31] The report went on to say that the training included the killing of animals and then eating them raw and drinking their blood to demonstrate courage. The extreme cruelty of this training, according to testimony received by the commission, was put into practice in a range of operations carried out by these counterinsurgency forces. The way they carried out these operations confirmed one point of their training Decalogue: "the Kaibil is a killing machine." The commissioners recommended that the Kaibiles be disbanded.

The report of the Archdiocese provides an example of this peculiar training method. After three months of training, the recruit arrived at the firing range.

> "[They] set us to grab three hundred dogs. We grabbed them. The army leader said, 'Okay, listen, this is the meat that we are going to eat today.' They took us to a firing range located in the gullies below the university, where they ordered us to kill the dogs. They filled a barrel with blood. All of us were given a disposable cup filled with dog blood, and we had to down it. Whoever didn't drink it was two-faced. They didn't serve us lunch that day in order to get us to eat that; our lunch was that cup of blood. During the meal [dinner] they gave us dog stew. This is the reason many deserted; they got sick. That is how they ended the course."[32]

THE REPORT OF THE ARCHDIOCESE OF GUATEMALA CITY

The team representing the Archdiocese came to conclusions very similar to those of the United Nations report. This team interviewed 5,465 witnesses and documented 14,291 incidents of human rights and humanitarian law violations.[33] These incidents produced 52,427 victims. This compares with 42,275 victims referred to in the United Nations report. The most frequently reported violations found by the team that produced the report of the Archdiocese were individual or collective murders. These produced 25,123 victims or 47.92 percent of the total. If the percentage of those who were forcibly "disappeared" (and who presumably did not later "reappear") is added, this percentage augments to some 54 percent of the total victims. Their number becomes 28,301. The comparable figure in the United Nations report was 29,830, or over 70 percent of the crimes committed. The predominance of murders led to the somewhat exaggerated saying that Guatemala had no political prisoners, only political corpses. A convenient way of estimating the sample size of the report of the Archdiocese is to compare this number with the 200,000 estimated to have been killed. The sample size thus derived is 14.15 percent, very close to the size estimated for the United Nations report. No matter which kill rate is accepted, 70 percent or 54 percent, the repression in Guatemala was extraordinarily lethal.

The report of the Archdiocese found the army, police forces, civil patrols, military commissioners, death squads, and paramilitaries responsible for 95.19 percent of the victims. This compares with 93 percent found in the United Nations report. The report of the Archdiocese identified the army as the chief transgressor, having committed 62.9 percent of the crimes by itself and another 20.22 percent in conjunction with other transgressors. The guerrillas were charged with having committed 4.81 percent of the violations. This is certainly consonant with the three percent found in the report of the United Nations. These figures thus answer one of the three central questions asked by the study: was the terror committed in the country under review state terror committed by the government, or private terror committed by the guerrillas? The evidence provided by the truth commissions indicates that it was state terror committed by the government. The violations of the guerrillas were divided into three parts of almost equal proportions: killings, cruel treatment, and threats against groups or institutions, *i.e.* against paramilitary organizations or communities considered hostile. Their kill ratio was thus lower than that of the army and its affiliated agencies.

The number of those murdered, as of the report of the Archdiocese, was followed by other victims in this order: victims of attacks, irregular detentions, threats, torture, forced disappearances, abductions (who later reappeared), and rapes. A few comments about this list are warranted. The report immediately pointed out that the number of rapes was under-documented. The shame attached to it by the victim, the victim's family, or even the community accounts for this. Torture was also under-reported. The majority of those who were subsequently killed or forcibly disappeared were first tortured. These victims were put under the kill category. Attacks were seen as actions committed against individuals with the purpose of causing them harm or of intimidating them so as to modify their behavior. Nearly all of these attacks were committed by the army (91.16 percent), in the context of such operations as the bombings of communities. The guerrillas were found guilty of 2.92 percent of the attacks, committing such actions as attacks on installations and the harassment of communities.[34]

Impunity was the silent and constant accomplice of repression and the army relied upon the former to accomplish the latter.

The two reports that provide the chief documentary basis for our presentation agree that impunity was the silent and constant accomplice of repression and that the army relied upon the former to accomplish the latter. The creators of the report of the archdiocese were impressed with the pervasiveness of governmental impunity. It affirmed that: "The term 'impunity' appears throughout this book to describe a pervasive reality in which government agents operated, and continue to operate, without fear of punishment." The testimony of Professor Philip Heymann, a professor of law at Harvard, the Director of the Center for Criminal Justice there, and former head of the Criminal Division of the U.S. Justice Department, is used here to bring home the point.

In his testimony before the subcommittee on Western Hemisphere Affairs July 17, 1990, Professor Heymann affirmed that he was about to terminate "a very sizeable administration of justice program in Guatemala" that had been in operation for over two years.[35] Paid for by USAID, the program's purpose was to help "the new democracy" in Guatemala to deal with ordinary violence and with political violence. The reason for the termination was the way the government was dealing with, or actually not dealing with, political violence. The professor drew attention to the fact that the courts and the prosecutors could not handle political violence alone, "especially if there is a strong suspicion that the nation's security forces, police, or military are behind it." They need the strong support of the police and "someone with guns on their side." Heymann added that the decision to leave actually was made the previous fall after the forced disappearances of twelve students, whom he presumed to be dead.

Heymann went to see the then Defense Minister General Gramajo and the Minister of Government as well. He told Gramajo that he did not want the army to investigate the crime, but what he wanted was a vigorous statement that the army was strongly supporting such an investigation and that it would offer any information collected by army intelligence. He warned the Minister of Government that unless a vigorous effort was made to investigate the crimes, he and his staff would leave. Neither of his demands was met, so he decided to terminate the project, seeing "no point in building half of a criminal justice system, one that dealt only with street crime and not with important people either in the administration or in the security forces or private industry."

Professor Heymann could recall from his experience only one case of violence that seemed to be politically motivated that was seriously investigated.[36] He assured the subcommittee that there were hundreds, perhaps thousands of such cases not investigated. This led Representative Kostmayer, who was chairing the meeting, to turn to General Gramajo, and say, "Now, General, you do not agree with that?"

To which the general replied, "No."

Yes—General Gramajo was in the subcommittee room. After thirty-three years in the Guatemalan army, General Gramajo retired in May of 1989, having held the positions of Chief of the General Defense Staff and Minister of Defense. He had spoken to Professor Heymann just a few months before as Minister of Defense. At the time of his appearance before the subcommittee he was a Fellow of the George Mason Program at the Kennedy School of Government which is affiliated with Harvard University. General Gramajo had not been subpoenaed to appear before it. He volunteered. Given the close connection between the Guatemalan army and the atrocities committed there and the positions he held in the army, he certainly should be considered to be an expert witness. He held the two positions referred to above from January, 1986 until his retirement in May, 1989—not the period of the great massacres, but during a period of the selective repression of political and social activists, such as the twelve "disappeared" students mentioned above.[37]

The reader may remember that in the discussion above concerning the School of the Americas, General Gramajo argued that Sister Ortiz was "self-abducted" and that the 111 cigarette burns she received were the result of a failed lesbian love affair. This charge contains the standard allegation leveled at priests and nuns by the Guatemalan government: that their torture or demise was some-how related to homosexual activities. The other testimony of the general before the subcommittee was predictable and equally unenlightening. To the question why are there no major left-of-center candidates running for the presidency of a country that has so many poor, he answered alternately that there were, maybe two, but their parties are new and badly organized, and they lack the ability to deliver their message to the people.[38]

> Question: "Is there any possibility that their lives [those of left-of-center candidates] might be in danger?"
> General Gramajo: "I do not think so. Not at this stage."

Congressman Kostmayer next turned to Mr. LaRue, a former labor lawyer living in Guatemala.

> "Mr. La Rue how do you account for this lack of left of center candidates in the election?"
> "Well, the two social democratic candidates, historic candidates, were assassinated in 1979, Alberto Fuentes Mohr and Manuel Colom Argueta."

Mr. LaRue went on to assert that the social democrats were the historic democratic party of the country, and that no candidate from this party or any other left-of-center party has been willing to risk his life by running for office. The general agreed that this type assassination could happen again. When asked why, he retorted "Because political killing is a way of life in Guatemala." He did not inform the subcommittee how it became that way or who or what made it so.

The general and the labor lawyer disagreed also on whether the latter would be safe if he returned to Guatemala. The general said "yes." LaRue disagreed. That is not what he heard from his friends in that country.

This section ends with the testimony of the two "colleagues" from Harvard, one an expert on criminal justice systems, the other who appears, by the facts presented above, to be an expert practitioner of state terrorism. They faced off on the subject of the "disappeared students." Professor Heymann alleged that they had been killed and that the military was involved. No, he couldn't prove it. But then how could you prove it? He added:

> "My basis, Mr. Chairman, is a fairly universal opinion of very well-informed people in Guatemala. This is not proof. This is not evidence. But it is a fairly universal opinion of a large number of highly placed people in Guatemala. Large number being five or six sources highly placed. I believe that for that reason. I also believe that because I believe some of the students were picked up in the presence of police with no police response. I think that is true.[39] "

General Gramajo's explanation was at variance with this. In fact, it was in the same vein as his explanation of the rape and torture of Sister Ortiz. The students were "self-abducted" in the sense that these twelve students had been forcibly disappeared by other students. Perhaps this explains the general's use of the term in relation to the rape and torture of Sister Ortiz: she was raped and tortured by other nuns!

> Congressman Kostmayer: "General, are you telling the sub-committee that the students killed the students, other students killed these students?"
>
> General Gramajo: "The evidence that we had in those days indicate that. We are saying that, sir. Yes."

He went on to explain that the student unions would not join the teachers strike that had been going on for a long time and that was designed to destabilize the government. The students were ordered to join the strike by the Marxist-Leninist guerrillas, they refused, and thus they disappeared. Their disappearances had been brought about by other students, evidently also Marxist-Leninist. He went on to explain to his American audience that:

> "Here it is outrageous to think that the students kill each other in the college environment of the United States. But if you are familiar with Latin America or you are familiar with Guatemala, this is an event that you do not have a doubt that it will happen."[40]

THE CHARGE OF GENOCIDE

The authors of the United Nations report went beyond accusing the state of committing terror to what is often considered to be a more grievous and heinous level, the ultimate charge of genocide. The authors of the UN report devoted no less than sixteen paragraphs (numbers 108 to123) of their conclusion to substantiate this charge. They first cited the Convention on the Prevention and Punishment of the Crime of Genocide, the United Nations-sponsored treaty that had been ratified by Guatemala. The convention pictures genocide as having two sides: that of actions and that of intention. Article II expresses evidence of the intention of this crime as "to destroy, in whole or in part, a national, ethnical, racial, or religious group, as such." Five actions are identified as characteristic of genocide, and the commission found that the army of Guatemala was guilty of three of these.

1) Physical destruction in whole or in part

The first action is killing, causing serious bodily or mental harm to, and deliberately inflicting on the group conditions of life calculated to bring about its physical destruction in whole or in part. The commission found that the intention of the Guatemalan army was to go beyond targeting guerrilla sympathizers, combatants, or militants to include specific ethnic groups as such. The commission continued by pointing to the period 1981 to 1983 when the Guatemalan army targeted Mayan ethnic groups in four geographical regions that the commission identified. It charged that despite the fact that the state had several options for combating insurgency, it "chose the one that caused the greatest loss of life among non-combatant civilians."[41] The commission put the killing of minors and Mayan leaders by the Guatemalan army and its allied agencies in the first category as well. Moreover, the way in which the army conducted massacres revealed its intention of killing as many Maya as possible. Prior to the massacres, the army almost always carefully gathered all the members of the community together, surrounded them before the killing started, or chose a market day or a day of celebration in which they were already gathered together.[42]

2) Systematic torture

With respect to the second type of genocidal action, the commission charged that the army and the civil patrols systematically committed acts of extreme cruelty, including torture and inhuman and degrading acts.

3) Destruction by means of conditions of life

The effect of systematic torture is to terrorize the population and destroy the foundations of social cohesion. The commission argued that the destruction of this cohesion was intended to annihilate the group physically and spiritually. This third type of action entailed the deliberate attempt to inflict on the target group conditions of life calculated to bring about its physical destruction in whole or in part. The commission emphasized that the massacres committed by the army and its allies and collaborators typically were accompanied by the razing of villages. This was most evident in the Ixil region, where 70 to 90 percent of the villages were destroyed. Moreover, the properties of the displaced peasants were burned as well, including their harvests, leaving the communities without food. And the displaced persons were bombed. Those who gave themselves up continued to be violated despite their condition of being completely under army control.

The Intent to Commit Genocide

The overall conclusion of the commission was "that agents of the State of Guatemala, within the framework of counterinsurgency operations carried out between 1981 and 1983, committed acts of genocide against groups of Maya in the four regions analyzed."[43] The commissioners who wrote the report went on to say that they had received information that similar acts had "occurred and were repeated" in other regions inhabited by the Mayan people. They added that, aside from the culpability of the actual perpetrators of the crimes, the state of Guatemala was also guilty of genocide, "because the majority of these acts were the product of policy pre-established by a command superior to the material perpetrators." Moreover, the state was charged with contravening the Convention on the Prevention and Punishment of the Crime of Genocide by failing to investigate and to punish acts of genocide committed on its territory.

The report of the Archdiocese charged that "counterinsurgency violence acquired certain genocidal characteristics."[44] The context for the charge was the attack upon the social fabric of societies by the attempts to kill women and children. The latter were pictured as "the vessels for the continuity of life and the transmission of culture." In another section, the report characterized some counterinsurgency violence as including "certain aspects of genocide."[45] Specifically mentioned was violence directed at religious and ethnic groups. But the report stopped short of charging the Guatemalan army and its allies and associates with genocide on the grounds that an analysis of intentionality and the decisions underlying this violence merited further study beyond the scope of research based solely on the testimonies of the victims.[46]

McClintock provided evidence that he judged demonstrated that the Guatemalan government's policy of extermination in the Indian highlands in the eighties fits the United Nation's definition of genocide as found in the treaty cited above. The Ixil were among the hardest hit.[47] In November, 1982 Americas Watch reported that the Ixil had been all but wiped out as a cultural entity. The previous month, the American Friends Service Committee had asserted that Indian cultures were beginning to disintegrate as a consequence of army policies. Indians stopped wearing their traditional dress, because it rendered them suspect. The Committee of Peasant Unity affirmed that Indians were hunted down and murdered not only in their native villages, but also in the cities. The report of the Archdiocese saw religion as an important motive for the government repression. The report charged that the army considered the Catholic faith to be a "subversive doctrine," and, therefore, the army encouraged the spread of some Pentecostal Churches in order to control the population.[48] This charge was not leveled at all Protestant churches, many of which stood up to the army.

Father Falla rejected genocide as the central motive for state action. He found race (ethnicity) and religion as motives for the massacres, but subsidiary ones. The major motive for the massacres in his view was class: the military acted to prevent basic changes in the structure of society. He went on to explain, however, that ethnicity did play a role in the massacres. The upper classes and the upper echelon in the army are proud of their European ancestry. They are Ladinos (mestizos), not to be confused with the Mayan majority. It is not that the army and its accomplices hesitated to kill mestizo guerrillas, labor and peasant leaders, or other "subversives." But it was easier to kill Indians, because of the belief among the socially dominant groups that they are vile and despicable creatures whose lives are worth less than those of "real people." Moreover, these groups saw the Maya as being by nature treacherous and deceptive, and required little evidence to prove it.

My view is that the conclusion that terrorism was committed in Guatemala does not exclude the view that genocide was committed there as well. But genocide was restricted to the Ixil and perhaps a few other Mayan groups. They were the target groups devastated by the Guatemalan army to the point of destruction. Fortunately, other target groups and sections of Guatemalan society were not devastated to this point, even if they were ravaged or merely terrorized. I agree with Father Falla that the **The basic motive for the government terrorism in Guatemala was the determination of the upper classes working through the government, and particularly the army, to maintain their power and their possessions.** basic motive for the government terrorism in Guatemala was the determination of the upper classes working through the government, and particularly the army, to maintain their power and their possessions. They sought to maintain this power and these possessions against the Maya, an unassimilated cultural group located at the bottom of the social and economic order, that several times has revolted against them. The revolts of the Maya together with the repression of the upper classes and their allies appear to be instances of class struggle, but they also are struggles between cultures. Because the center of power in Mayan culture has been at the local, village level, the Spanish and their mestizo successors have never been able to destroy it as was the case with centralized Inca governance.

Other motives besides class were at work in the terrorist process, including the prejudice against the Maya that could lead to the desire to exterminate them, and a diminished sense of culpability for so doing. The two motives were compatible, working in the same direction: the realization that the Maya are "revolutionaries" who desire and work for social change, and the prejudice that the Maya are a vile, treacherous, and deceitful group that should be eliminated.

The concept of genocide is less applicable in relation to the targeting of Ladinos by the Guatemalan government. This is more easily explained by the concept of terrorism, insofar as the purpose of the terrorism is assumed to be to preserve the status quo rather than to destroy a target population. The terrorism concept explains what happened to Guatemala considered as a whole. Genocide does not. It has a more limited application, to one or more Mayan groups.

THE KEY ROLE OF THE ARMY AND INTELLIGENCE AGENCIES

The United Nations commission found that the hostilities in Guatemala could not be reduced to a struggle between two armed parties. Such an interpretation fails to explain the persistence of political and economic forces on each side. The commission argued that between 1978 and 1982 citizens from broad sectors of society mobilized in opposition to the established order. These sectors included parts of the Catholic Church, labor union and peasant leaders, teachers, representatives of the liberal professionals, and many Maya. The relationship of the former to the insurgents was often problematical. Nonetheless, they were targeted. This was encouraged by counterinsurgency doctrine which insisted on the very broadest definition of the enemy and its agents. It lumped together all opposition to the status quo as insurgency, leaving no room for a third force.

The commission argued that the state's response to the guerrillas was totally disproportionate to any threat they posed. It charged that the army knew of the military inferiority of the insurgents, but exaggerated their military capability. It waged an internal war, a campaign of terror, against those who were against, or seemed to be against, the status quo. All opponents were considered to be under one banner, and the state set out to annihilate or terrorize them. Washington taught counterinsurgency and provided the wherewithal to implement it in the Guatemalan setting where those wielding power divided society along rigid lines into the ins and the outs along both class and ethnic lines.

The army knew of the military inferiority of the insurgents, but exaggerated their military capability.

The United Nations commissioners turned to the army and to the intelligence services to identify the state institutions directly responsible for state terrorism committed in the country in the sixties, the seventies, and halfway through the eighties. They charged that the Guatemalan army deliberately militarized the country in stages, culminating in the eighties in the penetration and absolute control of state institutions.[49] Military intelligence structures played a decisive role in the process. The result was that these structures controlled the population, the state institutions, and the army itself. This control depended not merely upon its formal structures, but also upon an extensive network of informants who infiltrated a variety of social institutions. The evidence pointed to the military intelligence agencies as being involved in widespread covert, irregular, and unconventional operations. Their control of state institutions assured their immunity. The commissioners specifically fingered the army intelligence agencies G-2 and the Presidential General Staff as the agencies that prepared the lists of those to be captured, interrogated, tortured, forcibly disappeared, or executed. They concluded that the majority of atrocities committed in the country took place with the knowledge or by order of the highest authorities of "the state."

WASHINGTON'S COMPLICITY

The United States government gave military assistance to Guatemala. In the early stages, the emphasis was on the teaching of counterinsurgency doctrine and on building an infrastructure for its application. Moreover, Washington's aid was specifically concentrated on the growth and improvement of local communications and intelligence agencies, the very institutions that the UN commissioners found were guilty of most of the crimes.

As is usually the case with truth commissions, the UN Commission on Guatemala had little to say about Washington's support for the government under review. But, after stating that the United States demonstrated that it was willing to provide support for military regimes in its strategic backyard, it found room for this charge:

> In the case of Guatemala, military assistance was directed towards reinforcing the national intelligence apparatus and for the training the officer corps in counterinsurgency techniques, key factors which had significant bearing on human rights violations during the armed confrontation.[50]

The report of the archdiocese re-enforced this charge by adding further evidence and its authority to the indictment. It spoke of marked changes in the structure of the Guatemalan government that occurred "with meddling by the United States."[51] Army size doubled, and special counterinsurgency units were created within the regular army structure. The Mobile Military Police was formed and stationed primarily in rural areas. The National Police and the army were put under a single command structure. The communications network was modernized, and it was made to extend throughout Central America. An agency was set up to coordinate police and military intelligence.

After 1963 military aid from Washington was used primarily to strengthen specialized counterinsurgency units that became permanent auxiliary forces to the regular army. This aid was channeled through the Military Assistance Program of the United States, aid that increased after 1960. This program sponsored training in counter guerrilla techniques and small-unit tactical operations. Suitable weapons were provided, and the army's communications and transportation systems were upgraded. Guatemalan forces were trained by mobile teams, advisors and military schools located both in Panama and in the United States. Eight thousand men were added to the regular army, together with more than one thousand mobile military police, and nine thousand military commissioners. The army gained the capacity to organize an intelligence and control apparatus in rural areas, two key elements in counterinsurgency war. The presidential intelligence apparatus maintained a communications link with the United States base in Panama and with its counterparts in other Central American countries. Since the mid-sixties, army intelligence through its international section maintained the same connections.[52] They were used to track those who committed an offense in one Latin American country, but who fled to another. For example, a fugitive wanted by the Guatemalan government and thought to be in El Salvador could be tracked directly by communications links to that country or indirectly through the United States base in Panama.

Moreover, Washington provided aid to Guatemala, even if the amount involved never approached the extravagant levels it reached in El Salvador. In the period 1981 to 1990 Guatemala received 778 million dollars in aid.[53] True, only 31.4 millions of this was in the form of military aid. But most aid, like money itself, is fungible or substitutable. If the aid itself could not be used directly for the military, it could be used to substitute for non-military expenses and thus free up funds for use on the military. The Carter administration suspended military aid to Guatemala in 1977 in response to reports of human rights violations as well as to pressure from London due to Guatemala's claims to Belize. Military aid resumed in 1985. During the time when Washington's military aid was cut off, its allies took up the slack. This military aid was then provided by Israel, Taiwan, and Argentina "rather than directly from the United States."[54] It was at this time that Guatemala received Bell helicopters, the Israel Galil rifle, Pilatus aircraft, and Israeli Arava cargo planes.

In 1981 and 1982 the Reagan administration sought to justify the behavior of the Guatemalan government and army. Consistently, the administration downplayed the scope of the massacres and excused the Guatemalan army.[55] For example, in 1981, the Deputy Assistant Secretary of State blamed the guerrillas for the wholesale slaughter, and a human rights report of the State Department blamed most of the violence on self-appointed vigilante groups. In contrast to this, the United Nations report pointed to the period 1981 through 1983 as that period during which the "State of Guatemala.. committed acts of genocide against groups of Guatemalan people."[56]

In February 1981 Amnesty International issued a report stating that since President Lucas Garcia had taken office in July 1978, the organization had learned of the seizure without warrant, and subsequent killing, of some 5,000 Guatemalans. Contrary to claims by successive Guatemalan governments that the death squads were not under official control, the report concluded that there was no evidence of pro-government, clandestine groups operating *independently* of government control. The organization stated that the links between the death squads and the authorities had been particularly blatant during the presidency of Lucas Garcia, and that officials at the highest level had been involved in orchestrating a centralized program of illegal actions. The "disappearances" and killings continued throughout 1981. Incomplete records assembled by Amnesty International list a minimum of 2,011 people killed between January 1 and June, 30 1981. In the period from July 1 to December 31 Amnesty International recorded a minimum of 2,569 killed.[57] In 1981 the Inter-American Commission on Human Rights of the Organization of American States presented a well-documented report that concluded that an alarming climate of violence had prevailed in Guatemala in recent years, either instigated or tolerated by the government which had proved itself unwilling or unable to contain it.[58] At a more general level, the Amnesty International report published in 1983 revealed that "Guatemala has appeared again and again in the reports of human rights watchdog organizations, and on the agendas of international and regional bodies."

On March 10,1999 the United States government released a memo of January 4, 1966 from a U.S. State Department security official which dates from the Johnson administration. The security official described how he set up a "safe house" in the Guatemalan presidential palace for use by Guatemalan security agents and their U.S. contacts.[59] The safe house became the headquarters for Guatemala's "dirty war" against leftist insurgents and their suspected allies. Three months after the above cable was sent, on March 6, 1966 security forces arrested 32 suspected of aiding the guerrillas. They "disappeared." Kate Doyle, Guatemala Project director at the National Security Archive, commented: "I have never seen anything like it." This was her way of expressing her amazement at "our (Washington's) intimacy with the Guatemalan security forces."

A U.S. State Department security official set up a "safe house" in the Guatemalan presidential palace for use by Guatemalan security agents and their U.S. contacts.

In view of the military aid and training, economic aid, diplomatic support and obfuscation of the dreadful events in Guatemala, it seems clear that Washington facilitated state terrorism in that country.

THE AFTERMATH

The first recommendation of the United Nations report was that the president of Guatemala admit that the governmental repression outlined in the report had occurred and that he assume responsibility for this oppression, particularly for those crimes committed by the army and the state security forces. He did not assume this responsibility. On March 10, 1999, thirteen days after the United Nations released its report, President Clinton visited Guatemala City. In his speech there, he did recognize that repression had occurred. The American president, however, did not assume any responsibility for what had occurred, nor did he apologize—not for complicity in the commission of terrorism, before, after, or during its commission, or by any administration. He did admit that Washington "was wrong" to have supported the Guatemalan "military forces or intelligence units which engaged in violent and widespread repression of the kind described in the report."[60] He added that the United States must not repeat the mistake. Clinton aides said that the president had spent some time in deciding how to craft his statement. These words were uttered as the president made a four-day visit to Central America. He used the opportunity to praise the local governments for ending their civil wars and for establishing what he termed "democratic systems of government." Similarly, earlier in a speech given in San Salvador, he referred to the repression that occurred in that country but did not apologize for Washington's complicity in it. He boldly affirmed that over the past few years a battlefield of ideology in Central America had been transformed into a marketplace of ideas.

A Bishop Is Beaten to Death

Two days after the archdiocese of Guatemala issued its report, Bishop Juan Gerardi, the head of the project that produced it, was beaten to death with a cement block.[61] He had also served as the director of the Human Rights Office of Guatemala City's Archdiocese. Many other participants in the project received death threats, or their houses were broken into. Bishop Gerardi evidently heard a noise in his garage and went to investigate it. It was there that the assassin killed him. Shortly before this incident, the bishop said in a speech in which he presented the study that the church assumed the task of breaking the silence that thousands of the victims of the repression have kept for years.

The government first tried to pin the crime on a vagrant, but this claim was withdrawn when it was revealed that the accused could not lift the eight-pound cement block used as the murder weapon. Next the government shifted targets to a priest and accused him of homosexuality and of committing a crime of passion.[62] The government alleged that the priest's dog, an eleven-year-old German shepherd, was implicated as well. The bishop's body was exhumed, and no bites of a dog were found, thus exploding the government's allegation that the priest and his dog were the murderers. Human rights leaders and the head of the United Nations Mission in Guatemala believe that the government is involved and that it is engineering a cover up. More specifically, they point the finger of guilt at a colonel and his son, a captain in the air force whom they believe to be the killers. In March, 1999, Judge Henry Monroy who had been presiding over the investigation of the death of the bishop resigned. The reason he gave was the threatening phone calls he had been receiving.[63] He was the second judge to resign from the case in less than three months.

Edgar Gutierrez, executive director of the church project, expressed concern about those who gave testimony for the project. He said that the assassination of the bishop gives "a green light to all those in the military patrols who participated in the massacres or committed torture during the war."[64] Church and civil rights leaders argue that the murder was intended as a warning to the church, human rights activists, and the government itself. The killing of the bishop and the government's reaction to it help to confirm an assertion made in the report of the Archdiocese.

An Ongoing Atmosphere of Impunity

The term "impunity" appears throughout this book to describe a pervasive reality in which government agents operated, and continue to operate, without fear of punishment. A crack in this wall of impunity seemed to appear when in June 2001 a three-judge panel convicted the colonel and the captain referred to above plus a sergeant and a priest for the killing of the bishop. However, on October 8 of the following year an appeals court granted a new trial for the four men on the grounds that the lower court did not adequately verify the testimony of a star witness.[65] It seems that the crack in the wall may be repaired.

A *New York Times* editorial of July 19, 2002 remarked that Guatemala was "drifting back toward violence and misrule."[66] The army and its allies that acted before as death squads had gained strength, and they were again involved in criminal behavior. The editorial pointed out that the party of the sitting president was controlled by former military officers and led by General Efrain Rios Montt who served as dictator during the worst government repression in the eighties. Some four months later the United Nations mission set up to verify the Guatemalan government's compliance with the peace accords charged that that government had utterly failed to carry out the programs of reconciliation and social development mandated by these accords.[67] The mission attributed the "human rights crisis" existing in the country partly to this failure. It also faulted the government for increasing the role of the military in the country and for failing to investigate crimes.

The Central American project director of the Inter-American Dialogue pointed to Guatemala as the most corrupt country in the region.[68] It also has the widest gap between the rich and the poor.

The repression has left its victims with deep psychological scars, the particular victims being the Maya living in the villages.[69] These villages are trying to restore the cultural ties that once bound them together. Many villagers complain of migraines and body aches that medicines do not cure. In the early 1990's a nun and a psychologist established a mental health program called "good life" to cope with the problem. The program involves Eastern meditation and Mayan cosmology. The villagers are encouraged to say what they have held back for so long.

The allies of the army that served as death squads during the repression staged a mini-coup by taking over the province, Peten. Instead of arresting them, the president negotiated with them and promised to try to enact a tax to pay them for their "services" rendered during the repression. These so-called "patrollers" who "patrolled" villages and served as death squads in Guatemala submitted their names to the government and demanded payment for their services. President Alfonso Portillo is considering paying them $2,600 apiece.[70] The "patrollers" have maintained their structures, and assassinations and death threats continue in this unfortunate country. The military budget has been increased to the level of the repression at the expense of needed health and education programs while the reforms mandated by the United Nations peace agreement have been essentially scuttled.

Those who "patrolled" villages and served as death squads in Guatemala have since submitted their names to the government and demanded payment for their services.

Meanwhile, the victims of state terrorism have received no compensation for the terrorism inflicted on them. The peace agreements promised land and education for the majority Mayan peasants, the chief victims of the repression. This has not been done; even pilot projects that would improve their lot are behind schedule. Peasants continue to occupy the land of the plantocracy in order to eke out an existence on it. "Human rights advocates who have brought genocide charges against the country's rulers continue to face death threats."[71]

Since the mid-nineties, forensic anthropologists examined the remains of some 2,000 victims in 200 clandestine graves, thus providing evidence that could be used against the army and its allies. Clyde Snow, an internationally acclaimed forensics expert who helped start the program, said that the work was just getting close to incriminating former military officers, including Rios Montt himself, when an organized campaign to intimidate the forensic anthropologists was unleashed, and an accountant for a human rights foundation started by Rigoberta Menchu, a noted human rights activist and Nobel Peace Prize winner, was assassinated.[72] The police said the assassination occurred during a robbery. Human rights advocates doubt this. Four of the anthropologists decided to leave the country after their families were threatened with death, sometimes at gunpoint. The head of the program decided to leave after his brother was threatened by three armed men on the streets of Guatemala City.

In 2003, human rights groups inside and outside Guatemala, including Amnesty International, urged the establishment of another truth commission to investigate the persistent violations of human rights in the country. "Former members of the military close to the government have been linked to politically motivated assassinations and threats against people seeking to prosecute war crimes."[73] The Guatemalan human rights ombudsman asked the government to allow the United Nations and the Organization of American States to appoint the truth commission.

CONCLUSION

This, the last section of the chapter, presents fhe answers for Guatemala to the three central questions posed in the study. Two of the questions are easily disposed of. They are: was terror committed in the country, and, if so, was it state terror committed by the government or private terror committed by the guerrillas? Certainly, the chapter provided adequate evidence that terror was committed in Guatemala in the period under review. The excerpt from the research conducted by Father Falla should be fresh in mind, but the chapter is full of other examples. Deliberate acts took place—indeed, campaigns—of a physical and psychological nature designed to coerce and intimidate their victims, their immediate target groups, by causing them intense fear, anxiety, apprehension, panic, dread, and horror.

More importantly, the intent of these campaigns was to intimidate and coerce larger sections of society that were against the status quo or thought to be so by the Guatemalan elites. The report of the Archdiocese of Guatemala charged the guerrillas with having committed 4.81 percent of the violations. This finding is supported by the three percent found in the report of the United Nations. Both the UN Commission and the Archdiocese reports put over 90 percent of the infractions at the door of the government. The conclusion to draw from this is that the terrorism in Guatemala was overwhelmingly state terror committed by the government, with a small fraction being private terrorism committed by the guerrillas.

The third question concerns Washington's support for the government and the forms which this support took. One form well documented above is the counterinsurgency warfare training of Guatemalan security forces which later committed state terrorism. Washington's policy was a deliberate one of improving the very structures used in Guatemala's "dirty war." Moreover, Washington also provided diplomatic support and economic and military aid to the Central American government. The economic aid helped to finance the repression. When military aid was halted during the Carter administration, Washington's allies provided aid until the restriction on American aid was removed by the Reagan administration.

Another conclusion, also painful given the poverty of Guatemala and the condition of the Maya there, can be made at this juncture. The CIA planned and sponsored the coup d'état of 1954 that interrupted a program of reform for the Mayan majority, and darkened the possibility that this reform will take place in the foreseeable future. This also makes Washington a candidate for accessory to the violation of economic rights—which are widely considered as a component of human rights, the gamut of which are understood to be mutually supporting and indivisible.

CHAPTER 3

Chile: The Forgotten Past Is Full of Memory

WHY CHILE?

As noted at the outset of this volume, the terrorist attack on the World Trade Center took place on the 28th anniversary of the coup in Chile that deposed its president Salvador Allende and introduced the dictatorship of General Pinochet. The major part of this chapter is directed at terrorism as it subsequently played out in Chile. A major reason for the inclusion of Chile is to enhance the validity of the findings to be established in relation to the three central questions of this study. The situation in Chile following the ascendancy of Pinochet was sufficiently dreadful as to occasion the establishment of a truth commission. Much of the findings of this chapter are drawn from this truth commission's report entitled *Report of the Chilean National Commission on Truth and Reconciliation* and a much shorter report based on a review of CIA records mandated by Congress.

The report of the truth commission for Chile can hardly be accused of bias against the Pinochet dictatorship. Indeed, three of the eight commissioners who formulated the report had been members of that regime, and all eight signed the report. The commission was forced to operate within a limited time frame, without subpoena powers, and with a restricted scope for investigation. The political situation at the time was at best murky. The Pinochet constitution was still in force, and Pinochet himself remained the commander of the army. While the commission was formulating the report, he put the army on nationwide alert.[1]

While the Chilean truth commission was formulating its report, Pinochet put the army on nationwide alert.

The shorter report, based on CIA records, was mandated by Congress by virtue of the Hinchey Amendment (Section 311) to the Intelligence Authorization Act for Fiscal 2000.[2] It was prepared by the Intelligence community, led by the National Intelligence Council. Since the CIA represents a large portion of the intelligence community, I call it "a CIA report," and view it as a report card, whose author is the agency reported on. Named *CIA Activities in Chile* (hereafter referred to as *CIA Activities*), and numbering only 14 pages, it declared that it answered the questions posed by the Hinchey amendment "in an unclassified format." How much wiggle room this left for skewing or cooking the results is left to the imagination of the reader. There is merit in using it, however, in that this secret agency was forced to make a public confession, its admissions lending credibility to the accusations made in this chapter.

DENYING SOCIAL CHANGE THROUGH ELECTORAL PROCESSES

CIA Efforts to Prevent Allende Taking Office

CIA Activities granted that United States efforts to support anti-communist activities in Chile date to the late 1950's, but it confined the list of its covert actions in that country to the 1960's and 1970's. Listed were financial assistance to political parties in several congressional and presidential elections.[3] Data made available to a Senate committee revealed that 15 such payments were authorized by Washington for a total of $ 5.9 million.[4] The CIA revealed that as early as 1964 American businessmen with interests in Chile offered the agency money to prevent Allende from being elected. One such businessman was employed by the International Telephone and Telegraph Company. The agency refused the money, but advised the businessmen how they could funnel the funds to opposition candidates. It admitted secretly creating political action programs, political workshops, and "mechanisms" for "placements" in radio and news media, and conducting what it chose to call "spoiling operations" against the Allende forces. "The overwhelming objective—firmly rooted in the policy of the period—was to discredit Marxist-leaning political leaders, especially Dr. Salvador Allende, and to strengthen and encourage their civilian and military opponents to prevent them from assuming power."[5]

Nonetheless on September 4, 1970 Allende was successful in the general elections in his third bid for the presidency of Chile. While he garnered only 36.2 percent of the vote, it was a three-cornered race, and he received a plurality of the popular vote. The constitution of Chile required congressional approval before a plurality winner could assume office. On September 15, 1970 six weeks before the Chilean Congress was scheduled to vote, **President Nixon instructed the CIA to prevent Allende from coming to power or unseat him and authorized $10 million for this purpose.** "President Nixon informed the DCI (the Director of Central Intelligence) that an Allende regime in Chile would not be acceptable to the United States. He instructed the CIA to prevent Allende from coming to power or unseat him and authorized $10 million for this purpose.[6] "High level concern" in the Nixon administration resulted in the development of what the CIA chose to call "a more aggressive covert action initiative." This initiative called for both political action (track I) and a military coup (track II) to prevent an Allende presidency. The first track led the agency to pursue a variety of actions including placing "propaganda information" in local media, promoting opposition to Allende in leading newspapers, and stirring up Catholic opposition to Allende. The agency cooperated with the American Embassy in promoting a scheme whereby the Chilean Congress would elect one of the losing presidential candidates in the popular election (Alessandri) who would then resign. This to be followed by the other losing candidate (Frei) facing off against Allende in another popular election. The scheme failed when Frei refused to become a part of it.

"Under 'Track II' of the strategy, the CIA sought to instigate a coup to prevent Allende from taking office after he won a plurality in the 4 September election and before... the Chilean Congress reaffirmed his victory."[7] Numerous contacts were made with key military and national police officers to persuade them to carry out a coup. The U.S. Army's attaché was placed under the operational control of the agency, and he relayed similar messages to his military contacts. Four CIA officers were sent under non-official cover to meet with the most sensitive of the Chilean military officers who were plotting the coup. The agency worked with three groups of plotters. All three conspiring groups agreed that any successful coup would require the kidnapping of General Rene Schneider, a staunch defender of constitutional government. Although the agency agreed with this assessment and although it provided weapons to two of the groups, it could find no evidence that the agency or any of the groups sought to kill the general. He was mortally wounded by one of the groups that supposedly sought to kidnap him, evidently by the group led by General Viaux. General Schneider's death shocked the armed forces and those civilians intent on a coup, and plans for military action were put on hold.

On October 24, 1970 the Chilean Congress approved of Allende by a vote of 153 to 35, and soon thereafter he was inaugurated. Allende himself was a socialist and an admitted Marxist, and his coalition government included other leftists and the communist party. The CIA report reveals that the coming to power of this coalition government resulted in a shift in Washington's policy. Its long-term objective then became to keep the opposition active so that it would prove victorious in the 1976 election. The CIA's role "was primarily to provide funds and influence opposition political parties." It supported two conservative parties, and it continued its propaganda activities, inter alia by "media placements" in support of opposition parties and against the Allende regime. Covert funding during the Allende regime totaled $6.5 million. But a strategy of encouraging, supporting, or perhaps even inaugurating a coup was not ruled out. "The CIA was instructed to put the U.S. Government in a position to take future advantage of either a political or military solution to the Chilean dilemma, depending on how developments unfolded."[8]

Asserting that it did not instigate the successful coup of September 11, 1973, the agency allowed that it was aware of military coup-plotting. Indeed, it maintained ongoing intelligence collection relations with some of the plotters, and it "probably appeared to condone" the coup. If the CIA document was hesitant to state bluntly that Washington's policy was to support the coup, the issue was cleared up in a statement by Secretary of State Colin Powell in February of 2003. While trying to pressure Chile, then serving as a non-permanent member of the Security Council, to support a resolution calling for a war on Iraq, Powell admitted that encouraging the coup that brought Pinochet to power for 17 years was "not part of American history we are proud of."[9] Santiago expressed pleasure at hearing the remark.

The CIA document asserted that the day before the coup, a Chilean military officer informed the agency of the existence of a plot, and shortly before it took place the agency was informed of the exact date. When the coup was launched and during its immediate aftermath, the agency limited its activities "to providing intelligence and situation reports." Soon after the coup succeeded, the CIA closed down its covert action plans and activities in Chile. However, throughout the post-coup period it "collected and disseminated to the intelligence and policy communities extensive reporting concerning human rights issues in Chile."[10]

Making the Chilean Economy "Scream"

Washington's efforts to undermine the Allende government were not confined to the activities of the CIA. These efforts contained a large economic component. As the architect of "Nixon's secret policy" toward Allende, Kissinger originated the idea of an economic blockade The prospects for its success were good, since Chile depended upon the United States for supplies for its industries, finances, and foreign aid. Washington refused to grant new loans to Chile, demanded the repayment of old ones, and used its considerable influence in international lending institutions to convince them to deny new loans. From its founding in 1959 to 1970, the Bank for International Development had loaned $310 million to Chile, but during Allende's administration this fell to $11.6 million, which consisted of two loans to private universities.[11] The World Bank loaned $234 million to Chile prior to Allende, but

Washington sold its strategic copper reserve, which flooded the market with the metal, with serious consequences for the Chilean economy.

nothing after he became president. USAID, which had provided $540 million before 1970, provided no new loans during the Allende years. The Export-Import Bank granted no new loans to the Allende administration, despite the fact that it had loaned $234 million to a preceding regime in 1967 and another $29 million in 1969. Washington sold its strategic copper reserve, 258,000 short tons, which flooded the market with the metal and greatly lowered its price, with serious consequences for the Chilean economy.[12] Washington had little trouble enlisting private business interest in this blockade against the socialist president and his administration.

Strengthening the Chilean Military

In contrast to its economic policy toward Santiago, Washington did not reduce military aid and sales nor curtail its military training program during the Allende years. Actually, both were increased. The number of Chilean officers trained at the School of the Americas in Panama increased from 63 to 107 in the period from 1966 to 1969.[13] During the Allende years from 1970 to 1973 this number increased from 181 to 257. The number for 1974 was 260. Military assistance and sales totaled 3.2 million in 1970, increased to 8.9 million in 1971, and reached 13,5 million in 1972.

The purposes of the aid and training went beyond the functional and the technical, however, to include the establishment and maintenance of fraternal relations between the personnel of the two military establishments. In the words of Colonel Narin, the director of the School of the American Fleet, "We are in contact with our graduates and they are in contact with us."[14] Cooperation between Washington's and Santiago's military intelligence services was maintained and Washington's military attaches continued to have access to the highest Chilean officials. This was of use to Washington during the Allende years if only for the intelligence it made available regarding coups during that period. Of greater importance was the impact that training at American military institutions had on the ideology of the Chilean military and on their view of their mission. General Horacio Toro, who served the Pinochet regime during its first two years, affirmed that Chilean officers historically were called upon to fight neighboring countries in border disputes.[15] But what they were taught in American military institutions was that their mission was to destroy Marxism. They were also being trained in the methods of state terrorism later committed by the Pinochet government.

The Coup of September 11, 1973

On the morning of the coup President Allende arrived early at work in the La Moneda Palace, because he had been forewarned of troop movements in Valparaiso. At dawn the palace was surrounded by police forces and at ten A.M. by tanks from an armored regiment. After capturing a local radio station, the junta used it to announce its first decrees and to warn that the palace must be evacuated by 11 A. M. Otherwise, the palace would be bombed. The first decree of the junta was read by a military spokesman who said in part:

> First, the President of the Republic must immediately surrender his office to the armed forces and the carabineros of Chile. Second, the armed forces and carabineros are united in order to begin the historic and responsible mission to fight for the liberation of the Fatherland, and to prevent our country from falling beneath the Marxist yoke.[16]

Allende gave those in the palace the choice of staying or leaving. His closest aides, his security guards, and officials of the investigative police chose to stay. The bombing started at 11:52, and this set the palace on fire. Allende did have a chance to address the nation on television:

> This will be my last opportunity to speak to you...Given these developments I can only say to the workers: I am not going to resign. Set upon a historic path, I will pay for my loyalty to the people with my life...These are my final words, and I am certain that my sacrifice will not be in vain.[17]

These were, indeed, his final words to the nation. According to the *Report of the Chilean National Commission on Truth and Reconciliation*, he committed suicide a few hours after the successful coup to overthrow him. With Allende's death went the demise of what has often been called the first freely elected Marxist president. Also battered, if not murdered, was the Chilean myth that the inhabitants of this South American country are the "Englishmen of Latin America."[18] According to the myth, political violence, torture, and massive human rights violations are reserved for the "banana republics." The national anthem of Chile adds to the myth with the claim that the country is an asylum for the oppressed. This is, or was, a South American variation of the myth of national "exceptionalism," still in vogue in the United States.

The Pinochet Regime

The Pinochet dictatorship was installed in 1973, and it lasted until 1990. "Actually, however, what emerged was a new institution, unprecedented in Chile: the President of the Republic/Commander in Chief."[19] Pinochet ruled and administered the country and presided over the junta. Without him no laws could be passed, nor could the constitution be amended. He was also the commander in chief of the army, and his powers were enhanced by the fact that the country was in a state of emergency during practically the whole period. He took over the executive branch, dissolved the legislative branch, and prohibited leftists parties in 1973 and all other parties in 1977.

Pinochet preserved the judiciary, but the judiciary did not preserve the human rights of Chileans–this, because this branch of government lacked the necessary dedication to human rights and because of the restrictions put on it by the army. Most members of the Supreme Court sympathized with the dictatorship.[20] The dictatorship issued decrees, for example, forbidding habeas corpus for political crimes. The media were censored, recalcitrant newspapers were closed, and some journalists disappeared. Much of the media preferred to stay open by engaging in self-censorship. The class bias of the regime was shown by its treatment of labor unions. A decree of December 10, 1973 ordered labor unions to refrain from all political activity.[21] Meetings were allowed only if they were of an informational nature or if they were concerned with the internal management of the institutions. Moreover, the nearest police station had to be notified in writing two days in advance of such meetings. The president/commander in chief accepted an economic plan for the country formulated by a young group of liberal and neo-liberal economists who had done post graduate work in economics at American universities, notably the University of Chicago. Pinochet imposed the plan against all who resisted it, "granting its authors the power, support, and time they said they needed to apply it."[22] The Pinochet years thus represented a period of right-wing dictatorship, motivated by an anti-labor bias and the class struggle.

THE CHILEAN NATIONAL COMMISSION ON TRUTH AND RECONCILIATION

The possible pro-coup bias of the *Report of the Chilean National Commission on Truth and Reconciliation* is suggested by the fact that it maintained that "the armed forces and the security forces faced no organized rebel troops,"[23] –employing the term "rebel troops" for troops which would in fact have legitimately been supporting an existing and democratically-empowered government. This assertion is meant not so much as a criticism of the commission, but as an introduction to its "balanced" composition and its narrow terms of reference. In 1988 General Pinochet held a plebiscite on the continuation of his reign. To his surprise, he lost, but narrowly so. In order to participate in the election, however, the democratic forces aligned against Pinochet had to accept the dictator's constitution.[24] Many Chileans clung to Pinochet, fearing that his opponents would bring disorder to the country. The forces of the right claimed that remembering old wounds and divisions would not benefit Chilean society and that only the courts could investigate the violations of human rights of the past. The winning Christian Democratic Party presented this investigation as a means of achieving social peace and reconciliation. Some modification of the Pinochet constitution was made after the election, but the amnesty that the dictatorship decreed for itself in 1978 escaped unscathed. Its impact was enhanced by the fact that the Supreme Court applied the broadest meaning to this decree.

The commission consisted of eight members, three of whom held posts in the Pinochet government, and two who had been exiled by that government. The chairperson of the commission was Raul Rettig, whose name is customarily used to refer to the commission and to the report, and who served as ambassador to Brazil in the Allende government. Correa asserted that the members were "respected human rights figures" and added that by appointing a commission that was more or less evenly divided politically, the president indicated that the investigation of human rights was "too important to be pursued in partisan terms."[25] The commission was given nine months to complete its report, a deadline it met. All eight commissioners signed the report.

The politics surrounding the report were made manifest as well in the restricted mandate given the commission. It was authorized to investigate only the "most serious violations." These were defined as those acts, motivated by political reasons, consisting of forced disappearance or which resulted in death by torture, terrorism, or other means. Only those violations which led to the death or the disappearance of the victim were investigated. All others were excluded, no matter how barbaric the violation. Included were acts

Only those violations which led to the death or the disappearance of the victim were investigated. All others were excluded, no matter how barbaric the violation.

by the government, condoned by the government, or committed by the guerrillas. Excluded from investigation were acts no matter how horrendous such as torture that did not prove fatal, attacks that only wounded their victims, or cases of arbitrary arrest, detention, or exile. One estimate is that the military and the security forces "tortured tens of thousands of Chileans."[26] The report asserted that although the number of Chileans who left the country for political reasons during the military dictatorship cannot be determined exactly, "it is estimated that the figure cannot be less than 20,000."[27] The report merely gave this estimate, and then dropped the subject. The commission, therefore, was not allowed to investigate fully the political violations committed during the Pinochet dictatorship. The general was still the head of the army, and the right was too strong politically to allow a full disclosure. While the commission was sifting through its files, Pinochet put the armed forces on nation wide alert. Moreover, the commission was not given the power to subpoena witnesses, court records, or other documents. Cooperation with it was strictly voluntary.

The commission sought to fulfill its mandate first by compiling a list of all those who were killed or forcibly disappeared for political reasons during the period of the dictatorship. A list of somewhat more than 3,400 was compiled from the responses of the relatives of victims, the police, the armed forces, human rights organizations, the socialist and communist parties, the Unified Labor Federation, and the guerrilla organization, the Revolutionary Left Movement (MIR). The relatives of victims were interviewed, usually for from 45 minutes to an hour. The police were uncooperative, claiming that the documentation requested by the commission had been legally burned or that the case of concern was part of a judicial investigation and therefore information about it could not be divulged. The army claimed that such records had been burned in a terrorist attack in 1989. The navy was somewhat cooperative, but it was the air force that gave the commission permission to investigate all trial documents it requested. Those involved in the violations were asked to appear before the commission to give their version of what had happened. The commission requested that 160 members of the armed forces and the police testify before it. Only a few of those on active duty complied with the request.

The Victims of the Repression

The list of victims of the repression, "somewhat more than 3,400 names," was trimmed down to 2,279. This reduction resulted, for example, from taking off the original list such cases as duplicates, claims made without giving names, and those judged to have been killed or forcibly disappeared for other than political reasons. The names of the remaining 2,279 victims were listed in the original

Spanish edition of the commission's report. This number seems to be a bare minimum estimate. A public monument located in the General Cemetery of Santiago has the names of 4,000 victims who, for political reasons, were either executed or forcibly disappeared and never found.[28] Moreover, President Aylwin established the Corporation on Reparation and Conciliation in an effort to complete the work left unfinished by the commission and to consider new cases. The corporation issued an interim report in March 1994 which indicated that it was working on 2,119 cases, of which 55 percent were new cases that the commission did not know about.[29]

The commission gave a breakdown of the vital statistics of the victims. It found that a great majority of these victims were male (95 percent), a majority were married (52 percent), and most were young (59 percent between 21 and 35 years old).[30] More significant was the breakdown of the victims based on whether their death or disappearance was the work of the government or of the guerrillas. This provides crucial evidence in determining whether the 17-year dictatorship was a period of government repression or of guerrilla terrorism. The commission discovered that during the period from the end of 1977 to March 11, 1990 the three guerrilla groups operating in the country killed 93 people.[31] Most of them were killed by the Revolutionary Left Movement (MIR), the main guerrilla group. Fifteen of these victims were civilians, the majority of whom just happened to be present when a "terrorist attack" occurred—for example, when a bomb went off. The commission also used the term "terrorist attack" to describe the means by which the remaining 78 victims were killed. All of these victims were members of the armed forces, the security forces, or the police. Prominent among them were police who, in the words of the commission, "were doing their duty, standing guard, when they were ambushed and had no chance to respond to the aggression." The usual motive for killing them was not to do harm to them personally, but for its overall impact on society. The individual became, so the report said, "a mere instrument." The commission found that the guerrillas killed only six people in the earlier period January 1974 to August 1977.[32] Three were military, two were police, and one was from the investigative police. All were victims of MIR. As previously stated, the commission found that in the immediate aftermath of the coup "the armed forces and the security forces faced no organized rebel troops."[33] The term "rebel troops," as previously explained, referred to troops supporting Allende. This statement along with others of the commission leads to the conclusion that the guerrillas killed no victims in the period from September through December 1973.

The conclusion follows that the guerrillas were responsible for a total of 99 victims during the three periods into which the commission divided its study, *i.e.*, during the entire Pinochet dictatorship. These 99 victims constitute 4.3 percent of the total victims. The government was responsible for the remaining 2180 victims, 95.7 percent of the total. This provides evidence to answer one of the central questions posed in the study. The Pinochet years appear to be much better described as a period of government repression rather than guerrilla terrorism, similar to Guatemala and El Salvador. The evidence presented in the report undermines the Pinochet government's attempt to rationalize its repressive behavior by contending that it was engaged in counterinsurgency warfare, an unorthodox type of warfare, necessary because the enemy was insidious, subversive, and armed. The guerrillas in Chile were never able to control territory or to wage military operations in a sustained manner. Moreover, they did not initiate their activities on any noticeable scale until the beginning of 1979. The commission could find only six cases of the killing of government personnel by the guerrillas in the period from January 1974 to August 1977. The commission described this period as one "in which the regime's security forces enjoyed complete mastery over the political movements that had supported the previous regime and had some capacity for a violent response."[34] The MIR and the socialist and communist parties were under the harshest repression. "Their structures fell apart and their members fled the country or were under continual pursuit." By the beginning of 1979, the time when the guerrillas started to become active, the great majority of the killings and forced disappearances in the country had already taken place. No less than 1862, or 82 percent of the total number, occurred during the Pinochet dictatorship.

Of the 2,279 victims, 1,231 were found to have been politically active and their political orientation could be determined.[35] A breakdown of these victims and their orientation is as follows:

Socialist Party	405 or 33 percent of the total
MIR	384 or 31 percent of the total
Communist Party	353 or 29 percent of the total
Other Guerrilla Groups	43 or 3 percent of the total
Non-Leftist Parties	41 or 3 percent of the total
Christian Left	5 or 1 percent of the total

Nine-seven percent of the victims were from the guerrillas or leftist parties, only three percent from non-leftist parties. This is further evidence for the assertion that the principal terrorists during the Pinochet years were from the right—operating directly from within the Pinochet government without the smokescreen of intermediaries such as paramilitary groups—and not from the left and the guerrillas. This identification is based on the logical assumption that terrorists do not generally kill their own. They kill their enemies. The commission said of the victims:

> Most of those killed were officials in the previous government, leaders in organizations, or people identified with an overall political program as leaders, activists, or supporters. Their death amounts to a punishment for their involvement in that political program.[36]

Extending our breakdown of the victims tends to further validate the conclusion that the Pinochet repression represented a type of class warfare. This appears to have been the overall purpose of government repression in Chile. Workers and small farmers led the list with 686 of the total number of 2,279 victims (30 percent).[37] Students were second with 324 of the total (or 14 percent), followed by self-employed workers 314 (or 14 percent), private employees 305 (or 13 percent), and 132 (6 percent) from the military and the security forces. Again, the military and the security forces appear in the guise of oppressors rather than the oppressed. The commission found on the other end of the distribution 45 victims (two percent of the total) who were identified as high-level officials, either administrators 33 (or 1.5 percent of the total) or business

The breakdown of the victims tends to further validate the conclusion that the Pinochet repression represented a type of class warfare.

people 12 (or .5 percent of the total). They inhabit the other end of the class structure.

The commission addressed this general subject when it sought to assign motives for the violations it had investigated. It concluded that the government justified its efforts to destroy "the internal enemy," because this enemy assaulted higher and permanent values. And the Chilean National Intelligence Directorate (DINA) defined this enemy as MIR and the communist and socialist parties. The casualty figures cited above tend to substantiate this assertion.

The commission defined the modus operandi, the type of political action, adopted by the government to accomplish its objective in this way:

> Destroying political parties meant physically eliminating the activists who made such an organization possible. According to that logic, those who by their training and experience in the party, their positions in the party, and their personal qualities of education, training, persistence, or physical courage, were seen as dangerous and beyond redemption, and had to be physically eliminated. A prisoner's unwillingness to be forthcoming even under torture only confirmed that he or she was dangerous. This primary motivation or rationality, heavily imbued with ideology, is inherently contrary to those most basic values of justice and of respect for the rule of law from which human rights laws draw their inspiration.[38]

This modus operandi sounds very much like an excerpt from an encyclopedia of horror and a recipe for terrorism as well. The commission ascribed the use of forced disappearances rather than the simple killing of the victims, not only to its efficacy in intimidating other political activists, as simple killing would do, but to other reasons also. It allowed the government and its security agencies to cloak their activities, and it saved them the legal complications of court trials. Finally, it spared them the political and possibly future domestic or international legal ramifications related to having to explain to Chileans and others why they had arrested and executed so many people. This technique was used throughout the repression and at the expense of a variety of victims, but especially against the leadership of the communist party in 1976. The devastating impact of forced disappearances on the surviving family is discussed elsewhere in this study.

INTELLIGENCE AGENCIES, THE COUNTERINSURGENCY DOCTRINE, AND TORTURE

The National Intelligence Directorate (DINA)

The commission singled out a group within the military whose ideas and activities had a singular impact upon the human rights record of the Pinochet regime. Composed mostly of army majors and colonels, it was remarkably coherent in its anti-communist sentiments and later in its activities as well. Formed on the day of the coup, it was called the "colonels committee."[39] It functioned for a few weeks after that in the Military Academy, but it became the "DINA Commission" in November 1973, and in June 1974 it was upgraded to the level of a government agency and called the National Intelligence Directorate (DINA). An army officer, Lieutenant Colonel Juan Manuel Contreras, formulated the plan for its creation as a government institution, and he served as its head during the three years of its existence.[40] All three military branches gave their approval prior to its formation, and the police provided personnel as well. Civilians were hired, but the highest positions were held by army officers, and a few by navy and air force officers. The commission revealed that doctors were hired not merely to take care of sick victims, but also to assess the ability of victims to withstand torture.

DINA was an intelligence organization, responsible for collecting information, but it was also an operational institution. It was the agency directly responsible for most of the political repression that occurred during its life span, during the most oppressive years of the dictatorship. It was disbanded in 1977 and succeeded by the National Center for Information (CNI). Its speciality was forced disappearances, and it performed these heartless deeds in a premeditated manner, after prior planning and with centralized coordination. Some forced disappearances occurred before DINA was formally established, but the intent at that time had been simply to hide bodies, not to cause extra anguish for surviving friends and relatives. DINA had many contacts and collaborators in the media, both in Chile and among the press attaches in Chilean embassies abroad. It coordinated its activities with similar intelligence agencies in the Southern cone: those in Argentina, Paraguay, Uruguay, and Brazil. The commission concluded that the organization "should be seen as an agency which enjoyed almost unlimited power. The upshot was that it could infringe on basic personal liberties and use its powers to conceal its actions and to assure its impunity."[41]

Lieutenant Colonel Contreras, the founder and head of DINA, had attended the Army Career Officers School in Fort Belvoir, Virginia for two years.[42] It was not unusual for a Chilean officer to attend a military school in the United States. The CIA publication *CIA Activities in Chile* revealed that: "Thousands of Chilean military officers came to the United States for training, which included presentations on the impact of global communism on their own country."[43] A sizeable number attended the School of the Americas when it was located in Panama. Between 1966 and 1974 this number totaled 1,437.[44] Known for his no nonsense approach, Contreras served as the commanding officer of the Tejas Verdes army regiment in San Antonio. When the dockworkers in this pro-union and leftist port city went on strike because the military government banned all union activity, he ordered four union leaders to his office for a meeting. The following day the bodies of the four were delivered to their families in coffins. After the junta had agreed to the creation of DINA and Contreras' leadership of it, he habitually met with General Pinochet for breakfast and a briefing. Afterwards the two would travel in a chauffeured vehicle to Pinochet's office. If the briefing had not finished or if Pinochet had further orders, their meeting would continue in the president's office. Moreover, their offices were connected by a two way television system. DINA became Pinochet's personal tool to implement the early and bloodiest phase of his program of state terrorism. With Contreras at his side, or at least in constant communication with him, Pinochet directed this phase of the program. After Contreras was assigned to a different position and DINA was dissolved, Pinochet continued to give central direction to the program, which continued to live up to the definition of state terrorism.

The CIA admitted that the agency had contact with Contreras while he was the head of DINA and that this contact was approved by the "US Government policy community."[45] The agency maintained that the relationship was pursued for purposes of gathering intelligence. It claimed that it advised him to improve his record on human rights. Yet the relationship was maintained even after it became clear to the agency in December 1974 that Contreras was not going to improve this record. In fact, by April 1975 he was seen as "the principal obstacle to a reasonable human rights policy within the junta." Nonetheless, the U.S. ambassador to Chile recommended that he be received in Washington by Deputy Director of Intelligence Walters in the interests of maintaining good relations with General Pinochet. With interagency approval, he was welcomed as a guest by the deputy director in August 1975. He received one payment from the CIA before he was transferred to a function unrelated to intelligence.

After retiring from the army with the rank of general, Contreras set up a private security agency on Calle Londres in downtown Santiago.[46] He also headed the Council of Retired Army Generals, and from this position he attacked the report of the Commission for Truth and Reconciliation as being partial. He complained that the report did not give sufficient credit to the military for their patriotic sacrifices on behalf of the country. In March of 1978, however, the Chilean Supreme Court appointed a special investigating judge to look into the case involving the issue of false passports to Michael Townley, the American mercenary who killed the former Allende cabinet minister Orlando Letelier and his companion Ronni Moffit in Washington, D.C. on September 21, 1976. This crime had been a constant irritant in the relations between Santiago and Washington, but nothing could be done at first because of the power position of Contreras. He knew too much about important people, and he was a friend of Pinochet. But this changed after Alwyn became president. A few months after the issuance of the report of the Commission on Truth and Reconciliation, the president petitioned the supreme court to appoint another investigating judge to try Contreras and a subordinate as accomplices in the Letelier/Moffit murders. He was found guilty, but he appealed his conviction. The fourth section of the supreme court upheld it. But then Contreras refused to accept the judgment of the court, disappeared, and reappeared at a naval base. This led to a constitutional crisis, with the army pitted against the civilian authority. After lengthy negotiations involving the president, the army accepted the verdict of the court. Contreras was sentenced to seven years in prison for complicity in the Letelier/Moffit murders. He has not been tried for any of his other activities.

Evaluating the Extent of Washington's Complicity

Washington's training of thousands of military personnel from Chile who later committed state terrorism again makes Washington eligible for the charge of accessory before the fact to state terrorism. The CIA's close relationship during the height of the terror to Contreras, Chile's chief terrorist (with the possible exception of Pinochet himself), lays Washington open to the charge of accessory during the fact. That he was a graduate of an American military school and received at least one payment from the agency makes the charge more plausible.

But the extent of Washington's role was further clarified, albeit tangentially, as the commission examined the ideology of DINA. Since the commission did not find a written statement of the ideology of DINA, it sought to deduce it from DINA's behavior and from the information it received from outside the country. Of course, DINA was anti-communist. But the commission went beyond this obvious observation. It identified two ideologies which motivated DINA—a lesser one, national security and a major one, counterinsurgency doctrine. It characterized national security as a distorted doctrine, one that puts this value above ethics. Little more than a revival of what was once called *raison d'etat*, in extreme cases it allows the rights of the individual to be sacrificed by reason of an alleged general national interest. The commission pointed out that the counterinsurgency doctrine developed in Latin American against a background that featured the Cuban revolution, Fidel Castro, Che Guevara, and guerrilla warfare. Guerrilla focos (units or foci) were to be established by the likes of Guevara in many rural and urban settings in all of Latin America. There was also to be a coordinating agency for these guerrilla focos, either in Havana or Moscow. In this view, counter-insurgency would establish its

The United States took charge of the overall coordination of counterinsurgency efforts between all Latin American countries.

own focos in these settings. Then, in one of its few references to the United States, the commission mentioned almost in passing what is in fact a major indictment of Washington's role, not simply in training generations of officers, but in supervision of their activities related to the actual suppression of purported insurgencies in Chile and elsewhere. The commission noted that their anticipation of insurgency:

> led a number of governments, and especially that of the United States, to start a counterinsurgency drive. Just like the focos, counterinsurgency was both local in nature in each country and centralized through a degree of coordination between all Latin American countries. *The United States took charge of the over all coordination,* [italics added] and to that end it took advantage of the fact that generations of officers from the various Latin American countries were passing through its military training schools each year.[47]

Washington's service as the overall coordinator of state terrorism in Latin America demonstrates the enthusiasm with which Washington played its role as an accomplice to state terrorism in the region. It was not a reluctant player. Rather it not only trained Latin American governments in terrorism and financed the means to commit terrorism; it also encouraged them to apply the lessons learned to put down what it called "the communist threat." Its enthusiasm extended to coordinating efforts to apprehend those wanted by terrorist states who had fled to other countries in the region. This much is known. How centralized the coordination was is a more difficult question to answer. How much influence was exercised by Washington in the decision to commit terrorism is a much harder question to answer. Of course, the actual commission of state terrorist acts was in the hands of terrorist governments and their agents. The evidence available leads to the conclusion that Washington's influence over the decision to commit these acts was considerable.

Counterinsurgency Doctrine

The commission affirmed that counterinsurgency was a type of armed struggle against urban or rural guerrillas. It had "hidden within it" an implicit doctrine or philosophy, one that was not necessarily embraced by its instructors, let alone by all its students, "although events prove that it influenced many of the latter." Here the commission seems to be in general agreement with the above evaluation that Washington's influence on the commission of state terrorism was considerable. This time it is the students that are impacted, and the impacting agent is counterinsurgency doctrine. The commission asserted that events prove that the doctrine influenced many of them, even if it did not influence all of them or all of their instructors.

I am struck by the similarity between the doctrine or philosophy of counterinsurgency and that of counter-terrorism as embraced by the Bush administration. Just as counterinsurgency doctrine is designed to fight the guerrilla, so counter-terror doctrine is designed to fight the terrorist. Both rationalize the use by "our side" of what are said to be the terrorist tactics of the adversary. Guerrilla warfare, so the counterinsurgency doctrine alleged, is not a minor type of conflict as its name implies in Spanish or Portuguese. (After all, the word is the diminutive for *guerra*, whose meaning in both of these languages is war.) It is genuine warfare. Moreover, its practitioners are said to be hypocritical in that they do not declare it, or they even disavow it. The governments that promote it deny that they are in any way responsible for it. Guerrillas are seen as showing no respect for the laws of war or for ethical principles: they take no prisoners, and they torture, practice terrorism, and destroy productive property. Governments must be made to understand the threat posed by the guerrillas and to confront guerrilla warfare with its own methods lest these governments place themselves at a disadvantage. The fundamental values of the country, the nation, and the state are at stake.

The commission went on to say that counterinsurgency doctrine was reflected in the information and practice received by recruits in training sessions on anti-guerrilla warfare—courses such as interrogation techniques, special forms of killing, how to lay ambushes, and survival training. "All of this gradually accustomed the student to the fact that ethical limits were receding and diminishing, sometimes to the vanishing point." The counterinsurgents were thus taught to use the very techniques that the guerrillas were purported to use. This could make them heroes in the double sense that they not only risked their lives to save the values for which their country purportedly stood, but that they sacrificed their own integrity to do so.

The counterinsurgents were taught to use the very techniques that the guerrillas were purported to use.

Those studying counterterrorism in America's new war on terrorism will learn the same lessons and are likely to engage in the same type of immoral and terrorist activity.

CNI, The Successor to DINA

When high level officials in Santiago realized the harm that DINA was causing the regime, it was terminated, and a new agency was put in place to fulfill the same function. On August, 13 1977 DINA was replaced by the National Center for Information (CNI), which took over the staff, the buildings, and the other property of its predecessor, but was put under the authority of the Interior Minister rather than the junta.[48] CNI was mandated to gather intelligence, but also to safeguard national security and the established institutional order. If DINA was the chief instrument of terrorism during its existence, so was CNI from its birth to the end of the Pinochet dictatorship. It was headed by a military officer on active duty with the rank of general. It engaged in direct action against guerrilla groups that became active during its tenure. It engaged in infiltration, surveillance, arrest, torture, armed repression, forced disappearance, and killing. The commission charged that in such operations it enjoyed absolute impunity.

Terror and Torture by the Pinochet Regime

The CNI's use of torture was systematic, but more selective than that of DINA, an agency that tortured practically everyone that passed through its hands. Torture in its hands continued to be mainly the use of electric shocks especially on the sensitive parts of the body, beatings of all kinds, and threatened asphyxiation through emersion in water. Perhaps because it initiated the practice of torture immediately after the coup or because it did more of it, the commission spent more space on the torture activities of DINA than on those of the CNI. The former institution included, along with beatings, humiliations, insults, degrading conditions of confinement, being held blindfolded, and being fed poorly for an extended period.[49] Electric shocks were customarily administered with the help of the "grill," a metal bed spring to which the victim was tied. The electricity was applied to the sensitive parts of the body, favorite spots being the lips and the genitalia. By having a close relative or a favorite friend tortured close by, perhaps in the same bunk bed, a psychological dimension would be added to the operation. "Suspension" was an alternative manner of applying electrical shocks, and it could be used as a supplement to increase the pain of beating, cutting, and humiliating the victim. "Suspension" meant that the victim was hung by the wrists or by the wrists and knees for long periods of time. By hanging on the victim and thus adding their weight, the guards would increase the victim's pain. Threatened asphyxiation was applied by the use of the "submarine," a technique that immersed the victim's head in a pan of some liquid, usually filthy water, and holding it there to the point of asphyxiation. This was repeated over and over again. A variation of this was the "dry submarine." This technique consisted of putting a plastic bag over the head of the victim to cut off the supply of oxygen. Beatings were inflicted by fists, feet, rifle butts, and chains, and could be applied to all parts of the body. This could cause serious wounds or even death.

The commission stated:

> The Commission feels that it must make it clear that in many instances the killing was carried out with such forms of torture and with a viciousness whose only objective seems to have been to intensify the suffering of the victims to an unspeakable degree. The mother of Eugenio Ruiz-Tagle killed in Calama on October 19,1973, described the condition of her son's body in the following way. "An eye was missing, the nose had been ripped off, the one ear visible was pulled away at the bottom, there were very deep burn marks as though done by a soldering iron on his neck and face, his mouth was all swollen up, there were cigarette burns, and judging from the angle of the head, the neck was broken, there were lots of cuts and bleeding."

The Chilean government carried out its executions principally by the use of knives and automatic rifles with silencers. Most of the prisoners who had disappeared were taken from their secret locations and executed close to the places where their bodies were to be buried or thrown.[50] The commission added that witnesses testified to another method of execution. It "consisted in taking prisoners out while asleep or drowsy from heavy sedation and putting them onto a helicopter and dropping them

Prisoners were dropped from helicopters into the ocean after their stomachs were cut open with a knife to keep their bodies from floating.

into the ocean after first cutting their stomachs open with a knife to keep the bodies from floating."[51] Ridicule and mistreatment sometimes continued to the moment of execution. The bodies of the disappeared were generally buried secretly or thrown into the ocean or a river.

Located in the foothills of the Andes on a windswept rise, Villa Grimaldi served as DINA's most important secret detention and torture center. The villa had special places and equipment for various types of torture. Notable among these was the "tower," that in fact looked like a tower with a water tank on top. But it contained a torture chamber and ten strange structures, cells, each of which was 28 inches (70 centimeters) by 28 inches (70 centimeters), and 80 inches (2 meters) high.[52] Each had a tiny door at the bottom through which victims were forced to enter on their knees. When a single prisoner was put in one of these cells, he or she was completely isolated. But sometimes two victims were pushed and squeezed into one cell. It was difficult for them to fit, and especially difficult to sleep. This must have been pure horror for the claustrophobic. The commission concluded that apparently those who were taken to the tower were prisoners of importance whose period of "intensive interrogation" was at an end. They were marked for disappearance, and were never seen again. Among its victims was Ariel Marcilla, one of the main leaders of the socialist party, who was tortured, taken to the tower, and then made to disappear.

Marc Cooper, an American who had served in the Allende government, finally summoned the courage to visit the remains of Villa Grimaldi in the late nineties.[53] Too many of his friends had passed through the villa prior to their disappearance and extinction. By then the villa had been torn down, its grounds enclosed with a bright yellow fence, and it was renamed by human rights groups the Park of Memory. The stumps of the old villa's foundation still punctured the earth. Marc accepted the invitation offered the visitor to follow the narrow circular "path of brutality," where plaques marked the various torture facilities formerly offered by the villa: "the grill;" "electric beds;" "the tower: place of solitary torture and extermination;" "place of hangings;" etc. The path ended with a wall inscribed with over 200 names, These are the names of those who had passed through the villa from 1974 to 1978 before they were disappeared or executed. On the top of the list is the assertion: "The Forgotten Past is Full of Memory." Marc read the first name of the list, Rene Alberto Acuna, and the last, Mario Luis Quesada. But he lacked the courage to search through the rest of the list for the names of long-lost friends and colleagues.

Marc found the wall and the park in its entirety to be a quiet and deeply moving experience and a fitting monument to those killed by the Pinochet dictatorship. Indeed, it was quiet. Marc and his memories had the park all to themselves. The park is tucked away on a distant suburban hilltop, a place of memories for the few, safely segregated from the mainstream of Chilean society. The circular path shows little sign of foot traffic, as does the park in general. Some days the park is padlocked. Human rights activists planted rose bushes and saplings at the entrance to the park. Marc observed that they had survived, but barely. They were scrawny, overshadowed by the established vegetation, and seemingly unable to compete with it.

Internal Support for the Dictatorship

DINA engaged in disinformation campaigns aimed at encouraging the public to think that the disappeared Chileans had been killed in other Latin American countries, the victims of infighting among the left. Such a campaign was launched in July 1975 when DINA published two lists totaling 119 names of Chileans who had disappeared after arrest. The claim was that they

DINA engaged in disinformation campaigns aimed at encouraging the public to think that the disappeared Chileans had been killed in other Latin American countries, the victims of infighting among the left.

had been killed abroad by other leftists. The purpose was to shift the onus for the disappearances from the government and put it on the squabbles that broke out among the left. The Chilean press was quick to join in and to publish the news with sensational headlines. The campaign was a success, as the public became confused and the relatives of the disappeared were humiliated and isolated.[54] Those who defended human rights were discredited.

The casualty figures exhibited above, almost all leftists and almost all victims of the Pinochet dictatorship, suggest that the dictatorship was from the right. This is hardly a startling conclusion, and it is the logical one to draw from Decree Law No. 77 enacted in 1973. This decree/law prohibited "as illicit associations" all of the political parties of Allende's coalition government. Prohibited were all leftist parties and "all entities, groups, factions, or movements that advocate Marxist teaching, or by their aims or the behavior of their supporters are in substantial agreement with the principles and objectives of such teaching."[55] It was not until four years later that this prohibition was extended to include all other political parties. This section, however, is concerned with who or what supported the dictatorship, not against whom or what the dictatorship acted. The report of the commission deals with this issue, and thus provides the reality symbolized above by the plight of the scrawny roses and the saplings planted by human rights activists in the Park of Memory as they tried to compete with the established vegetation all around them.

The report speaks of internal and external groups that supported or opposed the dictatorship, the former providing the main subject matter for this section. The first of these internal groups discussed here are political parties. The commission concluded that the coup of September 11 was a military affair with political parties playing no role. So the reaction of political parties to the coup and the resulting dictatorship are the more revealing.

Immediately after the coup, the Christian Democrats in exile published a statement that raised the issue of human rights violations in Chile. At the same time prominent members of the party in Chile issued statements in support of the junta, claiming that the coup had saved Chile from a communist dictatorship. Members of rightwing parties made similar statements at this time, praising the junta's actions and alleging that it had saved the country from communism. These parties "unanimously supported the September 11 military intervention during this period"[56]—September through December, 1973. Representatives of rightwing parties took no position on human rights violations. While the leftist parties were abolished in 1973 and the remainder of the parties in 1977, the policies of parties in the early post-coup period had to be deduced from the statements of their leaders since all political activities were forbidden from the earlier date. This changed in the later periods of the dictatorship as the parties became more organized, even if their activities remained illegal. Their view of violence whether governmental or guerrilla, continued to be filtered through their particular ideologies. Right-wing parties condemned violations of human rights by governmental officials in theoretical terms, but failed to state clearly that such violations were actually taking place in the country.[57] In contrast, these parties openly and categorically condemned the terrorist activities of the guerrillas. The Christian Democrats, Social Democrats, and some socialist factions condemned human rights violations of the government and of all terrorists of the left and the right. From the beginning, political parties of the left condemned the violations of human rights by the government. After all, it was their rights that were being violated by the government. They did not take an equally clear stance toward the violence committed by the guerrillas. Indeed, many leftists, and finally, the communist party itself, participated in the guerrilla activity.

The policies of political parties in Chile thus created a familiar configuration, with the right wing supporting a military solution to the social movements which arose as a result of social inequalities, and which sought to challenge the status quo, in this case legitimately through the ballot box. When considered as a whole, the non-reaction of Chilean society to the coup and its immediate bloody aftermath was troubling. The commission found that these events "prompted almost no public reaction except from the churches, primarily the Catholic church."[58] This the commission explained by ignorance, the fear of being punished, and a national culture deficient in the area of human rights. Even when the public became aware of what was happening, major sections of it allowed, tolerated, supported, or concealed the violations of the rights of the former members or sympathizers of Allende's government. They justified these violations with the excuse that these victims were planning to kill their opponents. This was a rationalization based not on what the Allende people had actually been planning, but on what they were imaged as likely to have done. This type of logic echoes the counterinsurgency theory discussed above. There, the brutality of counterinsurgency was justified because of the supposed or anticipated brutality of guerrilla warfare. The commission found that as the instances of victims being arrested, tortured, executed, or forcibly disappeared became more widely known, the public made "feeble efforts" to defend human rights. The abolition of DINA in 1977 did not open a new era of public support for human rights. Chilean society did not react in open solidarity with the victims. "The prevailing attitude was rather one of indifference or unbelief, despite a gradual but slow growth in awareness on the matter."[59] An incipient, but clear, opposition to the military regime did emerge in the realms of labor, politics, academia, and others. It took two forms: one violent, one non-violent. The civic-oriented non-violent form expressed itself through the denunciation of human rights violations, primarily by human rights organizations; aid and support for its victims offered by these agencies and the Catholic Church; and the campaign to vote "no" in the September 11, 1980 plebiscite. This plebiscite was the Pinochet government's response to a General Assembly resolution of December 16, 1977 that condemned the government of Chile for human rights violations. Seventy-five percent of the participants voted "yes," and thus supported the Pinochet dictatorship against this supposed "attack from the outside." Partisans of the political left and center disputed the results, but the charge that the Chilean public was essentially indifferent to the violation of human rights by the government appears to be valid. The commission remarked:

> The deep conviction that every person's human rights must be respected, and especially the most essential of those rights, no matter what the accusations against such persons might be or the harm they are alleged to have caused, did not win the day in our country. It is not our role to take a position on the moral responsibility that may fall to society as a whole as a result of its failure to react in a timely and vigorous fashion to what was happening. Nevertheless we believe that what happened should lead all Chileans to reflect on the grave omission that was ours.[60]

A major cause of this "grave omission"—the public's permissive attitude toward government repression—was the condition and the attitude of the media. Immediately upon seizing power, the military government established control of the media. They were closed down or placed under a system of prior censorship, which was applied systematically until the end of 1973. The surviving media after that time were usually supporters of the military regime, and they uncritically published whatever the military handed them. Some of the handouts were disinformation that, for example, took the form of explaining the deaths of leftists as resulting from gun battles or guerrilla action, rather than their arrest, torture, and murder by the government. These media covered up for the government, misled the public, and acted as the accomplices to governmental repression. After the demise of DINA, the media enjoyed what the commission called "an incipient degree of independence," as shown by its permission to reprint information from abroad about the Chilean government's repression of human rights. Most censorship was self-censorship. "Nevertheless, as a rule the media continued to offer the regime virtually unqualified support, either because they were under restraint, or constrained themselves, or did so spontaneously."[61]

A major cause of the public's permissive attitude toward government repression was the condition and the attitude of the media. Most censorship was self-censorship.

Washington's Reaction to State Terrorism in Chile

Throughout the post-coup period, the CIA collected and disseminated extensive reporting concerning human rights issues in Chile to the intelligence and policy communities.[62] Washington thus was aware of the state terrorism and other forms of government repression committed by the Pinochet regime. The CIA produced its first report on what it prefers to call human rights abuses by the new Pinochet government on September 15, 1973, just four days after the coup.[63] This was followed a few days later by the report that security interrogation units dealt with suspects "in an extremely vigorous manner" and that the prisoners at the National Stadium were harshly treated. The agency's report of September 28 revealed that 27cadavers had been recovered from the Mapocho River and that they showed signs of torture and mutilation. *CIA Activities* lists three other specific reports it made in October and November 1973. They indicated that

Soviet non-diplomatic technicians in Chile were repeatedly threatened, abused, beaten, and injured; that General Stark had given orders that resulted in the killing of 21 political prisoners; and that 20 bodies with bullet holes in them were found in the San Carlos River.[64] In the months following the coup, the agency provided Washington with extensive coverage of "what the (Chilean) government charac-terized as activities necessary to restore order." It informed Washington that there were widely varying reports on the number of persons killed and arrested and that the military deliberately did not disclose accurate figures on these subjects. It reported extensively on the application of "military justice" (CIA's quotation marks) to civilian detainees and the types of punishment they were likely to receive. The agency revealed that "Plan Z" —supposedly a plan adopted by the Allende regime in its last days to assassinate important military and civilian leaders who were opposed to its leftist agenda—was probably "disinformation manipulated by the junta to improve its image and to provide justification for its activities." The agency denied that it had taken part in the hoax, but it admitted that military officers with whom it had contact helped draft the *White Book,* a publication in which Plan Z was featured.

The CIA confirmed that it had reported on what it called "human rights" abuses during the entire seventeen years of the Pinochet dictatorship. It expressed this idea this way. "Over the next 17 years, the CIA reported information available from its contacts concerning human rights abuses in Chile."[65] As suggested by several of the examples given above, some of these abuses qualify as state terrorism. It continued. "As the left later gained strength, intelligence reporting included the plans, intentions, capabilities and terrorist acts of the left." This statement seems to confirm the assertion contained in the report of the Commission on Truth and Reconciliation that the state terrorism practiced by the dictatorship predated by years the private terrorism on any significant scale practiced by the guerrillas. Note above that the offenses committed by the left were characterized as "terrorism," those by the government as "human rights abuses." This distinction in labeling is extremely important, for it is Washington's official vocabulary, the terminology in which it wraps its foreign policy. Its purpose is to absolve rightwing dictatorships of the Pinochet type from being viewed as terrorists. Even more significantly, it seeks to shield Washington from being called a supporter of terrorism. The CIA claimed credit for downgrading at the time what it characterized as a "ruse," namely the Chilean government's circular dated January 17, 1974 that prohibited torture. It stated: "CIA reporting indicated that the Chilean security forces did not, and probably would not, observe the stated policy." Although the State Department and the Embassy were primarily responsible for reporting on human rights abuses, the CIA did so because the clandestine nature of the Chilean security forces required it. In any case, it is fair to assume that the elites in Washington realized that the regime that they supported was guilty of state terrorism.

Given that they knew about the terrorism of this regime, what did the elites in Washington during the Nixon and Ford administrations do about it? The CIA report stated:

> After Pinochet came to power, senior policy makers appeared
> reluctant to criticize human rights violations, taking to task US

diplomats urging greater attention to the problem. US military assistance and sales grew significantly during the years of greatest human rights abuses. According to a previously released Memorandum of Conversation, Kissinger in June 1976 indicated to Pinochet that the US Government was sympathetic to his regime, although Kissinger advised some progress in human rights in order to improve Chile's image in the US Congress.[66]

The elites in Washington reacted by increasing U.S. military assistance and sales to the state terrorists, by covering up their terrorism, by urging U.S. diplomats to do so also, and by assuring the terrorists of their support, thereby becoming accessories to state terrorism before, during, and after the fact. The report of the Commission on Truth and Reconciliation painted a similar picture of Washington's early policy, but only after it had pointed

The elites in Washington reacted by increasing U.S. military assistance and sales to the state terrorists, by covering up their terrorism, by urging U.S. diplomats to do so also, and by assuring the terrorists of their support, thereby becoming accessories to state terrorism.

out the critical and negative reaction of other governments and institutions. Mexico broke off diplomatic relations, while Italy withdrew its ambassador. Relations with a number of other countries deteriorated as well. The "Chilean case" came to occupy a prominent place on the agendas of the United Nations, the Organization of American States, and such non-governmental organizations as Amnesty International and the International Commission of Jurists. Beginning in 1974, the United Nations Human Rights Commission issued special reports on the human rights situation in Chile, and the General Assembly followed through with condemnatory resolutions. The reaction of Washington and other countries to these resolutions is indicated in Table 1 below.

The Commission on Truth and Reconciliation suggested that the post-coup relations of Washington with the Pinochet regime "remained relatively normal."[67] This general, bland comment is followed by the revelation that aid from the United States to Chile increased several times in the period 1974-1976 compared with the pre-coup years 1971-1973. Military aid to Chile was banned in 1976, and the ban remained in force until 1981.[68] The report of the commission went on to say that the Nixon and Ford administrations helped Chile to re-negotiate its foreign debt. Actually, the coup brought an improvement in Washington's economic relations with Chile for two reasons. One reason was that Washington had been waging economic warfare against the Allende government, and the second reason was Washington's general preference for rightwing military regimes over leftist regimes. The commission contended that the election of President Carter affected American policy,[69] and indicated that pressure from Washington after the assassinations of the former Chilean foreign minister Orlando Letelier and his co-worker Ronnie Moffit led to the disestablishment of DINA and to some improvement in human rights.

The Republican administrations of Nixon, Ford, and Reagan were more supportive of the Pinochet dictatorship than the Democratic administration of Carter. Ensalaco points out that the Nixon and Ford administrations took no action to punish the Pinochet dictatorship for its human rights violations.[70] In fact they circumvented the efforts of Congress to curtail economic and military assistance

TABLE 1
Criticism of Chile's Violation of Human Rights:
Votes on Roll Calls in the General Assembly
1974-1989

COUNTRIES	19 74	19 75	19 75	19 77	19 78	19 79	19 80	19 81	19 82	19 83	19 84	19 85	19 86	19 87	19 88	19 89
Canada	Y	Y	Y	Y	Y	Y	Y	Y	Y	Y	Y	Y	Y	Y	Y	Y
Denmark	Y	Y	Y	Y	Y	Y	Y	Y	Y	Y	Y	Y	Y	Y	Y	Y
Finland	Y	Y	Y	Y	Y	Y	Y	Y	Y	Y	Y	Y	Y	Y	Y	Y
France	Y	Y	A	Y	Y	Y	Y	Y	Y	Y	Y	Y	Y	Y	Y	Y
Germany	Y	Y	A	Y	Y	Y	Y	Y	A	A	Y	Y	Y	Y	Y	Y
Iceland	Y	Y	Y	Y	Y	Y	Y	Y	Y	Y	Y	Y	Y	Y	Y	Y
Israel	A	A	A	Y	A	A	A	N	N	N	A	A	A	A	A	A
Netherlands	Y	Y	Y	Y	Y	Y	Y	Y	Y	Y	Y	Y	Y	Y	Y	Y
Norway	Y	Y	Y	Y	Y	Y	Y	Y	Y	Y	Y	Y	Y	Y	Y	Y
Sweden	Y	Y	Y	Y	Y	Y	Y	Y	Y	Y	Y	Y	Y	Y	Y	Y
UK	Y	Y	Y	Y	Y	Y	Y	Y	A	A	Y	Y	Y	Y	Y	Y
USA	A	Y	A	Y	Y	Y	Y	N	N	N	N	N	N	A	A	A
All	90	95	95	96	96	96	95	84	85	89	90	88	94	93	97	84
Members	8	11	12	14	7	9	8	20	17	17	13	11	5	5	1	2
	26	23	25	25	38	33	39	42	11	38	40	47	52	53	55	60

Y indicates an affirmative vote; N a negative vote, and A an abstention or an absence. The votes of all members of the General Assembly on a given roll call are given at the bottom of the table in the same order, with the affirmative votes first, next the negative ones, and in last place the abstentions.

Source: The editions of *The Yearbook of the United Nations* (New York. Department of Information) from 1974 to 1989.

to Chile. When the armed forces were in the first and worst phase of their repression, the Nixon administration arranged for $52 million in commodity credits. In 1974 Congress managed to restrict military aid to the South American country to less than one million of International Military, Education, and Training funds, and in 1977 a ban on all

When the armed forces were in the first and worst phase of their repression, the Nixon administration arranged for $52 million in commodity credits.

military assistance and sales went into effect after Carter had become president. President Reagan admired Pinochet as the ruler who had saved Chile from communism. Before Reagan appointed Jeanne Kirkpatrick as the United States ambassador to the United Nations, she had become famous for her benign view of rightwing dictators. In a visit to Chile in August 1981, she refused to meet with Jaime Castillo, the director of the Chilean Human Rights Commission. During the Reagan years the ban on military assistance and sales to Santiago was lifted, and joint exercises with the Chilean navy were resumed. But the Reagan administration became concerned when Pinochet re-instituted a state of siege in 1984. By 1986 the Reagan administration had become converted to the notion of a democratic Chile. Other countries in South America had already turned in this direction.

The votes on the annual roll calls cast in the General Assembly from 1974 to 1989 that criticized the Pinochet dictatorship for its human rights violations are displayed in Table 1. This type of evidence is included to further substantiate the firm factual basis of this study. None of the U.S. votes were cast during the Nixon administration, the first three were cast during that of Ford. One of these votes supported the resolution charging the Pinochet dictatorship with flagrant violations of human rights. But the U.S. abstained on two other resolutions which accused the dictatorship of the violations of human rights. The record of this administration contrasts with that of its successor, the Carter administration. Its delegate voted affirmatively on every one of the four condemnatory resolutions from 1977 to 1980. This behavior in turn contrasts with the voting during the Reagan years, a record that is the least supportive of human rights of the four administrations. Six of its eight votes were negative; two were abstentions. The abstentions occurred in 1987 and 1988, at a time when the Reagan administration finally became concerned with the absence of democracy in Chile. The Bush administration repeated this performance by abstaining on a similar resolution before the world body in 1989. The table also provides data to compare Washington's performance on human rights with that of other countries. The data allow comparisons with the average vote of the entire General Assembly; with three democracies—France, the United Kingdom, and Germany; with Israel; and with seven countries reputed to have good human rights records (see Table 1 on the previous page).

Although they are purported to be standard bearers of democracy, France, the United Kingdom, and Israel were suppliers of military hardware to the Pinochet dictatorship.[71] Israel was included, because other research has shown that Israel often supplies aid to rightwing dictatorships and is the country that votes most often with Washington in the General Assembly. The seven states chosen as the standard for upholding human rights were found in the study of Jack Donnelly entitled *International Human Rights*.[72] He discovered that this type of state is staunch in its support of traditional human rights, and is also hospitable to the idea of accepting economic rights as human rights. The seven states are

Canada, Denmark, Finland, Iceland, the Netherlands, Norway, and Sweden. Other evidence that at least the Netherlands and the three Scandinavian states Norway, Sweden, and Denmark should be eligible for nomination as good world citizens is provided by the level of their contributions to third world development. They were the only countries in 2002 that had fulfilled their promise of providing 0.7 percent of their gross domestic product for aid to such development.[73] Washington ranked 22nd on the list, contributing 0.1 percent of its gross domestic product to this cause. As shown in the table, the behavior of the seven proved to be a worthy standard for upholding human rights in Chile. Each of them voted 15 times in the affirmative on the 15 resolutions to criticize the state terrorism and the violations of human rights in that country. Their record is now compared with other states and other groups, and notably with that of Washington. The votes are broken down into the categories yes votes, no votes, and abstentions, and are expressed in percentages:

	Yes	No	Abstentions
The seven	100%	0%	0%
The three	88	0	12
All members	65	7	28
United States	31	38	31
Israel	6	19	75

These comparisons put Washington's record on condemnation of known human rights violations well below that of the seven, the three, and even below the average for all members of the world institution. This record is the worse because it primarily measures the policies of Republican administrations, only one Democratic. This divergence provides more evidence to support a general conclusion of this volume. Israel's voting record is also in accord with other findings in this study.

THE AFTERMATH

The General Visits, Shops, Has an Operation, Is Charged With Murder, Then Returns Home

Traveling on a diplomatic passport and accompanied by bodyguards, General Pinochet arrived at Heathrow Airport in London on September 21, 1998. Consistent with previous visits, he received red carpet treatment, met with former prime minister Lady Thatcher for tea, and went shopping at his favorite stores, Harrods and Fortnum and Mason's. On previous visits he had been welcomed by British Aerospace, Europe's largest arms manufacturer, and by the Conservative Party. Even after Labour came to power there was no attempt to block his entry, even though decades before he "had been a principal hate figure of the Labour Party."[74] This time the 82-year-old general, suffering from diabetes and wearing a pacemaker, entered the London clinic where he was operated on for a herniated disc. While the former dictator was still sedated and recovering, two plainclothesmen from the London police entered his room to inform him that he was under arrest for the torture and murder of Spanish citizens. They explained that they were acting in response to a warrant issued by Interpol on behalf of the Spanish authorities. His bodyguards were disarmed, and armed policemen were posted at the entrance to his room.

Thus started what seemed like a never ending legal process as the case wound its way through the labyrinth of the British legal system and presented itself for final decision on the desk of the Home Secretary, Mr. Jack Straw. Mr. Straw finally ruled that Pinochet was too ill to stand trial, and that he could not endure a prolonged judicial process. He left for home, where he received a joyous and triumphant reception from his followers. Before this occurred, however, the public in Chile divided along the lines already described above. Margaret Thatcher led the charge of an entourage of her Conservative colleagues as they attempted to protect the dictator from extradition and trial. But Switzerland, Belgium, and France backed Spain and lined up for their turn to prosecute the dictator for the crimes committed against their nationals. "The United States, however, has remained silent: a silence that has been interpreted around the world as support for Pinochet's impunity."[75]

The United States' silence has been interpreted around the world as support for Pinochet's impunity.

On returning, Pinochet faced the problem of hundreds of criminal complaints filed against him in Chile. Moreover, the courts there stripped him of his senatorial immunity and ordered his house arrest. The socialist candidate Ricardo Lagos became the president of Chile in March 2000, only a few days after Pinochet had been freed from house arrest in Britain. Everything seemed to be falling into place for the trial. But Lagos led a coalition government made up of his party plus the Christian Democrats, and he was in no mode to antagonize the armed forces. A confidant of the president revealed that he let it be known to the supreme court that he opposed the trial for Pinochet. In any case, this court ruled that the general was not well enough to stand trial.[76] The Lagos regime is a cautious, conservative one—maintaining good relations with Washington, promoting free trade, and purchasing airplanes for the military. The constitution still gives exceptional powers to the military, and the military has not fully cooperated in finding missing persons, despite its promise to do so.

CONCLUSION

For years, the Pinochet dictatorship engaged in a sustained and deliberate campaign of a physical and psychological nature whose purpose was to intimidate and coerce victims by causing them intense fear, anxiety, apprehension, panic, dread, and/or horror. The terrorism was under the overall supervision of General Pinochet himself, assisted at the height of the terror by his right hand man, General Contreras and systematically applied by the state for political ends. A measure of this terror was the means adopted for "destroying a political party" ---not merely by the destruction of the party's structure but by targeting and killing the party's activists in order to coerce and intimidate not only those party stalwarts who survived direct terrorist attacks, but also other less avid members and the public at large.

To what extent was the terror essentially state terror committed by the government or private terror committed by the guerrillas? The commission found that the former was the case, not the latter. Similar to the commissions in Guatemala and El Salvador, the data gathered indicated that the government was responsible for 95.7 percent of the victims identified, the guerrillas for the remaining 4.3 percent. Moreover, the commission concluded that those who were killed and disappeared were overwhelmingly leftists and guerrillas, which suggests that the perpetrators were predominately from the other end of the ideological spectrum. A further breakdown of the victims—workers and small farmers were at or near the top of the list, while high level officials and business people were found at the bottom—substantiates the conclusion that the Pinochet repression represented a type of class warfare. The commission found that these events produced little public response except from the churches, and of course from the guerrillas. The state terrorism of the government of Chile most probably produced some of the terrorism of the guerrillas, retail terrorism as a response to wholesale terrorism. I am reminded of Palestinian terrorists who terrorize Israel, whose government they see as a wholesale terrorist institution.

The third and final question is whether the government that perpetrated the terror upon its own citizens received support from Washington, and if so, in what ways was this support given? During its campaign of state terrorism, Chile received economic and military aid and diplomatic support from Washington. Military aid was significantly increased during the height of this campaign. The CIA publication cited above affirmed that Washington trained thousands of the Chilean military and that the training included the charge of the possible dire impact of global communism upon their country. Other sources indicated that this training was often in counterinsurgency warfare and that this prepared the students for the terror that they later committed. Recruits were taught that guerrillas show no respect for the laws of war or for ethical standards, took no prisoners, tortured and practiced terrorism. The recruits were taught to confront guerrillas with what were purported to be their own methods, lest they place themselves at a disadvantage. Gradually, the lesson was learned: ethical standards have no place in this work. They were inculcated with the maxim: "they'll do it to you, so you better do it to them first." The general findings for this chapter are the same as those of the two preceding chapters that dealt with terrorism in Guatemala and El Salvador.

CHAPTER 4

Argentina's Dirty War

ANOTHER COUP WAGING LAW AND ORDER

The dirty war in Argentina started in 1976 after a military coup on March 25 of that year brought General Jorge Videla to power. The coup was the military's response to the disorder and deteriorating economic conditions that preceded it. The disorder was marked by strikes and terrorism from the left and the right. The president of the country was Isabel Peron, who assumed office the year before upon the death of her husband. The first female president in Latin America, she had served as her husband's vice-president. He had been elected with over 61 percent of the vote. Many Argentinians were relieved by the prospect of a military government putting down the violence and restoring order and stability. The period preceding the coup was one of violence, but nothing approaching the retaliatory and repressive violence of the dirty war to be unleashed by the new regime. In late 1980 Videla stepped down in favor of Army General Roberto Viola. The dirty war was going well for the army, but the Argentine economy was doing badly. Under military management/mismanagement, the country fell deeply in debt, the currency depreciated, wages fell, inflation rose, and the labor unions started to regain their militancy. An early casualty was General Viola. After serving less than a year of his supposed four-year term and after suffering from a mild heart attack, he was pushed aside in a palace coup in favor of the Army Commander in Chief, General Leopoldo Galtieri.

The dirty war damaged the reputation of the junta, earning it the criticism not only of the human rights community, but also that of the United Nations, the Organization of American States, and much of the world at large. The Reagan administration tried to repair the damage, but without much success. It did manage to "end the junta's isolation through symbolic gestures that had great significance from the Argentine perspective."[1] The administration received members of the junta as honored guests, and it sent high-ranking officials to be honored in Buenos Aires.

Dr. Jeanne Kirkpatrick, U.S. ambassador to the United Nations and a noted apologist for supporting rightwing dictators, arrived in Buenos Aires on August 1,1981 on the second leg of her tour of Latin America. The Mothers of the Plaza de Mayo—a domestically notorious human rights group of brave women who demonstrated publicly for information on the disappearance of their loved ones—had prepared a long letter for her, and they asked for an interview. They were not accorded an interview by Kirkpatrick, nor did they receive a response to their letter.[2] Americas Watch did a follow-up check at the American embassy about the letter, only to be told that it had been misrouted within the embassy. This diplomatic snub contrasts with the treatment that the mothers received elsewhere. They were received at least once by the president of France, once by the prime minister of Spain, four times by the president of Italy, and three times by the pope.[3] At a press conference in Buenos Aires, Kirkpatrick dodged questions about the disappeared, but asserted that the governments of Argentina, Chile, and Uruguay had more elements of constitutionalism in their governance than many other countries. Next Kirkpatrick went to Chile, where she again antagonized human rights advocates, refusing to meet with Jaime Castillo, the leader of the human rights movement there. He also asked for an interview, but was granted one with one of her subordinates. Two days after Kirkpatrick left Chile, Castillo, together with three other human rights workers, were arrested and expelled from the country. Kirkpatrick's office issued no statement of regret at what happened.

The Reagan administration received General Viola with full honors on his visit to Washington in early 1981. He declared at the end of the visit, "I have encountered an understanding that exceeded my most exaggerated hopes." The retiring Argentine ambassador to the United States informed his countrymen, "Reagan is a friend of Argentina and of President Viola, and this sets a course toward future possibilities." In November of 1981 General Galtieri visited Washington. A luncheon he hosted at the Argentinian embassy was attended by Secretary of Defense Caspar Weinberger, National Security Adviser Richard Allen, and Assistant Secretary of State Thomas Enders. The general promised his distinguished guests that Argentina would join the United States in its crusade against communism in the Western Hemisphere, particularly in Central America. Weinberger and Allen were impressed and called him "magnificent."[4] Knowledge that he was an alumnus of the School of the Americas must have fueled their enthusiasm.

After returning to Buenos Aires, the general followed through by implementing his promise. Argentina proceeded to distance itself from the Non-Aligned Movement. Its ambassadors were withdrawn from Cuba and Nicaragua. Its instructors launched programs to train the Contras and Salvadoran security forces in the techniques of counterinsurgency warfare. It trained a thousand Contras in Honduras, preparing them for the war to be waged against the Sandinistas. Argentinian trainers thus substituted for American instructors, who were forbidden by Congress from continuing with such instruction.

NUNCA MAS: REPORT OF THE ARGENTINE COMMISSION ON THE DISAPPEARED[5]

Organization of the Commission

CONADEP consisted of ten members appointed by the president and three by the House of Deputies. Five of the members appointed by the president had been prominent in the civil rights movement, as was most of the staff that served the Commission.[6] At its first meeting on December 18, 1983, it chose as its chair Ernesto Sabato, a leading Latin American novelist. The Commission was charged with the duty of investigating and submitting a report to the president on the fate and the whereabouts of the disappeared, the *desaparecidos*, a word left in Spanish by the world press in its reports on Argentina. It worked initially from a list of six thousand *desaparecidos* provided by the Permanent Assembly on Human Rights. With no power to subpoena witnesses as human rights advocates wanted, its evidence came overwhelmingly from the victims. Forty-four of the torturers and their commanding officers were invited to testify. None of them accepted. The Commission spent nine months on the project, and then submitted its report to the president in September 1984. Its findings were summarized in a book entitled *Nunca Mas (Never Again)* which immediately became a best seller in Argentina.

The armed forces of Argentina did not cooperate in its preparation, behavior that duplicates that of other armed forces discussed in previous chapters. That the Argentine armed forces would not cooperate was suggested in 1981 in a statement made by General Viola in response to the question posed by a journalist concerning whether there was the need to have an inquiry into the problem of the disappeared. The general responded:

> I think you are suggesting that we investigate the Security Forces—that is absolutely out of the question. This is a war and we are the winners. You can be certain that in the last war if the armies of the Reich had won, the war crimes trials would have taken place in Virginia, not in Nuremberg.[7]

Of course, the general proved to be wrong. The security forces and the armed forces were investigated, but, as suggested above, without their cooperation. The Commission complained:

> We must point out, however, that our work was hindered by the destruction and/or removal of a vast amount of documentation containing detailed information on the disappeared. We appealed to various institutions and organizations of the military and security forces for instructions, organizational diagrams, orders and the names of certain members who, because of the central role they played in the repression, could have supplied us with vital evidence.[8]

The Commission sent out some 1,300 requests for information. The principal destinations of these requests were the ministry of defense (280), the federal and provincial police (200), and the national and provincial courts (290). The Commission went on to say that many of its questions remained unanswered "since the organizations connected to the armed forces did not reply satisfactorily to the Commission's request for information." It noted a similar lack of cooperation from some judges who returned its letters. The Commission appealed to the president to require that certain administrative and security bodies reply to its requests and to annul provisions of the regulations of the armed forces that allowed them to refuse to answer questions on grounds of national security.

Like the other truth commission reports on Latin American countries used in previous chapters, that produced by CONADEP is based on extensive research. This research resulted in the preparation of 7,380 files on the *desaparecidos*, consisting of testimonies of victims who survived and were released from detention centers, depositions of relatives, and statements by the members of the armed and the security forces which had taken part in the terror and repression.[9] Its report to the president came to over 50,000 pages. It discovered 340 detention centers used by the military and security forces for detaining and torturing their victims. It was able to identify 8,960 *desaparecidos*, i.e., those who had disappeared and were never found, but it had every reason to believe that the number was much higher. Estimates have varied between 10,000 and 30,000.[10] Some families were afraid to report disappearances, and they were under-reported in the poorer areas of the country.

As in other Latin American countries, the Argentine army claimed that its actions were a response to the terrorism of the guerrillas on the left. The report

J this claim, arguing that the "response" of the armed forces was "infinitely
ะ" than what they were combating.[11] Other sources have claimed that the
guerrillas never went beyond the stage of "armed propaganda." These statements indicate that the dirty war was more state terrorism carried on by the army
than private terrorism committed by the guerrillas. One source put the number of
guerrillas at 2,000, of whom only one-fourth were capable of fighting.[12] There
were two main guerrilla groups: the Peronist Montoneros and the Trotskyist
People's Revolutionary Army (ERP).

In drawing up the report, the Commission dealt with a general problem
that has confronted me throughout the study. The Commission wondered how it
could deal with the repression in Argentina without making its report an encyclopedia of horror. It found no way to avoid this.[13] It justified its presentation of this
encyclopedia as necessary for understanding the physical and mental suffering
of the victims and for informing the reader of the methods used by the torturers.
There appears to be no alternative to this practice if the human and inhuman
aspects of what was done are to be fully realized. The cold statistics have a place,
They tell their side of the story. The encyclopedia is no less essential; it completes
the picture. The encyclopedia records those unspeakable actions meant to intimidate and coerce victims, their supporters, and their potential followers by
inflicting on them intense fear, anxiety, apprehension, panic, dread, and horror.

ARGENTINIAN STATE TERRORISM

The Commission was empowered to investigate only cases of disappearance. Since the guerrillas made little if any use of this practice, the report is
mostly about the actions committed by the security forces under the direction of
the army. The Commission thus did not make numerical estimates of the comparative number of victims produced by the army and the guerrillas, estimates
that had been made by the truth commissions in El Salvador, Guatemala, and
Chile. Actually, the Argentine public had already been apprised of the actions of
the guerrillas by a number of TV programs, a multitude of newspaper and magazine articles, and a book published by the military government that enumerated,
described in minute detail, and condemned the terrorism of the guerrillas.[14]

The report found a contradiction between the military's constant disre-
spect for human beings and its advocacy of what it called a Western, Christian life
style. A month after the military coup, Colonel Juan Bautista Sasiain, who later
became Chief of the Federal Police, affirmed that "the army values a man as such,
because the army is Christian."[15] The Commission charged that the army practiced
state terrorism, made possible by the power and the impunity of a military dictatorship "which they misused to abduct, torture, and kill thousands of human beings."
It went on to ask what else were the tortures but a display of the most grave and
perverted acts used by military governments that lacked legitimacy to dominate the
people? The report indicated that there were only 600 abductions before the military
coup of March 24, 1976, and that the military courts that were set up after that date
to try terrorists actually brought suit against only 356 defendants. The military and
the security forces ignored the courts in favor of "disappearance."

The Victims

The Commission found that the vast majority of the 8,960 victims were
not only innocent of acts of terrorism, but even of belonging to guerrilla organiza-

tions. They were trade union leaders struggling for higher wages for workers; youngsters who belonged to student organizations; journalists who did not support the military regime; professionals who belonged to suspicious organizations; young pacifists, nuns, and priests who were inspired by the teachings of Christ and who took this message to the poor; friends of these people; or others whose names were given to the security forces out of vengeance or by the kidnapped under torture.

As impressive as the combined size of the groups targeted for direct attack may seem, the reader is reminded that state terrorism in Argentina sought to intimidate and coerce a much larger audience, namely those sectors of society that longed for social change. Furthermore, a quantitative breakdown of the victims points to the class nature of this case of state terrorism and to the prominence of students as victims. The largest percentage (30.2 percent) were blue collar workers; the third largest (17.9 percent) white collar workers; and the seventh largest (3.8 percent) maids.[16] Students were second, accounting for 21 percent of the victims, and one-third of these were also employed. Notable among the other groups were professional people (10.7 percent); teachers and professors (5.7 percent); the religious (.3 percent); and the self-employed and others (5.0 percent). Businessmen did not rate a separate category, but they seem to have been included in the category self-employed and others. The type of victims they produced is evidence of the nature of the oppressors. The statistics enumerated here suggest that the oppressors were rightwing and anti-labor, and that the dirty war was essentially a form of class warfare.

Despite the fact that Jews constitute only one percent of the population of Argentina, an estimated ten percent of the victims of the dirty war were Jews. That this war had an anti-Semitic side is attested to by CONADEP, which devoted a section to illustrate this point. It is illustrated, to quote the report, by the "particular brutality in the treatment of prisoners of Jewish origin."[17]

Jews were not only tortured, but the torture often took on an anti-Semitic form. The torturers painted swastikas on one Jewish prisoner's back with a sharp pointed marker. Another torturer who called himself the "great fuehrer" made Jewish prisoners shout "Heil Hitler." A Jewish woman on her way to an excursion in Israel was called by her abductors "a Yid," and subjected to the cattle prod. They wanted information from her and from her files on Jews. She was told that the Jewish problem was second only to the problem of subversion. Later, they told her that her abduction was a mistake and to forget it. In one torture center Jews were made to raise one hand and to shout "I love Hitler." One prisoner remembered the ordeal of another prisoner, a Jew nicknamed "Chango," at the hands of his torturer called "Julian the Turk." Julian always carried a key ring with a swastika and wore a crucifix around his neck. He made Chango bark like a dog, wag as though he were a dog wagging his tail, and lick his boots. Chango did very well at this. If he didn't, Julian would beat him. CONADEP concluded that:

> All kinds of torture would be applied to Jews, especially one which was extremely sadistic and cruel: "the rectoscope," which consisted of inserting a tube into the victim's anus, or into a

woman's vagina, then letting a rat into the tube. The rodent would try to get out by gnawing at the victims's internal organs.[18]

Class War

A CIA analysis of the situation in 1976 concluded that the labor movement and Peronism were the major targets of this early stage of the dirty war. It was also impressed with the brutality with which the army and the police waged the dirty war. It declared:

> The army is responding to this threat with corresponding brutality. As one headline expressed it "Guerrillas in Argentine Battle Army In A War Without Prisoners." Torture, battlefield "justice," a fuzzing of the distinction between active guerrilla and civilian supporter, the use of arbitrary arrest and imprisonment, and the support of right wing death "squads" have all been noted as increasingly common army (and police) tactics. As more and more police and military are exposed to the notion that all means are justified in order to eliminate subversion and the threat to the state posed by guerrilla/terrorists, the previously obeyed norms on expected treatment of political opponents seem likely to erode further.

> Labor strife and the specter of uncontrollable agitation is causing a hardening of attitudes towards unionized workers among the military and security services, both of which have recently been involved in breaking strikes declared "illegal and subversive" by the government. Generally opposed to Peronism as a political movement, a growing number of officers are beginning to perceive workers and even their "normal" economic demands as a threat to national security which must be suppressed. One Argentine general is quoted as having said that "in order to save 20 million Argentines from socialism, it may be necessary to sacrifice 50,000 lives."[19]

The Church

Figures cited above indicated that 0.3 percent of the victims were religious. Hardly two months after the coup, the bishops of the Catholic Church of Argentina condemned the repressive measures taken by the military dictatorship as being "sinful."[20] They repeatedly condemned these repressive measures. Members of the Catholic Church and other churches dedicated to helping the least fortunate or who denounced the violation of human rights were kidnapped, beaten, tortured, and in many cases killed. The report found it regrettable that, despite this, some individual members of the clergy—by their presence, their silence, or their statements—supported the actions that the bishops condemned. Charges concentrated on the role of military chaplains and on priests who were present in prisons where inmates were tortured. But there were other complaints. The Cathedral in Buenos Aires was usually closed to the Mothers of the Plaza de Mayo when they demonstrated for their disappeared relatives. The Catholic Church publicly served the government with mass and participated in public ceremonies.[21] Conservative Catholic thinking tended to support the army against "the Marxist, atheist" guerrillas. One of the few priests who in 1983 refused to give the sacraments to members of the junta posed this question:

> I wonder what would have happened if, in April 1977, when the first note of the military junta had appeared, one threatened the excommunication of the junta, the renunciation of the military vicar and the renunciation of all military chaplains and the total rupture with the government.[22]

The Systematic Sowing of Terror

Ernesto Sabato, the chair of CONADEP, drew a distinction in the prologue of the report between the way his country and postwar Italy dealt with terrorism. The European country also experienced terrorism, in its case from the Fascists, the Red Brigades, and other private groups. After the kidnapping of Aldo Moro, a member of the Italian security forces suggested to General Della Chiesa that he should have tortured a prisoner who evidently knew a lot. The general responded that Italy could survive the loss of Aldo Moro, but not the introduction of torture. In contrast, the military government in Argentina responded with an organized state campaign of torture and terror infinitely worse than that of the guerrillas. In the words of Sabato, the government "brought about the greatest and the most savage tragedy in our history."[23] It went beyond the criminal to the realm of crimes against humanity.

What was done was not haphazard, but systematic, according to a common pattern of kidnapping, torture, and terror implemented throughout the country. Sabato asked rhetorically how this could be attributed to anything but a common methodology of terror (una metodologia del terror) conceived by the military high command? The reader is reminded that Sabato was the chair of CONADEF and that in the paragraph just ending he accused the Argentine government of having waged a campaign of organized terrorism.

What was done was not haphazard, but systematic, according to a common pattern of kidnapping, torture, and terror implemented throughout the country.

The abductions were precisely organized, whether they occurred at work, in the street, or at the home. When the victims were abducted at home at night, the security forces would force their way into the house, terrorizing relatives and children who were often gagged and forced to watch. They would seize the victims, beat them mercilessly, hood them, and drag them off to their cars or trucks. Meanwhile, other members of the security force almost invariably would ransack the house and carry away everything that was transportable. Silence was the response of the authorities to any inquiries or writs of habeas corpus about the *desaparecidos*. An ominous silence engulfed them. No information was available on where they were or why they had been abducted. A widespread feeling of uncertainty and vulnerability engulfed Argentine society. No kidnapper was ever arrested, never was a detention center located, and never was there news that those responsible for any of the crimes were punished. This is, indeed, a description of terrorism.

How Impunity Functions

The main body of the report returned to the question of state terrorism, and it used this very term "terrorismo del Estado." The report emphasized the impunity that state terrorism affords its practitioners and the defenselessness that it instills in the target population. The concern associated with impunity when practiced by normal criminals assumes alarming proportions in the hands of the state. This, because impunity is both a necessary and a planned component in the execution of the crimes of this type of terrorism and constitutes an integral part of its modus operandi. Furthermore, the criminals enjoy the full weight of the power and prestige of the associate state in covering up their deeds. This emphasis on impunity in the report seems natural, given that disappearances are its central focus. The authorities had no intention of delivering dead bodies to their loved ones. True, it is harder to solve a murder in the absence of the corpus delicti. But the state has so many other ways of covering its tracks. Therefore, the report dwells on the feeling of total defenselessness of the population in the face of the overwhelming power of the state. None of the classical methods of protection, judicial or social, were available. The report indicated that the public's conviction that nothing can change the course of events is a great advantage in implementing a policy of state terrorism.[24]

The Government Tortures and Disappears Its Victims

The first sentence of the report challenges the reader with the sentence, "Many of the events described in this report will be hard to believe."[25] It explains. The reason for this is that Argentinians have heard of such horror only in reports from different places. I would find it hard to believe had I not done the research for the other parts of this study. The authors of the report found it hard, after their long and difficult search for disappeared persons, to accept the fact that they were dead and that their bodies could not be found. They found it to be incredible that the victims were tortured, and then after being killed or while still alive, thrown into the sea. They also concluded that torture was an important element in the methodology of government oppression.

In almost every case that came to the Commission's attention, the victim spoke of torture. Granting that the government's way of disappearing victims was scarcely believable, the authors asserted that it was mentioned by many witnesses, some because they heard about it, others because of direct reference by their captors. In addition, there were bodies that washed up on shore. They judged that "this savage repression" for those who practiced it "was just one more method among many with the same purpose."[26] The report referred to an article that appeared in the newspaper *Clarin* on December 30, 1983. The article reported that 38 corpses had washed up on the beaches of Santa Terisita. They had been discovered by voluntary firemen in the mid-1976 period and had been buried in unmarked graves. All came from far out at sea. Some bodies showed unmistakable signs of violence, and the salt water and predatory fish had disfigured nearly all of them. In the opinion of an expert, they could have fallen from a ship or been thrown from an airplane. A local doctor filled out appropriate death certificates, all with no names.

The Commission recorded another way that bodies were disposed of. They were burned in pits or traps. Juan Carlos Urquiza, a member of the provincial police, testified that he saw in a detention center in San Justo traps or pits fifty to sixty centimeters deep and two meters long. One night he saw the fires. "They put human bodies inside these pits, sprinkled them with petrol they brought from the tanks and burnt them to ashes." A guard named Luis Vera testified that dead prisoners were placed in a ditch and that their cremation was disguised by burning tires along with the bodies. "It covered up the smell and smoke peculiar to cremation. I can affirm, as I saw it myself, that there were clear signs, evidence of charred bodies, in the ditch." Antonio Cruz was a member of the Gendarmeria who worked as a guard in a detention center in Tucuman province. He said that one night three prisoners arrived in a civilian car. He managed to overhear that two of them were father and son. The three were lined up at the edge of a pit, and immediately they were shot by revolvers at point blank range. Two died immediately, but the older man, evidently the father, was still alive. Antonio asked the assassins to finish off the old man as an act of charity and not to burn him alive. "But they carried on with their task without paying any attention."

Three women who were freed from the Navy Mechanics School made the following declaration:

> On the day of the transfer we were very tense. We didn't know if it would be our turn that day or not... they began taking prisoners by number...They were taken to the first aid room in the basement, where a nurse was waiting to give them an injection to send them to sleep, but not kill them. They were taken out by the side door of the basement like that, alive, and put on a lorry. They were driven to Buenos Aires Airport half asleep, put into a plane which flew southwards out to sea, and thrown in alive. Captain Acosta forbade any mention of the subject of "transfers" from the start. In moments of hysteria he would say things like "Anyone who makes trouble gets given a pentothal and sent aloft." [27]

All the attempts of the father of Elena Arce Sahores to recover her were in vain. Through a couple he knew, however, he obtained an interview with a colonel who promised to look into the matter. The father continued with the story:

> He did so, and her arrest in an anti-terrorist operation was confirmed, though the details were not clarified and he ended with a sentence which has been burnt into my memory. "Do not look for Elena any more, her sufferings are over. God rest her soul." He explained the technical side of this kind of operation, which he described as "in white" or "in black" according to whether the people carrying it out were in uniform or not. In short, it was a cruel account. A few days later, when I had recovered from the shock, I contacted him again at his home and claimed the body of my daughter. He replied: "Bodies are not handed over..."[28]

The authors of the report asked themselves why the bodies of the victims were treated in this way? Was the reason the same as that of an individual criminal who tries to wipe out all traces of his crime? The authors responded to their own question by affirming that this was not a sufficient explanation. The reason they added has been cited previously—that this procedure adds to the horror of families by denying them closure. The authors explained that disappearance increased family anxiety by first allowing the family to hope that the kidnapped victim would be freed and returned home, only to have these hopes overcome by doubt and ultimately dashed. But the period of hope, gradually clouded more and more with doubt, prolonged and increased family anxiety still more. Moreover, the giving of some hope to the family paralyzed public protest, at least for a time. It frightened the family into avoiding anything that might antagonize the government and thus lead to the death of the loved one. The Commission went on to ask what else were the tortures but a display of the most grave and perverted acts that military governments that lacked legitimacy used to dominate the people?

WASHINGTON'S SUPPORT FOR STATE TERRORISM IN ARGENTINA

Aid Replacement and Increased Trade

Early on in this chapter the attempt of the Reagan administration to repair the diplomatic damage inflicted on the junta by the world community was recorded. What was presented was mainly the comings and goings of junta members and of Ambassador Kirkpatrick as they were feted and honored in each others' capitals. This was a type of diplomatic support given by the Reagan administration to the junta as it engaged in state terrorism. The Carter administration did not engage in this activity, and thus did not support state terrorism in this way. This distinction between Democratic and Republican administration has been noted in other chapters, the Republicans emerging as the greater supporters of terrorist regimes.

The Congressional Research Service collected data less useful though germane nonetheless in drawing this distinction. But the data was essential in providing a composite view of Washington's support for Argentine state terrorism. These data consist of the aid that Washington gave to Argentina and the trade between the two countries in the crucial period of the dirty war and in the years preceding and following it. The aid figures are so arranged that they reflect the year for which the aid was committed, not the year in which it was disbursed. They are expressed in constant 1989 dollars. These data indicate a dramatic change in military aid with the onset of the dirty war, such that it fell from $70.4 million in 1976 to $1.4 million in 1977, to be followed by ten years for which no military aid was contracted.[29] Washington contracted for only $198,000 of military aid in the third quarter of 1976. This was during the last year of the administration of President Ford. The coup that led to the dirty war took place on March 24 of that year. Military aid was resumed only in 1988. Although nonmilitary aid followed a different trajectory, its pattern leads to a similar conclusion. Small amounts of nonmilitary aid were contracted by Washington during five of the eight years of the dirty war: the amounts ranging from $29,000 to $212,000.

In 1976, backing the Humphrey-Kennedy amendment to the Foreign Assistance Act of 1976, the Carter administration placed an embargo on the sale of arms and spare parts to Argentina and on the training of its military personnel. This resulted in the absence of military aid contracted by Washington in the period of the dirty war, including the Reagan years. Upon assuming office, the Reagan administration did not think the political climate was such that it could resume military aid. It did reverse the negative voting policy in multinational development banks of the Carter administration. And it continued with the "symbolic gestures" that helped to lessen the junta's diplomatic isolation

Before too much is made of Washington's cutting off military aid and maintaining nonmilitary aid at modest levels during the dirty war, aid replacement by its allies must be considered. The absence of aid from Washington was compensated for by its allies, no doubt at least in the Reagan years with encouragement from that administration. From 1978 to the early eighties these allies sold an estimated two billion in arms to Argentina.[30] Notable among the suppliers was Israel. Argentina became Israel's largest South American customer, accounting for over 30 percent of Israeli weapons sales. Israel claimed that such sales served American policy by containing communism in the southern hemisphere and that the sales saved hundreds of Jews from military jails. These claims were evidently made privately, because the Begin government, the government of the time, refused to comment on the matter, at least publicly.[31]

Trade figures, especially U.S. exports to Argentina, followed a different path from aid figures. Exports rocketed from $544 million in 1976 to $2.625 billion by 1980, and then dropped back sharply to $965 million in 1983.[32] U.S. imports from Argentina mounted steadily every year from 1976 to 1982, from $308 million to $1.128 billion. They dipped the next year to recover in 1985 at $1.069 billion. These economic indicators thus suggest that Washington was not so taken with human rights that it decided to punish the dirty warriors by trade boycotts or by the refusal to buy from, or to sell to, the errant nation. This conclusion has a bipartisan edge, applying both to the Carter and the Reagan administrations. The question arises as to why, in a period when military aid was prescribed, U.S. trade with Argentina should rise so dramatically, then subside quickly once the dirty war was terminated. Did Washington intend thereby to facilitate the dirty war by bolstering the domestic economy and freeing up resources for military use?

Why, in a period when military aid was prescribed, should U.S. trade with Argentina rise so dramatically, then subside quickly once the dirty war was terminated?

Military Support

Washington's economic and military aid to Buenos Aires prior to the dirty war was substantial, and this leads to the suggestion that Washington was an accessory before the fact. Between 1960 and 1975 military aid totaled $810 million , and nonmilitary aid between 1946 and 1975 came to $863 million dollars. Again, was Washington's intention to prepare the Argentine army to engage in such an enterprise? The short answer to this question is implicit in statements made by General Ramon Camps, the head of the police force of Buenos Aires province, a famous state terrorist organization. The general himself was equally famous as a state terrorist. His statements appeared in one of a series of articles published in the January 4, 1981 edition of the newspaper *La Razon* entitled "The Defeat of Subversion. The Rise and Fall of Guerrilla Groups in Argentina." General Camps wrote:

> In Argentina we were influenced first by the French and then by the United States. We used their methods separately at first and then together, until the United States' ideas finally predominated. France and the United States were our main sources of counterinsurgency training. They organized centres for teaching counterinsurgency techniques (especially in the US) and sent out instructors, observers, and an enormous amount of literature.[33]

In 1967 a group of officers from intelligence schools in Argentina collaborated on a joint guide for the evaluation of their work against what they termed "subversion." The reader by now no doubt realizes the significance of the intelligence component in identifying the enemy in state terrorist operations and often in "neutralizing" this enemy. The article was a systematic treatment of the geography, state organizations, the enemy, and the strategic aims of such operations. It pointed out that the question of suppressing subversion had not been pursued sufficiently in the literature in Argentina, because "our rules" do not deal with the problem in sufficient detail and because there is doubt about how the problem should be confronted. Of some 60 sources cited in the article, 19 were from the U.S. military and four from the French.[34] The four French sources included material on counterinsurgency operations, pursuit operations, strategy, and the Indochina war. The nineteen American sources included course material used at Fort Bragg for teaching counterinsurgency, counter-guerrilla warfare, anti-bandit warfare, and requisites for resistance movements and guerrilla operations. Also included was material from the School of the Americas on the nature and threat of communist insurgency, counter-guerrilla operations, the theory of communism, and the improvement of intelligence.

When President Kennedy became concerned with the threat from Cuba and communism in general, he insisted on developing a counterinsurgency capability and studies for the countries so threatened. One such study written in 1961 by the State Department pointed to the continuing threat to the Argentine status quo stemming from rising demands for social change and improved living conditions, and from the inadequacy of the armed forces and the police in dealing with the resultant widespread civil disturbances and guerrilla warfare. The study warned that the communist party could become more influential through the formation of a popular front with the Peronists and other leftists. It concluded by discussing improvements needed by the armed forces in training, communications, and transportation. It recommended the strengthening of the civilian police, particularly outside the Federal District, as well as closer coordination within the embassy "to ensure that the fullest advantage is taken of existing US facilities to further US objectives in the internal security field in Argentina."[35] A threat assessment by the State Department in 1963 warned that the communist party in Argentina, with its membership of some 60,000, was the largest in Latin America. It declared that although the potentiality for serious communist infiltration and subversion existed, there had been no serious upsurge in communist strength. It argued that the greatest potential threat to internal security came from the left elements of the Peronist movement, which was a democratic electorally-oriented movement.

Teaching Them "How We Think"

U.S. military aid to Buenos Aires made its debut in 1960 with the modest sum of 1.1 million dollars. In the succeeding six years, it climbed from this base to 15.8; 115.5; 83.6; 38.7; 62.2; and 100.3 millions, only to assume an erratic course until commitments were stopped in 1977.[36] They were resumed in 1988 again at a modest level. At the swearing in ceremony of President Johnson in 1963, Secretary of Defense Robert McNamara told Congress:

> Our primary objective in Latin America is to aid wherever necessary, the continual growth of the military and paramilitary forces so that, together with the police and other security forces, they may provide the necessary internal security.

Somewhat earlier in 1963 when President Kennedy was still alive, McNamara told Congress:

> The best return on our investment in military aid probably comes from the training of selected Army officers and key specialists in our military academies and training centers in the US and abroad. These students are carefully selected by their countries so that they in turn become instructors when they go home. They are the leaders of the future, the men who have the skills and will instruct their own Armed Forces. I don't need to dwell on the value of having people in positions of power who have a first-hand knowledge of how we think and act here in the United States. For us having these people as friends is invaluable. [37]

Four thousand and seventeen military personnel from Argentina were trained by the United States in the period from 1950 to 1979.[38] Actually, Argentina ranked ninth among Latin American countries. By 1975, 600 had graduated from the School of the Americas where they received training in counterinsurgency warfare. Since that year Argentine attendance dropped off dramatically. Notable among the School's graduates were Generals Viola and Galtieri, two of three Argentine dictators during the dirty war. The former took a course for cadets at the school in 1971, and Galtieri took engineering there in 1949. The Argentine police participated in the dirty war, and they were under the general jurisdiction of the army at that time. Washington's police assistance to Argentina was initiated in 1962, a year after the study mentioned above, with the training taking place in the United States.[39] Eighty-three members of the federal police were trained at the International Police Academy and other United States institutions. Washington's police aid to Argentina seems to have been limited, but training and consultation with those who built the police infrastructure for the dirty war and who later participated in this war has been confirmed.

Diplomatic Support

According to a stipulation in the legislation passed by Congress, before military aid could be sent to Argentina the administration had to certify that human rights there had improved. In 1982 the Reagan administration made this certification. On March 2 of that year Secretary of State Haig argued before a Congressional committee for the resumption of military aid. The war over the Falklands Islands intervened, however, and the Reagan administration laid aside this plan. Early in February of the ensuing year, the administration repeated the certification that human rights had improved in Argentina. Support for this assurance was contained in the annual country report of the State Department on Argentina, which included an assertion that "The Argentine government has received approximately 6,000 requests for information on the whereabouts of disappeared persons and is believed to have provided information to family members on the deaths and in some instances the location of the remains of the disappeared in about 1,450 cases."[40]

This assertion was counter-indicated by what was happening in Argentina at the time. In the negotiations between the military and the political parties for the resumption of civilian rule, the military was insisting that there be no investigation of the disappeared by the civilian government. Moreover, the appearance of the State Department claim induced the Center for Legal and Social Studies, a local human rights group, to conduct its own study of the problem. It mailed out 1,100 questionnaires to the families of the victims from the 4,464 cases of disappearances that it had in its files. To its surprise, it received 607 answers. Of these, only 18 said that they had been contacted by the government, and of these only two had been able to recover the remains of their loved ones.[41] One observer explained the strange story of the Reagan administration's determination to support the junta that was generally hated locally and whose days of rule were numbered. The explanation centered on the unflinching support of the American embassy in Buenos Aires for the junta. Loyal to the end, embassy personnel "struggled to present the best possible case for the Junta and to keep embarrassing disclosures to a minimum."[42] The ambassador's report to Washington on Argentina in 1983 "was full of subtle distortions intended to show the Junta in the best possible light: little phrases, such as 'disappeared persons had been killed at the hands of the terrorist groups' which were hard to disprove, hard to spot."

THE AFTERMATH

The Theory of the Two Devils

On December 15, 1983 just five days after his inauguration as president of Argentina, Raul Alfonsin announced the creation of the National Commission on Disappeared Persons (CONADEP). He was the winner in a race in which he ran on a platform of human rights in the first free election since the military coup of March 24, 1976—the last of the coups in the Southern Cone of South America. Preceded by coups in Brazil (1964) and in Chile and Uruguay (both in 1973), the 1976 coup in Argentina deposed President Isabel Peron and ushered in the "dirty war" that lasted for eight years. In his inaugural address, Alfonsin promised to prosecute both military and guerrilla leaders who had "sowed terror, pain, and death throughout Argentine society."

Three days after his inauguration, he ordered the trial of seven guerrilla leaders and of nine members of the three juntas that had ruled Argentina from 1976 to 1983. Some two years later the verdicts were handed down on the nine members of the juntas. Two of them (including General Videla) received life imprisonment; General Viola 17 years; one eight years; one four and one half years; and four were exonerated.[43] Hebe de Bonafini, the President of the Mothers of the Plaza de Mayo, arrived to witness the sentencing session of the trial. She was wearing a white scarf, the symbol of the organization she headed. As she entered, the proceedings stopped. She was told that the scarf was a political symbol and that the session could not restart until she took it off. After she saw how the sentencing was going, she put it back on. She chose the scarf and left.

In April 1987 Colonel Aldo Rico staged an insurrection and demanded a total amnesty. President Alfonsin met with the rebels, and he claimed that he made no concessions. Two months later, however, he effectively yielded by proposing a law that was essentially a total amnesty. Once passed, this proposal became a law which virtually exonerated all military personnel, because it exempted all but the most senior officers from prosecution on the grounds that those under these senior officers were merely carrying out orders—contrary to the Nuremburg Principles of international law which explicitly refuted similar arguments put forward by German generals at the close of World War II. In 1989 President Menem granted pardons to 39 military officers and more than 200 leftists guerrillas and other military personnel. The following year he pardoned the convicted leaders of the juntas. In 2003 both houses of the Argentine congress repealed the amnesty laws that prevented the prosecution of the military officers who terrorized the population during the dirty war. It is up to the Supreme Court to decide if these officers can now be tried. Argentina thus seems to have gone further in punishing state terrorism than most countries examined in this volume. Like most post-terrorist governments described in this volume, these governments in Argentina followed "the theory of the two devils." Both state terror and anti-state violence were punished.

Some Closing Remarks for the Chapter

This chapter answered the three central questions posed by the study in the affirmative. Yes, the Argentine government did practice state terrorism. It tortured practically all of those it detained, and it "disappeared" thousands of its citizens. The Commission found that the vast majority of the government's victims were not only innocent of acts of terrorism, but even of belonging to guerrilla organizations. It felt helpless in depicting what this government had done without writing what it described as "an encyclopedia of horror." This horror resulted from deliberate campaigns organized and directed by the Argentine army designed to intimidate and coerce that part of society that desired social change. CONADEP concluded that the governmental terror was infinitely greater than that committed by the guerrillas. The terrorism that occurred in Argentina was state terror committed by the government, much more than private terror committed by the guerrillas. The dirty war was a war waged essentially by the Argentine army, not by the guerrillas. It was such a one-sided contest as hardly to deserve the name "dirty war." If it takes two sturdy contestants to engage in warfare as it does two agile partners to tango, then the contest could better be called government repression. An analysis of its victims suggests that it was a class war, waged against organized labor and those demanding social change. It looked at first as though Argentina would be different from its neighbors and that the perpetrators of state terrorism would be punished. But after a few short years and an army rebellion, Argentina joined the ranks of its merciful neighbors.

Washington's military and economic aid to Buenos Aires prior to the dirty war was substantial, military aid alone amounting to $810 million between 1960 and 1975. Moreover, it trained 4,017 Argentine military personnel during several administrations in the period 1950 to 1979; many of the personnel were trained in counterinsurgency warfare. The evidence indicates that the training given was intended for such an eventuality as the dirty war and that Washington is guilty of being an accessory before the fact. With the onset of the dirty war, military aid dropped dramatically and then no more of this type of aid was offered by Washington. This was the work of the Carter administration, which provides additional grounds for believing that Democrats were more supportive of human rights than Republicans. The Reagan administration sought to provide military aid to the junta, supported

Neither the Reaganites nor the Carterites were so taken with human rights that they resolved to punish the dirty warriors by trade boycotts or by the refusal to buy from, or to sell to, these state terrorists.

it diplomatically, and covered over its atrocities. It was thus an accessory to state terrorism during and after the fact. The Carter administration did not engage in these activities, and thus did not support state terrorism in these ways. However, neither the Reaganites nor the Carterites were so taken with human rights that they resolved to punish the dirty warriors by trade boycotts or by the refusal to buy from, or to sell to, these state terrorists. Imports from, and exports to Argentina increased during both administrations.

Moreover, the absence of military aid from Washington was made up for by its allies, no doubt, at least in the Reagan years, with encouragement from that administration. Friendly countries and allies rushed in to provide the weapons needed. From 1978 to the early eighties these allies sold an estimated two billion in arms to Argentina.[44] Notable among the suppliers was Israel. Israeli sales are hard to understand, or to justify, given the fact that the dirty war was in part anti-Semitic, as evidenced above. The stark realism of Israeli policy may help in understanding Washington's policy: at least this commitment to the realism of the Old Testament puts Washington's approach in a comparative perspective.

Bits of information continue to surface. While valuable, they are not sufficient to provide the whole story, nor are they widely publicized. For example, in December 2003 the National Security Archive, acting in accordance with the Freedom of Information Act, received two memoranda of the conversations between former Secretary of State Henry Kissinger and the visiting Argentine Foreign Minister indicating Kissinger gave his approval to the forthcoming "dirty war." The secretary urged his guest to act before Congress resumed session, but assured him that Washington would not cause "unnecessary difficulties." Kissinger had already been implicated in connection with the 1973 coup in Chile.[45]

This chapter answered the three central questions posed in the study in the same way that they were answered in the three preceding chapters for El Salvador, Guatemala, and Chile.

CHAPTER 5

South Africa, Apartheid and Terror

APARTHEID

The Western democracies considered the Portuguese colonies of Angola and Mozambique, the white-ruled colony Southern Rhodesia, and the Republic of South Africa to be their outposts in southern Africa. But the key country in the region, the rock upon which Western interests were thought to rest, was the Republic of South Africa, a country whose racial policies were so extreme as to invite comparison with those of the Nazis. This was a country that, during the period of white domi-nance, constructed six atomic bombs, dabbled in the fabrication of chemical and biological weapons, and according to a United Nations task force brought about the deaths of an estimated 1.5 million people in surrounding countries.

The South African apartheid government brought about the deaths of an estimated 1.5 million people in surrounding countries.

I begin the unbelievable tale of the Republic of South Africa in 1949, the year the Nationalist Party came to power and prepared to formulate and to insti-tute its policy of apartheid. The term itself means "separateness" in Afrikaans. It sought to impose extremes in segregation to an already segregated and racist society. Apartheid aspired to create a total pigmentocracy created by, and com-bined with, massive oppression and exploitation. The tale told here ends in an improvement—the death of apartheid—but with the majority in South Africa still in poverty. The termination of apartheid was finally achieved through the suffering and deaths of the brave in that country, but without the tragedy of the much-predicted racial holocaust. Unfortunately, this last assertion is in need of major qualification. No such holocaust occurred in South Africa itself. But massacres and wholesale starvation did occur in surrounding countries, a result of the "total strategy," a murderous scheme adopted by Pretoria after a coup d'état in Lisbon resulted in the independence of Angola and Mozambique.

The Nationalists came to power in South Africa in 1949 with great expectations to institutionalize white domination of blacks, but without having spelled out just how apartheid was to be achieved. With larger and larger mandates in subsequent (white-only) elections, they pushed through progressively restrictive legislation enforcing racial segregation in white areas for Africans, the colored, and Asians. And they sought to establish separate Bantustans for the separate tribal development of the Africans. Ideally, they would force all Africans into these "homelands," each one restricted to one of the many ethnic groups into which the Africans at one time were divided. The Bantustan was a centerpiece of the apartheid plan to remold and to restructure the racial architecture of South African society. The plan was to pretend that the Bantustans were to become, or at least would seem to become, separate, sovereign nations. But it was too late for this "ideal" solution. The majority of Africans had left the countryside to work in white factories, farms, mines, and homes. Their cheap labor was too valuable to be dispensed with. Regulations formulated in 1967 forcing Africans not born or long domiciled or employed in urban areas to return to rural areas, notably the Bantustans, turned their victims into migratory laborers. Labor officials in the Bantustans sent the worker to a particular job, and normally he was required to return to the Bantustan within a year. Usually, the worker left his family behind to live in an all male dormitory in the city. The African family was thereby victimized as well. Prostitution and homosexuality flourished, and this in a country where the dominant elites were self-proclaimed Christians. Actually the few Bantustans that were created simply became the satellites of the South African government. Racism apart, their development served the white economy and the policy of divide and rule.

Inter-racial marriage, and even inter-racial intercourse were made illegal. The colored who had been allowed to vote in Cape Province were taken off the rolls. The government divided cities into racial areas for ownership, occupancy, and commerce. When outside their homelands, the movement of Africans was tightly controlled. They had to carry passes and receive permission to change jobs. The ultimate goal of the Population Registration Act and the Group Areas Act was to restrict each racial group to specific regions in or near cities for purposes of residence, ownership, and commerce. To accomplish this end, the burden fell on the three dominated racial groups, who were uprooted and made to move to less desirable areas. More than three million were "ethnically cleansed" in this way. Education was put in the hands of the central white-ruled government, and Africans were trained for inferior roles in society. The few non-whites who sought a university education were forced to do so by correspondence or obliged to attend segregated institutions staffed mainly by Afrikaners.

The Terrorism Act was passed in 1967, but was made retroactive to 1962. It viewed this phenomenon so broadly that virtually any political or social act came under its purview. Cooperating with UNICEF to reduce infant mortality or revealing the misconduct of a state official could be construed as "terrorism," indicating again, the flexibility of the term and the political purposes for which it can be used. The act denied the accused the right of habeas corpus, and the accused were guilty until proved innocent beyond reasonable doubt.

Cooperating with UNICEF to reduce infant mortality or revealing the misconduct of a state official could be construed as "terrorism".

The policy of apartheid obviously was propelled by the ideology of racism, but it was prodded on by economic considerations as well. Apartheid maintained low wages for the Africans, low costs for South African industry and agriculture, and also for maid service. It preserved the existing governmental policy that was highly discriminatory against labor. Though they outnumbered other workers, Africans were excluded from the category "employee" as found in the Industrial Conciliation Act. They thus had no right of entree to, and membership in, the industrial councils that worked out the differences between labor and management. Nor could they directly participate in negotiations over wages. Moreover, strikes were forbidden from 1942 until 1973, and were so hedged in with restrictions when they were allowed in that year as in effect to continue the prohibition. Most of the Africans lived in the "white" part of the country, and most of these lived in urban townships on the edges of cities rather than on white farms. Africans outnumbered whites in virtually all urban settings. These townships served as dormitories and warehouses for the black bodies and hands that supported the mines, factories, stores, and kitchens of the whites. Despite the restrictions placed on residence in these townships, their African populations increased. It was the African youth from these townships who since the mid-seventies so persistently demonstrated and rioted.

Although Africans outnumbered whites more than four to one, the Bantustans were to constitute only 13 percent of the land and were to include some of the most arid and infertile land. No major cities or mineral deposits were included. The land set aside for them was scattered and non-contiguous, origi-nally consisting of 110 separate pieces from which the nine homelands were to be patched together. The number of separate pieces would be reduced to 36. One Bantustan thus constructed, KwaZulu, would still feature ten disconnected patches, divided by white-owned farms. To transit these farms, Africans would require special papers. The average density of population in the homelands in 1972 would have been 46 per square kilometer, compared with 13 for white South Africa, which had all the industry, valuable land, and mineral deposits. These rural slums, besides accommodating the white elites' peculiar view of race, were meant to be appendages of the white economy. They were designed as holding tanks to serve the white economy with cheap labor and as breeding grounds to assure the future supply of such labor. They were the rural counterparts of the African-populated townships.

The Truth and Reconciliation Commission report (TRCR) concluded that the policy of establishing homelands "was an extension of a colonially estab-lished practice of 'divide and rule'." The report is hereafter referred to as the TRCR. Their establishment was meant to protect the privileges of the whites and to inhibit the attainment of democratic rights by the black majority. The report accused the homeland governments of gross violations of human rights, the subject of the next section. These governments were charged with attempted killings, conspiracies to kill, actual killings, arson, abductions, and the torture of their enemies and opponents as well as covering up the crimes committed by the friends of the homeland governments. The report revealed that the police force in KwaZulu cooperated with the South African police and military intelligence in covert activities and projects aimed at destabilizing popular opposition to the state and homeland governments.

Archbishop Tutu argued that the racist convolutions brought about by the apartheid system would have been utterly ridiculous except that they had ghastly repercussions. Visiting Japanese businessmen were classified "honorary whites." A person of Chinese origin born in South Africa was a non-European. If born in China, he or she was a European. The South Africa racial classification scheme led some South Africans to commit suicide because they had been put on the wrong side of the social divide, since worth and privilege depended so much on one's racial classification. It determined where a person could live, what schools he or she could attend, whom the person could marry, what job the person could have, and finally where he or she could be buried.

THE TRUTH AND RECONCILIATION COMMISSION REPORT

Introduction

What was required to institute and maintain such a racist system to which there might well be expected to be both violent and nonviolent resistance?

No description of apartheid can leave unexplored the terrorism and the gross violations of human rights committed in South Africa in pursuance of this racist policy, as they were inseparable from it. I rely here primarily on the findings of the TRCR for the exposure of those committed from 1960 to 1994 at least. President Mandela appointed 17 members to the commission that wrote the report, and Archbishop Tutu, who won the Nobel Prize for Peace in 1984, served as its chairperson. Both de Klerk and practically all of the notables in the National Party plus those in Inkatha opposed the establishment of the commission. Although it was first proposed by the ANC, this party later tried, unsuccessfully it turned out, to block its publication. The TRCR's investigation was limited to what it called "gross violations of human rights" that occurred during that period. These violations were defined by the TRCR to mean killings, abductions, torture, and severe ill treatment of any person, or any attempt, conspiracy, incitement, or command to commit such acts. Included also is what this volume calls terror.

Exempted from the commission's purview were acts committed in any other period and such terrible abuses as the forcible removal of millions of Africans from their neighborhoods for racial reasons, the arrest of millions of Africans for pass law violations, and the use of detention without trial. Included were violations committed not only by the state and its security forces and any such forces by the homelands, but also those committed by the liberation movements. This was the so-called "two-devil policy," a policy objected to by guerrilla and liberation movements. The African National Congress (ANC) objected to this provision on the grounds that the fight against apartheid by these movements was a just cause and that therefore their violations of human rights were of less moral significance than those committed in support of an unjust system. The commission granted that the ANC and the PAC (Pan African Congress) were internationally recognized liberation movements and that apartheid was a crime against humanity. But it drew a distinction between a just war and the means of fighting such a war. It concluded that liberation movements were not allowed to commit gross violations of human rights in pursuance of their just cause.

Before agreeing to the death of apartheid and the birth of majority rule, de Klerk insisted on amnesty provisions. These were written into the new constitution. There is doubt that he would have agreed to the new dispensation without these provisions. The political situation of the time as well as the commission that wrote the TRCR were subject to cross pressures, not unlike those existing at the initiation of other truth commissions. The Africans had the votes, but the whites had the guns and the economy. The whites were generally unrepentant, sometimes arrogant, hidden away as they were in their all-white neighborhoods and generally unaware of the plight of the Africans. The possibility of a coup existed. Whites learned from the hearings that were held of what had been done in their name, that is, if they bothered to listen. Samples of the applications for amnesty were televised during the first weeks of the hearings. White viewership increased as the program progressed. Amnesty also became part of the terms of reference of the TRCR. The commission established a special organization to deal with it. Other special features of the commission were its power to subpoena and its holding of public hearings. Only individual applications for amnesty were considered, and then only if the violation had been committed for political reasons, not for personal ones. The panel had to be convinced that the applicant had made a full disclosure. The commission reported that of the 7000 applications that it had received, only some 150 had been granted amnesty with 2000 still to be considered.

Anyone could come to the commission to lodge a complaint, to fill out a statement about gross violations of human rights. During the two years from the time the commission began work until the cut off date in December 1997, some 21,296 took advantage of this opportunity to file a statement or complaint about what happened to the one making the statement, the deponent, or someone else. The sample that resulted was self-selective, and the commission made no attempt to collect a representative or random sample from which a total of violations could be "scientifically" deduced. Eighty-nine and nine tenths percent of the statements or complaints were made by Africans, with much smaller percentages (in order) by the colored, whites, and Asians. The low percentage for whites (1.1 percent) relative to their percentage of the South African population was explained by the commission in two ways: white hostility to the commission and the fact that the repression during apartheid was not aimed directly at whites. All complaints were investigated, and a finding was made in each case, together with a recommendation for reparations. The commission gathered evidence from other submissions, amnesty applications, and documents to which it had access. The total number of reported violations, whether gross violations or other was 46,696, of which 36, 935 were judged to be gross violations.

The number of victims was found to be 28,750, with the average victim having received 1.6 violations. Of the gross violations, 9,980 were killings. Most of those who suffered gross violations were men, whereas most deponents were women. The commission divided the violations into four periods. The last two -- from 1983 to 1989 and from 1990 to 1995--experienced many more violations than the previous two periods. The dramatic increases occurred during the administrations of Botha and de Klerk. The commission heard testimony from every part of the political spectrum. It interviewed generals, policemen, murderers, former guerrilla leaders, saboteurs, and torturers, and it searched through government documents. Yet much of the record was denied to it. Apartheid governments shredded tons of documents, and even as the commission investigated, the security establishment continued to shred despite orders to the contrary by the Mandela government. Having noted that the submissions by the officials of the former government were often deliberately intended to be of little assistance, the commission estimated that the destruction of state documents did more to undermine the work of the commission than any other single factor. A large number of investigations of gross human rights violations were hampered by the absence of documentation.

Gross Human Rights Violations: Pretoria and the Inkatha

Nonetheless, the report of the commission was voluminous, consisting of no less than 2,759 pages, distributed in five volumes. Despite the deficiencies noted above, the commission expressed confidence in the validity of its findings. I regard it as a fine basis, the best I have seen, upon which to evaluate the terrorism and the violations of human rights that occurred in South Africa from 1960 to 1995. The commission found that "the predominate portion of gross violations of human rights was committed by the former state through its security and law-enforcement agencies." This is the beginning of an answer to a central question posed by this study: whether the terrorism committed in South Africa was state terrorism committed by the government or private terrorism committed by the opposition. Moreover, in the period from the late seventies to the early nineties the state "became involved in activities of a criminal nature," including the extra-judicial killing of political opponents. In doing so, the Botha and de Klerk administrations acted in collusion with other political groupings, most notably the Inkatha Freedom Party.

The commission went on to explain that the administrations before Botha killed opponents, but not in the systematic way introduced by his administration. During its first five to seven years in office, the Botha administration implemented its "total strategy" by invading neighboring countries and waging counterinsurgency warfare against them. This strategy led to the deaths of some 1.5 million victims in neighboring countries. The TRCR mentioned this slaughter only in passing. Its estimates were confined to what had happened within the Republic of South Africa itself. When the conflict intensified within South Africa itself in the mid-eighties, the tactics that worked abroad were applied domestically. A military style of opposing internal dissent became the hallmark of the State Security Council, whose decisions were almost always accepted by the cabinet. Actually, all of its key members sat on the council as did the leadership of the security forces. The South African military began to play an increasing role in domestic security, and the military way of destroying the enemy was transferred from the external to the internal and became more and more common practice within the country. The public rhetoric of the cabinet and security forces as well as their internal documents mirrored this change as they began to be laced with terms such as "take out," "neutralize," "wipe out," "remove," "eliminate," "cause to disappear," and "destroy terrorists." The word 'terrorist' was used constantly, but never defined. Botha himself called Mandela a "communist terrorist." No distinction was drawn between activists engaged in military operations or acts of terrorism and those who opposed apartheid by lawful and peaceful means. All were lumped together as one target, a single category of persons to be killed. The kill rate perpetrated by the government increased accordingly, as did the use of torture, abduction, arson, and sabotage. The commission alleged that Botha, as head of the state and as chairperson of the State Security Council, contributed to a climate in which gross violations of human rights could and did occur. It concluded that he was responsible for such violations.

Archbishop Tutu tried to get Botha to appear before the commission, and the commission subpoenaed him to appear. By then 81 years old with a heart problem and recovering from a hip operation, he steadfastly refused to do so. He maintained that he was a follower of Christ, that he was innocent of any wrong doing, and that the conflicts in which he was involved were directed against Soviet imperialism. He did, however, dispatch a 1,800-page submission to the commission in which he accused it of being involved "in a transparent attempt to finally discredit the Afrikaner and its former leadership corps." He was brought to trial, found guilty, and fined 10,000 Rand, the equivalent of $1,320. His sentence was overturned on a technicality.

One of the witnesses at the trial was Eugene de Kock, a highly decorated police colonel and former commander of the counterinsurgency agency at Vlakplaas, He had worked closely with Botha as a "foot soldier," and was said to be involved in the murder of at least 70 victims. He was sentenced for only six of these murders, but also for conspiracy to murder, attempted murder, culpable homicide, abduction, assault, possession of illegal arms, and sixty-six charges of fraud. He was sentenced to 212 years in prison. Declared sane in a psychiatric examination, he characterized himself as a loyal defender of the white state. "I'm a relentless hunter who stays on the track until the problem is solved." He claimed that he received his orders from police generals, who in turn received their orders from the highest levels of government. De Kock looked straight at Botha at the latter's trial and declared that politicians who refuse to take responsibility for the illegal actions of their followers are cowards. "The politicians wanted lamb, but they didn't want to see the blood and guts."

In the closing pages of his book, de Kock declared that "the person who sticks most in my throat is former State President F.W. de Klerk." This was not because he failed to take responsibility for the death of this person or for that particular raid or even because of the holier than thou attitude he assumed before the commission. The former police colonel, now a convicted killer, said that it was because de Klerk did not have the courage to admit that "we at the top levels" condoned what was done on our behalf by the security forces; that if we did not give the orders, we turned a blind eye to what happened; that we did not stop what was happening; and that we did not declare that "the foot soldiers" be excused. De Klerk put in a mixed performance before he appeared before the commission. He earned the respect of much of the world when he released Mandela from prison, lifted the ban on the African National Congress, the Pan African Congress, and the Communist Party, and opened the way for a negotiated settlement. In 1993 he shared the Nobel Prize for peace with Mandela. On the other hand, he had been a stalwart supporter of apartheid and a member of previous racist governments, even before his own government came to power. This government was marked by some of the worst human rights abuses, the realm of criminal misconduct extending into his period of office. But the violence of the period was not a monopoly of the state security apparatus. It was also perpetrated by the ANC and Inkatha.

In his appearance before the commission, de Klerk acknowledged that many "unacceptable things" occurred during the rule of the National Party and that they caused immeasurable pain and suffering to many. But he denied being any part of a decision to commit gross violations of human rights. He granted that things happened that were not authorized, not intended, "or of which we were unaware." But he wrote these off as the unauthorized actions of rogue elements. He claimed never to have condoned gross violations of human rights, and he rejected any insinuation that it was ever the policy of his government or his party. He repeatedly proclaimed his innocence and characterized accusations to the contrary as lies. The commission found that de Klerk failed to make a full disclosure of the gross human rights violations committed by the senior members of the government and the police. Therefore, it found him to be an accessory to the commission of gross violations of human rights. The generals and the politicians that had run the security establishment were equally unhelpful in describing their role and unwilling to accept responsibility. Most of them showed hostility to the commission.

The commission returned to its principal charge against the South African state. It used these words: "The state—in the form of the South African government, the civil service, and its security forces—was, in the period 1960-1994, the primary perpetrator of gross violations of human rights in South Africa, and from 1974, in southern Africa." It re-asserted this accusation in its discussion of apartheid, which it characterized as a crime against humanity. The commission found this extreme form of racism, sometimes called "evangelical racism," to be "the motivating core of the South African political order." It was adopted to preserve the power and the privileges of the white minority, and as a consequence of this racism the white citizens in general "adopted a dehumanizing position toward black citizens" to the extent that the state "largely labeled them as the enemy. This created the climate in which gross atrocities committed against them were seen as legitimate." This allowed torture, abduction, killing, and other gross violations of human rights as well as the creation of an authoritarian state. In one of its rare references to the West, the commission charged that the racism that served as the motivating core of the South African political system was in the period 1960 to 1990 "largely endorsed by the investment and other policies of South Africa's major trading partners."

The commission reminded its readers that four former National Party cabinet members agreed before the commission that apartheid had no moral basis and that De Klerk himself admitted that the system brought suffering to millions of its victims. The commission granted, however, that some whites at the time honestly believed that apartheid was an acceptable way to solve difficult racial problems. It conceded that a virulent form of anti-communism had become widespread in South Africa after the National Party's electoral victory in 1948. By the sixties virtually any opposition to the government was labeled communist. Former Minister of Law and Order Adriaan Vlok testified before the commission that the ANC and the PAC were correctly seen as tools and fronts of the Marxist-communist threat to the country. He continued: had the communists taken over, they would have made South Africa a backward country with an atheistic ideology. He saw it as his duty to fight against such thoughts, programs, and initiatives. Craig Williamson, former intelligence officer and bomber, admitted that the members of the South African security system paid little attention to the personal political motivation of the liberation forces beyond regarding them as a part of the Soviet onslaught against the civilized, free, and democratic Western world. This belief made it easier for these forces to take the most violent action against the liberation movement, because the action was seen as being taken against a foreign enemy.

Archbishop Tutu argued that Soviet communism played a pivotal role in the politics of the apartheid era, with nations defining themselves in terms of their relationship to communism. The communist threat was regarded as being so serious that prominent democracies such as the United States supported the world's worst dictatorships, such as that of Pinochet, rather than countenance social change on the scale that communism promised. Similarly, so the Archbishop charged, the United States had been willing to subvert democratically elected governments merely because the governments were communist-influenced. And the United States did not care much about the human rights records of their surrogates. The Archbishop concluded that the South African government in its own crusade against communism was far from being an exception.

The commission rejected the notion that communism and its opposite, anti-communism, together constituted the central issue in South Africa during the apartheid era.

As indicated above, the commission rejected the notion that communism and its opposite, anti-communism, together constituted the central issue in South Africa during the apartheid era. It was rather a Cain-and-Abel dialectic that pitted an oppressive, illegal, and inhuman apartheid system against those struggling for a just cause. For decades the struggle was non-violent, at least on the part of the liberation forces. Only when non-violence failed was armed resistance used. The commission found that the moral position of those who sought to uphold apartheid could not be equated with that of those who sought to undermine it. Nonetheless, the commission argued that a just cause does not exempt the organization from pursuing its goals through just means. It does not legitimize the perpetration of gross violations of human rights. But the commission held the government to a higher moral standard than private organizations, because of its privileges and superior resources.

The commission portrayed the Inkatha (IPF) and its leader Buthelezi as allies of the Botha and de Klerk governments. Posing as a liberation movement, the IPF sought to crush the ANC and to disrupt the elections held in 1993-1994. It received financial and logistical support from these governments. The special forces unit of the South African army in 1986 trained its hit squads in the Caprivi strip under a plan whose code name was Operation Marion. In addition, the South African Army provided financial, logistical, and behind the scenes training. The activities of these hit squads were notorious in KwaZulu and Natal. "The Commission received evidence from thousands of people about attacks and massacres perpetrated by IPF (Inkatha) supporters over the twelve year period after April 1983." It found Buthelezi responsible for making speeches that incited supporters to commit violence, for authorizing paramilitary training intended to disrupt the 1993-1994 elections, and for numerous violations of human rights including murder. As indicated below, the Inkatha was found to be the foremost perpetrator of murder within the country.

Gross Human Rights Violations: The ANC and PAC

The commission was critical of some of the violence committed by the ANC. Condemning the atrocities committed by liberation movements is not uncommon for truth commissions. It is in accord with the "two-devil principle" that the activities of liberation movements as well as those of governments must be investigated and judged. But the truth commission for South Africa was appointed by the former head of the ANC who had been sentenced to life imprisonment because of the violence committed by the ANC. The commission first congratulated the ANC for its "openness" to the commission, by

The ANC signed the Geneva Convention on the conduct of wars of national liberation and made a conscious effort to conduct its armed struggle within the framework of international humanitarian law.

providing two full submissions and making available its inquiry reports on alleged violations in exile camps. It noted also that the ANC signed the Geneva Convention on the conduct of wars of national liberation and made a conscious effort to conduct its armed struggle within the framework of international humanitarian law. In general it was not ANC policy to target civilians. The commission observed, however, that ANC guerrillas killed more civilians than security forces. In the period 1985-1987, these guerrillas laid mines in the rural areas of Northern and Eastern Transvaal, designated as "military zones" by the government, where farmers were trained and equipped to operate as an extension of the military. The commission held the ANC responsible for the resulting deaths of civilians killed or injured by these mines, the victims including farm laborers and children—this despite the fact that the government had blurred the distinction between military and "soft targets" by establishing these zones and arming the farmers living there. The commission granted that the ANC leadership instructed the guerrillas to abandon the land mining program when it became clear that innocent civilians were being killed and injured by the mines. Nonetheless, the commission held the ANC responsible for the atrocities already committed. Although the commission found that torture was not the general policy of the ANC, it concluded that torture was used against suspected agents and routinely by its security department in its camps. In contrast to the behavior of the government, the leadership of the ANC accepted responsibility for all the actions of its members in the period 1960 to 1994.

The Pan African Congress (PAC) was an all African institution that differed from the ANC in that it refused to accept whites as members. The commission recognized it as a liberation movement, but it proved to be less open to, or cooperative with, the commission than the ANC. It differed with the ANC also when the latter suspended its armed struggle in 1990. It vowed to fight on, to continue with a protracted people's war, and it launched Operation Great Storm that targeted whites at random and white farmers in particular. In a hearing before the commission, Brigadier Mofokeng explained that the enemy of the liberation movement and of the people was always the white settler colonial group. He charged that the pillars of the apartheid state against the "black danger" were not only the military, but also the "arming" of the entire white population. "This militarization, of necessity, made every white citizen a member of the security establishment." Despite this contention, the commission applied to the activities of the PAC the same moral and legal yardstick used in measuring the behavior of the ANC. It charged that the targeting of civilians was a gross violation of human rights and a violation of international humanitarian law. It rejected PAC's claim that its killing of white farmers constituted acts of war. It held the PAC accountable morally and politically for this killing.

In July 1993 operatives of the PAC struck the St. James Church in Kenilworth. One of them entered the church firing his automatic rifle; the other threw hand grenades coated with nails at the assembled worshipers. After the second assailant ran out of grenades, he fired as well. Eleven were killed and fifty-eight were injured. Ironically, the church was integrated, and Russian sailors were regular visitors. Four Russian sailors were killed. In July 1997 the two assailants plus their driver asked for amnesty before the TRCR. They claimed that their attack was politically motivated, inspired by PAC's attempt to get the land back from the whites. They charged that whites used churches to oppress the blacks. "They took our country using churches and bibles."

One of the three parishioners who opposed the amnesty was Dawie Ackermann whose wife had been killed in the attack. His lawyer argued that there was no reasonable connection between the slaughter of those assembled in a racially integrated church and any defined political goal. Ackermann told how he had walked to the back of the church searching for his wife Maria who was seated there. He had to step over a dead Russian seaman and pools of blood before he saw her sitting upright. He thought she might have survived the attack, but she was dead. He broke into tears as he pointed to the three assailants and declared that he was not angry with them, but with his own family. He said that it was hard to say, but he wanted the assailants to know that since the death of his wife, he fights more with his children, and over stupid things. He asked if the assailants would turn around and face him. They did. After he observed that this was the first time that they had the opportunity to look each other in the face and talk, he turned to the assailant who had entered the church first and asked him if he had killed his wife. "My wife was sitting right at the door when you came in; she was wearing a long blue coat; can you remember if you shot her?" Ackermann added that he did not know why this was important to him, but it just was. The assailant answered by declaring that he pointed his gun at the congregation, and he fired some shots, but he did not know who he shot and who he did not shoot. Ackermann accepted this statement. He then observed that the lawyer for the three assailants had said "we apologize," but Ackermann wanted to hear it from each of them. "I would like to hear from each of you, as you look me in the face, that you are sorry for what you have done, that you regret it, and that you want to be personally reconciled." The three complied, but the first qualified his apology by pointing to the situation as it existed in South Africa. "We are asking from you, please do forgive us. All that we did, we can see the effects today." Ackermann responded.

> I want you to know that I forgive you unconditionally. I do because I am a Christian, and I can forgive you for the hurt that you have caused me, but I cannot forgive you for the sin that you have done. Only God can forgive you for that.

The TRCR granted the three assailants amnesty.

The Guilt of Civil Society

The commission quite wisely concluded that civil society was also guilty, through acts of omission and commission, of supporting an apartheid regime that committed gross violations of human rights. Quite appropriately, the commission introduced this subject with a quote from Major Craig Williamson made at a commission hearing on the armed forces. He was "handled" by General Johan Coetzee, who later became the commissioner of the police. A member of the security forces, the major allowed himself to be recruited by the ANC. He then set up what was ostensibly an ANC cell, but actually it consisted entirely of members of the security forces. A specialty of the major was to provide pamphlet bombs to the ANC. This procedure led to entrapment operations in which ANC operatives were caught and killed. At the hearings the major said:

> It is therefore not only the task of the security forces to examine themselves and their deeds. It is for every member of the society which we served to do so. Our weapons, ammunition, uniforms, vehicles, radios, and other equipment were all developed and provided by industry. Our finances and banking were done by bankers who even gave us covert credit cards for covert operations. Our chaplains prayed for our victory, and our universities educated us in war. Our propaganda was carried by the media, and our political masters were voted back in power time after time with ever-increasing majorities.

The commission granted that the sectors of civil society generally were not directly involved in the gross violations, but they were structurally part of a system that was. At the broadest level, the white electorate gave the National Party the mandate to do what it did, and this party's popularity increased after the 1948 elections as it embarked upon its program. Singled out for specific blame and mention were the health sector, organized religion, business, the media, and the judiciary. The media and organized religion exerted immense influence on the formation of ideas and moral codes, as did professional bodies of doctors and lawyers who were often seen as the custodians of scientific knowledge and impartiality. Although there was little evidence of direct involvement of health professionals in gross violations, they failed, among other things, to provide adequate health care for black South Africans and to draw attention to the negative

Singled out for specific blame and mention were the health sector, organized religion, business, the media, and the judiciary.

health effects of apartheid, torture, and solitary confinement. The commission took organized religion to task for promoting the ideology of apartheid in a range of different ways that included biblical and theological teachings. The churches provided chaplains who wore the uniforms of the police and armed forces, enjoyed the ranks of armed personnel, and some even carried side arms. On occasion they accompanied the troops engaged in internal conflicts or invasions of bordering countries.

Having pointed out that South African society was divided not only on racial lines, but on class lines as well, the commission argued that business was central to the economy that sustained apartheid. Most businesses benefited from operating in a racially structured context—those especially favored were mining, white agriculture, and the industry that supplied the military. The commission noted in its hearings that the business sector failed to accept responsibility for its involvement in state security initiatives. More than 100 laws were passed to restrict the media, their impact after 1985 amounting to pre-publication censorship of information about state-sanctioned violations. The commission found that the racism that permeated white society permeated the media as well. Moreover, mainstream English-language media adopted "a policy of appeasement towards the state, ensuring a large measure of self-censorship." With rare exceptions, the Afrikaans media provided direct support for apartheid and the activities of the security forces.

The commission criticized the judiciary for its collusion with the police regarding the torture of detainees and its collaboration in producing the highest capital punishment rate in the" Western world," an execution rate that overwhelmingly impacted poor black males. It found both the judiciary and the organized legal profession "locked into an overwhelmingly passive mind set" in the face of the injustices of apartheid. They had a choice of opposing such injustice, or taking the honorable way out by resigning.

APPLYING TERROR

Killings

The reader must be warned not to draw the conclusion from the above discussion that the liberation forces or the government featured domestic killing as a principal means of accomplishing its goals. South Africa was not Guatemala or even El Salvador—at least the commission did not find it to be. However, the impact of Pretoria's "total strategy" on neighboring countries is an entirely different and more lethal story, one that is recounted below. The commission estimated that in the period from 1960 to 1994, Inkatha was responsible for more than 4,500 deaths, the police for 2,700, and the ANC for 1,300. Expressed in percentages, this comes respectively to 53, 32, and 15 percent. As indicated above, Inkatha was allied with the Botha and de Klerk governments and received financial and logistical support from them. The ANC was its enemy. The conclusion to draw from this is that most of the killing done in the period 1960 to 1994 must be put at the door of the government and its ally, leaving 15 percent for the account of the true opposition, the ANC. This percentage is greater than that found for the opponents of the governments in Guatemala, El Salvador, and Chile. Nonetheless, this kill ratio is further evidence that what happened in South Africa was more government terror than private terror. The relatively small number of killings by the ANC is suggested also by police statistics. They indicated that for the period from 1976 to 1986, 130 people were killed by "terrorists." True, only some thirty were said to be members of security forces and some hundred were said to be civilians, but the total number for the two is low.

An examination of the graphs contained in the TRCR representing the known organizational affiliation of the victims who suffered gross violations of human rights also suggests that what happened in South Africa was more state terrorism committed by the government than private terrorism committed by the guerrillas. This conclusion is again based upon the logical inference that organizations terrorize and violate the human rights of enemy organizations. In this example, most victims were affiliated with the ANC and other liberation organizations, much fewer with government institutions and their ally, the Inkatha Freedom Party (IFP). Therefore, the conclusion is warranted that it was the government and its ally that committed most of the violations. The graphs in the TRCR do not provide exact numbers, but they are sufficient for what is being done here. The one depicting the numbers killed whose known organizational affiliation could be determined indicates that those with an affiliation with the ANC were far and away the greatest number: some 2,900. The IFP placed second, with approximately 750; followed by the United Democratic Front (UDF), a liberation organization, with 550; and non-partisan, nonaligned organizations with perhaps 400. The other four organizations barely made an impression on the graph. Notable among these was the SAP (the South African Police), which placed seventh, second from the bottom. The graph on severe ill treatment tells the same story. ANC affiliates again are in first place (some 5,000 victims), UDF (1,400), IFP (1,200), the non-partisan-nonaligned (700), PAC 300, and unions (200). Again, SAP placed seventh, too small to estimate, followed by another liberation organization. The breakdown of the graph depicting the affiliation of torture victims leads to the same conclusion, with liberation organizations placing first, second, and third, and the SAP not finding a place on the graph.

Detention Without Trial

The usual way the government treated dissidents was to imprison them and hold them without trial. The commission found that the period 1960 to 1994 saw "the systematic and extensive use of detention without trial" and that this "frequently led to the gross violation of human rights." Government detention and torture was not confined to any part of the country, and its perpetration was not the work of only one of the security forces. The commission concluded allegations of torture formed a large percentage of the violations reported to it and that most of those who said they had been detained added that they had been subjected in the process to some form of assault or torture. It estimated that from 1960 to 1990, eighty thousand were detained, of whom 10,000 were women and 15,000 were under the age of 15. Detention without trial represented the first line of defense by the security forces, and it was only after it seemed to fail that the tactic of killing increased. A law enacted in 1963 allowed the police to hold detainees in solitary confinement without access to lawyers or family until they answered all questions satisfactorily. Their period of detention was initially set at 30 days, then extended to 180 days, but it could be renewed indefinitely by the police.

Torture

According to a study based on fieldwork conducted in 1983 and 1984 by Foster and his associates, in 83 percent of the cases the detainee was physically tortured. The researchers interviewed 158 persons formerly detained by the government from all parts of South Africa who had experienced detention 176 times, some undergoing multiple detentions. The most frequent form of physical torture they endured (75 percent) was beating. This

In 83 percent of the cases, the detainee was physically tortured.

included punching, hitting, kicking, and slapping, sometimes with the help of implements. The second most widespread form of physical torture (50 percent) was forced standing for long periods of time. This meant maintaining abnormal body positions, such as holding a position as though sitting on a chair or standing tiptoe with the arms outstretched. Twenty-five percent reported that they were subjected to electric shock torture, 18 percent to strangulation either by hand, cloth, or towel, and 14 percent to suspension. The commission found that during the period 1960 to 1994 the most common form of torture by the security forces was beating, followed by electric shock treatment, suffocation techniques, and forced standing for long periods of time. According to the study by Foster and his associates, the percentage of females tortured was less than for men and much less for whites than for other races. Whereas only 31 percent of the whites claimed to have been tortured, 93 percent of the blacks and 83 percent of the Indians made the same claim. That racism followed the victims to the torture chamber seems logical in an apartheid society,

The study by Foster and his associates provides, in its own words, "clear and definitive evidence that physical torture occurs on a widespread basis and constitutes a systematic and common experience for those detained for interrogation purposes under South African security legislation." The study went on to claim that the frequency and range of torture used contradicted the standard claim of state officials that torture did not occur in South Africa aside from a few isolated cases. The data "show that it is a standard form of treatment during detention, particularly in the case of young black detainees." A study released two years before the one quoted above came to very similar conclusions. It also found that 83 percent of those in its sample were tortured, and many of the forms of torture catalogued in that study were the same as those found in the report of the commission.

The study by Foster and his associates reported that not one of the detainees interviewed reported an entire lack of psychological abuse. Eighty-three percent were subjected to false accusations; 79 percent to solitary confinement; 71 percent to verbal abuse; 64 percent to threats of violence; 41 percent to threats of execution for themselves or their families; 23 percent to constant interrogation; and 15 percent to sleep deprivation. Only four percent of the sample reported that they experienced no health problems during their detention. Examples of these problems were difficulty sleeping (60 percent), headaches (53 percent), weight loss (45 percent), appetite loss (44 percent), and nightmares (41 percent).

On June 14, 1986 three people were killed and some sixty-nine were injured when a car bomb exploded at Magoo's Bar on the Durban beachfront. This attack was carried out by a three-member cell of the Umkhonto We Sizwe (MK), the military wing of the ANC. One member of the cell turned state witness. Another, Ms. Greta Apelgren (later known as Zahrah Narkedien) broke down after being tortured, gave the police the information they wanted, and was acquitted. The third was Robert Mc Bride who was convicted and sentenced to death but later released during negotiations between political parties in the early nineties. In its first submission to the commission, the ANC maintained that the attack was a mistake and that the real target was the nearby Why Not Bar. The latter was often frequented by the security police. Mc Bride maintained that he parked the car with the bomb in it directly opposite the Why Not Bar and that Magoo's was never an intended target.

Before being acquitted, Narkedien was detained, tortured for seven days, and held in solitary confinement. She told the commission that what made her break down and talk was the threat to kidnap her four year old nephew, Christopher, and throw him out the window on the thirteenth floor. She figured that she could risk her own life and "let my body just be handed over to these men to do what they liked, but I couldn't hand over someone else's body so at that point I co-operated." During her detention she was kept in solitary confinement for seven months in a cell the size of a small bathroom with high walls. She described her ordeal this way:

> I don't even want to describe psychologically what I had to do to survive down there... It did teach me something and that is that no person can live alone for more than I think a month... I felt as the months went by that I was going deeper and deeper into the ground. I felt so psychologically damaged that I used to feel that all these cells are all like coffins and there were dead people in there, because they were not there, no one was there. It was as if I was alive and all these people were dead. I'm out of prison now for more than seven or ten years but I haven't recovered and I will never recover... I have tried to and the more I struggle to be normal, the more disturbed I become. I had to accept that I was damaged, a part of my soul was eaten away as if by maggots... and I will never get it back again.

Haroon Aziz, a local leader of the ANC in Natal was arrested, detained, and given the "invisible chair" treatment. He was made to squat in thin air as though he was sitting on a chair. He had to hold his hands out and click his fingers. He was interrogated as he was forced to assume this position. Directly behind him was the wall, but he was not allowed to touch it. Special branch policemen placed in front of him took turns holding a knife at his navel to prevent him from lunging forward. If his tormenters were not satisfied with his answers, they hit him on the penis or squeezed it. When he did fall forward, they withdrew the knife, but they then kicked him. The kicking went on while he screamed and hollered, and they laughed at him like mad hyenas.

Frank Bennetts, a former member of the Durban Riot Unit, provided the commission with a description of what was alternately called the "helicopter," "boeing" or the "aeroplane." The victim would be handcuffed with his hands behind his back, and his feet would be handcuffed at the ankles. He then would be laid down on his stomach with his feet in the air and a broom or piece of wood would be put between his ankles and pushed through under the handcuffs on his wrists. Each end of the broom or piece of wood would be placed on a desk. He would then dangle between the two desks, the result being similar to crucifixion. His muscles would be pulled taut, his chest closed, with the result that he could not breathe. Mr. Bennetts assured the commission that if left there long enough, the victim would talk.

The commission held Jeffrey Benzien's amnesty hearing in Cape Town in 1997. A former warrant officer, he was still employed by the police air wing. By his own admission, he was Cape Town's most successful torturer. His former commanding officer characterized him as "the best exponent of unconventional methods of extracting information from suspects." His specialty was the wet bag, a technique that he described to the commission at the request of Tony Yengeni. The latter was a former guerrilla commander, and at the time of the hearing, a member of parliament. Benzien had used the wet bag on him, but he was blindfolded at the time. He had never seen it used on anybody else; in fact, he had never seen the wet bag. He requested that Benzien demonstrate its use. Benzien obliged, using a volunteer from the audience to demonstrate how it was done. Benzien explained:

> ... it would be a cloth bag that would be submerged in water to get it completely wet... I get the person to lie down on the ground on his stomach... with that person's hands handcuffed behind his back. Then I would take up a position in the small of the person's back, put my feet through between his arms to maintain my balance and then pull the bag over the person's head and twist it closed around his neck, cutting off the air supply to the person... On occasions people have, I presume, and I say presume, lost consciousness. They would go slack and every time that was done, I would release the bag.

Asked about the reaction of the victim, Benzien replied:

> There would be movement, there would be head movement, distress. All the time there would be questions asked— 'Do you want to speak?'... and as soon as an indication was given that this person wanted to speak, the air would be allowed back... the person would moan, cry.

Benzien assured the commission that, with a few exceptions, there would be results within half an hour.

Yengeni pressed him: "And you did this to each and every one of us?"
Benzien replied: "To the majority of you, yes..."

Then Yengeni asked Benzien what was his reaction to the torture, to which Benzien responded that he did not remember except that Yengeni took the police to the house where the guerrillas kept their weapons. Yengeni then asked:

> What kind of man uses a method like this one of the wet bag, to people, to other human beings, repeatedly and listening to those moans and cries and groans and taking each of those people near to death? What kind of a man are you?... I want to understand

what happened... I am talking about the man behind the wet bag. When you do these things, what happens to you as a human being? What goes through your head, your mind?

Benzien did not really confront these questions. He said that he had also asked himself what kind of a man he was and that he had approached a psychiatrist with the same question. He granted that he was raised in a privileged white neighborhood and that he wanted to preserve these privileges. Another former guerrilla commander pressed Benzien to remember the details of his torture, but the former warrant officer remained "the professional," insisting on speaking in the abstract about methods, not remembering specific cases. He refused to remember the details of this man's torture, despite the victim's strong desire to hear Benzien admit and confirm them. This second guerrilla commander had tried to commit suicide rather than face another torture session. He finally did get Benzien to admit that at one torture session Benzien threatened to take him to the verge of death as many times as necessary to get him to talk.

WASHINGTON'S POLICY TOWARD SOUTH AFRICA

Introduction

Apartheid was a highly imaginative policy, so audacious, thorough, and ruthless as to challenge the human capacity to believe. Although less lethal, it shared this with Hitler's earlier "final solution of the Jewish problem." Another parallel is that between Schmitz's view of Washington's earlier policy in Latin America and Minter's view of its policy toward South Africa between 1960 and the late 1980's. The views of the two scholars are strikingly similar—despite differences in time frame and geographical reference.

Both Republican and Democratic administrations subordinated foreign policy issues to Cold War requirements and to the prevention of social revolution.

Minter characterized the policy pursued by Washington toward South Africa in the period indicated above as "conservative Realpolitik or pragmatism." He judged that both Republican and Democratic administrations subordinated foreign policy issues to Cold War requirements and to the prevention of social revolution. Like Schmitz for the earlier period, Minter found a continuity in Washington's policy. He argued that the faith that the Reagan administration put in white Pretoria was not an innovation. Indeed, all administrations supported anti-communist allies, even though they were rightwing dictatorships, white settler regimes, or colonial powers. Certain parameters were observed, limits beyond which no policy would be pushed. No administration imposed serious sanctions on Pretoria, nor did any openly proclaim its support for apartheid. Even the arms embargoes adopted in 1963 and 1977 by the Kennedy and Carter administrations due to domestic pressure were largely symbolic and hemmed in with numerous qualifications. Within these limits, certain policy variations did occur, depending upon outside circumstances, the give and take within the administration in question, and private actors.

Minter identified two liberal variations of the central theme, what he calls "interludes". He dates them at the beginning of the Kennedy and Carter administrations. They lasted for brief periods of less than two years. And they "promised far more than they delivered; each time, the image of pro-African liberation dissolved to reveal business-as-usual ties with the white regimes." These symbolic variations did offend Pretoria, but they were intended primarily to ease the discomfort and to attract the votes of African Americans and domestic human rights advocates. Minter concluded that no adjustments to Washington's policy were made out of concern for rising African nationalism, racism, or human rights violations. These would have been considered to be "sentimental distractions from the real business of defending US interests." Later, Washington did switch to embrace these "sentimental distractions." But this became serious policy only after South Africa's racists saw the necessity of doing the same. Minter's reference here seems to be the sanctions imposed by Congress in 1986 that did appear to be serious.

From Truman to Carter

Despite changes in administrations Washington supported a racist Pretoria from 1960 to the late 1980's. In 1950 Washington's delegate opposed a United Nations General Assembly resolution that faulted racial segregation on the grounds that it was discriminatory. The resolution also called upon South Africa not to implement the Group Areas Act, a law that became a centerpiece of its apartheid policy. Given that the American variation of apartheid (segregation) was still in existence at the time, opposition to the resolution seems logical. It is true that President Truman integrated the armed forces. But it is also true that in private conversation he used the word "nigger" to describe African Americans. He held to the racial stereotypes and categories that he had learned as a youth. In 1950 Secretary of State Acheson gave a short lecture in world politics to a gathering at the White House. He chided those "democratic purists who were repelled by some of the practices reported in Greece, Turkey, and North and South Africa." Such a posture he labeled "escapism," avoiding building foreign policy with the materials at hand. Later, as elder statesman, he opposed criticism of apartheid and Portuguese colonial policy and supported the white minority government in Rhodesia. He denounced the United Nations for interfering in the internal affairs of weak white nations.

In 1952 the United States delegate in the General Assembly proclaimed his government's respect for the sovereignty of "the great Union of South Africa" with which it had long been associated in friendly relations. He declared his delegation's determination not to criticize it. The same year Asian and Arab members of the world institution proposed the creation of a commission to study the question of race conflict in South Africa resulting from the policy of apartheid. The United States plus all other Western states abstained on the enabling resolution. The resolution passed because of third world and communist bloc support. Through 1958 U.S. delegations continued to abstain on anti-apartheid resolutions on the grounds that the world institution lacked the legal competence to make such judgments. The conclusion from this is obvious. Both the Truman and the Eisenhower administrations rendered diplomatic support to Pretoria in this early part of the cold war period.

Washington provided military support as well. In this period, the South African military bought arms in the United States as a matter of course. Such a deal in October 1952 provided for a purchase of $112 million in weapons, and the contract specifically noted that the weapons could be used for internal security. In a visit to the United States in 1950, the South African finance minister failed to get the full amount of a projected $70 million loan he sought. But after the two countries and Britain agreed to the development of South African uranium production, the financing was forthcoming from the World Bank and other sources. The 1950 agreement on the development of South African uranium was followed by years of nuclear cooperation between the African country and the West. In 1976 Dr. Roux, President of the South African Atomic Energy Board, ascribed "our" degree of nuclear advancement "in large measure to the training and assistance so willingly provided by the USA during the earlier years of our nuclear programme."[53] With help from the West, Pretoria did develop a nuclear bomb, a subject discussed below.

In his study of Washington's policy toward South Africa in the Truman years, Borstelmann argues that Cold War concerns led that administration "into a close embrace of the imperial authorities in southern Africa, and the outbreak of war in Korea resulted in a series of agreements with Pretoria that bound the United States government to the apartheid regime." It was the period of the emergence of the Cold War and "the tendency of Americans to view it as a struggle of transcendent good and evil guaranteed all opponents of the Soviet Union a warm welcome in Washington."[54] Despite this bonding with South Africa, the Truman administration and its successors attempted to distance themselves from the extreme forms of racism practiced there. This was crucial, given the racial discrimination and segregation that existed in the United States itself. White rule in South Africa was preferred not only because it was adamantly anti-communist, but also because it brought stability to the country. This was good for business and trade, and investments in South Africa grew apace. Moreover, South Africa was strategically located, and had sizeable uranium deposits. In an address to a branch of the African National Congress in 1953, Nelson Mandela reminded his fellow party members that "there is no easy walk to freedom anywhere." Borstelmann concludes that for most people in southern Africa, the Truman administration "had proven itself willing only to increase, not lighten, the load to be carried."[55]

In 1955 Washington's delegate to the United Nations warned against what it termed were "ringing resolutions to correct overnight situations which have existed for generations." The reference was to racial conditions in South Africa, and the delegate was part of, and spokesperson for, the Eisenhower administration. He expressed the hope that the General Assembly would not bring up the question again, because South Africa seemed "deeply aggrieved" by the proceedings. He proposed that the world institution focus its attention on human rights violations in the communist world. "South Africa continued as a military ally of the West during these years, although neither Britain nor the United States acceded to South African proposals for a formal defense pact." South Africa's friendship was of more concern than the policy of apartheid. To Eisenhower and to his secretary of state, John Foster Dulles, "South Africa was one more ally in the struggle against international communism."

In August 1963 the Security Council passed a resolution that called for a voluntary arms embargo on Pretoria. It called upon the members not to sell and ship arms, ammunition, and military vehicles to South Africa. The embargo was voluntary, allowing those nations not so inclined to ignore it. Not so obvious was Washington's successful insistence that the resolution not refer to a "threat to the peace," an assertion that could logically lead the Security Council to impose compulsory sanctions. This protected governments such as those of Britain and France that refused to accept the embargo. Adlai Stevenson, the Kennedy administration's ambassador to the United Nation at the time, observed that existing contracts for defense against external threats would be honored. He added that if it should prove necessary for the common defense the United States would feel free to provide equipment to South Africa. Washington voted in favor of a Security Council resolution in March 1961 that called for an inquiry into the Angolan situation. The resolution was introduced immediately after the guerrillas began their uprising. The resolution did not pass because it lacked the votes, including those of France and Britain. But the Portuguese were furious. Of course, none of this stopped Lisbon from using its U.S.-supplied weaponry from responding to the uprising. Washington approved of two other resolutions of similar caliber in April and June of the same year. In the first the General Assembly called upon Portugal "urgently" to consider reforms in Angola. The second was a Security Council instrument that deplored "the severely repressive measures" used in Angola. While deliveries of weapons under the Mutual Security Program were cut from $25 million to $3 million in 1961, official aid figures indicate that Portugal received $39.1 million in military aid from 1962 to 1968. Washington never used the leverage of cutting off spare parts, despite the fact that the Portuguese air force in 1961 depended primarily upon United States equipment. In an internal memorandum in April, 1964, G. Mennen Williams, head of the Africa Bureau of the State Department, referred to "Portugal's diversion and continued use of vast amounts of U.S. MAP (Mutual Assistance Program) equipment in Portuguese Africa." Two months earlier in a letter to a critical Methodist minister in Oregon he asserted that charges of such use "were completely unfounded." This occurred during the Johnson administration.

Criticism of Portugal did not lead to an attempt to cripple the colonialist counterinsurgency war that it launched to contain the African guerrillas. In fact, the Kennedy administration retreated from its early policy of strongly criticizing Portuguese policy. The acceptance of the critical resolutions in the first half of 1961 led to a policy review. Officials dealing with Africa and the United Nations came out in favor of a continuation of the policy. This was opposed by the Defense Department and the National Security Council, both of which argued that criticism should be muted. This view prevailed, and it was expressed in National Security Action Memorandum 60 of July 14, 1961. Washington did give material aid to the guerrilla movements, but it was minuscule compared with that delivered to Portugal. The purpose of the aid was to buy influence with the guerrillas, not to tip the balance of forces in their favor. The fact was that a guerrilla victory was not thought possible. Washington preached reform to both sides, and deplored violence. It looked to Portugal to help bring stability to southern Africa.

Toward South Africa, the Kennedy team followed a policy that it chose to call "bifurcated." It distinguished between non-cooperation in matters directly or indirectly related to apartheid and cooperation in all other matters. "Other matters" turned out to be a spacious category. In June 1962 an agreement between the two countries allowed NASA to set up a tracking station in the African country. It also allowed South Africa to purchase American arms "for use against communist aggression," but not to enforce apartheid. This distinction did result in the denial of sale of police and infantry type weapons, but not in the rejection for export of air-to-air sidewinder missiles and anti-submarine weapons. However, Washington continued to buy uranium from South Africa and to provide aid for its nuclear program. In 1961 Allis-Chalmers sold its first nuclear reactor to Pretoria. South African scientists came to study nuclear physics in the United States, and American warships continued their visits to ports in South Africa. In 1961 and 1963 American warships joined with the British in participating in joint naval exercises with the African country. American private investments grew apace, and the International Monetary Fund and the World Bank provided additional funds to South Africa.

That the Kennedy policy toward Portugal was adopted by the Johnson administration is suggested by the contents of an African Bureau Action Memorandum of April 29, 1964. The memorandum assumed that a stalemate existed in the fighting and that the Portuguese would eventually have to negotiate a solution. The immediate problem was to prevent the nationalists from mortgaging their future to the communists and from reaching a stage "where they no longer will be disposed to negotiate a moderate and evolutionary settlement when Portugal comes around to offering one." The memorandum concluded that the United States should encourage the guerrillas to turn to non-violence. This would in turn encourage Portugal to offer the moderate and evolutionary settlement referred to above.

An immediate issue the Johnson administration faced was the independence of Namibia (then called Southwest Africa). What should be done to procure its independence in the face of a hostile Pretoria? Minter reveals that sanctions were ruled out in favor of encouragement of South Africa to modify its policy toward the former mandate that, according to the United Nations, Pretoria was occupying illegally. Washington did not challenge the legitimacy of South African control. It abstained on a resolution to establish a council to rule Namibia. This was after the General Assembly had, on paper, removed the colony from South African control. In 1968, the Security Council passed by a unanimous vote a resolution that condemned the guerrillas as terrorists. But no sanctions were imposed. Sanctions were also ruled out when Pretoria issued the report of the Odendaal commission that sought to promote the establishment of Bantustans. President Johnson signed option three of National Security Council Action Memorandum no. 295. It authorized diplomatic activity and pressure designed to prevent the implementation of the plan. Washington continued on with most routine measures of cooperation with South Africa, including the shipping of nuclear fuel. Coker describes the policy of the Johnson administration as one of marking time, occupied as it was with Vietnam.

In February 1970 President Nixon accepted as official American policy the creation of closer ties with the white regimes in southern Africa. This policy was based on what by then was the time-honored assumption that constructive change could come about only through cooperation with the white regimes in control in South Africa, Namibia, Southern Rhodesia, and Portuguese Angola and Mozambique. No hope was seen for the attempts of Africans to gain political rights through violence. Such attempts would lead only to chaos and increase the opportunities for the communists. The policy was expressed in National Security Council Memorandum 39 (NSCM 39). It served as the inspiration for the policy of the Nixon administration toward the region, but previous policy had been similarly inspired. The memorandum was nicknamed with the racist epithet "tar baby".

Washington continued to export dual-use equipment to South Africa. The agreement with Portugal that extended Washington's base rights in the Azores provided for, in addition to other benefits, $400 million in export-import credits. Washington provided civilian aircraft used by Portugal **The Nixon administration openly and illegally violated the sanctions imposed upon Northern Rhodesia by the Security Council.** in Africa to transport its troops, and Germany and France provided weapons to use against the guerrillas. The Nixon administration openly and illegally violated the sanctions imposed upon Northern Rhodesia by the Security Council. Washington did vote to affirm the non-recognition of South Africa's mandate in Namibia. It abstained, however, on a resolution that recognized "the legitimacy of the struggle of the people of Namibia against the illegal presence of the South African authorities in the territory." In December 1973 Kissinger offered Portugal new military equipment to fight its wars in Africa. With strong backing from the Ford and Carter administrations, the International Monetary Fund made substantial loans to South Africa. This backing came on the heels of the Soweto uprising, an explosion that was sparked by an incident involving the killing of a student demonstrator on June 16, 1976. The uprising featured African youth in confrontation with the police. Six months into the uprising, one thousand demonstrators lay dead, half shot in the back.

The Carter people adopted a policy that combined a symbolic disassocia-tion from Pretoria with the same basic contention that no reforms were possible in southern Africa without the consent and cooperation of the controlling white rulers. If the Nixon and Ford people had Kissinger to advise them, Carter had the counsel of Brzezinski. Both were European born, but more importantly, both were cold warriors and realists in the strongest sense of the term. Economic sanctions for Pretoria were ruled out—for the purported reason that reforms were expected to come through greater economic ties with the outside capitalist world. U.S. exports to South Africa jumped from one billion dollars in 1977 to $2.5 billion in 1980. Aircraft and computers led the list of export categories.

The symbolic disassociation of the Kennedy administration was continued by the Carter team, but at a higher decibel level. The "preaching" was provided by Carter himself, Vice President Mondale, and Andrew Young. In his inaugural address the president made human rights the cornerstone of American policy. He affirmed, "Because we are free, we can never be indifferent to the fate of freedom elsewhere." In his first years in office he looked to revolutionary changes in the third world as not favoring Soviet interests. But by 1979 the goal of containing the Soviet Union, particularly in Africa, re-emerged as the priority. Once again, the emphasis was not on sanctions, but on the supposed beneficent effects of enlightened capitalism. Not coincidentally, the president, the vice-president, the United States ambassador to the United Nations, and others in the administration were members of the business-oriented Trilateral Commission. Young advised Africans to use the non-violent methods of the U.S. civil rights movement and to abjure armed struggle and demands for international economic sanctions.

The Carter administration, however, did approve the Security Council resolution which in 1977 imposed compulsory military sanctions on the errant country. Minter is not impressed with this action, characterizing the sanctions as being "blatantly porous." Their enforcement contrasted with the strict system set up by Washington for the Soviet bloc. Minter exemplifies the porous nature of the sanctions with the example of the export of long range 155 millimeter shells by the Space Research Corporation, a Canadian-American company. Pretoria made contact with this company through a CIA source. From 1976 through 1978 the company exported 6,000 shells to South Africa and provided technical assistance as well. Reporters who investigated the case affirmed that these exports could not have happened without U.S. officials being aware of them. Yet no action was taken until after the clandestine operation began unraveling when dockworkers in Antigua reported the transshipment of the shells in October 1977. No shipments were blocked until the next year. The Stockholm International Peace Research Institute revealed that a large number of military items were sold by the United

States to South Africa in the early seventies, including tanks, armed personnel carriers, 155 millimeter self-propelled guns, and helicopters. The Justice Department disclosed in 1978 that at least 178 of South Africa's 578 military aircraft had been purchased from the United States since 1963 and that of those purchased since 1972 some were clearly military aircraft. The above information indicates that all of the administrations from Truman to and including that of Carter provided support for a racist Pretoria and for other racist and colonial regimes in southern Africa. This support increased during the Reagan years.

Reagan and Botha: "From Repression to Criminal Activity"

Soon after taking office, President Reagan strongly endorsed friendship with South Africa on nationwide TV. He initiated a policy that his administration called "constructive engagement." He asked rhetorically, "Can we abandon a country that has stood by us in every war that we have ever fought, a country that is strategically essential to the free world"? The South African Broadcasting Company praised these remarks, adding that they cleared up the ambiguity and veiled hostility that had characterized Washington's attitude in recent years. The broadcast was followed by an unofficial visit to the United States of five high-ranking South African military officers. They conferred with the National Security Council, Pentagon officials, and Kirkpatrick, the U.S. Ambassador to the United Nations. Reagan's remarks were similar to those of his Undersecretary of State William Clark. Clark raised his glass to Foreign Minister Pik Botha at a reception in Washington in May, 1981 with these hopeful and generous words: "Let this be the new beginning of trust and confidence between the United States and South Africa, old friends, like minister Botha, who are getting together again." The reference was to the hopes for a new policy between two countries, but it also took account of the fact that Botha had been South African ambassador to the United States from 1975 to 1977. Chester Crocker, Assistant Secretary of State for Africa, provided the rationale for establishing more friendly relations with Pretoria. In a scope paper for internal consumption, Crocker affirmed that U.S. policy in Africa was designed above everything else to stop Soviet encroachment. The paper went on to say that Pretoria shared this priority, and that a new U.S. policy toward South Africa should be based upon this common objective. The new relationship with South Africa "should be based upon our shared hopes for the future prosperity, security, and stability of southern Africa, constructive internal change within South Africa and our shared perceptions of the role of the Soviet Union and its surrogates in thwarting those goals."[74]

Archbishop Tutu declared that this was a period in which Washington enthusiastically supported any government however shabby its human rights record was so long as it declared itself to be anti-communist. "Thus the apartheid government benefited hugely from President Ronald Reagan's notorious 'constructive engagement' policy." While paying lip service to anti-apartheid sentiment, the Reagan administration said that it could more likely bring about change by maintaining relations with Pretoria than by isolating it. After receiving the Nobel Prize for peace in 1984, the archbishop engaged in some private diplomacy in Washington and London. He tried to get both Reagan and Thatcher to impose economic sanctions on South Africa. He met with Reagan and his cabinet, but to no avail. The president was a bit shocked when the archbishop showed him his travel document. He was not allowed a regular South African passport. The shock was caused by the entry in the space for nationality. The entry read "Undeterminable at present." He had an hour-long tea with Prime Minster Thatcher. Although she "oozed oodles of charm," the archbishop failed again. He added that "the people in both countries eventually heeded our pleas, some sanctions were imposed, especially by the United States, and they contributed very substantially to the demise of apartheid." This development is recounted below.

Some two and a third years before Reagan was sworn in as president, P. W. Botha on September 29, 1978 became the prime minister of South Africa. He remained in that office until 1989, when he was replaced by de Klerk. As indicated above, the Truth and Reconciliation Commission charged that with Botha's ascendancy to power, Pretoria left behind government repression and entered "the realm of criminal misconduct." The new government adopted a policy called "total strategy," a cruel policy that resulted in the widespread use of torture, abduction, arson, sabotage, and the killing of its opponents. The terror committed by Pretoria before was dramatically increased, and the Reagan administration reacted by offering its friendship and support.

South Africa's "total strategy" for preserving apartheid at all costs was a total, holistic strategy that brought together the internal and the external, as well as the economic, military, political, and diplomatic institutions of the country.

"Total strategy" was laid out in a defense white paper in 1977 and adopted as official policy after Botha became prime minister. It was a strategy for preserving apartheid at all costs, and its application was accompanied by an effort to gain legitimacy for a cosmetic version of this extreme type of racism. It was a total, holistic strategy that brought together the internal and the external, as well as the economic, military, political, and diplomatic institutions of the country. To assure the coordination of the strategy, the government created the Joint Security Management System with a military structure, and put it directly under the powerful State Security Council.

Total strategy was adopted in the wake of the independence of Angola and Mozambique, two colonies originally envisaged as part of the group of political entities necessary for the protection of the apartheid state. After independence, these former colonies, now states, were seen as the enemy. The original group of political entities so considered included Namibia and Southern Rhodesia. In 1980 Southern Rhodesia, now renamed Zimbabwe, elected an African government. It was then switched to the list of enemies. The dominoes were falling, and the arrival of the Reaganites in Washington was welcomed as good news by the white elites in Pretoria. Their total strategy was many-sided, however, and it made provision for such unwelcome contingencies as falling and fallen dominoes. Better to have friendly white neighboring governments, but if they are or they turn black, make them dependent surrogates, politically submissive, through trade or other economic means. Failing this, reduce them to impotent enemies.

Botha at first called for the formation of a southern African "constellation of states," one dominated by Pretoria. The dark side of the strategy was the one implemented—at tremendous cost to the Africans in neighboring countries. Pretoria thus was engaged in a war on two fronts, an internal war with the domestic majority and a more lethal external one with neighboring countries. South African forces and their surrogates invaded and/or committed acts of sabotage, terror, and destruction against South Africa's neighbors—Angola, Mozambique, Botswana, Lesotho, Swaziland, Zambia, and Zimbabwe. They assassinated political opponents and sought to destabilize regimes. Favorite targets were transportation systems, but other economic assets were destroyed, including food supplies. The destruction of transportation facilities in Angola and Mozambique forced other surrounding land locked states to use South African ports. The transit states lost revenue, Pretoria gained revenue. The total strategy of horror and terror continued to be implemented until 1988, with a tremendous cost in wealth, human life, and misery.

Botha did not have to build his total strategy from scratch. In fact, throughout the seventies the South African army taught courses and gave lectures in counterinsurgency to the security and non-security forces of the nation. It was during this period that General Jannie Geldenhuys introduced the South African military to the ideas of the American security theorist J. J. McCuen. Even before this in 1962-1963, General Magnus Malan was exposed to counterinsurgency theory in the United States where he completed the regular command and general staff officer's course. He became chief of the South African Army and from 1980, Minister of Defense. As the officer in charge of the South West Africa Command from 1966 to 1968 he conducted a war largely on the principles of counterinsurgency. Some suggestion of the brutality of that campaign is recorded in a different part of this chapter. During his tour of duty as chief of the army from 1973 to 1976, he established a series of joint inter-agency counterinsurgency agencies. Counterinsurgency thinking had an impact on the patterns and modes of human rights violations by South Africa. It introduced a regional component to the government's struggle and became important domestically as an inspiration for devising new and more repressive measures

The CIA gave the government information that led to capture of Nelson Mandela.

for domestic crowd control. Moreover, this manner of thinking legitimized the establishment of covert governmental units and inspired the abduction and killing of political activists. "Further U.S. influence was evident in the co-operation between the security forces and the Central Intelligence Agency (CIA) which considered South Africa a local ally against the Soviet Union." The commission gave as examples the information the CIA gave the government that led to capture of Nelson Mandela and the training given to General Van den Bergh prior to the creation of BOSS, the national intelligence agency of South Africa. The general became its first head.

A prime component in total strategy was the strengthening and expansion of the military and the police. The military budget showed dramatic expansion even before Pretoria adopted this strategy. This resulted in great part from the impact of counterinsurgency thought. The budget continued its upward thrust after the acceptance of total strategy as well. It jumped from 44 million Rand in 1960 to 1.3 billion Rand in 1977. The budget was estimated at 4.274 billion Rand for fiscal 1984-1985. The budget thus increased over three times during the period of the new strategy. In 1985 the government announced that it was going to expand its police force from 45,000 by 11,000 during the next 17 months. South Africa developed the world's tenth largest arms industry, with sufficient capacity to manufacture for export.

Just days after President Reagan was inaugurated, Pretoria launched an attack on Maputo, the capital of Mozambique. It appeared as though the South African elites were testing the validity of the friendlier attitude expressed by Washington. The operation was a small part of the implementation of the total strategy of the apartheid regime. Twelve people in the capital city were killed. The incursion followed a speech in which the new Secretary of State Haig condemned rampant international terrorism and promised that a priority of the new administration was to fight it. Pretoria justified the attack as an attempt to root out the terrorist bases of the African National Congress located in the Mozambican capital. When the Security Council attempted to condemn the attack, the American delegate vetoed the draft resolution. Even before the advent of the Reagan administration, Washington had crafted a definition of "terrorism" such that attacks like these by allies and friendly states were exempt from criticism by definition.

Two months later Mozambique expelled several U.S. diplomats on the grounds that they were part of a CIA network that was targeting the government as well as South African exiles. Washington retaliated by cutting off food assistance. Later in August 1981 Pretoria sent a force of 11,000 to occupy the southern part of Angola. Secretary of State Haig justified this invasion and occupation as a defensive maneuver intended to protect against the threat of Cuban forces and Soviet weapons and advisers. Washington broke with its allies to veto a Security Council resolution that would have condemned this invasion and occupation of Angola. This operation was also part of the implementation of total strategy. In a major foreign policy speech two days before the veto, Undersecretary of State Crocker argued that the United States should sustain those who "would resist the siren call of violence and the blandishments of Moscow and its clients." He went on to imply that South Africa's actions were defensive and blamed the Warsaw Pact for supporting the guerrillas in Namibia and South Africa. He noted that Pretoria "clearly signaled its determination to resist guerrilla encroachments and strike at countries giving sanctuary." Export controls on security items and on nuclear-related items were loosened despite the fact that Pretoria refused to sign the Nuclear Non-Proliferation Treaty. In November 1982 Washington used its influence and its vote in the International Monetary Fund to help improve the economic situation in South Africa. The year before the General Assembly had deplored the increased political, economic, and military assistance rendered South Africa by "certain Western countries." It demanded that this assistance be terminated as well as aid from the International Monetary Fund.

Clearly, the Reagan administration gave its blessing to the Pretoria regime, to its continuing nuclear program, and to the way the "total strategy" first unfolded. Minter observed "the signals from Washington shone brightly green." The Reaganites provided diplomatic, military, and economic support for a terrorist Pretoria. Minter also accused Haig of "racial insensitivity" —the Secretary of State playfully beat the table like a jungle drum whenever African topics were discussed at meetings of the National Security Council. The Reagan administration continued the policy of granting scholarships for South African blacks to study in the United States. It offered this aid as an alternative to sanctions. The president demonstrated that he did not always keep up with things when he declared in a radio interview on August 24,1985 that South Africa had "eliminated the segregation that we once had in our own country." Violent demonstrations in South Africa escalated to the level of civil war. Human rights groups estimated that between September 1984 and mid 1986, 2,500 were killed, nearly all Africans. At least 30,000 were detained, including 300 youngsters under eighteen. These demonstrations were triggered by a new constitution that provided for Indian and colored representation, but not for African representation and by a defiant speech delivered by Botha. The violent street reaction in South Africa was matched in the United States by peaceful demonstrations

The Reaganites provided diplomatic, military, and economic support for a terrorist Pretoria.

instigated by African Americans, students, churches, and others. Some six thousand protestors were arrested picketing the South African embassy and its consulates, including eighteen members of congress, one being a Senator (Senator Weicker). Pressure was put on universities, local government, and businesses resulting in divestiture and the refusal of banks to role over loans for South Africa. More than half of the American firms with direct investments in South Africa withdrew them between 1984 and the end of 1986. The value of the rand plunged. A declining economy and a volatile political situation induced South African business to pressure the government for change.

Washington finally imposed sanctions on South Africa in 1985 and 1986. The first imposition was by the Reagan administration, intended to ward off more serious action by Congress. It banned the sale of Kuggerrands in the United States, incorporated the Sullivan principles into law, and restricted bank loans and technological exports. The sanctions were subject to discretionary reversal by the president. The Reagan administration showed its limited commitment to the new dispensation when in November of the same year it vetoed a Security Council resolution that mandated compulsory sanctions for South Africa because of its continuing occupation of Namibia. On October 2, 1986 Congress overrode a presidential veto to impose the first substantive, albeit not comprehensive, sanctions of the United States on South Africa. This did not occur before the administration vetoed another attempt by the Security Council to impose sanctions. The sanctions imposed by Congress banned new investments and loans as well as imports of coal, iron, steel, uranium, agricultural products, and textiles. They also prohibited the right of South African Airways to land in the United States. The legislation threatened to cut off military aid to those countries that breached the international arms embargo against Pretoria. This could have been a warning to Israel because that country had become an important source of arms and military expertise for South Africa. The sanctions legislation did not confine its criticism to the government that had instituted apartheid, but included the two African parties, the African National Congress and the Pan African Congress as well. The Inkatha Freedom Party, responsible for much of the ongong violence within South Africa, was not mentioned. The Reagan administration showed its disagreement again by vetoing a sanctions resolution in the Security Council and by its lax enforcement of the sanctions legislation passed by Congress. The resolution it vetoed was almost identical to the legislation passed by Congress. The administration continued to provide aid to UNITA and did not criticize Pretoria as the latter repeatedly attacked neighboring countries and implemented other aspects of its total strategy.

In 1987 for the first time the U.S. representative to the United Nations Human Rights Commission submitted a resolution that criticized Pretoria's policies. It called for the release from prison of Mandela and other political prisoners and condemned the widespread incarceration of children under the apartheid system. Human rights groups in South Africa estimated over 25,000 people had been incarcerated since June 1986 under the State of Emergency Act. Ten thousand of these were children. Finally, Reagan's ambassador to South Africa "was activated." At first, Edward Perkins, the first African American ambassador to Pretoria, kept a low profile. As his tenure progressed, he became more visible, attending the treason trials, protesting the jailing of dissidents, and authoring an article in a local journal that seemed to call for majority rule. He went so far as to be labeled "too outspoken" by Pretoria. Washington's conversion to a new policy toward apartheid had been long in coming and was shaky at best. Moreover, it seemed to be driven by the realization that apartheid was being killed at the local level and that realism dictated that its death be accepted at other levels as well.

The Republican platform for 1988 opposed sanctions; the Democratic platform called for comprehensive sanctions and named South Africa a "terrorist state."

The Republican platform for the 1988 election reaffirmed its support for the Reagan administration's policies in South Africa and opposed sanctions. In contrast to this, the Democratic platform called for comprehensive sanctions and named South Africa a "terrorist state."

In 1989 T.W. de Klerk replaced P.W. Botha as head of the ruling party in South Africa and as head of the government. The Botha government had waged a war on the home front and one abroad as well. It invaded neighboring countries, pillaging and terrorizing their civilian populations. On the home front, Africans had become more and more militant, and were in open rebellion. The government declared martial law and states of emergency, detained prisoners without trial and tortured them, censored the press, banned political meetings, committed political murders, and organized death squads. Domestic support for apartheid was dwindling, and the Reagan administration, despite its own feelings and policies, was forced by Congress to impose meaningful economic sanctions. One of the last straws occurred when the Dutch Reformed Church, a beacon of moral leadership for most Afrikaners, switched theological positions on apartheid. Whereas before the church argued that apartheid had been mandated by the Bible, after the switch the church declared apartheid to be immoral. It was in this context that apartheid legislation was repealed and Africans and other non-whites were allowed to vote.

De Klerk released top African leaders from prison, including Nelson Mandela, the head of the African National Congress. He then initiated negotiations with the former "saboteur," "terrorist," and prison inmate, to lay the groundwork for a democratic regime. Mandela had served some 28 years of a life sentence under the Suppression of Communism Act for involvement in sabotage. Just four years and two months after his release from jail, he became the president of South Africa. This turnabout was accomplished without the usually predicted racial war. True, an estimated 15,000 were killed in the violence that pitted supporters of the African National Congress against those of the Inkatha Freedom Party. This latter party was a surrogate of Pretoria, and it drew its support from the Zulu living in the "homeland" Kwa Zulwi. But apartheid was scrapped without the usually predicted white-on-black/black-on-white holocaust. This heartening conclusion drawn by the media and others did not take into account the massacres and terror that Pretoria inflicted on its neighbors as it implemented its total strategy on them. Nor did it expose the recklessness of the West in helping a desperate Pretoria succeed in developing weapons of mass destruction.

THE IMPACT OF PRETORIA'S TOTAL STRATEGY ON NEIGHBORING COUNTRIES

The commission reminded its readers that while its focus was understandably on what happened inside South Africa, this represented somewhat of an historical distortion because most of the violations had occurred outside, in neighboring countries. These countries, some of the poorest nations in the world, "bore the brunt of the South African conflict and suffered the greatest number of individual casualties and the greatest damage to their countries' economies and infrastructure." Again, the commission charged that it was the state that was primarily responsible. "The state—in the form of the South African government, the civil service, and its security forces—was, in the period 1960-1994, the primary perpetrator of gross violations of human rights in South Africa, and from 1974, in southern Africa." It re-asserted the gravity of what Pretoria did to its neighbors when in another context it charged that a majority of the victims of the South African government's attempt to stay in power were outside of that country. "Tens of thousands of people in the region died as a direct or indirect result of the South African government's aggressive intent toward its neighbors." One of its conclusions was that the South African government's military in Angola between 1977 and 1988 led to gross violations of human rights "on a vast scale." As though to confirm this, it quoted an estimate of UNICEF that at least 100,000 Angolans died between 1980 and 1985 mainly as a result of war-related famine. The cumulative effect of the devastation of the economy and the infrastructure in that period produced an even greater escalation of the death rate. Between 1981 and 1988, again according to UNICEF, 333,000 Angolan children died of unnatural causes.

A 1982 visit by Archbishop Hurley from the Southern African Catholic Bishops Conference resulted in a detailed study of torture based on interviews with 180 South West Africans (Namibians). The Archbishop was charged under the Police Act for making the study, and newspapers in South Africa and South West Africa were threatened with prosecution if they published its findings. The charges against the Archbishop were dropped because of international protests. The Bishops Conference reported in 1982:

> The Security Forces will stop at nothing to force information out of people. They break into homes, beat up residents, shoot people, steal cattle and often pillage stores and tea rooms. When the tracks of SWAPO guerrillas are discovered by the Security Forces, the local people are in danger. Harsh measures are intensified. People are blindfolded, taken from their homes and left beaten up or even dead by the roadside. Women are often raped... There is no redress because reporting irregularities or atrocities to commanders is considered a dangerous or fruitless exercise.

When Pretoria failed to create a guerrilla group in Namibia that would do its bidding, it decided in 1978 to establish Koevoet (Special Operations K Unit of the South African Security police). Koevoet patterned itself after the Rhodesian Selous Scotts, the organization that taught most of its original organizers their counterinsurgency skills. Louis le Grange, the Minister of Law and Order, described the organization as: "The crowbar which prises terrorists out of the bushveld like nails from rotten wood." John Deegan, one of its members, described its activities this way: "We were basically automatons. We would just kill. That's how we got our kicks. We were adrenaline junkies."

At peak strength, the unit numbered one thousand—250 white officers and the remainder local Africans from South West Africa. Broken down into mobile units of ten to fifteen locals and one white officer, it roamed the bush in Casspirs (specially designed armored personnel carriers) to gather intelligence, track guerrillas, and kill them. Koevoet borrowed the practice of "turning" from the Rhodesian Selous Scotts. Captured guerrillas (members of SWAPO) were offered the choice of joining with them or summary execution. Those who turned often committed atrocities that were then blamed on SWAPO. The commission revealed that there existed extensive documentation that confirmed the activities of Koevoet. These activities included the destruction of property, sexual assault, solitary confinement, hooding, electric shock, submersion in water, mock burials, roasting over fire, and sleep, food, and water deprivation. Rape was common, and women and girls of all ages were its victims. The records indicated that the unit's personnel raped an eighty-year-old woman and a four-year-old girl.

Captured SWAPO guerrillas were offered the choice of joining with Koevet or summary execution. Those who joined often committed atrocities that were then blamed on SWAPO.

The authorities devised a unique method of rewarding the members of the unit, and the method bore bitter fruit. They were rewarded on a sliding scale for discovering caches of arms, capturing guerrillas, or killing them with the largest reward going for killing. In the mid-eighties Koevoet killed from 300 to 500 per year. "Corpses were... used for purposes of spreading terror and intimidating villagers." Rough body counts were issued by military headquarters, but there never was independent confirmation to determine how accurate the figures were or whether the corpses were those of SWAPO members or civilians. A document obtained by the commission suggested that the bounty for killing achieved its apparent purpose. In the engagements listed, 3,323 "insurgents" were killed, but only 104 were taken prisoner—the ratio of those taken prisoner to those killed being about one to thirty-two.

Two main sources are used here in an attempt to assess the general impact of Pretoria's total strategy upon neighboring countries. Both were commissioned by United Nations agencies. The first is named *South African Destabilization: The Economic Cost of the Frontline Resistance to Apartheid.* Initiated by an economic task force appointed by the Secretary General, its purpose was to determine the impact of South Africa's total strategy on the prospects for development of the region. The second source is entitled *Children on the Frontline: the Impact of Apartheid, Destabilization and Warfare on the Children of Southern Africa.* It was commissioned by the United Nations Children's Fund (UNICEF). Its publication resulted from a decision made by UNICEF's executive board in 1986 to assess the impact of military and political activities in the region upon women and children. It has four authors. They are Reg Green, a fellow at the Institute of Development Studies of the University of Sussex; a UNICEF staff member; a UNICEF project officer; and the UNICEF representative for Mozambique and Swaziland. The preface to the report enlarged upon the reason for the initiation and publishing of the report. It alleged that apartheid itself and South Africa's incursions into surrounding countries have been universally condemned. But it went on to say:

> But the extent to which South Africa's policies of apartheid, economic disruption and de-stabilization have seriously affected the lives, health, and welfare of children in other countries of southern Africa has been hardly reported upon, and almost certainly too little appreciated. To help remedy this situation, UNICEF has commissioned this paper.

The above quote singles out children as the victims of these massacres since UNICEF's mandate is with these innocents. Obviously, the massacres affected adults as well, and their fate was not widely advertised either. The ignoring and minimizing of the massacres and terror committed by Pretoria against neighboring African populations is an extremely significant point. Despite my longstanding interest in Africa, I was unaware of its extent. But these phenomena of minimizing and being ignorant of abuse have come up again and again in connection with other massacres and terror described in this volume. The report returned to this subject a few pages later, but from a new angle. Its reference shifted from the exclusive concern with the welfare of children, the chief human victims of the total strategy, to reflect on the general situation in Angola and Mozambique, the chief territorial victims of the strategy. The report declared:

> Since independence Angola and Mozambique have been beset by internal fighting and external attacks from South Africa. Hardly a week has been passed in peace.
> The widespread and continuing conflict in these two countries has been virtually ignored as most of the world has concentrated its attention on events within South Africa and Namibia. It is necessary to outline here its instruments, its economic and social costs to the region and, above all, the human costs in the lives of the region's children.

Tom Brennan, a consultant to the U.S. Committee for Refugees, complained of the lack of coverage of the violence in the American media. He registered this complaint in a publication written in 1986, affirming that the crisis had been ongoing for eleven years and had steadily grown more violent. He asserted that human suffering and human displacements were truly massive in scale in the entire southern third of the African continent and that there existed a potential for catastrophe. He continued:

> Until very recently, however, little has appeared in the American media regarding the domestic situations in Mozambique or of the other nations in southern Africa, or regarding their relationships with each other and with the South African government. Even less has appeared on the impact that the existing and potential armed conflicts in the region—stemming from ideological as well as ethnic and racial differences—are likely to have on the civilian populations of the area as the struggle to eliminate apartheid gains momentum.

The UNICEF report indicated that Mozambique and Angola had the highest infant and children mortality rates in the world. This is ironic since these two countries gave priority in the post independence period to public health measures designed to improve the health of the population, especially infants and children. Their governments created networks of health centers and posts, thousands of health workers were trained, and mass vaccination programs were implemented. The groundwork for this ambitious public health program was laid in the immediate post colonial period. It took root and blossomed in 1979 and 1980, only to be poisoned after that. It is no accident that this setback occurred at the very time that Pretoria started seriously to apply its total strategy. The UNICEF report charged that the war and the destabilization campaign (total strategy) chose health and educational facilities as targets. It offered as examples the 718 health posts and centers destroyed in Mozambique since 1981 and the schools for 300,000 primary school children. The destruction of the health posts and centers deprived two million people of health care. In areas of southern Angola and in much of rural Mozambique vaccinations were no longer given because of lack of security. Many health workers were maimed, wounded, kidnapped, or killed. The result was that easily preventable diseases and curable illnesses "are now taking a hideous and rising toll on the vulnerable age group of infants and children under five."

In 1986 one hundred and forty thousand children under the age of five in these two countries lost their lives because of South Africa's "war and destabilization" campaign, what we refer to as its "total strategy." The number of deaths was expected to increase in 1987. But it was not merely the state of the children in these countries that "is grave and getting worse." All fifteen million children in the region whose countries border South Africa were considered to be in the same perilous situation. They were caught up in the throes of an external civil conflict and an economic de-stabilization campaign (total strategy). While the report set forth a number of conditions responsible for undermining the health of children in these two countries and the others in southern Africa, war and de-stabilization were identified as the major causes. And the report concluded that all countries in the region suffered economic losses either directly from South African aggression or from its destabilization campaign or indirectly by having to spend more on defense. Mozambique spent 42 percent of its budget on defense, one of the highest percentages in the world. This diminished the revenue left over for social services, for example, for children. The dislocation of the population also contributed to malnutrition and starvation. This was particularly evident in the case of Angola and Mozambique where 9 million people became refugees at one time or another. After 1981 sabotage units were particularly active. The principal targets were transportation and power infrastructure, but major production units came under the gun as well, especially those earning foreign exchange. The destruction of the transportation systems of neighboring countries made these countries more dependent on South Africa's system for the export of their commodities.

The UNICEF report argued that what is called here Pretoria's "total strategy" went beyond seeking merely to destroy military and economic targets to include those that sustain the very social fabric of nations. The report gave as examples of the fruit of this objective the destruction of health and educational facilities, the dislocation of communities, the loss of food production, and the reduction of the health and water budgets because of expenditures for defense. In another section, some of this type of destruction appeared again, but as the result of mass terrorism:

UNICEF: Pretoria's "total strategy" went beyond seeking merely to destroy military and economic targets to include those that sustain the very social fabric of nations.

> One of the deadliest weapons of the war is the mass terrorism carried out by forces which have burned crops and farm houses, pillaged and destroyed schools, clinics, churches, mosques, stores and villages, poisoned wells by throwing bodies down them, and attacked the transport system which is a vital part of rural life. Members of religious orders, mainly

Catholics, have been murdered and kidnapped. So too have foreign aid workers from both West and East. In Angola and Mozambique teachers, nurses, agricultural technicians, engineers, and geologists have also been killed and kidnapped, maimed and mutilated.

The carnage has been indiscriminate, with infants and children not exempted. The results are clear and tragic: death for many, and for the survivors fear and flight, destruction and displacement. About 8.5 million Angolans and Mozambicans—roughly half the rural population of the two countries—have been displaced or are internal refugees in their own countries.

The costs of the war are cumulative, have been escalating since 1981, and are likely to continue to do so.

South African Destabilization, a report initiated by a task force appointed by the Secretary General of the United Nations, provides an estimate of the total economic and demographic cost to the victims in neighboring countries of the implementation of South Africa's total strategy. Its purpose was to provide a synthesis of the impact of South Africa's total strategy upon neighboring countries. It concluded that the cost to these countries from 1980 to 1988 was over $60 billion at 1988 prices, reflecting the loss in gross domestic product attributed to the implementation of this strategy by South Africa and its accomplices. The report added that the losses promise to extend beyond 1988. The report indicated that Pretoria's strategy killed the inhabitants of neighboring countries in three ways. The first was directly by war or terrorism, the victims being military personnel or civilians. The second was through a combination of malnutrition, disease, and the destruction of rural health networks. Those killed by this method were usually infants and young children. The third consisted of famine-related deaths as a result of the lack of food caused by drought in combination with general insecurity. The report concluded that by the end of 1988, 1.5 million had been killed in these three ways. Over half of the fatalities were infants or children under five. The report estimated that almost half of the populations of Angola and Mozambique had been driven from their homes at least once, usually with the loss of possessions. It calculated that at the time of the writing, 1.5 million were refugees abroad and 6.1 million were displaced internally.

The estimate of the task force that 1.5 million were killed can be compared with a 1988 study commissioned by the U.S. State Department that concluded that the guerrilla group, the Mozambican National Resistance (RENAMO), alone killed 100,000 civilians in Mozambique. By the time of the study Washington was supportive of the Mozambican government, rather than opposing it as before. This guerrilla group was established by Southern Rhodesia's intelligence organization around 1975, and after that colony became African-governing in 1980, the South African Army adopted it. Until the middle of 1979, it had little more than nuisance value. But with South African supplies and support it witnessed a marked improvement in its destructive power. It became active in all parts of Mozambique and, besides its propensity to kill, it was responsible for much of the damage to the country's transportation system. RENAMO carried on guerrilla operations differently from the way the Front for the Liberation of Mozambique (FRELIMO) did when it was leading the fight against Portuguese rule. FRELIMO sought only to disrupt economic activity and used a selective targeting system for civilians. In contrast, RENAMO "has often completely destroyed economic infrastructure and has been generally indiscriminate in its attacks on the civilian population."

WASHINGTON, SOUTH AFRICA AND WEAPONS OF MASS DESTRUCTION

Chemical and Bacteriological Weapons

The commission discovered that the apartheid governments developed a chemical and bacteriological warfare (CBW) capability. The TRCR based its investigation of the CBW program on more than 150 documents, affidavits, amnesty applications, and interviews. Given the code name Project Coast, this program was under the general management of the chief of staff of the defense force, the chief of staff of intelligence, the surgeon general of the army, and Dr. Wouter Basson, the project director. Its goals included the manufacture of cholera, botulism, anthrax, chemical poisoning, drugs of abuse allegedly for crowd control, lethal micro-organisms for use against individuals, and "applicators" (murder weapons) developed for their administration. As examples, anthrax was "applied" in cigarettes, botulism in milk, and paraoxon in whiskey. A company was enlisted secretly to act as a front for the project. The commission concluded that toxins had been used by the security forces against anti-apartheid activists. Although the production of a thousand kilograms of methaqualone (mandrax) was started, its production was stopped in 1988, because its ability to incapacitate was found to be too slow to act as an efficient agent for crowd control. Work on its analogues continued. A British scientist alleged that South African troops used a chemical agent against guerrillas from Mozambique in a military encounter along the South African-Mozambican border in January 1992. Other investigators, including the United Nations, could not verify the charge. The commission concluded that the matter remained unresolved.

The apartheid governments developed a chemical and bacteriological warfare (CBW) capability; the security forces used these toxins against anti-apartheid activists.

The commission concluded that "without some level of foreign assistance, the (CBW) programme would not have been possible." The assistance was forthcoming from Belgium, Israel, the United Kingdom, and the United States. In the early eighties, Dr. Basson attended a conference on the subject held in San Antonio. "Other documents reveal links between the surgeon general (of the South African army) and Americans who were part of the United States CBW programme, and demonstrate their willingness to assist South Africans." Dr. Basson visited the United States in 1981, and later Dr. Knobel, the surgeon general, had contact with scientists who were part of the American CBW program. As 1993 drew to a close and the ANC seemed closer to taking over the government, both the Unites States and the British governments expressed concern lest a government under the control of the African National Congress take over the program. At a hearing of the commission both Dr. Basson and Dr, Knobel testified that these governments told them that they did not want this to happen.

Nuclear Weapons

Much earlier Washington helped Pretoria develop a nuclear capability. In 1957 Washington signed a 50-year agreement for nuclear cooperation with

Pretoria, and the latter has received "extensive assistance in the nuclear field" from the United States. In 1961 South Africa purchased a Safari 1 research reactor from the United States. There has been some variation between administrations in the intensity of the collaboration. The Carter administration sought to impose more restrictive parameters on the sale of nuclear technology than the Reaganites. They approved the sale of vital equipment that could be used, for example, to simulate nuclear explosions and to test warheads and re-entry equipment. A study by the General Accounting Office found that in 1981 South Africa was the second leading country purchasing "dual-purpose, nuclear related" equipment from the United States. In 1984 a substantial number of the licenses issued by the Commerce Department for export to South Africa were for material that could be used in producing or testing nuclear weapons despite the fact that Pretoria had refused to sign the Nuclear Non-proliferation Treaty. Britain, West Germany, France, and more recently Israel were heavily involved in assisting as well. When challenged, the political elites of each country insisted that their collaboration was for peaceful purposes only. The General Assembly of the United Nations on numerous occasions called for a stop to such collaboration, but it continued. Efforts to exclude South Africa from the International Atomic Energy Agency failed, because of the opposition to exclusion by the Western nations. There was evidence that Pretoria conducted nuclear tests in 1979, 1981, and 1987. Despite strong evidence to the contrary, Washington claimed that there was no "corroborating evidence" for the first test or that the evidence was "inconclusive". In like manner, it shrugged off the other reported tests as well.

Western collaboration with South Africa continued, and "it paid off." In August 1988 Foreign Minister Pik Botha announced that South Africa had a nuclear capability, and in March 1993 President de Klerk acknowledged that the apartheid state had produced six nuclear bombs in 1989. He asserted that the bombs had been dismantled by the time of his announcement and that the pilot enrichment plant necessary for their production had been decommissioned. The white government seemed determined not to see this nuclear prize fall into the hands of a black government. And so with the aid and silence of Washington and its Western allies, white Pretoria went nuclear, but only temporarily. The silence was deafening, in view of Washington's continuous warnings and condemnations of the efforts of states such as Iraq and Iran to go nuclear. Minty finds the nuclear collaboration of the Western powers in the last days of apartheid to be "a dangerous and puzzling policy given the instability and desperation of the apartheid regime." They

The nuclear collaboration of the Western powers in the last days of apartheid was "a dangerous and puzzling policy given the instability and desperation of the apartheid regime."

certainly knew of the nuclear capability of Pretoria, and of the testing as well. In particular, he indicts the Reagan administration, because it increased nuclear collaboration during the last days of apartheid, the most sensitive period. As they must have been aware, some desperate racist could have unleashed a nuclear holocaust to accompany the non-nuclear one that had already been unleashed by the apartheid state in its neighboring countries. Fortunately, by the time the white elites in South Africa had developed an atomic bomb they decided not to use it. They should be congratulated for this. Unfortunately, by then the holocaust unleashed by their total strategy had already cost the lives of a reported 1.5 million inhabitants of neighboring countries.

BRIEF COMMENTS ON THE CHAPTER

The answers to the three central questions posed in this study are clear. Yes, the South African government did commit terror, and, yes, this state terror was much more widespread and grievous than the private terror committed by the opposition forces. Certainly, the administrations in Washington provided diplomatic, military, and economic aid to the South African state terrorists, including assistance in constructing weapons of mass destruction. The encyclopedia of horrors catalogued above points to the existence of a centralized governmental program that, by deliberate acts of a physical and psychological nature perpetrated on select groups of victims, sought to coerce and intimidate these target groups and also the majority of society that was opposed to apartheid. The government caused both groups, especially the target groups, intense fear, anxiety, apprehension, panic, dread, and horror.

The evidence leads to the conclusion that the South African government practiced terrorism much more than either the ANC, the PAC, or any other opposition group. It was not the general policy of the ANC to target civilians, whereas it was the policy of the government to target non-violent opponents. Torture was not the general policy of the ANC, but it was the general policy of the government, applied systematically throughout the country by the security forces against the opponents of the government. Detention without trial by the government was extensive and systematic, and two studies referred to above concluded that eighty-three percent of those detained by the government were tortured.

The commission concluded that the Pan African Congress "engaged in a limited struggle which resulted in a few human rights violations inside South Africa." It also concluded that "the predominate portion of gross violations of human rights was committed by the former state through its security and law-enforcement agencies." and that the state was the primary perpetrator of gross violations of human rights in South Africa. In the period from the late seventies to the early nineties the state "became involved in activities of a criminal nature."

South African society under apartheid was not only structured by race, but also by class. Africans were not only discriminated against socially and generally humiliated, they were found at the bottom of the national pay scale. At the other end was the business class, which benefited from the low wages that existed in the racist society. Especially favored were mining, white agriculture, and the defense industry. Besides criticizing business, the TRCR singled out for dishonorable mention organized religion, the health sector, the media, and the judiciary. The judiciary was charged with collusion with the police in the torturing of prisoners; the media with self-censorship or support for apartheid or repression; the health sector for not calling attention to the negative health effects of apartheid, torture, and solitary confinement; and organized religion for promoting the ideology of apartheid. Churches provided chaplains for the military and police forces, and sometimes the chaplains were armed.

One reason given for the establishment of a truth commission in South Africa was to inform the white population as to what had happened. Safely tucked away in their all-white segregated sections of the cities, the whites were unaware of what was happening in the African townships. I was reminded of the public in the United States separated by distance and propaganda from knowing that its government was helping rightwing governments commit state terrorism. In the case of South Africa, this help extended so far as to aid in the development of weapons of mass destruction.

CHAPTER 6

Indonesia:
Three Series of Massacres

THE ANTI-COMMUNIST MASSACRES: INDONESIA

It was reminiscent of what happened in El Salvador in 1932. The sequence was the same: small incident, large massacre. Only the place and the time were different. This was Indonesia in 1965. On October 1 of that year what some called an attempted coup occurred when an Indonesian army lieutenant colonel kidnapped six senior generals and killed them. This incident occurred as the Sukarno government of Indonesia was moving closer to China and also to the local communist party. The army seized upon this incident, pretended that the communist party was the chief conspirator, and used it as a way of destroying the power of this party, its chief political rival, over the objections of President Sukarno. I "seize" upon this incident and the larger story of Indonesia to broaden further the geographical scope of the study and to illustrate that the war on terrorism is following the lead of the Cold War by supporting rightwing violators of human rights, if not state terrorists.

Indonesia is an island nation in southeastern Asia, the fourth most populous country in the world and the most populous Muslim one. The Dutch had established their political and economic control over it by the end of the seventeenth century. Before that the country was the stakes of colonial rivalry among Portugal, Spain, Britain, and the Dutch East India Company. Aside from a brief interlude in the nineteenth century, the Dutch maintained their hegemony until the Japanese invasion. In 1927 the Indonesian Nationalist Party was founded with Sukarno at its head. Two years later he and other leaders of the party were arrested by the Dutch because of their agitation for independence. He spent two years in jail and more than eight years in exile. He became the chief advisor to the Japanese during their occupation, and after their defeat declared Indonesia to be independent. There followed two unsuccessful attempts by the Dutch to regain control, followed by their formal recognition of Indonesian independence on December 27, 1949. Sukarno served as president of the country until he was deposed in a coup in 1967. He adopted a neutral policy toward the Korean War and the Vietnam conflict and became a strong supporter of the Nonaligned Movement.

The PKI: An Historic U.S. Obsession

American administrations dating from that of Eisenhower were obsessed with the neutralization of the Communist Party of Indonesia (PKI). Their moral code was in accord with that recommended by General Doolittle. "There are no rules in such a game. Hitherto acceptable norms do not apply." By the fall of 1957, the Eisenhower administration decided to back the rebellion of the colonels and civilians in Sumatra and Sulawesi. The insurrection was aimed at toppling the Sukarno government, which was friendly to the PKI and dependent upon its support. The rebel colonels made anti-communism their main issue. Washington provided money, arms, munitions, training in communications, and finally air support to this failed attempt to overthrow the Sukarno regime.[1] The United States Seventh Fleet, with marines aboard, was sent to the area. Of course, President Eisenhower and Secretary of State Dulles denied involvement. On February 15, 1958 the rebels announced the formation of "The Revolutionary Government of the Republic of Indonesia", and they asked for international recognition. This was not forthcoming, not even from Washington. The rebels had suffered several reverses on the battlefield, and Washington decided to look to other alternatives.

Washington provided money, arms, munitions, training in communications, and finally air support to this failed attempt to overthrow the Sukarno regime.

On May 6, 1958 Djuanda, the Indonesian Prime Minister, warned American ambassador Jones that the relations between their countries were at a crossroads. This because of "foreign support" of the rebels. Jones concluded that further aid to the rebels would be counterproductive. Admiral Feliz Stump, commander of United State forces in the Pacific, picked up on this theme and complained that United States support for the rebels might persuade the anti-communist elements in Djakarta to support Sukarno. He went on to say that further bombing was counterproductive at a time when the United States was trying to develop "a response and a sense of gravity to the communist danger among the anti-communist elements left in Djakarta." Soon thereafter Admiral Lawrence H. Frost, chief of U.S. Naval Intelligence, met with General Nasution, the chief of staff of the Indonesian army. The admiral concluded that the key to resolving the internal situation in Indonesia lay with the military. In his view Washington should show the Indonesian military leaders tangible evidence of its intention to support them.

This diplomatic activity induced Secretary of State Dulles to suggest the possibility of a "cessation of military activities in order to permit the anti-Communist elements in Djakarta to take the contemplated steps in attaining their objectives that in essence are the same as those of the dissidents."[2] He looked forward to a ceasefire during which time Nasution "would take such action as he contemplates to bring about a change in the cabinet and against the Communists." In return for this Nasution could be assured of receiving U.S. economic and military support. On May 13 Dulles instructed Jones to reiterate Washington's concern at the growing influence and ambition of the PKI. He promised that if the Sukarno government "takes definite measures for the elimination of the communist threat... we would use the full extent of our influence...to try to compose the situation", as well as extend economic aid, "and such military aid as would seem appropriate to maintain internal order as against any Communist subversive threat."

These steps toward a settlement between Washington and Djakarta failed, but success eventually emerged from an unexpected incident. On May 18 a B-26 bomber sank an Indonesian ship in the Indonesian port city Ambon, and then proceeded to bomb a church and the central market. There were heavy civilian casualties. It was a rebel plane piloted by a U.S. Army pilot, and it was shot down by anti-aircraft fire. The American pilot survived and was taken prisoner. Washington persisted in declaring that he was a soldier of fortune, notwithstanding the fact that he carried U.S. military identification papers and a current post exchange card from Clark Air Force Base in the Philippines. Djakarta reacted slowly and mildly, with diplomatic circumspection. It did not make a propaganda bonanza of this golden opportunity. It did not even announce the capture of the pilot until nine days later. This was followed two months later in August 1958 by aid to Indonesia's military and an increase in the number of Indonesian officers accepted for training in United States military schools. This aid, however, was a mere token when measured against the massive aid provided to the Indonesian army later that year and the ensuing year. Much of the aid was tagged "surplus" or from "excess stocks" so that dollar values mean very little. This new departure meant that military aid from Washington and its Western allies exceeded that of the Soviet bloc and that since that time "Indonesia placed its orders almost exclusively in Free World countries." [3]

This massive arms program, that in itself represented a shift in Washington's policy, was accompanied by a statement of the new policy by the National Security Council. This new policy, particularly its policy recommendations, has direct relevance to the 1965 massacre and to Washington's involvement in it. The nineteen-page National Security Council report indicated that it was still obsessed with the growing threat of communism in Indonesia but had charted a new course to deal with it. It virtually wrote off the rebels in Sumatra and Sulawesi. Moreover, Sukarno was pictured in a new light, as someone Washington could deal with. Most importantly, the army was depicted as "the principal obstacle to the continued growth of Communist strength" and as having "assumed an increasingly powerful position in the political arena including a growing policy-making role."[4] It concluded that Washington should maintain and strengthen its ties with the Indonesian police and military establishment and increase their capability to maintain internal security and combat communist activity by providing arms, equipment, and training on a limited but continuing basis. And it should "give priority to requests for assistance in programs and projects which would isolate the PKI, drive it into positions of open opposition to the Indonesian government, thereby creating grounds for repressive measures politically justifiable in terms of Indonesian self-interest." This last precept "in fact was to remain the hallmark of American policy toward Indonesia for the next six years."[5]

Washington was able to cash in on this policy after the assassination of the army commander General Yani and five other high-ranking generals. The official version of what happened, set forth by General Suharto and Washington, was that the communist party attempted a coup that failed and that the massacre that followed was for the most part an irrational act of popular frenzy. A more likely explanation is that the right wing of the army encouraged the assassination of the six generals. The six generals represented the moderate wing of the army loyal to Sukarno, and the communist party foolishly decided to participate in the coup. This more likely explanation maintains that the right wing of the army planned and directed the massacre of the communist party and its sympathizers that followed the assassinations.[6] This more plausible version also includes the charge that the CIA carried on two disinformation campaigns before the assassinations, one intended to convince the communists of their imminent suppression by the army and the other to emphasize to the army the danger of a communist takeover. The campaigns included the planting of information and articles in publications, some of which were CIA assets. On the one hand, the plants indicated that General Yani and a mythical "Council of Generals" were plotting to suppress the communist party. On the other hand, they stressed the imminence of a communist coup and the purported smuggling of arms into the country by communist China to facilitate the communist takeover.

A Political Party Falls Victim to Massacres

The massacres that followed the attempted coup of October 1965 presented Washington with the much desired opportunity of witnessing the physical destruction of the Communist Party of Indonesia (PKI). Two days after the coup of October 1, U.S. Ambassador Marshall Green, in a communication to Secretary of State Rusk, defined the problem as whether the army had the "courage to go forward against PKI."[7] The ambassador repeated this statement, and this elicited no disagreement form the State Department. Two days afterward, the army started the killing. Green then expressed concern that the army under Suharto would not stand up to President Sukarno. He was not to be disappointed. On the same day, reports of the killings were sent to Washington. These reports continued as the tide of destruction continued to mount through October. Mainly rightwing youth and Muslim groups, with aid from the army, began systematic sweeps in the cities and the countryside. They killed indiscriminately—communists, peasants who had alienated their landlords, apolitical persons denounced by their neighbors, religious elements the Muslims did not like, and others. The attempt to kill all communists resembled genocide in that it was intended to eliminate an entire group. Terrorism was also committed, because victims and their sympathizers were intimidated, and were meant to be, by the deliberate slaughter that produced fear, panic, and horror. Insofar as it was propelled by the army, it was state terrorism. The communists and their allies were too weak to defend themselves, much less terrorize their enemies. Experts at the State Department knew that the PKI had neither the arms nor the will to resist.

Contrary to President Sukarno's appeals for calm and restraint, "the army leaders deliberately fostered a highly emotional atmosphere in which the dominant theme was the call for revenge."[8] The army charged that the generals had been mutilated, that their eyes had been gouged out, and their genitals cut off. Given Islam's respect for the dead, this added to the outrage of those who sought revenge. However, photographs of the generals' bodies indicated that the mutilation had not occurred. Over the next several months the army itself, or Muslim or nationalist groups encouraged by the army, killed hundreds of thousands of communists, their sympathizers, and those thought to be, or accused of being, their sympathizers. An estimated 300,000 to 400,000 were killed during a few months after the killing of the six generals. The communists and their sympathizers were easy prey. They were prepared for demonstrations—nonviolent political protest—not for combat. Some have estimated that up to a million and a half political deaths occurred over the period 1965-1970.[9] This massacre is one of three perpetrated by the Indonesian military and presented in this chapter.

The communists and their sympathizers were easy prey. They were prepared for demonstrations—nonviolent political protest—not for combat. Up to a million and a half political deaths occurred over the period 1965-1970.

The U.S. Embassy received reports of the army's support for the massacres, and was relieved to hear that the army had resisted Sukarno's efforts to stop the slaughter. On October 28 Green told Rusk the cleanup would go on. The next day Rusk cabled back affirming that the campaign against the PKI must continue and that the military was the "only force capable of creating order in Indonesia" which it had to continue to do "with or without Sukarno."[10] Bluntly put, the Secretary of State under President Johnson expressed his approval of the practice of state terrorism by the Indonesian army. He added that the generals could expect

United States help for a major military campaign against the PKI. Green reported to the department that the army was helping Muslim youth in Java to take care of the PKI, and the army was doing the job directly in the outer islands. He further advised that the army was heavily engaged, attacking the PKI ruthlessly and "wholesale killings" were occurring. "[We have] made it clear that Embassy and USG [the United States government] generally sympathetic and admiring of what army doing [*sic*]."[11] He also mentioned that the army was contemplating setting up a military state in the future. In early November the generals requested arms to be used by Muslim and nationalist youth groups in Central Java against the PKI. Most of them had been using knives and primitive means to accomplish their goals. Small arms and communications equipment would expedite the killing. The United States immediately offered such aid. The aid was to be covert, and it was given the code name "medicines."

> Careful study of all declassified U.S. documents that bear on the physical elimination of the PKI disclose no instance of any American official objecting to or in any way criticizing the 1965-1966 killings. When later asked to comment on this finding, William Colby, who at the time served as head of the Far Eastern Division of the CIA 's Directorate of Plans (and later as the agency's director), concurred, stating that he had never been aware of any such objection or criticism.[12]

In his study of American foreign policy Kolko concludes in effect that Washington was an accessory to the state terrorism in Indonesia. His exact words are the following:

> The 'final solution" to the Communist problem in Indonesia was certainly one of the most barbaric acts of inhumanity in a century that has seen a great deal of it; it surely ranks as a war crime of the same type as those the Nazis perpetrated. No single American action in the period after 1945 was as bloodthirsty as its role in Indonesia, for it tried to initiate the massacre, and it did everything in its power to encourage Suharto, including equipping his killers, to see that the physical liquidation of the PKI was carried through to its culmination. Not a single one of its officials in Washington or Djakarta questioned the policy on either ethical or political grounds; quite the contrary. 'The reversal of the Communist tide in the great country of Indonesia' was publicly celebrated, in the words of Deputy Undersecretary of State U. Alexis Johnson in October 1966 as 'an event that will probably rank along with the Vietnamese war as perhaps the most historic turning point of Asia in this decade.'[13]

In December 1965, the generals and American ambassador Green discussed what they wanted from each other. The generals asked bluntly, what was it worth to have the PKI smashed?[14] They asked for more aid, preferably through third countries. They did not accept the U.S. request for a change in policy toward Vietnam and Malaysia. Green asked for the total purge of Sukarno and those friendly to him. This was done, and the former nationalist hero was put under house arrest until his death. The United States used international consortia and international banks as levers to rewrite the country's basic economic legislation. So-called "technocrats" from Western business and academic institutions wrote the rules that were

The United States used international consortia and international banks as levers to rewrite the country's basic economic legislation.

to direct the national economy. Djakarta joined the International Monetary Fund and the World Bank. A new investment code made the country a haven for foreign investors, and U.S. investments and trade with the United States grew apace. Donald R. Keogh, the president of Coca Cola, captured the spirit of the American entrepreneur with the following statement: "When I think of Indonesia—a country on the equator with 180 million people, a median age of 18, and a Muslim ban on alcohol—I feel I know what heaven looks like."[15]

The euphoria experienced by the Johnson administration at achieving the mortal wounding of the PKI can be fully appreciated in light of the ethics and the activities of previous administrations, reaching back to that of Eisenhower. This brand of ethics was completely compatible with serving as the accomplice to state terrorism. In the instant case, the Indonesian army and its allies unleashed an organized campaign that killed the bulk of the Indonesian Communist Party and its sympathizers and sought to terrorize the remaining party members and sympathizers. This was state terrorism with shades of genocide. The PKI was in no position to defend itself, much less to launch a terror campaign of its own. So what happened in Indonesia at this time was state terrorism, not private terrorism. Washington served as an accomplice by providing arms and encouragement before and during the slaughter.

Welcoming the Suharto Regime

The October 1 coup d'état and its aftermath drastically changed the political landscape. The crushing of the communist party and its allies led to the assumption of power in 1966 by Suharto, the head of the army. President Sukarno was eased out of office in 1967, and the New Order was formally proclaimed the following year. Beginning in 1966 and extending for at least five years the United States and its closest allies met to refinance Indonesia's debt and to grant economic aid.[16] This was a period during which the slaughter of the communists continued. President Nixon visited Djakarta in July 1969. He exclaimed that under Suharto's leadership the Indonesian government had become truly democratic. This endorsement helped to legitimize and buttress Suharto's political position. The year after this, in May 1970, Suharto visited Washington. These visits did underline the friendship that existed between the two regimes, but the Indonesian dictator took the occasion of his visit to affirm the existence of differences of outlook between Washington and Djakarta with regard to various world problems. After Nixon's visit in 1969 United States' aid increased. After the ceasefire in Vietnam four years later, Washington supplied more airplanes and ships. The United States became effectively the sole supplier of military equipment to Indonesia. By 1976 this type aid rose to over $40 million annually.[17]

Dr. Kingsbury, the executive officer of the Monash Asia Institute, compared the Indonesian politics of the time to a Javanese shadow-puppet play. Fortunately, he also compared it to the more familiar Mafia movie which he admitted might be more appropriate. He made the latter comparison this way:

Stand-over tactics and corruption, protection rackets, violence, pride, the location of power in the person of the boss, rigged ballots, and the chicanery of naked power all feature in a good Mafia movie, and they are not alien concepts in Indonesian politics either. The main difference between the two, perhaps, is that the Mafia do not work on the scale on which the Indonesian government operates. [18]

The New Order became even more centralized around one man than in the predecessor regime. The "boss" was the head of the army. The elimination of the PKI and the "retirement" of Sukarno were the last steps in the army's rise to power. With their elimination, "the army's domination of government was unchallenged."[19]

Sukarno had permitted a modicum of civil liberties, and allowed political parties to operate more freely. He co-opted many of his political opponents. Suharto put them in jail. Although the massacres of late 1965 eliminated much of the leadership of the PKI, the army's security and intelligence network continued to search out and capture the remnants of the party's activists.[20] Arrests continued for years. The estimate is that 200,000 were held as prisoners in the last three months of 1965. It should be emphasized that this government repression and terror was not in response to the violence of the PKI and its sympathizers. They offered virtually no resistance. In July 1966 the attorney general, Major General Sugih Arto, said the number of civilians held in detention was 120,000. Those classified as having been part of the revolutionary movement were eventually brought before military courts that sentenced them to death or to long prison sentences. There was only one recognized labor union, and it was government controlled. An independent union was formed in the 1990's, but it soon suffered from government repression. Its head was arrested for "sedition" and sentenced to four years in prison. Criticism of government policy could be interpreted as "subversion," a crime that could result in the death penalty.[21] Although seldom applied, this had a deterrent effect.

Suharto reigned for over three decades until May 1998. His political demise occurred not long after he had been re-elected for his seventh consecutive term. His domination was trilateral, grounded internally on a tripod of the military, the political, and the economic. He was the supreme commander of the armed forces which had crushed its main political rival, the communist party and its allies. As head of the army, Suharto appointed the officers he trusted to crucial positions, while exiling those who opposed him to peripheral posts or to retirement. He rotated senior regional officers so that they would not gain the loyalty of their troops. He had effective control of Golkar which, although officially not a political party, acted like one. It controlled the bureaucracy, and could deliver a large number of votes. In 1973 Suharto abolished the plethora of existing political parties and established two official ones in their place. Both were deeply influenced by the government and by the army, and both were subject to numerous restrictions.[22] Neither party was allowed directly to criticize the government or its policies. Rallies could be held only with government permission, and neither party was allowed to campaign in villages.

Suharto himself was incredibly rich, as were his family and close business associates. He was located among the super rich. In 1989 the CIA estimated his wealth to be as much as twenty billion dollars.[23] Others put it between thirteen and sixteen billions. His family was worth about the same amount. The army participated in this system of "crony capitalism" as well. It is said that old soldiers in Indonesia neither die nor do they fade away. They go into business. The wealth generated by this combination of Suharto, his family, and the military in business has been of such magnitude that its activities impact the Indonesian economy as a whole. And of course foreign capital has been welcomed, and it has enthusiastically responded.

THE FIRST EAST TIMOR MASSACRES

An unannounced three-pronged attack against Dili, the capital of East Timor, took place on the morning of December 7, 1975. Indonesian ships bombarded the city, a maneuver followed by the landing of seaborne troops and the dropping of paratroops in and behind the outskirts of the city. This was an Indonesian mini-version of Pearl Harbor, 34 years later and not as successful. The Indonesian Foreign Minister Malik characterized the invasion force as "volunteers" intent upon bringing stability to East Timor. But the "volunteers" did not plan the operation well. The parachute drop was designed to seal off the city, so as to surround and destroy the Revolutionary Front for Independent Timor (Fretilin) troops, the East Timorese forces that were determined to fight for the independence of East Timor. Unfortunately for the paratroopers, they were dropped on top of the retreating Fretilin troops and paid a heavy price. The Fretilin forces escaped to harass the Indonesian occupying army in the years to come. But this was of little consolation to the civilians left behind to face a ravaging Indonesian army. "The soldiers who landed started killing everyone in sight. There were many dead bodies in the streets. All we could see is the soldiers killing, killing, killing." These were the words of former bishop Monsignor Martinho da Costa Lopez.[24]

This Indonesian act of aggression terminated a process of decolonization begun following the Portuguese coup d'état of April 25, 1974 in which the Armed Forces Movement finally put an end to a half century of rightwing dictatorship. Guerilla warfare in Africa had put a terrible drain on an impoverished Portugal, and the policy of the new government to free all its colonies looked as though it would favor East Timor as well. Several independence movements were formed in the colony, Fretilin emerging as the strongest and most popular. Indonesia tagged it as a communist organization. In early November 1974, Indonesia and Portugal met in Rome to consider the problem, but the followup talks between the Timorese parties and Portugal never materialized. On the twenty-fourth of that month, Fretilin called upon the United Nations to demand that Indonesian troops withdraw from the colony. Four days later it declared the independence of East Timor.

"The invasion took place one day after Secretary of State Kissinger and President Ford had visited Djakarta, suggesting official American acquiescence in, if not approval of the invasion."[25] The above quotation is from Robert Pringle, a U.S. Foreign Service political officer who was stationed in the United States embassy in Jakarta from 1970-1974. Allan Nairn of *The New Yorker* magazine had an opportunity to quiz both Ford and Kissinger about the visit. His first encounter was with Ford in 1991. His question was whether Ford had authorized the Indonesian invasion. Ford replied, "very honestly, I can't remember exactly that detail."[26] He went on to say that Timor was a "lower echelon priority" on the U.S.-Suharto agenda. More central was the fact that the " Indonesians were anxious for greater military help and assistance". Ford recalled that "we were very sympathetic to their request." Nairn used the occasion to question the former Secretary of State when he was promoting his book on diplomacy in New York in 1995. In answer to a question posed by Nairn's friend during a question and answer period, Kissinger replied "Timor was never discussed with us when we were in Indonesia."[27] Kissinger next modified his statement. After saying that no one asked "our opinion" about the matter, he added: "It was literally told to us as we were leaving. When the Indonesians informed us, we neither said 'yes' or 'no'. We were literally at the airport, so that was our connection with it." Nairn claimed that he was carrying documents with him that showed that the question of Timor was discussed at the December 6 meeting and that the United States had given a green light to the invasion. Nairn then challenged Kissinger, asking him if he would facilitate the declassification of the meeting's minutes and support the convening of a United Nations war crimes tribunal on East Timor and abide by its verdict with respect to his own conduct. Kissinger editorialized by way of reply. "This sort of comment is one of the reasons why the conduct of foreign policy is becoming nearly impossible under these conditions."

Pringle asserted that the initial response of Djakarta to the East Timor case was probably indefensible on legal grounds. "The Indonesians' use of American equipment (in the invasion) violated the terms of the extant military assistance agreement, and hence U.S. law."[28] Washington did subject military shipments to "administrative delay" from January to June 1976. However, this was done "with such exquisite tact that the Indonesians were never aware that they were being chastised, nor was the Congress, and in fact some arms shipments appear to have continued throughout the period of suspension."[29] Pringle continued with a comment that has special relevance, given President Carter's vocal commitment to human rights:

> The executive branch has not applied human rights criteria either to Mindanao or East Timor. Although there has been an involvement of "advisers," the United States has continued to provide both Indonesia and the Philippines with military grant assistance of a specially counterinsurgency nature (*e.g.* T-28 and OV-10 aircraft) which as of 1978 was being used in both conflicts. In both cases, the Carter administration has maintained a policy which assumes that the broader political benefits accruing to us from such relationships outweigh whatever human suffering may result, and that other weapons would be used if ours were not.

Jardine charged that following the invasion the Ford administration more than doubled its military assistance to Indonesia to $146 million.[30] The Carter administration authorized a huge increase in commercial arms sales to $112 million. This occurred in 1977 when it appeared that Indonesia seemed to be running short of military equipment. Again, the Carter administration's commitment to human rights is called into question, as it is below. Military

Following Indonesia's invasion of East Timor, the Ford administration more than doubled its military assistance to Indonesia to $146 million.

sales peaked during the Reagan years, exceeding $1 billion from 1982 to 1984, not an unusual development for that administration. Jardine adds that over 2,600 Indonesian officers received training in the United States after the invasion of East Timor under the International Military Education and Training Act. A Congressional Reference Service study concluded that "the United States appeared to accept the results [of the invasion of East Timor] with equanimity. Indeed, in the case of East Timor the U.S. public stance, as measured by its abstentions from voting on UN resolutions which reproved Indonesia in relatively mild terms, would seem to have been on the side of the government acquiring territory by force."

But in fact, on December 22, 1975 the Ford administration's delegate voted for a Security Council resolution that deplored the intervention of the armed forces of Indonesia in East Timor and called upon Djakarta to withdrew its forces from the territory.[31] The resolution passed unanimously. Portugal had brought the issue to the United Nations to obtain an immediate cessation of Indonesia's intervention. Lisbon also broke off diplomatic relations with Djakarta. On December 12, 1975 the General Assembly passed a resolution similar to that of the Security Council, 72 to 10 with 43 abstentions. The delegate of the Ford administration abstained on this resolution. It is difficult to account for the difference in voting on the two resolutions since the resolution of the General Assembly was slightly tougher, "strongly" deploring Indonesia's intervention, whereas the Security Council merely "deplored" it. The next year, the Security Council followed through with a resolution very similar to the one of the previous year. This time Washington's delegate (still from the Ford administration) abstained. He then voted against the General Assembly resolution of December 1, 1976, a resolution that passed 68 to 20 with 49 abstentions.[32] Two years later the American delegate repeated this performance for the Carter administration, voting against the General Assembly resolution of December 13, 1978, an instrument that passed 59 to 31 with 44 abstentions.[33] The resolution was very much like those of previous years.

On November 23, 1982 the American delegate, this time representing the Reagan administration, voted "no" on still another General Assembly resolution quite unlike its predecessors. It not only referred to previous resolutions and to the right of decolonization, but it expressed concern at the humanitarian situation existing in the territory. It called upon the United Nations agencies dealing with food, refugees, and children "immediately to assist, within their respective fields of competence, the people of East Timor, in close consultation with Portugal, as the administering power."[34] The resolution thus pointed to the fact that the United Nations never recognized Indonesia's conquest of East Timor, although on July 17, 1976 Suharto declared East Timor to be Indonesia's twenty-seventh province. In the view of the world institution, Portugal remained the administering power.

Moreover, the resolution recognized the terrible economic plight of the Timorese. In a note verbale addressed to the Secretary General of the United Nations six weeks before the resolution was passed, Indonesia objected to the impression created by his working paper on East Timor. The impression created, according to the note verbale, was that "the Territory was famine stricken, subjected to major military operations against civilians, and the scene of widespread human rights violations."[35] Inadvertently, the Indonesian communication gave an accurate, if incomplete, indication of the fate of East Timor in the aftermath of the invasion. The Indonesian army faced years of guerrilla warfare, very successfully fought, at least at first, by Fretilin with the support of the Timorese population.

The strategy of the Indonesian army was classical counterinsurgency doctrine: to cut off the guerrillas from the supporting civilian population and to destroy their food supply. Many Timorese villages were destroyed, and thousands of Timorese suspected of helping the guerrillas were killed. Beginning in 1977, the Indonesian army inaugurated an "encirclement" policy that resulted in the uprooting of much of the population and moving them into designated

In 1977, the Indonesian army inaugurated an "encirclement" policy that resulted in the uprooting of as much as half of the population and moving them into designated hamlets.

hamlets. In 1979 the U.S. Agency for International Development estimated that half of the population had been moved to these hamlets. Many of those uprooted were resettled in agriculturally poor areas. Food production plummeted, and famine spread. As the army advanced against Fretilin, civilians were pressed into service to be used as human shields. This tactic, called "a fence of legs," forced the guerrillas to choose between holding fire and thus giving the army an enormous advantage, or shooting the civilians.

> Catholic clergy, Timorese refugees, and foreign aid workers estimate that more than 100,000 Timorese died in military actions or from starvation and illness in the period 1976-1980. Some estimates run as high as 230,000 out of a pre-invasion population of some 650,000. Although Jakarta disputes the number of Timorese that have died, Mario Carrascalao [the Jakarta-appointed governor of the territory] describes the estimate of 100,000 dead as 'credible.'[36]

The Santa Cruz Massacre

After two years of fighting, Fretilin was weakened, but not defeated. The fuel for resistance by the populace, however, lay just below the surface, ready to be ignited by the proper provocation. Anti-integration demonstrations erupted at the visit of practically every high profile visitor, including the Pope and the Jakarta-based papal nuncio. A major eruption occurred on November 12, 1991. The story is best told by Allan Nairn, a journalist and an eyewitness, whose description of the "eruption" won him several awards. Upon arrival in East Timor, he was immediately struck by a sense of fear such as he had never seen before on assignment in some of the world's most repressive dictatorships. [37] He did not meet any Timorese who had not lost family or friends. When he called upon Bishop Carlos Ximenes Belo, he was greeted with the warning: "There is intelligence everywhere, so people feel afraid to speak. I don't know if I can talk to you." His reference was to the intelligence branch of the Indonesian army. Nairn learned that virtually all Timorese institutions, except the Catholic Church, had been crushed. Peasant leagues, student groups, and political parties had been banned. The bishop's mail and phone were cut off. He had smuggled out a letter to the Secretary General of the United Nations declaring that the Timorese were "dying as a people and as a nation." He asked the Secretary General to organize a referendum on Timor's future.

Nairn also visited Mario Carrascalao, the Governor of East Timor, who had been appointed to this position by Indonesia. He lived up to his reputation of being outspoken. He confirmed that army intelligence maintained a series of houses of torture, where it used razors, electric shock, and iron bars on its victims. One could be called in for any of a variety of reasons—discussing politics, meeting in an unauthorized assembly, expressing enmity toward the state, listening to foreign radio broadcasts, or because an informer suspected the victim of thinking prohibited thoughts. Carrascalao added that torture was not within his jurisdiction. "That's the army's job," he explained.

The Indonesian army's brand of torture was essentially the same as that already encountered in this volume in other locations. Matthew Jardine, also a journalist, however, discovered a variation from the common standard on a visit to the eastern end of the territory less than a year after Nairn left. He met a nun, whose identity he shielded by calling her "Sister Maria."[38] She told him the difficulty the nuns were having trying to get Rosa, a young student, to accept the Christian concept of forgiveness. The young girl explained by telling the story of her older brother. Some years before, Indonesian soldiers came to her house and took him away. They accused him of having ties to the guerrillas. Afraid to ask about his whereabouts, the family did not know if he was dead or alive. A month later, the soldiers returned with a bag. Inside it was her brother's head.

Nairn concluded that if the Indonesian army's occupation was totalitarian, it was also unsuccessful. This was evident in the aftermath of the news that a delegation from the United Nations and the Portuguese parliament would soon arrive in East Timor. The army responded by threatening to kill any demonstrators or anyone who tried to speak to the delegation. The army hunted down those who were organizing demonstrations, and some two dozen of those being pursued took sanctuary inside the Montael Church in Dili. The army raided the church, dragged out the would be demonstrators, and at point blank range shot one of them, Sebastiao Gomes, in the stomach. He bled to death on the steps of the church. The delegation's visit was cancelled, and the Timorese learned that there was no sanctuary for them.

An underground organization loosely tied to Fretilin planned a demonstration for November 12, the fourteenth day observance of the death of the slain Gomes.[39] Moreover, the United Nations Rapporteur on Torture was scheduled to arrive in Dili on November 11. It was thought that the army would not move against the demonstrators while the Rapporteur was in town. There would be a procession across town from the Montael Church to the Santa Cruz cemetery. At dawn November 12, the army and the police were already lined up all along the demonstration route. Army vehicles were going up and back, with officers speaking in their walkie-talkies. It was a full mobilization of the army. There was an overflow crowd at the memorial mass at the Montael Church. About a thousand joined in the march to the Santa Cruz cemetery to lay flowers on the grave of Sebastiao Gomes. As the procession proceeded, more joined from homes, schools, and offices. Nuns were at the front singing hymns. As the crowd marched through the city, many of the participants unfurled homemade bed sheet banners that, along with other messages, insisted that Indonesia leave East Timor or referred to the 200,000 Timorese killed by Indonesia. Nairn sensed that this sent an electric current through the crowd. He felt that East Timor would never be the same again.

He and his companion Amy Goodman, then from WBAI/Pacific Radio, were talking to an old man in the street when suddenly he looked up and shouted "the Gestapo." Nairn turned to see Indonesian soldiers, with their American made M-16 rifles at the ready, arriving in trucks to seal off the escape route. He turned again to see a long column of soldiers in brown uniforms marching along the same route by which they had come, thus completing the encircling maneuver. They were marching in columns 12 to 15 abreast, and they were also wielding M-16s.

It was then that Nairn and his fellow journalists resorted to their own version of a human shield tactic, but this version had a far different purpose than the one that inspired the Indonesian army when fighting the guerrillas. They decided to stand between the crowd and the advancing troops. Nairn reasoned that the troops would see that he and his companions were foreign journalists, and they would not do anything rash for fear of the negative publicity. But he was mistaken. The troops continued to advance. The crowd was surrounded. No warning shots were fired, no command to disperse was given. The troops marched a pace or two beyond the journalists, raised their rifles to their shoulders, and opened fire on the crowd. Nairn describes it this way:

> "Though I knew the history of repression in East Timor and had dealt, after the fact, with many massacres in Guatemala and El Salvador, I couldn't quite believe in human terms that they were going through with this. I thought at first that the soldiers must be firing blanks. But then I saw people buckling and the blood spilling on the road. They were torn apart by the M-16s. The people we'd been talking to were dying all around us. The street was carpeted with bodies and growing slick with blood.
>
> The soldiers were firing and charging in unison. They leaped over fallen bodies. They aimed and picked off people in the back." [40]

Seconds after they started firing, the soldiers grabbed Nairn and his companion Amy Goodman and began to beat them. They confiscated their cameras and tape recorders. They fractured Nairn's skull with the butts of their M-16s, and they wrestled them to the ground. Seven or eight soldiers crowded around the reporters and pointed their rifles at their heads, all the time shouting "Politik, Politik". Nairn and Amy shouted back "American, American." When the soldiers realized that the reporters were Americans, they let them go. They left East Timor that afternoon.

There were seven foreigners present at the cemetery when the shooting started, and the six that survived immediately departed Dili and brought the news of the "Santa Cruz massacre" to international news organizations. A student from New Zealand was killed. An English cameraman smuggled out a videotape of the procession that contradicted the official Indonesian version of what had happened. The very next day the European Community strongly condemned the Indonesian government.[41] Within weeks Holland, Canada, and Denmark suspended aid programs. The Secretary General of the United Nations, Boutros Boutros-Ghali, visited East Timor in 1992 and asserted that the shootings by the soldiers were unprovoked, unnecessary and in utter disregard of the right to life. In June 1992 the United States House of Representatives voted to cut off military training funds to Indonesia. In March of the following year the United Nations Human Rights Commission censured Indonesia for its human rights violations in the territory. "Surprisingly, support for the resolution came from the United States. The newly installed Clinton administration, however, voted for the censure resolution and its example was followed by 21 other countries."[42]

The "Santa Cruz massacre" put East Timor back on the world's agenda. It also induced Djakarta to modify its policy in the occupied territory. It stiffened it in some directions and loosened it in others. It reduced the size of the army occupation forces. The public relations value of this was compromised, however, when the local military commander organized ceremonies in which thousands of youths were required to swear their loyalty to Indonesia by drinking the blood of chickens and goats.[43] It replaced Governor Carrascalao with a hardliner, and rounded up a group of suspected guerrilla sympathizers in Dili and "relocated" them in the interior. In 1996 Bishop Carlos Belo and Timorese resistance spokesperson Jose Ramos-Horta received the Nobel Prize for Peace. Djakarta was furious. It refused to attend the ceremonies. Because of its continued violations of human rights in East Timor, Washington vetoed the sale of F-5 jets to Djakarta. "Even so, it would be a mistake to exaggerate the impact of criticism from Washington. US trade to and investment in Indonesia helped Suharto much more than the occasional barb from Washington hurt him."[44]

Some Conclusions

Before leaving this section, I answer the central questions posed by the study. Yes, terror was committed in East Timor after the Indonesian invasion of December 7, 1975. The Indonesian army launched an organized campaign against the civilian population of deliberate acts of a physical and psychological nature designed to intimidate and coerce their victims by killing victims or other acts that caused intense fear, anxiety, apprehension, panic, dread, and horror. No estimate of the terrorism committed by the guerrillas is available, but it seems certain that whatever it was it did not compare with that inflicted by the Indonesian army. This state terrorism of this army was supported by at least three administrations in Washington—those of Ford, Carter, and Reagan. When the training and equipping of the Indonesian army is counted, previous administrations are accessories before the fact as well. Notable among the accessories is the Carter administration, which both sold Jakarta arms when they were needed and provided diplomatic support at the United Nations.

THE SECOND EAST TIMOR MASSACRES

Succumbing to pressure from the United States, on August 8, 1999 Indonesia held a referendum to determine if East Timor should remain a part of the country or should become independent. The United Nations helped monitor the referendum. Reportedly, 99 percent of the electorate turned out, and 78.5 percent voted for independence. The Timorese paid a heavy price for this act of defiance. The slaughter preceded the referendum of August 8, but it escalated dramatically after the vote. The killing fields were ploughed principally by militias recruited by the Indonesian army.[45] A spokesperson for the Secretary General of the United Nations estimated that nearly a quarter of the population was driven from their homes in four days.[46] This was not a spontaneous, merely emotional frenzy, but a planned, organized effort. The plan included as targets foreign journalists, United Nations personnel, and the local Catholic clergy including Bishop Carlos Belo. The United Nations personnel had acted as election observers, and they came under fire as they were fleeing to the airport. The bishop's residence was burned down—the bishop fled to Australia. Amnesty International estimated in September 1999 that since the 1975 Indonesian invasion of East Timor, 200,000 East Timorese had been killed by the Indonesian military or fallen victim to starvation and disease—a human tragedy that it characterized as one that "defies belief."[47] Moreover, this organization accused the United States government of having given a green light for the 1975 invasion and for having followed this with more than one billion dollars worth of weaponry and millions more in aid and training.

There is an obvious parallel between the crimes committed by the Indonesian army in East Timor and those committed earlier by the Serbs in Kosovo. In the words of a *New York Times* article, however, Washington moved "gently" in East Timor, avoiding the threat of sanctions.[48] Clinton's National Security Adviser Sandy Berger commented: "Because we bombed in Kosovo does not mean that we should bomb Dili." In fact Washington left at least its early negotiations with Djakarta to the Defense Department, because of the latter's longstanding comfortable relations with the Indonesian Army. On September 6,1999 the United Nations sent a team to negotiate with Indonesia to see if that country would accept a peacekeeping force for East Timor. Portugal's representative to the world organization complained that these discussions should have started weeks before.[49] His comments are the more pertinent since he helped negotiate the agreement to hold the plebiscite on independence. He asserted that the Security Council did nothing—its members offering various excuses. Portugal was the first to ask for a peacekeeping force, but it was only two or three days after Britain had been persuaded that such a force was necessary that the momentum changed in favor of such a force. By this time (September 6, 1999) Secretary of State Albright had accepted the idea, but only if violence continued and only if Indonesia gave its consent.[50] She had finally recovered from the myopia for which by then Washington was so famous. The Secretary General later complained that the Security Council waited for an Indonesian invitation and that it did not take preventive action despite reports reaching the world body and government capitals about the threats from the militias.

The United Nations Commissioner for Human Rights Mary Robinson accused the Indonesian army of being directly behind the militias that terrorized the people of East Timor. She advocated the creation of an international force to stop the "deliberate policy of terror and displacement of the population of East Timor."[51] She later negotiated an agreement with the Indonesian Prime Minister for an investigation of military abuses in East Timor that she said might lead to war crimes trials. This led James Fox, an expert at the Australian National University, to observe that this was "really scary" for the military, because for the first time ever the Indonesian military might be held accountable for its deeds.[52] The International Red Cross, whose personnel were present in East Timor, asserted that there were no safe places left in the territory. The Vatican's Foreign Minister Archbishop Jean-Louis Tauran declared: "We are facing another genocide, a genocide that does not spare the Catholic Church."[53] The Catholic Church argued that its institutions had been singled out for attack by the militias. There were reports of nuns being killed and of the wounding of the Bishop of Baucau. East Timor is the only Christian province in Indonesia. Bishop Carlos Belo, the local Catholic leader and the co-winner of the 1996 Nobel Prize for Peace, called for the creation of a war crimes tribunal to bring charges against Indonesian military commanders and militia leaders.[54] He put the death toll in the thousands, perhaps 10,000, and he asserted that as he spoke the killings continued both in East Timor and West Timor. He charged that the Indonesian military commander General Wiranto had been directing the violence in East Timor.[55] He proposed the establishment of a United Nations war crimes tribunal similar to those already established for the Balkans and Rwanda. Of course, this was not done. On December 27, 2002 the Indonesian officer formerly in charge of Dili received a five year sentence for crimes against humanity.[56] This was the first army officer to be convicted for the crimes committed in East Timor in 1999, and it occurred after ten military and police officials had been acquitted. Human rights groups dismissed the conviction as tokenism.

The United Nations envisaged a peacekeeping force of from seven to eight thousand. It put an Australian general at its head, and the troops came mostly from Australia and nearby countries. Washington's insistence persuaded Jakarta to accept the force, and it was public relations that changed Washington from an opponent to an advocate of the force.[57] Washington warned that it would block aid from the International Monetary Fund if Indonesia did not acquiesce. Washington did cut off military aid. When the first peacekeepers arrived in Dili on September 20, 1999, they found the city to be looted, burned, evacuated, dead. The terror that had begun some two weeks before when the government announced the results of the plebiscite had taken its toll.[58] Actually, the formation of the peacekeeping force was the second step in the plan agreed upon by Indonesia, Portugal, and the United Nations. The first step had been the supervision of the plebiscite on August 8. The third step was the transfer of the administrative and security measures of East Timor to the United Nations and after that to the East Timorese. The Secretary General estimated that this third stage might require two or three years, for East Timor had become an empty shell completely ravaged by the militias.[59] The civil administration was no longer functioning, the judiciary and court systems no longer existed, and such vital services as water and electricity were in real danger of collapse. The three-step plan was based on the assumption that East Timor would not be reduced by the Indonesian militia to an empty shell and that United Nations governance would be brief and inexpensive. However, Portugal's warning had not been heeded and East Timor had been reduced to an empty shell. Estimates of the cost of administering it ran as high as one billion dollars.

U.S. military aid was sharply curtailed in the early 1990's and terminated in 1999.[60] Under a law authored by Senator Leahy, such aid was not to be resumed until the military officers thought to be responsible for the slaughter in East Timor were brought to justice. Although the trial of only a few mid-level military officers was held, military aid to Indonesia resumed. In March 2002 the Bush administration sent proposals to Congress to help train Indonesian police in counterterrorism.[61] Some five months later on August 2, Secretary of State Powell announced that the Bush administration would resume direct military aid to Indonesia. Although Suharto no longer runs the country, his successors have shown little regard for human rights. The reader will notice that those who are waging the war on terrorism are following in the footsteps of their Cold War predecessors. Powell said that the administration planned to provide some $50 million over a two-year period for counterterrorism programs. Virtually all of the funds were appropriated, and most of it is for police and civilian training. Human rights groups promptly criticized this resumption of aid. The director of the Indonesian Legal Aid and Human Rights Association said that Indonesia will use this to justify its past repression. The administration skirted the Congressional ban on providing military aid to Indonesia by taking the money from the Pentagon's funds, not from the State Department's foreign operations account. But there is growing support in Congress for aid to Indonesia. The month before Powell's announcement, the Senate Appropriations Committee set aside $400,000 for Indonesian military aid for the coming fiscal year. The Indonesian army has been accused of serious human rights abuses in its attempts to counter the secessionist guerrillas in Aceh, a province of Indonesia. President Megawati re-enforced the army in the province, and she advised the army to uphold the law, but not to worry about human rights issues.[62] "You can do your duty without worrying about being involved in human rights issues."

CONCLUSION

I answer for this section the three central questions posed in this study by emphasizing what has been said above: that terror was committed in East Timor after the holding of the referendum in August 1999 and that it was committed by the militias supported by the Indonesian army. The Secretary General of the United Nations found that East Timor had become an empty shell completely ravaged by the militias. When the first peacekeepers on September 20, 1999 arrived in Dili, the capital of the unfortunate country, they found the city to be dead. As noted above, Amnesty International estimated in September 1999 that since the 1975 Indonesian invasion of East Timor, 200,000 East Timorese had been killed by the Indonesian military or fallen victim to starvation and disease. It described the situation in East Timor as a human tragedy that "defies belief." This was, indeed, wholesale terrorism and it assumed an anti-Catholic and anti-Protestant bias. The Vatican's Foreign Minister spoke of "genocide" that did "not spare the Catholic Church." Bishop Carlos Belo called for the creation of a war crimes tribunal to bring charges against Indonesian military commanders and militia leaders.

But the Clinton administration would have none of this. It seemed not to hear. It moved "gently" in the face of terrorism in East Timor, avoiding until the last minute the threat of sanctions. Clinton's National Security Adviser Sandy Berger commented: "Because we bombed in Kosovo does not mean that we should bomb Dili." In fact, Washington left at least its early negotiations with Djakarta to the Defense Department because of the latter's longstanding comfortable relations with the Indonesian Army. Washington was reluctant to authorize the formation of a United Nations peacekeeping force there, despite the many warnings voiced by the Portuguese ambassador to the world body. The force arrived much too late to prevent the slaughter. Washington's consent to establish the force came late, and it was contingent upon the previous consent of Djakarta. This adds up to diplomatic support. Moreover, Amnesty International found that Washington approved of the 1975 invasion and after that it provided more than one billion in weaponry and millions more in aid and training. The evidence provided here leads to the conclusion in the instant case that Washington was an accessory to state terrorism before, during, and after the fact.

This chapter answered for Indonesia the three central questions posed in the study in the same way that they were answered in the five preceding chapters for El Salvador, Guatemala, Chile, Argentina, and South Africa. Each of the six case studies found Washington acting as an accessory to state terrorism during the Cold War.

CHAPTER 7

The Root Doctrine
and Some Notorious Instances
of U.S. Support for Dictators

The purpose of the present chapter is to broaden the scope of the study both chronologically and geographically to enhance its validity by including more instances of administration support for rightwing dictatorships--and even state terrorists on the left, as the varying needs of U.S. interests abroad required. This support can be traced back to 1922 when the Root doctrine which rationalized this support was formulated, and the historical record amply demonstrates that since then virtually every administration has been faithful to it. The primary force driving American policy has been and remains—as the following chapters related to the war on terrorism demonstrate—the protection of U.S. economic interests, irrespective of the undemocratic nature or human rights record of the groups and governments with whom it has allied.

THE ROOT DOCTRINE

Schmitz makes it clear in his book *Thank God They're on Our Side: the United States and Right-Wing Dictatorships 1921-1965*[1] that Washington's support for rightwing dictators during the Cold War was a continuation, an elongation and an intensification of a policy developed during the early part of the century. That policy placed the fear of communism, socialism, and the spread of disorder as the centerpiece of its formulation. The Cold War demanded new and expanded tactics, approaches, and procedures, "but the ideological basis and fundamental assumptions remained remarkably consistent."[2] By casting the hegemon in the role of the supporter of rightwing dictators, Schmitz contradicts the traditional "triumphalist" interpretation of the way Washington waged and won the Cold War: that victory came to the United States because its governments followed a policy of containment as well as a steadfast adherence to the promotion of democracy and liberalism. Concentrating on the period since 1921, Schmitz argues that since that date authoritarian regimes that have promised stability, anti-communism, and investment and trade opportunities for American business have received American support. While critics argue that this behavior violates the stated ideals of the country, the leadership often embraces it because, so it reasons, business is business. Or, stated differently, politics is power politics; morals are secondary, if they apply at all.

The overarching rationale for accepting and sustaining rightwing dictatorships was written in 1922 by Elihu Root. A Nobel prize winner and senior policy spokesman for the Republican Party, he described the "right of self-protection" in a presidential address to an audience at the American Society of

International Law. The former U.S. secretary of state proclaimed the sovereign right of a state to take early action to "prevent a condition of affairs in which it will be too late to protect itself."[3] Root justified support for right-wing dictatorships with the argument that the populace in the victim country was incapable of democratic rule. They hadn't learned the knack of it. But no matter: the Italians had undertaken to govern themselves without having learned the knack of it, Root averred, singling Mussolini out for praise as the man of the hour, under whose dictatorship Italy had experienced a revival of prosperity, contentment, and happiness.[4]

The Root Doctrine proclaimed the sovereign right of a state to take early action to "prevent a condition of affairs in which it will be too late to protect itself."

While this might be projected as the Republican reaction to Wilsonian idealism, Wilsonian idealism remains open to question, at least in Wilson's dealings with Latin America, where he invaded no less than four countries in the region—Mexico, Haiti, Cuba, and the Dominican Republic—at the behest of American interests. In fact, it seems reasonable to presume that the Root Doctrine has been operational throughout United States history, both long before its articulation and to this very day.[5] Prior to the Spanish American War, the United States carried out 103 interventions; between the end of that war and the Great Depression, it sent troops to Latin America 32 times.[6] In any case, the Root Doctrine would soon become bipartisan, and it was touted as being more cost-effective than invasions.

The Good Neighbor policy of Franklin D. Roosevelt was entirely compatible with the Root doctrine. It simply required that Washington substitute support of local dictators for its previous policy of invasions and occupations, the latter being the ultimate forms of interference forbidden by the new policy. Keylor ascribes the adoption of this new policy to Washington's embarrassment at the obvious similarity between its previous invasions and occupations of Latin America and the then current aggression of Japan in China.[7] The parallel was too obvious, and compelled the implementation of a new way to maintain hegemony in the hemisphere.

The new policy was initiated by the Hoover administration, and taken up and "completed" during the succeeding Roosevelt administration. By 1934 all American troops had been withdrawn from Latin America, except for those at the military and naval bases maintained in Panama and in Guantanamo Bay in Cuba. The financial supervision of Haiti, the Dominican Republic, and Nicaragua was phased out between 1936 and 1940. Washington relinquished, at least on paper, its right to intervene. For direct forms of dominance, it substituted indirect ones, reminiscent of but less formal than those employed in British indirect rule in Africa. Central to this new scheme was support—economic, military and diplomatic—for local autocrats—for their currencies, their national constabularies, and their personal greed. In return, these autocrats suppressed local communists and radicals,

No need to invade to change unwanted regimes. Better to support the local military that would make the changes for you.

protected American business, and performed other favors when called upon to do so. The good neighbor policy and the Root doctrine not only accomplished the same essential goals, but the latter was generally more cost effective and presented a smoother surface. No need to invade to change unwanted regimes. Better to support the local military that would make the changes for you.

The facility with which President Roosevelt made such deals in Latin America was once again enhanced by the widely held belief that the people there were inferior. While serving as the assistant secretary of the navy, he used this type of argument to justify the invasion of Mexico. This intervention would serve to civilize "backward people."[8] He characterized Haitians as "little more than primitive savages," *i.e.*, before the arrival of the United States invasion forces. He was capable of supporting European fascism as well. In fact, he developed his policies toward other rightwing regimes on that continent based upon the apparent success of his approach to Fascist Italy. His approach to Hitler is too complicated to describe here. Suffice it to say that he, along with the leaders of France and Britain, was often an appeaser, who believed that the real threat came from the Soviet Union.

World War II marked a significant deviation in policy insofar as President Roosevelt saw fit to join with the Soviet Union to defeat the Axis powers. By 1948, however, events in the world and rumbling in the State Department brought Washington's policy back to its moorings in the Root Doctrine. In any case, the cleavage that separated the Truman from the Roosevelt administration can be overdrawn as the Roosevelt regime did support some dictators. In February of the previous year Secretary of State Acheson explained to Congress that the civil war in Greece was like one rotten apple in a barrel of apples. If Greece should fall to communism, the infection (his metaphor switched from fruit to bacteriology) would spread to the Middle East, Africa, and to Europe. The same theory was later applied to Vietnam, and relabeled the "domino theory." Only the United States could prevent this from happening. The next month President Truman announced the doctrine that bears his name. He found the world divided between incompatible ways of life: the free world and totalitarian communism. The Truman administration felt free to put rightwing anti-communist dictatorships in the free world camp.[9] But the tie to European fascism remained. In 1952 the Truman administration provided Export-Import credits to the Franco regime, though it was left to Eisenhower, his successor, to conclude a formal alliance with the dictator.

In 1948 when the military overthrew the democratically elected governments in Peru and Venezuela, Washington recognized both resultant dictatorships. In 1952 both Trujillo (Dominican Republic) and Somoza (Nicaragua) were hosted at the White House. Both were dictators whom, five years earlier, had been pressured into making reforms and holding elections. Nonetheless, State Department papers charged that the latter ruled through "repression and trickery" while Trujillo was characterized as a "ruthless and unprincipled dictator."

Again, the role of racism in facilitating negative human rights outputs in U.S. policy decisions cannot be ignored. Internal documents of the time reveal that the Truman administration maintained the tradition of basing policy on racism and ethnic stereotypes. Truman himself clung to the racism of his youth, and in private, he used the word "nigger".[10] He found Latin Americans to be "like Jews and the Irish," very emotional and difficult to handle. His Secretary of State Dean Acheson believed that the problems in Latin America stemmed from Hispano-Indian culture—or the lack of it. State Department records of the time are riddled with similar ethnic jabs. An example: to try to reason with Latin Americans is "like consulting with babies as to whether or not we should take candy from them."

The role of racism in facilitating negative human rights outputs in U.S. policy decisions cannot be ignored.

Kolko argues that General Eisenhower inaugurated "the era of the generals" in the realm of policy. Eisenhower preferred generals and helped them to take over because they preserved traditional values (a phrase which largely, as we have seen, serves as a euphemism for elite dominance) and brought order to situations plagued with disorder and the threat of social change. His administration also relied more heavily upon the CIA than previous administrations in the conduct of foreign policy.[11] The agency did not concentrate its efforts on collecting data to the neglect of subversive activities. Its size and the scope of its activities increased dramatically in the fifties. Despite the new reluctance towards invasion, the Eisenhower administration demonstrated an ongoing penchant for military interventions in preservation of US interests evidenced by forays into Burma, Cambodia, Indonesia, Laos, Vietnam, and the Philippines. During this administration the CIA formulated the plots that overturned the regimes in Guatemala and Iran and supported the rightwing dictatorships that took their place. With credentials like these, the Eisenhower administration demonstrated its allegiance to the Root doctrine.

The cases of Nicaragua and the Congo provide particularly noteworthy evidence of Washington's attachment to the Root Doctrine. These countries were chosen because in both instances many administrations followed the same policy, thus adding to the contention of this study that human rights compunctions had little impact upon the generation of policy for either Republican or Democratic administrations. The Khmer Rouge were leftwing terrorist fanatics who killed between one half and a million and a half of their fellow Cambodians, but their alliance was rather with China than the Soviet Union. Their story is included to show the extent of ideological stretch Washington was willing to encompass in its effort to defeat the Soviet Union. It was also chosen because the administration of President Carter, the primary American administration to be widely known for its verbal dedication to human rights, gave support to these genocidal terrorists.

NICARAGUA, THE SOMOZAS, AND THE SANDANISTAS: FROM COOLIDGE TO BUSH, SR.

A revolt in 1912 induced the president of Nicaragua, Adolfo Diaz, to request military aid from Washington to maintain order. The marines were sent, and they remained until 1925. When they withdrew, however, another revolt occurred, and the marines returned the next year. It was during this occupation that the Coolidge administration insisted on the establishment of a Nicaraguan national guard to be trained by the marines. It handpicked Anastacio Somoza as the commander of the guard, which in turn facilitated his accession to political power. A former latrine inspector, Somoza spoke fluent English, and he impressed Colonel **The Coolidge administration handpicked Anastacio Somoza, a former latrine inspector who spoke fluent English.** Stimson, a former secretary of war, who had been sent to Managua to find a solution to the Nicaraguan problem. President Hoover withdrew the marines from Nicaragua in 1933. Because the dictatorship of Somoza provided stability in the Central American country and protected Washington's interests, they were no longer needed. Eleven administrations followed the example of Coolidge by honoring the Root Doctrine in Nicaragua.

The elder Somoza and his two sons, Luis and Anastacio, Jr., used the national guard as the vehicle to maintain their reign until the last Somoza (Anastacio) was forced to resign in 1979. Washington was aware of the corruption of, and the repression practiced by, the Somozas. In 1939 Somoza was invited to visit Washington, where he had an audience with President Roosevelt and was given the honor of speaking to a joint session of Congress. U.S. military and economic assistance to Nicaragua increased steadily between 1945 and 1975, even as Somoza's sons refined and expanded the repression and corruption that had characterized their father's rule.[12] The Somozas reciprocated, with Nicaragua assuming the role of client state by providing a training ground and a launching pad for the intervention in Guatemala in 1954 and the invasion of Cuba in 1961.

When a devastating earthquake hit the country in 1972, Somoza reacted by siphoning off much of the relief money for himself and his cronies. On June 28, 1979 the United States Ambassador Lawrence Pezzullo cabled Washington that he had met with Somoza and suggested that "we" design a scenario for his resignation.[13] Having put the elder Somoza on the throne, Washington took his son off it 46 years later. On July 17 of the next month Anastacio, Jr. left for exile in Miami. He was compelled to step down as part of a scheme of the Carter administration to form a provisional government of moderate leaders to prevent the Sandanistas from coming to power. The Sandanistas were to be excluded from the coalition, and the national guard was to be preserved. Finally the Organization of American States was asked to form a peacekeeping force with the United States at its head to provide the muscle for the transitional period. A large majority of Latin American states, however, rejected this proposal. The scheme fell through, the national guard disintegrated, and Sandanistan troops marched into Managua unopposed.

The Reagan administration waged a low intensity war against the Sandanistas with the avowed purpose of driving them from power. This type of warfare is many sided, and it has been called total war at the grassroots level. The CIA was ordered to organize the Contras, a guerrilla force that consisted of former national guard officers and disaffected civilians. A liaison officer from the National Security Council serving with them characterized their leaders as liars motivated by greed and the desire for power, and charged that the war had become a business for them.[14] They attacked bridges, electric generators, but also state-owned agricultural cooperatives, rural health clinics, villages, and non-combatants. CIA commandos launched a series of sabotage raids on Nicaraguan port facilities. They mined the country's major ports and set fire to its largest oil storage depot.

Washington imposed a complete trade embargo on the Central American country, pressed allies to do the same, and used its influence in intergovernmental agencies to cut off all aid. It built up its military forces in neighboring Honduras and conducted joint war games near its border with Nicaragua to create the fear of invasion. It instituted an economic de-stabilization program, as well as a propaganda war directed at Nicaragua, but also at the Western allies and (illegally) at the United States itself. According to the General Accounting Office, the propaganda campaign extended to the point of engaging in prohibited, covert propaganda activities designed to influence the American media and the American public to support the Administration's Latin American policies.[15]

Washington engaged in prohibited, covert propaganda activities designed to influence the American media and the American public to support the Administration's Latin American policies.

In 1984, Congress cut off aid to the Contras, at least it thought so. But the Reagan administration resorted to illegal means to aid them. Thus the notorious Iran/Contra scandal, a caper not elucidated here. However, rather than the disclosure of the illegal aid leading to a stricter prevention of U.S. interference in Nicaragua, in 1986 Congress appropriated $100 million in lethal and non-lethal aid for the contras and lifted all restrictions on the participation of the CIA and the Defense Department in the paramilitary war.

On April 9, 1984 Nicaragua filed an application before the International Court of Justice, charging that in dealing with the Central American state, Washington had violated general and customary international law as well as the terms of several bilateral treaties. The application asserted that the United States had the duty to cease the use of force and to pay for the damages that had resulted from its illegal activities. It asked the court for immediate relief by specifying provisional measures to prevent further damages. A month later the court did so by directing "the United States to respect the sovereignty and the political independence of Nicaragua and to cease action affecting Nicaraguan ports, in particular the laying of mines."[16] Using a series of technical arguments and seemingly extraneous ones, a representative of the United States government responded by denying that the court had jurisdiction. The court rejected these arguments one by one, and held by a unanimous vote that it had jurisdiction. In a letter dated January 18, 1985 Washington informed the court that it would not participate in any further proceedings in connection with the case.

The court proceeded without a representative of the United States government present and on June 26,1986 rendered its verdict, a judgment in favor of Nicaragua. Washington was found guilty on several counts: illegally arming,equipping,financing, encouraging, and supporting the Contras; attacking several Nicaraguan cities and a naval base; directing over flights of its territory; laying mines in its territorial and internal waters; and declaring a general embargo on trade with it.[17] The court determined that all but the last type of activity violated customary international law. The latter two actions contravened the Treaty of Friendship, Commerce, and Navigation concluded between the two countries in 1956. The court affirmed that the United States was responsible for the damages generated by its illegal behavior and that the court would determine them, failing mutual agreement between the parties. When the Chamorro government replaced the Sandanistas at the polls in war-weary Nicaragua, the payment of damages became a moot question.

Washington refused to abide by the 1984 or the 1986 judgment of the court. On July 31, 1986 the Security Council voted on a draft that called for compliance with the latter judgment. Eleven members voted in the affirmative and three abstained, but the draft was rendered null and void by the U.S. veto. On November 3 of the same year, the General Assembly, where there is no veto, considered a similar resolution. It was accepted by a vote of 94 to three with 47 abstentions.[18] The three negative votes were those of Israel, El Salvador, and the United States.

The administration of the elder Bush employed a softer, more delicate, but time tested, approach to the Nicaraguan problem. It organized the electoral opposition to the Sandanistas and fashioned a campaign strategy for its presidential candidate, Violeta Chamorro. The CIA funneled money to former contra leaders, and the Congress openly authorized nine million dollars to aid her campaign as the opposition candidate. She started her campaign in Miami, and went on to win the election. The Sandanistas stepped down. A peaceful transition like this, without benefit of a coup d'état, is a rare phenomenon in Nicaraguan history. Whatever leftist or communist leanings the Sandanistas may have had, they in no way impaired their demonstrably greater commitment to democracy.

THE CONGO: FROM KENNEDY TO BUSH, SR.

Immediately upon independence in 1960, the Congo was beset by a struggle for power between President Lumumba, supported by the Soviet Union, and Prime Minister Kasavubu, supported by Washington. The CIA characterized Lumumba as another Castro. However, Mobutu, the head of the Force Publique (a combination army and national police) ultimately won the power struggle and ruled the country with help from Washington for 32 years. The Senate Intelligence Committee concluded that the evidence permitted a reasonable inference "that a plot to assassinate Lumumba was authorized by President Eisenhower."[19] The CIA had one of its science advisers, Sidney Gottlieb, assemble an assassination kit that the agency sent to Leopoldville by diplomatic pouch. The kit included a poison that produced symptoms similar to an indigenous African disease. Gottlieb was sent to explain to the local CIA station chief that the poison had to be put in Lumumba's food or on his toothbrush. Neither was done, and it is not known for sure who killed him. There are many versions of how it happened and who did it. Each version exonerates the narrator.[20]

Early in his career while in the Force Publique, Mobutu was an informant for the Belgians. Later, he became one for the CIA. After independence, he consolidated his power position through his control of units of the army loyal to him. Washington trained, armed, and paid these units. At the Security Council, UN Secretary General Dag Hammarskjold asked how Mobutu could come to power without outside financial and technical assistance? Dayal, who later became the civilian head of the United Nations peacekeeping force in the Congo, reported that United Nations military personnel had seen Western military attaches regularly visit Mobutu. They carried with them bulging brief cases containing thick brown packets, whose contents could only be guessed.[21] Mobutu visited President Kennedy in a successful bid for military aid, a visit that initiated a tradition that lasted for 26 years. The president complimented Mobutu: if it had not been for "you, general," the whole thing would have fallen apart, and the communists would have taken over.[22] Civil rights groups, and sometimes Congress objected, and the Carter Administration had second thoughts about the relationship, though it made no significant effort to change its terms. Between his first visit and his last with Bush in 1989, Washington supported the dictator, both Republican and Democratic administrations, over a period extending more than thirty years.

Mobutu took over in a coup d'état that "neutralized" the two chief contestants for power, Lumumba and Kasavubu. He closed down the parliament, and established in its place "a College of Commissioners." This was a group of students chosen from those who had studied abroad. Mobutu also closed the Soviet and Czechoslovak embassies. The CIA regarded Mobutu as an asset, and the agency certainly was an asset for him. Several times it provided him with crucial information that helped to extend his tenure as dictator. Israel was again involved. It trained Mobutu's own presidential guard.[23] After taking over the government, Mobutu no longer depended upon the fees paid him as an informant. He amassed a personal fortune from local sources estimated at between three and five billion dollars. *Fortune Magazine*'s regular list of "the world's richest people" in 1987 included businessmen, kings, queens, and sultans, but not that of Mobutu. His name was reserved for the list "The Wealth That Leaves No Tracks." This list is set aside for members of the Mafia, cocaine smugglers, and several foreign leaders.[24] The magazine estimated Mobutu's wealth at five billion dollars. The relationship between Washington and Mobutu began to sour after the African dictator's visit to President Bush in 1989. By the time of Kabile's revolt in October 1996, only France stood behind him, a distance behind him.

At the capital, Mobutu stayed on his yacht so much of the time that the public nicknamed him "Noah."[25] His whereabouts became harder to predict, especially at night. It was then that his yacht sailed up the Congo River, and his helicopter took off. It was not possible to determine if he was aboard the yacht or the helicopter. That way potential assassins and plotters had a harder time determining his location. These precautions proved to be successful. He died of prostrate cancer.

THE KHMER ROUGE: FROM CARTER TO BUSH, SR.

The Khmer Rouge came to power in Cambodia in 1975 following the disarray resulting from the secret illegal U.S. bombing of the country, and were removed from power by an invasion from Vietnam in 1979. During their reign, they slaughtered anywhere from one half million to a million and a half of their fellow citizens and were accused of committing genocide. They cut the country off from the outside world, emptied the capital city, banned foreign and minority languages, closed the schools and hospitals, abolished the currency, militarized the economy and the labor force, and attacked neighboring countries.[26] The Khmer Rouge were a strange brand of leftist radicals, usually denominated communist, but in reality were rather more nativistic, chauvinistic and anti-modernist. Since they were anti-Soviet, they received Washington's support as long as the Cold War continued. Paradoxically, when it ended, Washington called for the trial by an international tribunal of Pol Pot and other top leaders of the Khmer Rouge. The support resulted from the Cold War configuration at the time, in which the Soviets backed Vietnam and the government it imposed on Cambodia, while China and Washington backed the Khmer Rouge, the enemy of Vietnam. Washington's support for the Khmer Rouge was more egregious, given that its beneficiary was consistently charged with committing genocide. Moreover, the support came even from the Carter regime despite the fact that President Carter ran on a platform that featured the promotion of human rights. The Carter administration helped arrange continued Chinese aid to the Khmer Rouge when it was fighting the government installed by the invading forces from Vietnam.

Kiernan referred to Washington's support in this way:

> Along with China, which supplied arms, and Thailand, which supplied sanctuary, the United States was instrumental in rescuing the Khmer Rouge army from its 1979 defeat by Hanoi. From 1979 to 1981, the United States led Western nations in voting for the Khmer Rouge to represent their Cambodian victims in the United Nations.

In 1982, Washington helped prod two small pro-American groups into a Khmer Rouge-dominated alliance, and for more than a decade the United States has rejected all opportunities to take individual or collective action against the Khmer Rouge. Former U.S. national security adviser Zbigniew Brzezinski says that in 1979: "I encouraged the Chinese to support Pol Pot....Pol Pot was an abomination. We could never support him but China could." They both did. The United States, Brezezinski says, "winked semi-publicly at Chinese and Thai aid for the Khmer Rouge."[27]

Washington also pressured United Nations agencies to provide food assistance to the Khmer Rouge. This pressure yielded over $12 million in aid from the World Food Program alone when it was most needed, after the defeat by Vietnam. The Western media and Western intelligence supported the Khmer Rouge as well. Washington and its Western allies voted to give the United Nations seat to the Khmer Rouge when it ruled alone, and after 1983 when it ruled in coalition with other parties. The coalition was called the Coalition Government of Democratic Kampuchea (CGDK). Washington rejected any attempt to brand the Khmer Rouge as "genocidal" until the beginning of the Paris peace process in 1989.[28] It claimed that such a charge would be "counterproductive". With the end of the Cold War, Washington's support eroded. In July 1990, after eleven years of diplomatic support, Washington pledged that it would vote to deny the Cambodian seat in the United Nations to the Khmer Rouge. But in 1993, Kiernan observed that "in the fourteen years since the Pol Pot regime's occupation of Cambodia's U.N. seat was first challenged, not a single Western country has voted against its right to represent the victims of its genocide."[29] The same regime continued to control and operate from the Cambodian mission in New York City.

In his small book on the subject based on over one hundred interviews that he had with key decision makers, diplomats, journalists, and scholars, Haas paints the same general picture, but the details are different.[30] Haas traced the origin of Washington's aid to the diplomacy of Carter's National Security Adviser Zbigniew Brzezinski, who talked Thailand into being a conduit for Chinese aid to sustain Pol Pot's forces against Vietnam and their internal enemies. Thus began "the Faustian pact," whereby Washington became "the ally twice-removed" of the Khmer Rouge.[31] Actually, the pact, as already demonstrated, involved direct diplomatic support. The Carter administration honored the pact when in 1979 it voted to seat the Khmer Rouge representative to the United Nations. The rival candidate was backed by Vietnam. Washington also provided aid to the "non-communist resistance" (NCR), a misnamed organization that funneled aid to the Khmer Rouge. Generated by Brzezinski, the pact was continued and upgraded by the Reagan administration, which continued to vote to seat the representative of the Khmer Rouge in the United Nations. U.S. military and non-military aid that ultimately went to the Khmer Rouge was increased. It was channeled through various organizations (for example the NCR) and by various means so as to hide its source. Although a CIA report in 1980 concluded that the Khmer Rouge was responsible for the deaths of 1.5 million people during Pol Pot's rule, the Reagan administration steadfastly refused to acknowledge it.[32]

The motion picture *The Killing Fields*, released in 1985, had a chilling effect upon American and other audiences. It exposed the brutality and the horror of the Khmer Rouge. In the words of Haas, its message "was that something had to be done to stop the Khmer Rouge, who were still alive and well. That U.S. aid was ending up in the hands of the Polpotists was still a secret."[33] Something was done, but later. By 1997 the Vietnamese had withdrawn from Cambodia, the Cold War had ended, and the Khmer Rouge were in disarray. It was only then that Washington gave the signal to go after Pol Pot and his comrades. One news report found Washington urging the Security Council to establish a three-person tribunal to try the leaders of the Khmer Rouge.[34] Another pictured Washington making plans to apprehend Pol Pot in order to have him stand trial before the tribunal set up for the former Yugoslavia at The Hague.[35] Either proposal in 1998 was in accord with the hegemon's general policy of putting its enemies in the docket while protecting its allies and clients. But death intervened in the case of Pol Pot. His comrade followers claimed that he died of a heart attack. His body was shown to newsmen in his jungle hideout, and then cremated. The rumor spread that he had been killed by his former followers, a step in their process of inducing the world to forgive and to forget. Over the years since the four-year slaughter they renounced communism, renamed their party, and affirmed that Pol Pot was no longer their leader.[36]

In November 2002, the General Assembly passed a resolution calling for the resumption of negotiations for the establishment of negotiations to establish a special tribunal to try the surviving leaders of the Khmer Rouge.[37] Following years of failed negotiations, this effort was led by Australia, France, Japan, and the United States. The resolution was criticized by human rights advocates because it did not contain explicit language guaranteeing that the trials would meet international standards. It gave the Cambodian government ultimate control over the jurisdiction of cases with the privilege of overriding decisions of the United Nations.[38] Meanwhile the top leaders of the Khmer Rouge continue to live openly and freely in the country; some of them are included in the present government. The trial courts would be set up by the Cambodian government, and their jurisdiction would be limited to the senior Khmer Rouge leaders and those responsible for the crimes of the Pol Pot regime committed between 1975 and 1979.[39]

CONCLUSION

The present chapter enlarges the research landscape of the study by reaching back to 1922 and by adding more countries and more administrations. It was in 1922 that the Root doctrine was formulated, a formulation that rationalized Washington's support for rightwing dictatorships. The chapter gave examples to show that the thirteen administrations from Harding to Bush have honored this doctrine, a record that serves to enhance the validity of the study. So also does Washington's support for the notorious regimes of Anastacio Somosa, Mobuto Sese Seko, and Pol Pot of the Khmer Rouge.

CHAPTER 8

The Roots of the War on Terrorism: Washington's Policies in the Middle East

The purpose of this chapter is to expose the roots of the present war on terrorism. This is accomplished by examining Washington's support for the Shah of Iran, for Saddam Hussein who after the Iranian revolution invaded Iran and fought a bloody war with it for eight years, and for Israel that has fought and terrorized the Palestinians for over half a century. The chapter concentrates on the postwar period as it relates to the Middle East, and serves as a bridge between Washington's policies of counterinsurgency, and developments leading to the new war on terrorism. During the Cold War/counterinsurgency period, Washington viewed its enemy as communist-inspired insurgencies—as well as political movements charged as being so inspired or simply leftist movements. However, even prior to the collapse of the Soviet Union, and the events of September 11th, 2001, the primary American enemy was evolving from Communism to resurgent Islam. Both, albeit from differing perspectives and ideologies, challenged the legitimacy of the social order in place—an order maintained largely by governments which were viewed by Washington as sympathetic—and both promised (though this has been less explicit in the latter instance due to the fact that resurgent Islam's political ideology is religiously and culturally imbedded) a reshaping of national economies and priorities to suit the well being of the domestic peoples rather than external interests.

The secular bent of the Shah as well as his oppression and dictatorial ways alienated many Iranian groups, allowing radical Islamists to overthrow the dictator and install a radical Islamic state in its place. The new regime held Washington accountable for its years of support for the Shah, and relations between the two countries deteriorated as groups of Iranians took over the American embassy in Teheran. Perhaps it was revenge, but more probably it was the hope of stemming the tide of a radical Islam that led Washington to aid Saddam Hussein after he invaded Iran in 1980 soon after the Iranian revolution. That this aid included the wherewithal to produce weapons of mass destruction is recounted below, followed by an account of Washington's support for Israel, whose governments are popularly elected, but guilty of state terrorism and the wholesale repression of the Palestinians. Because of the massive aid bestowed upon successive Israeli governments by Washington, the Palestinians as well as many Arabs and Muslims hold the United States responsible as an accomplice to this repression and terrorism. Support for Israel is a major cause of Arab and Muslim terrorism aimed at the United States.

WASHINGTON INSTALLS AND SUPPORTS THE SHAH OF IRAN

In 1953 the CIA formulated a coup d'état against the Mossadegh government in Iran that returned the Shah to the throne inherited from his father in 1941. The target of the communists on the left and conservative clerics on the right, the

Shah had managed to survive during the rest of the forties. But in 1951 he was forced to go into exile, because of the rise to power of the popular and charismatic Mohammed Mossadegh. The most notable act of this government was the nationalization of the Anglo/Iranian Oil Co. After the 1953 coup the Shah re-established a dictatorship that ruled the country until 1979. Born and raised in a military family, the Shah had pursued a military career; as the Shah, he became supreme commander and the major decision maker of the armed forces. He "consolidated his undisputed authority through a huge military bureaucracy which denied any civil liberties" in the country.[1]

In 1957 Washington helped the Shah create SAVAK, the notorious secret police force,[2] which silenced those who criticized the Shah or the regime. The Shah followed the trail of so many other dictators by creating a military intelligence agency. The repression was particularly brutal in the period from 1970 to 1976. He dropped any pretense of reform and adopted

In 1957 Washington helped the Shah create SAVAK, the notorious secret police force.

a policy of stifling police rule. The press was censored, people were arbitrarily arrested and harassed, and prisoners were systematically tortured. Concessions whetted the resolve of opposition forces, and the repression resulted in over 10,000 martyrs for their cause.[3] Shiite clerics were favorite targets. Many were arrested and imprisoned, and some were executed. Religious publishing houses were closed down, mosques were infiltrated, and religious student groups were disbanded. The entire religious establishment was alienated, and it turned its support to the Ayatollah Khomeini.

Because of its burgeoning income from petroleum sales, Iran became a special type of third world country—a rich one. By 1967 the United States terminated all economic and military aid to the country, passing all costs of its military buildup to the country itself. In 1972 President Nixon approved the sale of all types of weapons systems to the repressive regime, no matter how sophisticated the weapon, with the exception of nuclear weapons. With the huge hike in oil prices in 1973, the Shah was able to satisfy his insatiable appetite for weapons (which served in turn as a mode of transfer of Iranian oil wealth to American defense contractors). Between 1970 and 1978 he ordered $20 billion of arms from the United States.[4] He became the largest importer of U.S. military hardware. The aftermath of the 1953 coup saw a dramatic increase in the presence of American military advisors. Samardar named them "dependency engineers," concluding that by 1976 Iran had become a dependency of the United States.[5] Washington never forged a formal alliance with the Teheran regime but did cooperate with the Baghdad Pact, of which Iran as well as the United Kingdom was a member.

The Shah dealt with eight American presidencies, but only the six that followed or planned the coup of 1953 are of concern here. One "arranged" the coup (that of Eisenhower), and the five following administrations—those of Kennedy, Johnson, Nixon, Ford, and Carter—maintained support. Three of the six were Republican, three Democratic. Republican administrations in general were more generous with economic aid than were Democratic ones.[6] Moreover, the Kennedy administration pressured the Shah into re-distributing some land. To indicate that its reform proposals were serious, this administration reduced military aid and increased economic aid. Nonetheless, there remained a striking consistency in the adherence of the two parties to the Root doctrine.

During the presidential campaign against Ford, candidate Carter ran on a platform of upholding human rights. He singled out Iran as a country where their abuse was widespread. He criticized the Ford administration for its arms sales, specifically those to Iran. Once in power, however, the Carter policy makers continued on the same track as their predecessors.[7] The first year of the new administration witnessed arms sales at the same level as in previous years. Ironically, the record year for military purchases occurred during the Carter administration. The overall conclusion is obvious. Washington remained faithful to the Root Doctrine.

On New Year's Eve, 1978, the Shah provided a royal reception for the visiting President Carter. The President complimented the Shah with this extravagant toast:

> "Iran, because of the great leadership of the Shah, is an island of stability in one of the troubled areas of the world. This is a great tribute to you and to your majesty and to your leadership and to the respect, admiration, and love which your people give to you."[8]

One year and 15 days later, the Shah was forced into exile by a combination of religious and nationalist leaders, with the cooperation of the Iranian air force. Corruption and repression had become the defining characteristics of his regime during its last two years. The gap between the rich and the poor increased, and the Shah turned SAVAK loose on his enemies. The Iranian revolution has been described as a multi-class uprising in which the lower classes and the burgeoning middle class joined hands against the Shah.[9] Shiite religious leaders became the organizing nexus of the revolution. A charismatic cleric, the Ayatollah Khomeini, returned from exile to become the head of an Islamic government. The Shah was seen as having been too friendly to the United States, which became the chief enemy of the new government. The Shah sought refuge in Egypt, Morocco, the Bahamas, Mexico, and the United States, before returning to Egypt where he died of cancer on July 27, 1980.

SADDAM HUSSEIN, 1979-1990: "OUR S.O.B."

In the summer of 1979, Saddam Hussein became the president of Iraq, chair of the Revolutionary Command Council, and the commander in chief of the armed forces. On February 1 of the same year, the Ayatollah Khomeini had returned home from exile to head the revolutionary government of Iran. Saddam marked his success by unleashing "the bloodiest purge yet, executing hundreds of party officials and military officers, some of whom were close friends and associates."[10] He also used his connection with the Baath party and with military intelligence to solidify his position. This party's chief ideologue was Michel Aflag, who was attracted to fascist ideas when he was a student in Paris in the late twenties and early thirties,[11] and saw Nazi Germany as a model for his ideas. The Baath party seized power in 1963 with the initial support of those who were opposed to the local communist party. This included the business community and the Sunnis in Iraq. The Baathists came to power with the help of the CIA. The agency provided lists of communists whom the party then hunted down, tortured, and killed.[12]

The Baathists came to power with the help of the CIA. The agency provided lists of communists whom the party then hunted down, tortured, and killed.

Saddam posed as a charismatic leader; his picture was everywhere in Iraq. In his hands, terror became a routine instrument of state policy intended to promote a climate of suspicion and to undermine the formation of groups that would oppose him. Torture was an instrumental part of this terror. In April 1985 Amnesty International listed 30 types of torture used in the country: ranging from beatings to burning, administration of electric shocks, and mutilation.[13] His victims were tortured, killed, and their bodies were either returned to their families or put on public display. Either method of exposure was intended to strike terror in the target audience. Saddam's way granted closure to the surviving family, but it had its own horror, illustrated by the experience of an Iraqi mother who in September 1982 went to a Baghdad morgue to receive her son's remains. This was the year in which the Reagan administration took Iraq off of the list of countries aiding terrorism. The boy had been arrested the previous December and held without charge or trial, and the family did not know his whereabouts. Here is part of the mother's testimony:

> "I looked around and saw 9 bodies on the floor stretched out with him... but my son was in a chair form... that is sitting form, not sleeping or stretched. He had blood all over him and his body was very eaten away and bleeding. I looked at the others stretched out on the floor alongside him... all burnt... I don't know with what...another's body carried the marks of a hot domestic iron all over his head to his feet...At the mortuary the bodies were on the floor... one of them had his chest cut lengthwise into three sections... from the neck to the bottom of the chest was slit with what must have been a knife and the flesh looked white and roasted as if cooked... Another had his legs axed with an axe...his arms were also axed. One of them had his eyes gouged out and his nose and ears cut off... One of them looked hanged... his neck was long... his tongue was hanging out and fresh blood was oozing out of his mouth."[14]

As the above narrative indicates, children and young adults were not exempt from Saddam's policy of torture and terror. A former prisoner reported in 1988 that young girls had been hung upside down during their menstrual period, and the hymens of young women have been broken with sharp objects.[15] Iraq is an Arab country where virginity is particularly prized and where girls feel extra sensitivity during their menstrual period.

The First Persian Gulf War

In a surprise attack on September 22, 1980 Saddam Hussein invaded Iran, and thus began the first Persian Gulf war. He wanted to make Iraq the dominant power in the Persian Gulf, and in the Arab world. He was also afraid that the Shiite majority in Iraq would be persuaded to revolt by the fiery rhetoric of the Ayatollah Khomeini. The sheiks in the Gulf shared this fear, and for this reason they supported Saddam. He successfully posed as the protector of the weak Persian Gulf sheiks, and accordingly was rewarded with their financial support during the war. The first Persian Gulf war was a fierce struggle between Iraq and Iran that lasted until 1988.

The Reagan and the Bush administrations supported the dictator in his war against an Iranian government dominated by an Islamic clergy. They feared that the Iranian revolution would spread throughout the Middle East to the detriment of Western interests. But Bush switched policies late in the year 1990, and waged war against Saddam in 1991, in the second Persian Gulf war. The switch in Washington's foreign policy was accompanied by a switch in propaganda campaigns. Whereas in the eight-year period from 1982 to 1990, Washington tried to cloak the evil nature of Saddam Hussein's regime, during the second Persian Gulf war it exposed Saddam as the monster he is and waged a full scale propaganda war against him. Once again, a compliant media followed the lead of Washington as it changed directions, rarely mentioning the support that Washington gave Saddam during the first Persian Gulf war. Now, Washington's support was not motivated by the anti-communist policies of the two Republican administrations of the period, but by the fear of the spread of resurgent Islam.

When the first Persian Gulf war seemed to go badly for Saddam in its initial years, Washington shifted in his direction to support him. Geoffrey Kemp, then head of the Middle East section of the National Security Council, explained:

> "It wasn't that we wanted Iraq to win the war, we did not want Iraq to lose. We really weren't naive. We knew he was an S.O.B, but he was our S.O.B."[16]

In 1982 the State Department took Iraq's name off of its list of states aiding terrorism, and two years later it extended formal recognition.[17] This was followed by the extension of credit and a flood of exports that included agricultural products and dual-use equipment to be used by Iraq in fabricating missiles and enhancing its nuclear, bacteriological, and chemical war capabilities. A Commerce Department report to Congress revealed that it had approved 241 dual-use exports to Iraq in two years, while denying only six applications. Approved were precision machine tools to be used on SCUD missiles; special digital computers for use on missile ranges; computers for chemical weapons production; equipment for the Iraqi Atomic Energy Commission; bacterial and fungus cultures; and high speed oscilloscopes that could be used to pick up the brief signals from nuclear weapons tests.[18] Seventy helicopters of the type used in Vietnam were also exported. According to U.S. intelligence sources, several American-made helicopters were used by Iraq to spray mustard gas on the Kurds.[19] "One of the Reagan administration's last acts was to allow the export of military equipment ordered by Saddam Hussein for his personal protection."[20] France supplied weapons, and Germany served as the chief source of support for the Iraqi chemical warfare industry.

The U.S. approved 241 dual-use exports to Iraq, among them precision machine tools to be used on SCUD missiles, computers for chemical weapons production, and bacterial and fungus cultures.

Washington provided diplomatic support for Saddam and became an active partner in Saddam's "oil war" with Iran. Iraq was clearly the aggressor, but the United Nations did not brand Iraq in this way. This strange behavior on the part of the world institution was due in large part to Washington's influence. Iran was especially bitter about a Security Council resolution passed soon after the invasion, calling for a ceasefire in place, while Iraqi troops were still occupying Iranian territory. The United Nations kept pressing for a ceasefire, not an unusual step for the world institution. But in this case a ceasefire was in line with the policy of Iraq, the aggressor, not that of Iran, the victim of aggression. Therefore, the threat of "further steps" in a Security Council resolution to be taken against the state not complying with a ceasefire seemed to call for action against the victim of aggression, not the aggressor.

The two adversaries fought the war not only against each other's armed forces, but also against each other's oil facilities. The Reagan administration became a co-belligerent with Saddam later in the war. In 1987 and 1988, Washington sent additional ships to the Gulf and carried out a number of attacks on Iranian oil platforms and ships.[21] It destroyed two oil platforms and sank six Iranian ships. These ships constituted one-half of the Iranian fleet. Washington gave orders to the navy to begin escorting Kuwaiti tankers through the Persian Gulf. The tankers were re-registered and re-flagged as U.S. commercial vessels, thus assuring their safety against Iranian attack. The safety of Kuwaiti tankers was essential to Saddam's war effort, because Kuwait was a generous contributor to this effort.

The Reagan administration became a co-belligerent with Saddam later in the Iran-Iraq war.

Saddam was ruthless in dealing with the Shiite population of his country. The deportation of the Shiite community began in 1979 and escalated during the war with Iran, *i.e.*, during the time of Washington's support. Ultimately some 300,000 were forced out of the country to become exiles in Iran. The Kurds living in Iraq were victimized as well, victims of chemical attacks. Hundreds of thousands of them were forced to flee. A visiting U.S. Senate staff delegation reported in the fall of 1987 that hundreds of Kurdish villages had been leveled. Its members found the aftermath to have an eerie deserted quality about it. "Fruit trees, graveyards, and cemeteries stand as reminders of the absent people and livestock."[22]

WMD For Use Against Iran and the Kurds

By this time Iraq had become the greatest possessor and producer of chemical weapons in the third world, both in quantity and quality. Its production of these weapons began in earnest in the mid-seventies, relying mainly upon the importation of dual-use equipment from West Germany. In its 12,000-page declaration to the United Nations on December 7, 2002, Iraq detailed the history of its chemical weapons program before the 1991 Persian Gulf war. Thirty-one major foreign suppliers were identified, along with the exact amount of equipment and poison chemicals that they provided. Fourteen of the major companies were German, three each were located in Holland and Switzerland, and two each in France, Austria, and the United States.[23] United States firms provided chemicals used in producing mustard gas and 60 tons of a chemical used for producing sarin. Sarin is an extremely toxic chemical warfare agent. Patrick L. Sloyan had already reported in *Newsday* in 1996, "*Newsday* has found that the nonprofit Rockville, Md., firm [American Type Culture Collection] made 70 government-approved shipments of anthrax and other disease-causing pathogens to Iraqi scientists between 1985 and 1989, according to congressional records." Further, ATCC "shipped 'bacillus anthracis,' twice—in May, 1986, and September, 1988. There were also two shipments of clostridium botulinum—a bacteria used to make botulinum toxin—on the same dates. The batches, frozen in tiny vials, were shipped to Baghdad's Ministry of Education."[24] United Nations weapons inspectors in Iraq in 2003 found the so-called "air force document" which indicated that the Iraq air force dropped 13,000 chemical bombs on its victims in the period from 1983 to 1988.[25]

In March 1988 the Iraqi air force attacked the Kurdish city Halabja with mustard gas and nerve toxins. Entire families were wiped out, and the streets were littered with the corpses of men, women, and children. Other forms of life in and around the city died as well—horses, cattle, and house cats. When the world first heard of the raid, Iraqi spokesmen blamed it on Iran. Dr. Fouad Bahan, who has studied the victims, identified 250 cities and villages and 31 suspected Kurdish guerrilla bases that Iraq gassed in 1987 and 1988. Halabja was the hardest hit. According to some sources, 5,000 people were killed.[26] The United Nations found evidence that Iraq used chemical weapons against Iranian soldiers four times—in 1984,1985,1986, and 1987. Saddam repeated this on a greater scale in 1988. This led the United States Senate to pass the Prevention of Genocide Act of 1988. It was aimed at Iraq, specifically forbidding oil imports, credits, and exports of dual-use equipment. The Reagan administration and elements within the House opposed the bill despite the fact that Secretary of State Schultz divulged that U.S. intercepts of Iraqi military communications confirmed that chemical weapons had been used.[27] The president threatened to veto any bill sent to him. All attempts at compromise failed. The Reagan administration argued that sanctions were premature and that they would be counter-productive.

On October 26, 1989 President Bush signed National Security Directive 26. It affirmed that the goal of U.S. policy toward Iraq was to achieve normal relations between the two countries. This to be accomplished by a strategy of using economic and political incentives to moderate Iraq's behavior and increase U.S. influence.[28] The directive called for strengthened military ties with Baghdad. One representative in Congress called the directive "more of the same under a new number." But this should not be taken to mean merely a continuation of the past, without an increase in support. At least this was true for agricultural credits and high technology exports.[29]

President Bush signed National Security Directive 26 in the wake of the *Anfal* campaigns, a series of seven military offensives designed to drive the Kurds from the villages Saddam considered to be located in strategic areas. Some of the villages were controlled by guerrillas, others were not. *Anfal* in Arabic means "spoils," the name of the eighth chapter of the Quran. In this chapter Muhammad and his followers are enjoined to fight courageously against the unbelievers until victory is attained or until the unbelievers have accepted the faith. (The reader is reminded that Saddam and the Baathist regime were secularists, who may have been attempting to exploit the "*anfal*" label to confer Islamic legitimacy on their actions. The Kurds are not unbelievers, but Muslims.) Saddam put his cousin in charge of the program and gave him the absolute power to achieve its objectives, including the right to override the decisions of other civilian or military authorities. It was after this appointment that poison gas was used and that Kurd villages beyond thirty miles from the border with other countries were cleared. Villages were destroyed, possessions were looted, and Kurds were relocated or worse. One such village was Halabja mentioned above as having been razed to the ground. A new town of concrete blocks named "New Saddam City Halabja" was erected for the survivors. In all, some 5,000 villages were destroyed.[30] The *Anfal* lasted until at least the middle of 1989. Kurdish society and culture were dealt a heavy blow. "Members of a medical relief organization who visited the area in November 1989 reported that little of the old society remained."[31]

The *Anfal* was thus in progress while National Security Directive 26 was being formulated, and the members of the medical relief organization mentioned above made their report a month, give or take a few days, after the signing of the directive. Certainly, the Bush administration knew of the horror resulting from the implementation of Saddam's *Anfal* strategy, even if it may have been unaware of the exact extent of it. This horror only received widespread publicity long after the event, after the allied victory over Saddam and the establishment of safe havens for Kurds in northern Iraq. Interested researchers used the opportunity to inter- view survivors and to examine truckloads of captured Iraqi Security Police and intelligence documents. Middle East Watch, a private human rights organization, attempted to coordinate the research. It concluded that the number of victims executed by the *Anfal* "cannot conceivably be less than 50,000, and it may be twice that number."[32] The *Anfal* was not intended and implemented as straight- forward ethnic cleansing. Its intent was not merely to instill terror in the victims, to scare them so that they would abandon their villages, homes, and major posses- sions. Its intent and implementation were much more lethal. Virtually all the men and some of the women and children were killed. They were buried in mass graves near the Saudi Arabian frontier.

On December 9, 2002 the Kurdish news media reported that the Deputy Prime Minister of Iraq for the first time admitted that his country had used chemi- cal weapons against Iran and the Kurdish city Halabja during the first Persian Gulf war between Iran and Iraq. The inhabitants of the Kurdish city now living in a self-governing enclave in northern Iraq received this admission with "knowing disgust".[33] They still bore the marks of the vicious Iraqi attack: darkened eyes, scorched limbs, hacking coughs, and involuntary shakes, as well as heightened rates of respiratory ailments, skin diseases, mental illness, and blindness. Esti- mates of the dead caused by the attack range from 3,200 to 7,000, of the injured from 15,000 to 20,000.

The Second Persian Gulf War: Washington Turns on Saddam

The end of the first Persian Gulf war did not mean the end of Washington's support for the Saddam Hussein regime. The Bush administration continued this support until after the invasion of Kuwait. As indicated above, President Bush signed National Security Directive 26 on October 26, 1989 that defined the objec- tives of American policy as striving to achieve normal relations and strengthening military ties with Iraq. This explains U.S. ambassador Glaspie's interview with Saddam Hussein after American intelligence had detected Iraqi troop move- ments on the border with Kuwait, and after Saddam had accused Kuwait of steal- ing $2.4 billions in oil from his country. Glaspie was conciliatory. Impressed with Saddam's sincerity, the ambassador did not threaten war or sanctions if Iraq invaded Kuwait. She told the Iraqi dictator that her government had no opinion on such inter-Arab disputes as the Iraqi problem with Kuwait. While this interview has been widely cited as offering American approval of an Iraqi invasion of Ku- wait, which Washington would subsequently use as a casus belli against Iraq as Glaspie explained later to a Congressional subcommittee, her remarks were fully in line with the existing policy of the United States. On the same day the State Department prevented the Voice of America from declaring that the United States was "strongly committed to supporting its friends in the Gulf."[34] Six days later John Kelly, the Assistant Secretary of State for Middle Eastern Affairs, added that the United States had no formal commitment to defend Kuwait. Two days after that, on August 2, 2000, Iraq invaded Kuwait.

Iraqi forces quickly overran the tiny oil sheikdom. Attempts at mediation failed, and the Security Council authorized member states to use "all necessary means" to induce Iraq to withdraw its troops if it had not done so by January 15. The next day the second Persian Gulf war was launched in earnest. For 38 days "U.S.-led coalition forces obliterated Iraqi resistance with the most intensive bombing campaign since World War II."[35] Flying an average of 2,000 sorties per day, the air armada dropped an estimated 700,000 tons of bombs on Iraq. The world was encouraged to watch this high-tech air show on TV brought to them courtesy of the United States government. The first day of the bombing knocked out the power and water facilities of Baghdad, causing enormous suffering for the inhabitants of the capital city. This led to epidemics of cholera, typhoid fever, and gastroenteritis, particularly among children,a probability of which the U.S. military was fully aware when it targeted them. The air offensive was followed by a 100 hour ground offensive, a cleverly conceived military strategy that provided a "turkey shoot" for coalition forces as they mowed down the retreating Iraqi conscripts, some 25,000 of whom were killed while fleeing on Iraqi highways according to US military reports.[36] Some 200,000 Iraqis, civilian and military, were killed during the war

The trade embargo imposed on Iraq before the second Persian Gulf war remained in force after the conflict ended. This embargo added to the suffering of the Iraqi people as they struggled to cope with the results of the war. It was not until May 20, 1996 that Saddam agreed to a program whereby Iraq was allowed to export oil in return for the importation of food, medicine, and medical equipment. Before the agreement and even after it went into effect, "hundreds of thousands of Iraqis [had] suffered from disease and malnutrition, and many [had] died from lack of proper medical treatment."[37]

Once the administration of the elder Bush turned on Saddam and determined to fight him, it mounted a full-fledged and extremely successful propaganda war against the Iraqi dictator. Instead of covering up for him, it painted him as the monster he was, but if possible, even worse. The public clarification of the grim realities of the Saddam regime was now carried on with the cooperation and support of a compliant popular media but at the expense of the American public's right not just to know, but to understand. The popular media "forgot" the eight years of Washington's support, along with that of Western Europe, for Saddam. Inclusion of it would have detracted from the high moral purpose said to motivate the democracies as they prepared their first attack upon Iraq. As indicated elsewhere in the present study, the administration of Bush's son had a harder time in 2003 selling a preemptive war, the third Persian Gulf war, to the American public. Saddam had to be taken down because, it was argued, he had weapons of mass destruction, and it was only a matter of time before he would use them, or give them to others to use, against the United States. Most religious leaders in the United States who spoke out questioned the morality of such an aggressive act. But the popular media again suffered from amnesia and myopia, failing to point out that the Western democracies helped the monster develop weapons of mass destruction in the first place.

President Mohammad Khatami of Iran used his visit to Spain in October 2002 to further his campaign for a "dialogue among civilizations," a campaign that he had introduced at the United Nations four years before. A mid-level cleric who studied philosophy, he noted in a speech at Complutense University in Madrid that modern Don Quixotes who lack the kindness, mercy, and humanitarian nature of the legendary hero "ruthlessly assassinate and annihilate people with their huge war machines." He asserted that his country opposed the proposed war against Iraq and charged that Washington's misguided war on terrorism had strengthened support for Osama bin Laden in the Muslim world. He likened the logic of President Bush to that of bin Laden. Whereas the latter says "whoever is not with me must be destroyed,"

> [T]he voice from Washington says "whoever is not with us is against us." The Iranian President rejected both options, indicating both would lead to horrendous consequences. The former logic leads to the most atrocious forms of terror, the latter to the worst atmosphere for waging war. He reminded his audience that after Saddam Hussein invaded Iran, he used chemical weapons against it and even against his own people. He contrasted the extraordinary reaction against Hussein's possession of these weapons now and the world's inaction in the face of his use of them then. He asked rhetorically, "If chemical weapons are bad, why, when they were used against us or Iraqi citizens, wasn't Iraq condemned and pressured?"[38]

WASHINGTON'S COMPLICITY IN ISRAELI STATE TERRORISM

The Partition of Palestine

At the request of Britain, a special session of the General Assembly met on April 28, 1947 to discuss and to recommend the fate of Palestine that at the time was a British mandate (a colony). The General Assembly established the United Nations Special Committee on Palestine (UNSCOP) to investigate the conditions in the mandate and to make recommendations as to its future.[39] After three and a half months spent conducting hearings and making field trips, the committee presented its findings and made its recommendation. Sensing that the committee would recommend the partition of the mandate, the Arab Higher Committee, which represented the Palestinian Arabs, refused to cooperate with the commission. The Palestinians opposed partition, the Jews (Zionists) supported it. The majority of the commission recommended the partition of the mandate into two states, one Jewish, the other Palestinian. To this day a Palestinian state has not been established. A minority of the committee (India, Iran, and Yugoslavia) recommended the preservation of the mandate as a federal state. The majority viewpoint was accepted by the Assembly on November 24, 1947 by a vote of 33 to 13 with 10 abstentions. This resulted in part from pressure bought to bear by Washington on several reluctant states. Europe and Latin America made up twenty of the affirmative votes—all Arab nations voted in the negative. But there can be no denying the fact that the General Assembly underwrote what was essentially the Jewish (Zionist) position, and thereby gave legitimacy to the existence of Israel. But it also gave legitimacy to the existence of a Palestinian state that has not as yet been established.

Even these terms established by the General Assembly's recommendation were not carried out. The Assembly called for a Jewish state of 5,700 square miles and an Arab state of 4,300 square miles. Thus a majority of the land was to go to the Jewish state, which had a large Arab minority within it, while the Jews were a minority in the Palestinian mandate. The actual division of land was decided by the war that followed, not by the resolution. Israel obtained 7,000 square miles, while Jordan and Egypt held 3,000 square miles for the Palestinians.[40] The Assembly recommendation called for an economic union between the two states, which of course was not established. Nor did Jerusalem become a trust territory with the United Nations as its administrator, as the resolution recommended. At first the city was partitioned—the old city put under Jordanian control, the new city under Israeli control. After the 1967 war, Israel took over the old part as well, and now insists on keeping it.

The Ethnic Cleansing of the Palestinians

Herzog argues that the British decision to bring the Palestine question to the General Assembly was caused by an uprising among the Jews in Palestine.[41] Some 30,000 Jews from Palestine had served in the British armed forces during World War II, and the British government did not wish to maintain a force of 100,000 troops in Palestine to deal with the anticipated conflict. Nor did the British enforce the Assembly's resolution. The rebellion occurred after the British government rejected President Truman's call in 1945 for the admission of 100,000 Jewish refugees from Europe. There were three Jewish military groups in the mandate—the Haganah, later to become the backbone of the Israeli army, and two splinter groups, the Irgun Zvai Leumi (also simply called the Irgun), and the Stern Gang. The three groups engaged in what Washington and the Israeli and Western press would later call "terrorism" when practiced by the Arabs. The Irgun blew up the King David Hotel, the British headquarters in Jerusalem, with heavy loss of life. In November 1944 the Stern Gang assassinated Lord Moyne, the British minister resident in Cairo, and later it killed Count Folke Bernadotte, the United Nations Mediator. Later still, from 1977 to 1983 a leader of the Irgun, Menachem Begin, served as Prime Minister of Israel. Yitzhak Shamir was a leader of the Stern Gang, and from 1983 to 1984 and again in 1986 he was the Prime Minister of Israel. These matters are presented in order to suggest how hollow the charge is to pretend that the Arabs have been the sole or even the major source of terrorism in what was Palestine during the British mandate.

The Irgun and the Stern Gang collaborated in the killing of 250 Arabs in the Palestine village Deir Yassin on April 9, 1948.[42] The purpose of the massacre was to strike terror in the surrounding Palestinian population so that they would leave to make room for returning Jewish immigrants. This form of terrorism was named "ethnic cleansing" when later used by the Serbs against the Albanians in Kosovo. The incident occurred during the first Arab-Israeli war, a two-year encounter that lasted from 1947 to 1949. It started as a series of bloody city riots, urban encounters, and hit and run operations between local Jews and Arabs. The local Jews were victorious despite the intervention of five Arab States. While this intervention could be considered as an invasion from the outside, the Arabs excuse and praise it as a manifestation of Arab brotherhood in defense of legitimate Palestinian rights. The fighting resulted, as we have seen, in the emergence of a Jewish state larger than the one projected in the General Assembly resolution. In 1948, during the fighting, Israel unilaterally declared itself to be a state. The Truman administration immediately recognized it.

The purpose of the Deir Yassin massacre was to strike terror in the surrounding Palestinian population so that they would leave to make room for returning Jewish immigrants.

The Fate of the Palestinians

At the time of the hostilities described above, Palestine was predominantly an Arab state. Prior to the influx of European Jews, the inhabitants had been overwhelmingly Arab. UNSCOP estimated that in 1922 Jews represented 13 percent of the population of Palestine, a figure which through immigration rose to 33 percent by 1946.[43] The estimate is that two-thirds of the Jews resident in Palestine in 1922 had immigrated there or their forebears had done so in the previous forty years.[44] The Jewish residents before that time, only some 4 or 5 percent of the population, were predominantly part of a culturally and linguistically assimilated community of orthodox Jews of long standing who saw their presence in Palestine as a religious obligation rather than as expressing a national claim. This group was Jewish, but not Zionist.[45]

The Zionist movement was founded in Vienna in the latter part of the nineteenth century. Once the world realized the horror of the Holocaust after World War II, Zionism received support not only from Jews, but from many other quarters as well. Many concluded that Jews must have their own country, if only so that those who survived could protect themselves against such future horrors. The Palestinians rejected Zionism's claim that Jews had the right to return to what was essentially a Palestinian state after being absent for centuries. Rome conquered Palestine in 63 BC, put down a rebellion there in 66 AD, destroyed the Jewish state in 70 AD, and expelled the Jews from Jerusalem in 135 AD, after which they lived for centuries scattered around the world in a Diaspora. Moreover, the Holocaust was a genocide committed by Europeans; the Palestinians had played no role in it.

UNSCOP put the number of Arabs displaced in the first Arab-Israeli war (1947-1949) at 750,000, some 59 percent of the Arab population of the mandate. Traditional Israeli historiography maintained that this mass exodus resulted from the urgings of Arab leaders, beseeching the Arab population to leave. Recent research, including that by the Israeli scholar and journalist Benny Morris, revealed that this is largely a myth. Morris maintains that the vast majority of Palestinians were expelled by the Israeli military and Jewish terrorist forces.[46] In 1967 Israel expanded by taking over the West Bank, the Golan Heights, the Gaza Strip, and the old city of Jerusalem. This led to the displacement of over half a million Palestinians—220,000 of whom were uprooted for the second time. The displacement of these people was deliberate Israeli policy intended to make room for incoming Jews from the Diaspora. In 1950 Israel enacted into law "the right to return," which it had been practicing since 1948. The law guarantees the right of every Jew throughout the world "to return," to become an Israeli citizen. Included are recent converts to the Jewish faith, regardless of their race, ethnicity, or culture.

The fate of the displaced Palestinians remains an obstacle to any settlement of the Arab-Israeli question. The Arabs argue for repatriation—that Israel must accept these displaced refugees and recognize their right of return. Israel refuses to accept them, arguing that they should be relocated in Arab countries. The Israeli refusal adds weight to the charge that the Palestinians were forced to flee in the first place to make room for immigrant Jews. Israel has rejected the many General Assembly resolutions that have called for repatriation or compensation to the refugees for their losses. The United Nations could not, the great powers would not, force Israel to repatriate them or even to compensate them.

Violations of the Rights of the Palestinians

The United Nations Relief and Works Agency for Palestinian Refugees (UNRWA) was created in 1949 by the General Assembly to provide aid to the displaced Palestinians. In its first years it concentrated on immediate relief in the form of food, clothing, and shelter. Later, it steered its program away from basic needs, so that by 1982 the emphasis had shifted to education and health. It was established without prejudice to the rights of the refugees to repatriation or compensation for the property they had left behind.[47] Many of the refugees live in camps, glorified slums maintained by the organization, from which terrorists have been recruited. The Israeli state often responds to terrorist acts perpetrated against Israelis by bombing these camps.

The 1986 edition of *Everyone's United Nations* characterized UNRWA, with its 17,000 employees, as "the largest operation in the United Nations system."[48] This was before the establishment of the large and very costly peacekeeping forces set up in the post Cold War period. The budget of the organization for 1995 was $307.7 million.[49] With help from UNESCO, UNRWA operates 654 elementary and preparatory schools. They have a teaching staff of over 10,000 and a total enrollment in excess of 345,000. UNRWA's workers are overwhelming Palestinian. They have diplomatic immunity, a special status not recognized by the Israeli government. International law forbids a government from even arresting those who enjoy this status. At its 37th session the General Assembly condemned Israeli policies in the Occupied Territories and urged Israel to release UNRWA workers. Israel later detained 104 UNRWA employees in the period from June 1990 to June 1992 in the Occupied Territories of the West Bank and Gaza. In the first year of that period, 160 UNRWA employees were arrested or detained in all of the Occupied Territories. One hundred and ten were subsequently released without charge or trial, whereas seven were sentenced to various terms of imprisonment.[50] Since the start of the first Palestinian intifada in December, 1987, UNRWA has reported extreme difficulties in meeting refugee demands for basic needs in the camps of the Gaza Strip because of curfews, the beating of refugees, and restrictive economic policies imposed by the occupying Israeli authorities.[51] Israel closed schools during much of the period from 1987 to 1990, which entailed the closing of 98 UNRWA schools with 40,000 students.

Naturally UNRWA goes where the Palestine refugees are, *i.e.* to Lebanon, Jordan, Syria, and Egypt, and it has had to deal with the Arab governments of these countries. Since the territorial expansion of Israel in 1967 and its occupation of Southern Lebanon, the institution has had to deal with the Israeli government as well. Although problems have been encountered with Arab governments, relations with Israel have been the most difficult. Largely because of the difficulty of this relationship, UNRWA has the dubious distinction of being that United Nations agency having the worst relations with host governments. When Israel invaded Lebanon in June 1982, UNRWA's infrastructure there was largely destroyed by the Israeli bombardment. Seven of the 13 Palestine refugee camps in Lebanon sustained heavy damage, while those used by the PLO as military assets were virtually destroyed.[52] Twenty-six of a total of 2,300 UNRWA employees were killed in the violence.

Also noteworthy was the massacre of over 2000 Palestinians in the Lebanese refugee camps at Sabra and Shatilla. *The New York Times* reported that from 5-5:30 a.m. low level flights of Israeli planes over Sabra and Shatila took place, after which shelling promptly commenced.[53]

> The Israelis established observation posts on top of multi-storey buildings in the north-west quadrant of the Kuwaiti Embassy. From these posts, the naked eye has a clear view of several sections of the camps, including those parts of Shatila where piles of bodies were found.[54]

sraeli facilitation of the massacres carried out by Christian Phalangists under their control became impossible to deny. "Throughout the night flares lit up the sky. They were fired at the rate of two a minute, as reported by an Israeli soldier from a mortar unit."[55] The Kahan Commission, appointed by the Israeli Cabinet to investigate responsibility for the Sabra and Shatilla massacres, conducted an extensive, independent, judicial inquiry, reporting back on 8th February 1983. While arguing that the actual numbers killed were lower than widely accepted figures, the Kahan Commission nonetheless found Israeli Prime Minister Menachim Begin responsible for not exercising greater involvement and awareness in the matter of introducing the Phalangists into the camps. Ariel Sharon, then Minister of Defense, was found responsible for ignoring the danger of bloodshed and revenge when he approved the entry of the Phalangists into the camps as well as not taking appropriate measures to prevent bloodshed.[56]

The Israeli government also violates the rights of those Arab Palestinians who have remained in Israel by treating them as second-class citizens. The Security Council passed more than sixty resolutions that condemned such Israeli behavior in the period to January 1992.[57] Such condemnations require at least the passive consent of the three Western democracies which are members of the body, notably that of the United States. Any of the three—France, the United Kingdom, or the United States—could have used its veto to block the adoption of the resolutions, but did not. The violations must have been egregious in these sixty cases if we credit a 1998 report of Amnesty International which castigated Washington's "refusal to criticize blatant human rights violations by Israel against the predominantly Muslim Palestinian population."[58] Until December 1, 1966, Palestinians living in Israel were under military law. They could be arbitrarily jailed or deported. Their economic activities were limited, and their freedom of movement was restricted. Even after martial law had been abolished in 1966, the Palestinians did not attain first class citizenship. They continue to be discriminated against in such matters as social and educational funding and employment opportunities. The records of the world institution are full of the violations that the Palestinians have endured. A comprehensive Bibliography of such violations is available in *Palestine, Palestinians and International Law* by Francis A. Boyle.[59]

The Israeli Nuclear Bomb

Several times the Arab League and the General Assembly of the United Nations have insisted that Israel sign the United Nations Nuclear Non-Proliferation Treaty. This treaty was promoted by the Eisenhower administration and its successors to prevent non-possessing states from developing nuclear weapons. By signing the treaty, non-possessing states promised not to adopt a nuclear weapons program and to allow United Nations inspectors to verify that they have not done so. Israel has consistently refused to sign the treaty. The reason for these refusals became obvious when on October 5, 1986 the Sunday edition of the *London Times* broke the story of the Israeli possession of nuclear weapons. The final decision to publish the three-page exposé was re-enforced by the successful attempt of Israeli Prime Minister Peres to censor the local press by instructing Israel's leading editors to steer clear of the story.[60] The exposé was based on the testimony of Mordechai Vanunu, who for eight years had worked as a technician at Israel's top secret plutonium separation plant in Dimona, located in the Negev Desert. He produced photographs and was able to convince scientists with experience in the field of the authenticity of his claim. After the exposé, a female agent of Mossad, the Israeli intelligence agency, lured him to Rome, where he was kidnapped by that agency and taken to Israel to stand trial for treason and espionage. After a secret trial, he was sentenced to 18 years in prison. Israel probably has a chemical warfare capability as well.[61]

Washington's Support for Israel

The above testifies to the diplomatic support, both inside and outside the United Nations, that Washington has given Israel. By 1989 Washington had used its veto in the Security Council 23 times to block resolutions critical of Israel. One would imagine that the special relationship between the two countries would show up in the proceedings of the United Nations. It has.

Washington adopted a two-faced policy of insisting on marginalizing the UN in dealing with Israel, while at the same time fighting the second Persian Gulf war against Iraq in 1991 using its banner.

In 1986 the two nations voted together 91.5 percent of the time, an extraordinary congruence surpassed only by the behavior of the now defunct Soviet bloc. Washington has almost always overlooked Israel's miserable human rights record and state terrorism committed against the Palestinians. Israeli nuclear weapons have remained a non-subject in Washington and in most of the American media.

Washington's material aid to Israel is extraordinary, especially if the postage size of the country and its small population are considered. This aid from 1948 to 1991 amounted to $53 billions, and after 1985 all of it has been gifts not loans.[62] By 1998 this aid to Israel, both economic and military, amounted to $3 billion per year, the most given to any country. In 1978-1979 this aid represented 43 percent of all American foreign aid, and by the mid 1980's Israel was receiving an annual subsidy of $1,500 for each of its men, women, and children. Israel has also received the most sophisticated weapons from Washington, and has been the beneficiary of intelligence gathered by the CIA.

By 1998 aid to Israel, both economic and military, amounted to $3 billion per year, the most given to any country.

The "Peace Process"

The "peace process" was a form of mediation, pitting Israel against the Palestine Liberation Organization (PLO) and the Syrians in a series of bilateral negotiations pushed forward by Washington. It was initiated at the Madrid Conference of October and November 1991. The Arabs had insisted on a United Nations sponsored peace conference attended by all parties to the conflict and chaired by all five permanent members of the Security Council.[63] Israel rejected the notion of United Nations sponsorship of the conference, protesting its pro-Arab bias. American Secretary of State Baker worked out a "compromise," whereby the conference was sponsored by the United States and the Soviet Union and attended by representatives from the United Nations and the European Union. This conference adjourned leaving it with no authority or influence over the negotiations that followed. The same was true of the United Nations. Israel insisted that the world organization play no significant role in the negotiations and that they proceed on a one to one basis between each Arab party and Israel. This way the Arabs would be denied the added strength that follows from a united front of several countries being pitted against one adversary. The Israel position prevailed; the conference denied the Arabs a united front and the support of the world organization. The United Nations was shunted to the sidelines in a quarrel in which it had been involved for nearly half a century, as Washington adopted a two-faced policy of insisting on marginalizing the world organization in dealing with this problem, while at the same time fighting the second Persian Gulf war against Iraq in 1991 using its banner.

A delicate question at Madrid was Palestinian representation—the PLO having been seen and depicted for so long by Israel and the United States as a terrorist organization, despite its recognition as a legitimate liberation organization by the UN, which had accorded it Observer Status in 1975. The PLO was excluded from the negotiations at Madrid, though it did attend and advise. Moreover, Israel successfully insisted that no Palestinian either from East Jerusalem or outside the Occupied Territories could attend. The PLO seemingly had graduated in Western eyes from a terrorist institution to an acceptable polity of some type. And again in Western eyes, Yasir Arafat seemed to have made the metamorphosis from terrorist leader to an acceptable political leader.

The peace process made little progress until the Labor Party in Israel replaced the conservative Likud party in July 1992. Labor announced a negotiating strategy of "land for peace," without specifying how much land it was willing to bargain away.[64] This became the modus operandi of the peace process with the Palestinians. The land to be negotiated was from the Gaza Strip and the West Bank, land that Israel took in 1967. The negotiations proceeded in stages in a double sense. Only a slice of land at a time, and the "give back" went through stages as well: from complete Israel control; to Palestinian civil control, but Israeli security control; and finally to complete Palestinian control. By April 1998 Israel had withdrawn from most of the Gaza Strip and from eight cities on the West Bank.[65] Another 27 percent of the West Bank was under Palestinian civil control, with security handled by the Israelis. The final settlement was to have been completed by May 1999, but the process then stalled for over a year. By March 2000, 43 percent of the West Bank was under Palestinian control. This included most of the Palestinian population.[66]

The Israelis continued to prove that state terrorism is more lethal than private terrorism. In the two and a half years prior to March 2003, the Israeli army killed 2,100 Palestinians in a process of intensified occupation of their lands, whereas Arab/Muslim terrorists killed 700 Israelis.[67] In the meantime, the settler population in the West Bank and the Gaza Strip (the Occupied Territories) increased to an estimated 226,028, a six percent increase in the previous year alone.[68] The Palestinians regard these settlements as a provocation, not only because they infringe on the lands marked out for the promised Palestinian state, but because the interconnecting highways servicing their access to Israel carve Palestinian lands into a series of disconnected plots similar to the Bantustans of former apartheid South Africa. Meanwhile Arafat was surrounded by Israeli tanks, and held as a virtual prisoner in his office. Prime Minister Sharon refused to recognize him as the leader of the Palestinians, and Washington, after some hesitation, adopted this as its policy as well. Arafat was forced to accept a new constitution and the creation of the office of prime minister. Both the prime minister and the minister in charge of security were acceptable to Israel. No elections were held to determine the democratic will of the Palestinians as to who should represent them.

The Road Map

The "road map" was drawn up by the Bush administration in December 2002, but not formally released until April 30 of the following year—not until the Palestinians accepted the regime change mandated by Washington.[69] Although approved by the United Nations, the European Union, and Russia, it will be Washington that will decide how much pressure to put on the belligerents involved to achieve the goals of the plan. The plan calls for concessions on both sides in a three stage series of negotiations leading by the year 2005 to a sovereign state for the Palestinians and a secure Israel. The first stage requires that the Palestinians immediately undertake an unconditional cessation of violence against Israel, issue an unequivocal statement declaring that Israel has the right to exist, and engage in a comprehensive political reform of their government. Israel is required in the first stage to withdraw from the settlements that were occupied since March 2001.

The "road map" was drawn up by the Bush administration in December 2002, but not formally released until the Palestinians accepted the regime change mandated by Washington.

Unfortunately, the violence between the two parties continued after the road map was released, and Prime Minister Sharon has ruled out the withdrawal of the Israelis from the settlements.[70] The hard problems are left to the last stage of the negotiations. They include: the borders of the two countries; the fate of Jerusalem, the Jewish settlements, the Palestinian refugees; and the end of the Israel occupation of the land it took in 1967. Before that time, the land was being held by Arab states for the Palestinians. The road map does not require that Israel give up all of the land.

The Palestinian Authority quickly accepted the road map, but the Israeli cabinet did so only reluctantly and under pressure from Prime Minister Ariel Sharon. The Israeli cabinet did this in May 2003 by a vote of 12 to 7 with four abstentions and only with several reservations.[71] This was followed by inconsequential meetings of the two prime ministers. The Palestinians were represented by the newly appointed Prime Minister Mahmoud Abbas, not by Yasir Arafat.

One year after the 9/11 atrocity, Arab anger at the United States for its "unstinting support" for Israel at the expense of the Palestinians was reported to be at an all time high.[72] According to diplomats and analysts, this high state of anger was evident across the Arab world. It was compounded and re-enforced, especially in Egypt and Jordan, by the fear that Washington would invade Iraq. More so than in other times of anti-Americanism, all strata of Arab society, especially the educated, felt that President Bush had broken his promise to reach out to them after the first Gulf war. Rather than doing this, he had "assumed an unquestioned tolerance of the actions of Prime Minister Ariel Sharon of Israel against the Palestinians." Even the good will that the United States has enjoyed in Kuwait, whose monarchical regime the elder Bush saved in 1991, was in jeopardy. The head of this country's information department of its Ministry of Islamic Affairs declared, "I would be lying if I said I wasn't happy about the attack [of September 11]."[73] He went on to say that many Kuwaitis were delighted about what had happened to the United States and that he had attended parties held in celebration. "Only then did we see America suffer for a few seconds what Muslims have been suffering for a long time."

CONCLUSION

The present chapter served as a background for and link to discussion of the present war on terrorism. Support for the Shah led the revolutionary Islamic Khomeini regime to target Washington as its primary enemy. Support for Saddam Hussein in the 1980's was intended to prevent the spread of radical Islam, also a motive in the war on terrorism. The second and third Persian Gulf wars were not interpreted by radical Islamists as attempts by Washington to dominate the Middle East. Knowledge of Washington's support for Saddam in the 1980's is necessary backgound for interpreting its motives in arranging and fighting the second and third wars in the region. The claim that these wars were fought for idealistic reasons against a regime of incarnate evil rings hollow when it is recalled that the Iraqi regime received support from Washington prior to its attacks against and demonization of Saddam Hussein.

The last section of the chapter identified Washington's support for Israel as a main reason why radical Islamists hate the United States, but clearly Washington's actions against other Muslim populations in the region—Iraqi and Iranian, to name only two[74]—should also be regarded as part of this grievance. This support for Israel seems to have no limits, running the gamut from the diplomatic, to the economic and the military, including the protective silence shielding the Israeli nuclear arsenal. These Islamists recognize that the United States is the chief accomplice to Israeli state terrorism. It follows that a major way to reduce this hatred, and with it terrorism, is to stop filling this role. This idea is pursued in the following chapter.

If Washington is truly interested in eliminating weapons of mass destruction from the Middle East, it should insist that Israel disband its nuclear weapons program and destroy these weapons and other weapons of mass destruction. It should insist that Israel sign the Nuclear Non-Proliferation Treaty and carry out its provisions. This has been a demand of the Arab League, but Israel has ignored it. The fact that Israel has nuclear weapons and perhaps other weapons of mass destruction is the incentive for the Arab countries in the region to develop them to protect themselves. The desire to protect one's country against a possessing enemy has been the chief motive for the spread of these weapons in the post-World War II period. Even the motive of the first possessor, the United States, was similarly grounded. The Roosevelt administration launched a crash program to develop them, based on intelligence reports that Berlin had a nuclear program. The antagonism of the Cold War led Moscow, London, Paris, and Beijing to launch their own programs. India developed the bomb, leading its major antagonist Pakistan to do so also. One can understand why Syria, Iran, and other states in the Middle East might be similarly motivated by the threat from Israel.

CHAPTER 9

The War on Terrorism

The 2003 annual report of Human Rights Watch charged that "Washington has waged war on terrorism as if human rights were not a constraint." The overriding message sent in its bilateral relations "is that human rights are dispensable in the name of fighting terrorism." Washington has withheld criticism of abuses by numerous friends and allies, including Russia, Israel and Malaysia,[1] and certainly other countries could be added to that list. This chapter supports this charge, and, indeed, demonstrates that the Bush administration has remained faithful to the Root Doctrine by supporting countries that have violated human rights and practiced state terrorism. However, as this chapter will demonstrate, with the Bush administration's doctrine of preemption, the U.S. allegiance to the Root Doctrine has undergone a marked shift. While previous administrations did invade countries, they found pretexts in justification of their actions, rather than asserting any right to invade. But preemption is another word for aggression, and its open embrace by the George W. Bush administration represents an historic setback in the development of international law.

This chapter will also reveal the war on terrorism as a starkly more aggressive and globally dangerous policy than that employed during the Cold War. During the earlier conflict, Washington used surrogates to neutralize the opposition and occasionally engaged in direct aggressive behavior, but it rationalized the aggression. The George W. Bush administration, however, has openly declared that aggression is the national policy of the United States.

The Bush administration has openly declared that aggression is the national policy of the United States.

THE NATURE OF THE WAR ON TERRORISM

The Bush Administration Projects a Dangerous New World

Like the now defunct Cold War, the war on terrorism possesses features that predispose Washington to operate in direct confrontation of accepted norms of international law, and to overlook the deficiencies and the crimes of its co-belligerents. As portrayed by Washington, the new war is a messianic, apocalyptic struggle of blameless good against consummate evil. Its inspiration is not the real world with its shades of gray (and indeed, relevant histories and grievances), but the kind of struggles that used to play out in the cowboy movies. Little mention is made of the fact that the primary enemy is religious, actually intensely so sometimes to the point of intolerance, bigotry, and terror, and not atheist as the previous enemy was. There is no need to try to understand that this new enemy regards Israel as a state that practices state terrorism and that by supplying military and economic aid, Washington is an accomplice. Or to try to understand that this enemy believes that Washington should cut off this aid and declare war on state terrorists as well as private ones. Those on "our side" are seen as being good, or at least infinitely better than the enemy. It is a war of no negotiations with the enemy, no summit meetings, no compromise, and certainly no need to modify policies to accommodate the feelings and the policies of the enemy, or examine any just grievances that the enemy might possibly have. The enemy's soldiers will not be given prisoner of war status and will be tried in special military courts.

Similar to the enemies of the Cold War, the enemy in the new war is portrayed as sinister, cunning and underhanded. This time—and it is no insignificant difference—the enemy actually struck mainland America on September 11 and before, and is likely to strike again. The fear is that the enemy will develop and use weapons of mass destruction against us—nuclear weapons, or more likely, radiological dispersion devices, also called "dirty bombs" (conventional bombs to which radioactive material has been added). The result iwould be the spread of radioactivity over a large area. But we are advised that we should not panic. Just be careful and vigilant.

This war too, Washington advises us publicly and in advance, is a war of global proportions. It is an open-ended war with the world as its battlefield. The enemy assumes two general forms. One part is visible, above ground, represented by evil governments and reminiscent of the old Soviet bloc. So far only four of the enemy governments in the new war have been identified—the former governments in Afghanistan and Iraq, and two remaining "axis of evil" governments in Iran and North Korea. The other enemy component is invisible, consisting, we are told, of cells in some 50 or 60 mostly unnamed countries. These are not the cells of the communist party, but the underground organizations of what Washington chooses to call "terrorists". Whatever its form, whether bearing the legitimacy of government or existing underground, the enemy must be destroyed. To do this, we must sometimes act alone, unilaterally. Other times we can act with our allies.

Upgrading U.S. War-making Capacity

Two general ways of protecting the United States from terrorism, of "fighting the war on terrorism," have been identified. The first would "criminalize" terrorism as the way of protecting the country without recourse to war, whereas the second would adopt the same measures as the first except that it would add waging war.[2] The Bush administration chose the second way thus requiring that the military be expanded and that its mission and structure be changed. The estimate is that the military budget will expand some $48 billion for fiscal 2003 and reach $451 billions in 2007.[3] President Bush would increase the military spending over the next five years by a quarter of a trillion dollars. The annual defense appropriation signed by President Bush on October 23, 2002 was for 354.8 billion dollars.[4] The president took the occasion to complain that Congress did not add an additional ten billion to be used by the Department of Defense to fight terrorism. In May of the following year both House and Senate by lopsided majorities approved a defense budget of 400.5 billion.[5] Both houses acceded to the administration's request to lift the ban on research for developing low yield nuclear weapons.[6] Now research can proceed on producing nuclear weapons with yields of less than five kilotons that could neutralize caves and underground bunkers.

The Bush administration has tried to refashion NATO from an alliance directed against a Cold War enemy to one relevant to the war on terrorism. Early efforts have centered on a proposal to create a rapid response force that could be used against terrorists or those nations to whom the U.S. has decided to apply the term "rogue nations," whom it views as possessing or even threatening to possess weapons of mass destruction.[7]

The budget of the CIA—the agency that, together with special forces, played such a significant role in training state terrorists during the Cold War—has been substantially increased as well. Two days after the attack on the World Trade Center and the Pentagon, many senators and representatives declared that the ten billion the government already spends every year fighting terrorism was not adequate. Most preferred that the increases in intelligence be made in "old fashioned human spying" and more advanced computer tracking rather than in such areas as upgrading satellite capabilities.[8] Some three weeks later the House overwhelmingly approved legislation by voice vote that would "rescind restrictions on the hiring of unsavory foreign agents."[9] Speaker after speaker repeated the opinion that the CIA would have to change its methods if it were to cope successfully with terrorism. One Republican lawmaker from Nebraska remarked that the restrictions imposed in 1995 to rein in the sources that had violated human rights had produced a "chilling effect" on the use of agents who are effective in the battle against terrorism and drugs. The bill would also increase the intelligence budget by nine percent. (Although the amount spent on intelligence is classified, it was estimated to be between 27 and 30 billion before the increase.) Evidently, no consideration was given to negotiating solutions, discontinuing policies that generate or increase the enemy's anger and hatred, or adopting new policies that would decrease their numbers and help prevent the creation of new crops of terrorists.

No consideration was given to negotiating solutions, discontinuing policies that generate or increase the enemy's anger and hatred, or adopting new policies that would decrease their numbers and help prevent the creation of new crops of terrorists.

A Homeland Security agency was set up to fight terrorism at home, with a political friend of the president acting as its head and several agencies put under its jurisdiction. There is evidence that homeland security—whose purpose is truly defensive rather than offensive—is under funded. For example, port security has received only one-tenth the amount that the Coast Guard says is needed.[10] A major weakness in home security is the desperate financial position of state and local governments. Impoverished by a sluggish economy and the drying up of federal grants, they have been forced to reduce expenditures not only for education and welfare, but also for police and fire departments. The latter are the first line of defense against terrorism on mainland America, and their perilous financial position is related to the federal tax cuts, favorite items in the domestic agenda of the Bush administration which favors tax breaks for the rich as a way of stimulating the economy.

In his first State of the Union Address, President Bush said "I will not wait on events, while danger gathers."[11] Later, he directed his top security aids to formulate a radically new national security doctrine and strategy called "preemption".[12] The doctrine and the strategy were created for use against those designated as terrorist groups "of global reach" and such states as Iraq that were accused of aiding terrorists and attempting to develop nuclear weapons or other weapons of mass destruction. As explained by Condoleezza Rice, the National Security Adviser, preemption "means forestalling certain destructive acts against you by an adversary." She added that there are times when you cannot wait to respond. What she evidently meant is that "you respond first, before your adversary strikes." Put in more accurate English, you initiate the violence, an act that traditionally has been called "aggression." The war against terrorism thus includes the preemptive strike, in which Washington "responds" before an adversary, or even a suspected adversary, initiates an aggressive act. Bluntly put, Washington seeks to convey the notion that "the enemy" is so evil that aggression is an acceptable strategy to be used against him. In the case of Iraq, the range of such strategies has run from attempts to assassinate Saddam Hussein to a full-scale invasion of Iraq.

Preemption contrasts starkly with the non-aggressive deterrence doctrine that served both Washington and the Soviet Union during the Cold War. Deterrence sought to prevent an attack by an aggressor, notably a nuclear attack, by threatening to retaliate. Washington built a mighty nuclear and conventional arsenal with the declared purpose of dissuading the Soviets from striking the first blow. The arsenal was planned to be of such dimensions that a Soviet attack would not destroy it and that Washington could retaliate with crushing nuclear force. The Soviets built what they judged to be a similar arsenal.

Preemption contrasts starkly with the non-aggressive deterrence doctrine that served both Washington and the Soviet Union during the Cold War.

The George W. Bush administration also rejected non-proliferation as the way of preventing the spread of nuclear weapons, *i.e.* of preventing their spread by peaceful means only. It has reserved for itself the right to attack those nations that it accuses of seeking to develop nuclear weapons or other weapons of mass destruction. Washington did engage in preemptive attacks during the Cold War, two examples being Panama and the Dominican Republic. The difference in the George W. Bush era is that aggression is now Washington's announced, overt policy. In both eras Washington supported rightwing dictators who committed state terrorism.

AFGHANISTAN: NO END IN SIGHT

The Soviet Union invaded Afghanistan in 1979, only to be forced out ten years later by the guerrilla tactics of the *muhajidin*—local fighters or volunteers from abroad who later would be labeled "Muslim extremists." Initially called "freedom fighters" by the Reagan administration, they later would be called "terrorists" by subsequent administrations. Their victory was due in large part to the massive military aid they received from Washington. Funneled through Pakistan's interservices intelligence, this aid was a large part of what has been called "the biggest single CIA covert operation in the world."[13] The aid totaled some 2.8 billion. Washington worked together with Pakistan, Saudi Arabia, and Egypt in financing and transporting anti-communist fundamentalist groups in the Muslim world to take part in the anti-Soviet jihad.

It was in this way that the young Osama bin Laden came to Afghanistan. He later observed, "To counter these atheistic Russians, the Saudi Arabians chose me as their representative in Afghanistan."[14] He added that at first he set up camp where the volunteers were trained by Pakistani and American officers. The weapons were supplied by the Americans, the money by the Saudis. Bin Laden also used his own money for this project. The seventeenth child of multiple marriages that produced 52 children, he inherited a fortune which he increased many fold by shrewd investments. Eventually this process generated al Qaeda which in turn provided troops for the Taliban, both groups emerging from the anti-Soviet strife of the warlords sustained by aid from Washington. Bin Laden "learned" from the successful struggle that forced the Soviets to leave Afghanistan that the superpowers are not invincible. He thus resolved to take on the United States.

Al Qaeda was founded at a *mujahideen* camp in Khost, Afghanistan as a loose organization of Arab militants.[15] Its purpose was to wage war beyond the borders of Afghanistan, but it became operational as an international terrorist group later in the period 1991 to 1996 when bin Laden settled down in the Sudan. After the end of the war in Afghanistan, bin Laden returned to Saudi Arabia, only to be expelled from that country two years later in 1991. With his private fortune and his access to outside funding, he controlled the purse strings of al Qaeda. He has also been described as the face of the organization, the chairman of the board. Much of the leadership group consisted of members of the Islamic Jihad, which provided many professionals for the new organization. It was led by Ayman al-Zawahiri, an Egyptian physician, nationalist, and revolutionary, who in effect became a CEO of al Qaeda. He was a pioneer in the systematic use of suicide bombers, and in the practice of recording their messages before they embarked on their deadly missions. He imposed a blind cell structure on the organization, whereby the members of one cell did not know the identity or the activities of the members of another cell. Al-Zawahiri had reason for this precaution. Islamic Jihad was dealt a devastating blow when Egyptian authorities obtained the entire database of the membership. In the Sudan, bin Laden pursued the jihad in general and against the United States, combining this with his successful efforts to increase his wealth. He was joined there by al-Zawahiri, after the eclipse of Islamic Jihad.

"The Taliban, mysterious new actors, burst onto the chaotic Afghan political scene in November, 1994, by 'rescuing' a 30-truck Pakistani commercial convoy on its way from Quetta to Turkmenistan."[16] The convoy was intended by Islamabad to demonstrate the feasibility of trade between Pakistan and the central Asian republics, but it was halted before it reached Kandahar by warlords demanding ransom. Members of the Taliban from Pakistan freed the convoy and proceeded into Kandahar which they captured after two days of fighting.

Inspired by an extreme form of Islam, funded by the Saudis, and armed and trained by Pakistan, the Taliban became a military force that imposed its will on a country that had been torn apart by civil war, invasion, and anarchy. While not directly involved, Washington saw the takeover of Afghanistan by the Taliban as a way of containing Iran and as a step in securing an alternate land route for United States petroleum companies anxious to build a pipeline for exploiting the oil and gas reserves of central Asia. The Taliban were seen as providing security for this land route that would link the central Asian states to the international markets through Afghanistan rather than Iran. "The U.S. assistant secretary of state for south Asian affairs, Robin Raphael, went so far as to state that the Taliban capture of Kabul was a 'positive step.'"[17] The Taliban were expected to act like the Saudis—an emir, no parliament, the guise of a peculiar view of Islamic law, and petroleum companies and pipelines. Behind American policy toward the Taliban lay UNOCAL, a consortium of U.S. oil companies formed to exploit the petroleum reserves of central Asia. Working with its Saudi partner Delta, the American consortium "hired every available American involved in Afghan operations during the jihad years, including Robert Oakley, a former ambassador to Pakistan, and worked hand-in-glove with U.S. officials."[18] UNOCAL staff acted as an unofficial lobby for the Taliban, and were regularly briefed by the CIA and Pakistan intelligence. With the appointment of Madeleine Albright as secretary of state, Washington's policy shifted against the Taliban. The reason given was the terrible human rights record of the Taliban, but there was also the matter of the feminist vote in an upcoming election.

Taliban is the Persian plural of the Arabic word *talib* that refers to a religious student of humble social status who receives religious training based on the Quran, learned by rote in rural-based madrasas in Afghanistan or in Muslim areas of central Asia. They have been part of the landscape in this region since the Arab conquest. But the Afghan Taliban have known nothing but war. Most of them were born in refugee camps in Pakistan; some of them were orphans. They were educated in the madrasas of the Northwest Frontier Provinces of Pakistan or Baluchistan. If they spoke a second language, it was Urdu, not Persian, the lingua franca of their homeland. They were rootless, influenced by the ideology of the madrasa in Pakistan.[19] Their numbers were augmented by defectors from the warlords, and later by conscription. The leader of the Talliban was Mullah Mohammed Omar, chosen as leader because of his piety. The son of poor landless peasants, he became a village mullah and opened a madrasa.

Kabul fell in 1996, and the Taliban established control over most of the country, except for an enclave in the northeast ruled by warlords usually referred to as the Northern Alliance. The Taliban established a rigid Islamic theocracy and violated the rights of the Afghan people, especially women, who were required to wear the burqa and could only go outside if accompanied by a man. Non-religious movies as well as radio and TV were banned. A moral police force was formed, and it enforced the religious code with severity.

After terrorist experts determined al Qaeda was behind the 9/11 tragedy, Washington demanded that the Taliban government hand over Osama bin Laden immediately "as well as all the leaders of al Qaeda who hide in Afghanistan." On Sunday, October 7, Washington launched the war with a massive air attack—cruise missiles, carrier based aircraft, and land based bombers. After the attack, the Taliban government agreed to hand over bin Laden and his associates at least for trial before an international tribunal if Washington would stop its offensive. Sterba raised serious doubts that Washington's behavior satisfied the requirements of just war theory. He granted that Washington had a right to respond to the unjust 9/11 attacks, but doubted that it exhausted nonbelligerent correctives first. Moreover, did the response meet the requirement of proportionality demanded by just war theory? In measuring proportionality, the fact that Afghanistan had been at war for twenty-two years and had suffered a drought for three years had to be taken into consideration. [20] The second phase of the war was the ground offensive, a campaign fought mainly by the Northern Alliance with help from American and British troops. The Bush administration first named the war 'Operation Infinite Justice," but when objections were raised, it downgraded the name to "Operation Enduring Freedom." These military operations went remarkably well, and Kabul was taken on November 15.

Washington attacked the Afghan government only three weeks after the 9/11 tragedy. It thus demonstrated that it was determined to protect the nation against terrorism, "to fight the war against terrorism," not only by police measures—interpreting the determination to protect the nation as actions undertaken to constrain and apprehend criminals— but also by actually waging war against governments. This, despite the fact that former approach is recognized as the most promising way a government can use to protect its citizens against terrorism if that government is interested in peace.[21] Such an approach involves the kind of police measures actually adopted by Washington and other governments such as anti-terrorist measures affecting airplanes and airports, as well as foreign policy measures such as pulling troops out of Saudi Arabia, and threatening to reduce aid to Israel. The use of war, however, increases the damage to the victim country and the innocent parties therein. This increases the moral dilemma posed by just war theory, as well as increasing the hatred that can result against the perceived aggressor, as has been demonstrated in the recent war against Iraq.

Washington decimated Taliban resistance in the north of the country, thereby opening the route south for the Northern Alliance. Finally dispensing with the notion of returning an ousted king to a resurrected Afghani throne, the U.S. facilitated the establishment of the Afghan Interim Authority, consisting of those who had opposed the Taliban or who were in the diaspora. The Interim Authority elected Hamid Karzai as its chairman. This was to be followed by the writing of a constitution and nation-wide elections to be held in 2004.

However, the Bush administration's purported success in Afghanistan appears to be on the way to unraveling. A news report filed in Kabul on April 25, 2003 revealed that: "In a very real sense, the war here has not ended."[22] The report was filed some 17 months after the fall of the Taliban government and just six days before Defense Secretary Donald Rumsfeld, also in Kabul, would declare the end of major combat operations in the country and a shift to a new phase of stabilization and reconstruction. In fact American military forces were still engaged in major military operations with Taliban groups as large as 100 in the early months of 2003.[23] As though to further call in question the secretary's assertion, one month and one day after he made it, a U.S. military force of 500 launched an offensive against a Taliban and al Qaeda group in the Shahikot Mountains in southeastern Afghanistan.[24] The group was thought to be setting up a base camp either for ambushing foreign forces or aid workers or to engage American troops in another battle. It was here on March 4, 2002 that the Taliban/al Qaeda warriors had shot down two American helicopters, killed seven troops, and wounded eleven others.

The news report cited above revealed that nearly every day there are killings, explosions, shootings, and targeted attacks on American forces, Afghan officials, and foreign aid workers. There is continuous feuding among the warlords and no clear picture yet of who or what will stop the feuding and the violence, though it is unlikely to be the 11,500 American, Rumanian, and other foreign soldiers who spend their efforts mainly in hunting down the Taliban and al Qaeda forces or the 5,000 peacekeepers in the capital—the only territory in Afghanistan that could (with some stretching) be described as under the control of the Karzai government. As yet the Karzai government has no national army or police force; even the personal protection of Karzai himself has had to be undertaken by American forces. It is indeed strange that the American military base outside the city of Kandahar is protected by paid gunmen belonging to the local warlord. This is but one example of Washington's continued support for local warlords.[25] They were recruited for the war against the Taliban and provided the bulk of the ground forces for that war. They continue to receive Washington's support at the expense of the attempt of the Karzai government to unify the country.

The continuing airborne assaults and searches of homes are angering Afghan villagers, especially when fatal errors are made. No enquiries comparable to the lengthy investigation of the friendly fire deaths of four Canadians have been held for the accidental deaths of celebrating Afghani wedding guests mowed down by American firepower, or similar Afghan civilian casualties. There are still one half million internally displaced persons in the country. Most of these are in the south, and the vast majority are nomadic tribes people and farmers devastated by the drought. American soldiers at the Bagram Air Base near Kabul share many of the feelings of the Afghans. Insisting on anonymity, one soldier stated: "I don't feel comfortable watching us start on another war when this one remains unfinished."

Meanwhile, the Taliban have undergone a resurgence in the border regions of Pakistan, especially in Quetta. It is here that many of the Taliban took refuge after their government fell. They stay in sprawling refugee settlements in Quetta or with fellow tribesmen in remote villages. The main center of support for the Taliban, Quetta is a breeding ground for opposition to the American presence in Afghanistan and to the Karzai government. Taliban leaders are active, and they are recruiting young men to fight. They gather openly with growing confidence since an alliance of Islamic parties sympathetic to their cause won the provincial election in the fall of 2002. They launch attacks from their bases in Pakistan on targets in Afghanistan. Although 400 Taliban and al Qaeda members have been arrested in Pakistan, none of the senior Taliban leaders have been apprehended. "Those familiar with the situation contend that Pakistan's army and secret service are allowing the Taliban to operate in Pakistan, and even protecting them."[26] A former senator and opposition leader in Pakistan remarked: "America should have selected to crush al Qaeda and the Taliban in Pakistan rather than go to war in Iraq."

The Guantanamo Bay Prisoners:
A Public Assault on the Rights of Detainees

Washington decided to hold some 664 enemy combatants captured in the Afghan war and elsewhere in a prison in a United States military base located in Guantanamo Bay, Cuba, outside of the jurisdiction of the American court system. The largest group (150) are Saudis, followed by Yemenis and Pakistanis. The prisoners are held without formal charges being filed against them, and for lengthy undetermined periods, without access to lawyers. The Bush administration refused to grant them prisoner of war status, which would have given them, inter alia, immunity from prosecution for many acts committed during a lawful war. The government contends that they are "illegal combatants," which in actuality places them in a kind of legal limbo, drawing criticism from human rights groups. In a statement of February 7, 2002 President Bush announced that the Geneva Conventions would apply to the conflict in Afghanistan and to the Taliban detainees, but not to al Qaeda. However, neither the Taliban nor al Qaeda would be granted prisoner of war status.[27] The meaning of this statement is not clear, since prisoner of war status is one of the chief classes of norms contained in the Geneva Conventions.

Since the Bush administration is actively waging its own private war against the International Criminal Court (see Chapter 10), it has no intention of using that court to prosecute the prisoners held at Guantanamo Bay. Rather, it intends to establish special military tribunals for this purpose, an announcement that has sparked considerable controversy. Human rights advocates argued that the special courts would not only violate the civil liberties guaranteed under American law, but that they would breach international law guaranteeing fair treatment for prisoners of war, such as the Geneva Conventions.[28] Prisoners would not be allowed to appeal a decision from the military courts to civilian courts, a right guaranteed to Americans. While the Pentagon was ready in April, 2003 to establish the special military courts after some eighteen months of planning, this did not necessarily mean that any trials would take place soon, since the primary purpose of incarceration was to facilitate the extraction of as much information from the prisoners as possible,[29] rather than to prosecute them for crimes. Perhaps the Pentagon is hoping that the defendants will plea bargain by exchanging the maximum of information about al Qaeda for a reduction in their sentences. According to the Geneva Conventions, prisoners of war are not required to give more information than their name, rank, serial number, and date of birth.[30] The conventions forbid the torturing of prisoners either physically or psychologically. Attempts to obtain information from them through such means as placing them in overheated cells have resulted in convictions on war crimes charges.

Photographs released by the Pentagon itself indicate that the prisoners held in Guantanamo are being subjected to psychological torture. The photographs "showed some of the prisoners kneeling before their captors, their legs in shackles, bound in manacles, their mouths covered by surgical masks and their eyes blinded by large goggles with black tape."[31] Amnesty International pointed out that sensory deprivation, humiliation, the use of unnecessary restraint, and keeping prisoners incommunicado were classic techniques used to break the spirit of prisoners before interrogation. The evidence thus leads to the accusation that Washington itself is guilty of psychological torture. There have been 25 suicide attempts at the camp, and more than five percent of the prisoners are being treated with antidepressants.[32] Interviews with 32 Afghans and three Pakistanis in the weeks following their release from the prison on Guantanamo indicate that the prisoners there have been subjected to psychological torture. The uncertainty of their fate, combined with confinement at first in small wire-net cells with only a wooden roof to protect them from the elements, with only Arabic-speaking prisoners nearby with whom they could not communicate, led to suicide attempts.[33] One Pakistani tried to kill himself four times in 18 months. The prisoners ate, slept, prayed, and went to the toilet in their small cells. They were allowed to shower for five minutes and exercise once a week. The Pakistanis spoke of the overwhelming feeling of injustice experienced by the prisoners. Several governments have argued that the prisoners should be accorded prisoner of war status. The foreign policy chief of the European Union said that "changing our values and our way of life would be terrorism's first victory." Washington has also turned over terrorist suspects to countries like Egypt, Jordan, and Morocco whom it knows are willing to use "more aggressive questioning," or what human rights advocates term torture.[34]

Pakistan and Terrorism

Within 48 hours of the September 11 attacks, Secretary of State Powell telephoned General Musharraf, the president and dictator of Pakistan, asserting that he had to make a choice: either to cast his lot with the United States or have Pakistan remain an isolated, pariah state.[35] The general, who had been put in power by a military coup in 1998, chose the former option.

The case of Pakistan is fascinating in that it entails a dictatorship that had previously supported terrorism as defined by Washington being nonetheless invited by Washington to join the war against terrorism. The support for terrorism referred to here, of course, is the support that the Musharraf regime has given to the Kashmiri rebels who believe that Kashmir should not be a part of India, not to the support

The case of Pakistan is fascinating in that it entails a dictatorship that had previously supported terrorism as defined by Washington being nonetheless invited by Washington to join the war against terrorism.

that Islamabad gave to the Taliban or al Qaeda. Pakistan had been a supporter of the Taliban, and one of only three countries that established diplomatic relations with Kabul during the reign of that organization. In 1990 Washington imposed an embargo on military aid to Pakistan because of its nuclear weapons program. Economic sanctions were added after Islamabad tested nuclear weapons in 1998. The sanctions against Islamabad were lifted when Musharraf agreed that Pakistan would serve as a support and a point of entry for the war in Afghanistan. The Bush administration responded by putting together an aid package for Pakistan that is likely to total billions of dollars and that just might make that country a competitor with Colombia to become the largest beneficiary of American aid after Israel and Egypt.[36] Washington wrote down Pakistan's debt by one billion dollars,[37] signed a bilateral trade agreement with it, and Bush promised to ask Congress for 3 billion in aid.[38]

Pakistan supports Kashmiri terrorists in their attacks on India. Its intelligence service even used al Qaeda's camps in Afghanistan for training these terrorists. The State Department labeled the Kashmiri fighters "terrorists."[39] There is a striking parallel between the Indian-Pakistani dispute over Kashmir and the Israeli-Palestinian conflict. At independence, India took by force territory whose majority population was Muslim, and that therefore, according to the principle of self-determination, should have gone to Pakistan. Israel took by force most of what was Palestine, a British mandate whose population in 1946 was two-thirds Arab.[40] Both India and Israel designate as terrorists those who later use force to rectify what they regard as unjust.

Uzbekistan

Another front line state in the war in Afghanistan is Uzbekistan. While Musharraf is a dictator who assumed power in 1998, President Islam A. Karimov is a dictator left over from the communist era when Uzbekistan was a part of the Soviet Union. The government in Tashkent maintains an intense security system that tortures political dissidents. It represses democratic rights including the practice of Islam. Religious activity is allowed only in government-approved mosques, holy books cannot be widely circulated, and only clerics can wear religious garb.[41] Human Rights Watch has charged that at least 7,000 Muslims have been arbitrarily incarcerated in recent years. This led the late Senator Paul Wellstone, Democrat from Minnesota, to declare: "To ignore Uzbek abuses could add fuel to the fire that this is not truly a war on terrorism, but a war on Islam." Uzbekistan has become useful as a staging area in the war in Afghanistan. It has opened its airspace and an air base for use by the U.S. military. American military units, including infantrymen and Green Berets, are stationed in the country.[42] Some two and a half weeks after the September 11 tragedy, an undersecretary of state visited the country to consider what economic and security assistance should be provided.[43] The purpose of the visit was to increase aid from the United States which until then had been minimal.

An Afghan Warlord

The activities of General Abdul Rashid Dostum indicate that Wshington persists in supporting leaders who commit terrorism and suggest that the Taliban were not replaced by Afghani leaders with a commitment to human rights. Dostum is a notorious warlord and member of the Northern Alliance who fought as an ally of Washington against the Taliban and al Qaeda in Afghanistan. His special form of horror and terror is "death by container truck." Captured prisoners were herded together and crowded into sealed container trucks where they choked from lack of air while being transported to prison or to a mass grave. But this was not the only type of war crime that he committed. In January 2002, two investigators from the Physicians for Human Rights were shocked when they discovered 3,000 prisoners jammed sick and starving in Sheberghan prison, a facility meant for 800.[44] They had been captured by General Dostum's forces and surrendered at Konduz in late November. But they were the lucky ones. They were alive. Interviews with them revealed that hundreds of their fellow prisoners had been stuffed into sealed containers where they were left to die on the journey from Konduz to Sherberghan prison. They begged for water and air, but to no avail. Truck drivers who provided them with water or who punched holes in the containers to let in air were beaten by Dostum's guards. Overcome with thirst, they licked the sweat from each other's bodies. Some dead bodies were scorched black, the containers acting as ovens heated by the desert sun.

Dostom's special form of horror and terror is "death by container truck;" a means by which more than one thousand are estimated to have been killed.

Local aid workers and Afghan officials secretly confirmed the tragedy described above and revealed that the bodies had been buried in a nearby mass grave at Dasht-e Leili. An examination of a few of the bodies suggested that the cause of death was asphyxiation. The bodies revealed no gunshot wounds or other overt evidence of trauma. Although he granted that no one knew how many bodies are buried at the site, the director of Physicians for Human Rights exclaimed: "We are talking about a potentially enormous war crime."[45] The director of the Afghan Organization for Human Rights estimated that more than a thousand died in the containers.

U.S. special forces were in the vicinity when the death containers were delivered, and the Defense Department has obfuscated the issue and its "spokespersons have made statements (about it) that are false."[46] These troops "played a pervasive role in advising and coordinating the Northern Alliance troops of which General Dostum's units were a major part."[47] The Karzai government declared that the crimes detailed above have the appearance of a "horrible atrocity," and it agreed to support an investigation of it "and other similar atrocities." General Dostum has also promised to cooperate, but he has not initiated such an investigation, nor has he posted security to maintain the integrity of the mass gravesite, which is under his physical control. The United Nations special representative for Afghanistan has warned that any attempt to mount a full investigation, including the gravesite, "would pose serious risks to investigators and to witnesses."[48]

The Treatment of Arab and Muslim Immigrants in the U.S.

In fighting the war on terrorism, the Bush administration has discriminated against Arabs and Muslims—both those living abroad and those in the U.S. itself—and has thereby added to the anger that these targeted populations already feel toward the United States. In the weeks after the 9/11 attacks, the Bush administration rounded up a total of 762 illegal immigrants in the United States. All but 134 were from Arab and Muslin countries; only 11 were from Europe.

Jurisdiction over them was taken from the Immigration Department and put into the hands of the FBI. The Justice Department tried to cloak the activities of the FBI from an inquisitive media. But a report of the inspector general of that department in June, 2003 revealed that the FBI took 80 days to dispose of such cases, a task which would routinely be accomplished by the Justice Department in 24 hours. The report charged that the government considered these prisoners guilty until proved innocent and that every legal device, including some of questionable legality, was used to delay the process and even to delay the release of the prisoners after they had been ordered deported.[49] They were also delayed in obtaining an attorney.

The 84 prisoners who were arrested in New York City and incarcerated at the Metropolitan Detention Center in Brooklyn faced "a pattern of physical and verbal abuse" as well as "unduly harsh" detention policies. They were limited to one phone call a week, and they were put in handcuffs, leg irons, and heavy chains every time they were moved out of their cells. By June 2002, most of the 762 prisoners had been deported, yet not one was charged with being a terrorist. Questioned about the report of the inspector general, Attorney General Ashcroft stated, "we make no apologies" for holding suspects to see if they had links to terrorism.[50] He asked Congress for new, tougher laws for fighting terrorism, including the expansion of the death penalty.

The Bush administration required that foreign nationals from 25 Arab and Muslims countries residing in the United State register by April 2003. Eighty-two thousand did so. Of these, some thirteen thousand men over 16 were found to be living here illegally, and will probably face deportation. Many thought that the government would be lenient since they had cooperated by registering. But they were not promised leniency, and most officials believe that the bulk of them will be deported in what will be the largest wave of deportations following the 9/11 attacks. Only eleven of the total 82,000 who registered plus the tens of thousands of those screened at border crossings and airports in the first six months of 2003 were found to have links to terrorism.[51]

THE THIRD PERSIAN GULF WAR

Congress Approves Preemption, the UN Declines

At the same time that the new policies of preemption and counter-proliferation were being aired in the press, President Bush asked Congress for the authority to use "all means" he determined to be appropriate, including force, to disarm Iraq and to dislodge Saddam Hussein.[52] He added that if the United Nations did not authorize the operation, Washington would go ahead anyway. The Senate gave its approval on October 11, two days after the House approved. The vote in the former was 77 to 23, the vote in the latter was 296 to 133.[53] The joint resolution authorized the president to use the armed forces as he deemed necessary and appropriate to defend the national security of the United States against the continuing threat purported to be posed by Iraq and to enforce the relevant Security Council resolutions regarding Iraq. Immediately after the resolution passed, President Bush remarked that the Congress had spoken clearly to the international community and to the Security Council and that "America speaks with one voice." The Senate vote of over three to one, and the House vote of over two to one were impressive, and the American public in general seemed to go along with the authorization as well. That is not to say that there was not opposition in the United States and especially in Europe and the Middle East.

President Bush had less luck at the United Nations Security Council, where he met the opposition of China, Russia, and particularly that of France. He did get a resolution unanimously passed by the Council that called for a tough United Nations regime authorized to search in Iraq for the presence of weapons of mass destruction and the means to produce them. But the resolution did not mention regime change, nor did it call for "all necessary means" to enforce its terms, items originally insisted upon by the Bush administration.[54] Despite intensive diplomatic hardball, the U.S. administration was unable to round up sufficient support in the Security Council to pass a second resolution explicitly permitting its intervention: not among the permanent members, nor indeed, could it even be assured of the support of a numerical majority. So it decided to dispense with the process altogether, and simply proceed almost unilaterally, with its "coalition of the willing," composed overwhelmingly of American troops, some from Britain, and a token force from Australia, though the addition of numerous very small states making minor contributions of one kind and another permitted the administration to claim that it had assembled a sizeable coalition of states.

Protest by the Public and by International Lawyers

International Lawyers

The invasion of Iraq was condemned as illegal by the International Committee of Jurists in Geneva (the ICJ), 315 professors of law at 87 law schools in the United States, 43 members of Australia's legal establishment, and 31 professors of international law in Canada. In their declaration, the American professors stated that this invasion was in defiance of America's treaty obligations and a violation of American and international law[55] insofar as the United States Constitution holds that treaties are the supreme law of the land and that the United States government had ratified the United Nations Charter, which is a treaty. The Charter provides that except in response to an armed attack, nations may not threaten or engage in warfare without the authorization of the Security Council. The ICJ expressed "deep dismay" at what it charged amounts to "a war of aggression," and "a great leap backward in the international rule of law."[56] It dismissed the notion that Security Council resolution 1441 authorized the invasion, as the Bush administration maintained. It noted, moreover, that the illegality of the war was not merely an academic question. The German constitution expressly forbids any support for a war of aggression. Thus the German government could be held responsible for allowing the American military to use its airspace and territory in the prosecution of the war. For this reason, Chancellor Schroder referred to the war as being "not justified," not as being illegal.

In their open letter issued just before the war started, the Canadian professors condemned the war as a violation of the United Nations Charter and as a fundamental breach of international law "that would seriously threaten the integrity of the international legal order that has been in place since the end of the Second World War." They declared that this action by Washington and its allies "would simply return us to an international order based on imperial ambition and

The invasion of Iraq was condemned as illegal by the International Committee of Jurists in Geneva, 315 professors of law at 87 law schools in the United States, 43 members of Australia's legal establishment, and 31 professors of international law in Canada.

coercive force." The Australian jurists characterized the invasion as an open breach of international law and as a crime against humanity.[57] They added that the "coalition of the willing" had not provided any persuasive arguments that the invasion could be justified by international law and charged that the doctrine of preemption as elaborated by the Bush administration represented a repudiation of the United Nations Charter. They warned that Australia's participation in the war would make members of the government liable to prosecution before the International Criminal Court.

Religious and Ethical Opposition

A month before President Bush asserted that "America speaks with one voice," the Catholic bishops of the United States indicated that they spoke with a different voice. The bishops sent a letter to Bush in which they warned that any "pre-emptive, unilateral use of force to overthrow the government of Iraq" could not be justified at that time.[58] They used Catholic just war criteria to support their position, essentially the same criteria that Archbishop Tutu used in his moral evaluation of the violence that occurred in South Africa.

The bishops argued that there was no clear and adequate evidence of an imminent attack from Iraq or that this country was involved in the September 11 attacks. Catholic just war criteria require that the injury posed by the nation to be attacked must be certain, lasting, and grave; the bishops concluded that Iraq did not pose the probability of being able to inflict such an injury on the United States. Furthermore, they found that the proposed attack lacked "proportionality." The damage that such an attack would inflict on the people of Iraq was out of proportion to the damage posed by Iraq to the United States. The people of Iraq had suffered from two devastating wars, plus years of sanctions that alone resulted in the deaths of hundreds of thousands of children. These sanctions were imposed by the United Nations under pressure from Washington. Another war would increase their suffering geometrically. At their annual fall meeting two months later, the cardinal who introduced a resolution added that it did not ignore Iraq's dangerous behavior, intentions, and threats. The bishops debated an amendment that would have pledged "prayerful support" for those military personnel who "conscientiously dissent from a choice for war." The objection was raised that this would imply that the personnel that followed orders and fought the war were wrong. If the bishops had adopted this amendment, they would have taken a step in the direction of the path forged by Archbishop Romero of El Salvador when he forbade the military of that country to obey orders to commit atrocities. Instead, the bishops chose to compromise on this issue. They expressed support for those who seek to exercise their right to conscientious objection as well as those "who risk their lives in the service of their nation."[59]

The bishops' claim that Iraq presented no clear and adequate evidence of intending an imminent attack on the United States was supported by the CIA. The agency granted that Iraq's efforts to acquire nuclear weapons and to build its arsenal of chemical and biological weapons were a serious concern. In a letter dated October 7, 2002 addressed to the chairman of the Senate Intelligence Committee, the director of the agency also expressed the view that Saddam Hussein's likelihood of using weapons of mass destruction grows as his arsenal grows. But the letter declared that "Baghdad for now ap-

The bishops' claim that Iraq presented no clear and adequate evidence of intending an imminent attack on the United States was supported by the CIA.

pears to be drawing a line short of conducting terrorist attacks with conventional or C.B.W. (chemical or biological weapons) against the United States."[60] The letter continued, "Should Saddam conclude that a U.S. led attack could no longer be deterred, he probably would become much less restrained in adopting terrorist actions. Such terrorism might involve conventional means, as with Iraq's unsuccessful attempt at a terrorist offensive in 1991, or C.B.W." It added that Saddam might decide that assisting Islamic terrorists in conducting an attack with weapons of mass destruction against the United States would be his last chance to exact vengeance by taking a large number of victims with him. The CIA did not amend this public assurance—at least it had not by January 28, 2003.[61]

It was not solely the Catholic bishops in the United States that opposed this war, but "Christian leaders and ethicists who represent a broad swath of the nation's Protestant, Catholic, Orthodox, and African-American churches."[62] Included were not only the traditional pacifists, but also those who adhere to just war theory. Religious leaders who opposed the war greatly outnumbered those who supported it. The former included leaders representing the Catholic, the Episcopal, the Evangelical Lutheran, the Presbyterian, and the United Methodist Churches, as well as the United Church of Christ, the Evangelical Lutheran Church in America, the National Baptist Convention, the American Baptist Church, the Church of Christ, Greek, Syrian and Coptic Orthodox Churches in America, and some Muslim and Buddhist groups.[63] Their leaders were not convinced that the war was just, necessary, or wise. Exceptions were some large ministries, some conservative evangelical and Pentecostal groups, and the president of the Ethics and Religious Liberty Commission of the Southern Baptist Convention, who argued in a letter to President Bush that the war against Iraq was justified because it would be a defensive action against a nuclear or biological attack from Saddam Hussein. Jewish leaders were divided on the issue, with some of the Orthodox supporting a preemptive war even without a United Nations sanction.

Religious opposition to the war was not confined to the United States. Both the heads of the Church of England and of the Catholic Church of England faulted Prime Minister Blair for claiming that the invasion of Iraq was morally justified. They declared that his claim lacked "moral legitimacy."[64] Archbishop Tutu raised his voice in opposition to the war as well.[65] But it was the Pope who emerged as the foremost international moral voice against the pro-

Religious opposition to the war included Pope John Paul II, and the heads of the Church of England and the Catholic Church of England.

posed war. He also came out against the war against Iraq in 1991. In his annual address to scores of diplomatic emissaries assembled in the Vatican, he said, "no to war!" He said this in an exhortation in which he mentioned Iraq by name twice.[66] Wondering aloud about what to say about "the threat of war which could strike the people of Iraq," he added: "War cannot be decided upon, even when it is a matter of ensuring the common good, except as the very last option, and in accordance with very strict conditions, without ignoring the consequences for the civilian population both during and after the military operations." This was followed by an article that appeared in *La Civilta Cattolica*, a Jesuit magazine that is reviewed before publication by the Vatican's Secretariat of State and is said to reflect Vatican thinking.[67] It contained a point-by-point refutation of Washington's stated reasons for a military strike, arguing that none of them held up under close inspection. It gave as the real reasons for the military strike the interest in Iraqi oil reserves and the sense of a messianic vocation to "democratize humanity". The consumption of petroleum by the United States was outstripping what Saudi Arabia could provide, and thus the need to assure access to a supply from Iraq. A point of concern for the Vatican was that Washington would initiate war without the approval of the United Nations. Archbishop Jean-Louis Tauran, the Vatican's foreign minister, argued that this would open the way to the politics of the jungle.[68]

The Pope met with Deputy Prime Minister Tariq Aziz of Iraq and several days after that with Kofi Annan, the Secretary General of the United Nations. The meeting followed a month and a half campaign in which the Pontiff and Vatican officials repeatedly expressed opposition to a war against Iraq. This campaign included a visit from Joschka Fischer, the foreign minister of Germany. After the meeting, the two held a joint press conference in which they expressed their concern about the situation. Some three weeks before this, the Pope called a meeting at the Vatican of the religious leaders of the world. They represented Christianity, Judaism, Islam, Hinduism, Buddhism, Jainism, Zoroastrianism, and Sikhism.[69] They appealed to the believers of all faiths to work to avert a conflict in Iraq.

World Public Opinion and the War

It was not only the churches, the ethicists, and specialists in international law that opposed the war, but world public opinion as well. There were demonstrations against it on the five continents of the world. Appearing on CSPAN June 6, 2003, the political activist Arundhati Roy estimated that ten million people had participated in these anti-war demonstrations. That these demonstrations indicated that world public opinion opposed the war is consistent with the findings of worldwide

An estimated ten million people participated in anti-war demonstrations.

polls conducted by the Pew Research Center for the People and the Press before and after the war. By contrasting world public opinion on various issues as it existed before the war with this opinion after the war, the organization provided a way of judging the impact of the war on these issues. The nonpartisan organization polled 38,000 people in 44 countries in the summer and fall of 2002, followed by postwar interviews of 16,000 people in 20 countries and among the Palestinians.[70] The Pew Center's director commented: "The war has widened the rift between Americans and Europeans, further inflamed the Muslim world, softened support for the war on terrorism, and significantly weakened global public support for the UN and the North Atlantic alliance." Favorable views of the United States declined in nearly every one of the countries surveyed—from 60 percent to 43 percent in France, from 60 to 45 percent in Germany, and from 61 to 36 percent in Russia. On the other hand, the American view of France plunged from 79 percent favorable to 60 percent unfavorable. Seven countries still had a favorable view of the United States, but even in most of these nations this view had slipped.

Dislike for the United States spread in the Muslim world. The populations in seven of the eight Muslim countries polled felt that their countries might be threatened by the United States. They voiced the fear that Islam itself might be threatened. A large percentage of the Palestinians, Indonesians, and Jordanians expressed at least some confidence in Osama bin Laden. Those who expressed these unfavorable views toward the "United States" added that their views were directed "mostly at Bush," not at "America in general."

Another casualty of the invasion of Iraq was the war on terrorism. Majorities in Western Europe and Australia still backed it, but at reduced levels. Support dropped 15 percent in France and ten percent in Germany. Washington's four staunchest allies in this war were, in order, Israel, Italy, Australia, and Canada. In Muslim countries there was little support—fewer than 25 percent in Indonesia, Pakistan, Turkey, and Jordan, and only ten percent in Morocco. With the exception of the United States, every country surveyed, either by a majority or a plurality, thought that the United States "excessively" favored Israel over the Palestinians. Even 47 percent of the Israelis thought so, while 38 percent saw this policy as being evenhanded.

Operation Iraqi Freedom

On March 19, 2003, the third Persian Gulf war got off to an unexpected early start after a spy in Baghdad reported that Saddam Hussein and his two sons were attending a meeting in that city. The word of the meeting and its exact location were immediately passed on to President Bush who gave the order to bomb the location where the meeting was hopefully still in session. Whether this assassination attempt succeeded was not known; neither was it known whether Saddam was alive or dead. Thus started the third Persian Gulf war, which the Bush administration insisted on calling "Operation Iraqi Freedom." The military phase of it ended on May Day 43 days later, according to President Bush.

Bush made this assertion in a twenty-minute speech aboard the Aircraft Carrier Abraham Lincoln after a short flight in a navy refueling plane, with a navy pilot at the controls most of the time. In this carefully choreographed episode, the president was dressed in a navy fighter pilot uniform, complete with helmet as he walked across the flight deck. White House officials later admitted that they were mistaken when they told reporters that the president used the navy plane rather than a helicopter because the ship was too far off shore for the helicopter to make a safe flight. They admitted that he used the plane because he wanted to.[71] It was revealed also that the ship slowed down, so that the coastline would not appear on the TV screen as the president addressed the nation. In fact, the ship made "lazy circles" in the sea to avoid arriving too soon. This was the same day that Secretary of Defense Rumsfeld declared in Kabul that major combat operations in that country had ended. But major combat operations continued in Afghanistan, just as military operations continued in Iraq.

The war was originally planned as a *blitzkrieg* (a lightning war) that would use "shock and awe" to achieve an immediate victory. Although this strategy failed, organized resistance by the main body of the Iraqi army was short-lived. The war was actually a mixed match, the world's greatest military power against a country that was facing its third war in a quarter of a century, after 12 years of a crippling worldwide embargo, and almost a quarter century rule by a cruel dictatorship. The casualties of the coalition forces were kept low, although in its aftermath the number continues to rise. One hundred thirty-eight Americans were killed in the period ending May 1, 2003 when the war was said to have ended. The number of Iraqi casualties is not known—either military or civilian—although it is probably in the tens of thousands. The U.S. government has refused to count them. On the American side, the war was a technological wonder, presented in a sanitized manner by the American media. Some 500 reporters were "embedded" in the armed forces, and a host of ex-generals and lesser officers crowded the air ways. Few religious leaders, ethicists, or experts in international law were invited. Audiences in other countries, notably Arab and Muslim ones, received a different picture thanks to the Arab language network, Al-Jazeera, with the blood and guts of war exposed.

In Search of Weapons of Mass Destruction

Of the three reasons offered by the Bush administration for the invasion of Iraq: Iraqi possession of weapons of mass destruction—Iraqi ties to al Qaeda; and the need for regime change—only the last has been achieved. A *New York Times* editorial of May 26, 2003 remarked on the scantiness of the evidence unearthed by the military weapons inspectors contrasted with the fearful claims made by the administration before the war. The editorial identified these fearful claims as assertions that "Iraq had reconstituted its program to produce nuclear weapons, was continuing to make biological weapons and possessed a large stockpile of chemical agents some ready to be used against American troops or made available to terrorists." However, the only evidence to date that seemed to point to Iraqi WMD were, three mobile laboratories that some experts judged could be used for producing biological weapons.[72] Other experts argued that they were used for peaceful purposes.

The failure to find WMD has not been from lack of trying. The Exploitation Task Force, the first organization that searched Iraq for the weapons of mass destruction, investigated over 900 sites.[73] The great bulk of these were suggested by Washington's intelligence agencies the year before as areas where weapons of mass destructive were likely to be found. None were found. However before its demise, the organization shifted its operating procedure by checking the leads provided by the interrogations of Iraqi officials. This is the procedure to be followed by its successor organization, the Iraq Survey Group, and one that the administration advertises will be much more productive. The new group was to have three times the personnel of its predecessor.

Several prestigious newspapers in Europe were less kind in their criticism of the Bush administration than the *New York Times*. In a front page headline about the failure to find chemical and biological weapons in Iraq, the French newspaper *Le Monde* asked, "Did Bush and Blair lie about the Iraqi weapons."[74] It answered its own question in an editorial that asserted that the insistence by Washington and London that Iraq had such weapons amounted without doubt to "the biggest government lie in recent years." In a similar vein, the *Financial Times* assailed the Bush and Blair administrations. "It's time for a reality check," adding, "We have been deceived." After stating that to date no weapons of mass destruction had been found in Iraq, the *Frankfurter Allgemeine Zeitung* asserted that the Bush administration's justification for the war had crumbled and that American credibility had been weakened.

What looked more and more like an intelligence fiasco led the CIA to conduct a review of its prewar intelligence on Iraq. Intelligence officials revealed that several CIA analysts complained that senior Department of Defense officials and other officials in the Bush administration pressed them to produce reports favorable to the administration's position on Iraq.[75] Several current and former members of the agency were upset by the politicization of the intelligence concerning Iraq. The establishment of a special intelligence unit under the Undersecretary of Defense for intelligence created a furor in the intelligence community. It did not gather intelligence itself, but it reviewed the intelligence gathered by the intelligence agencies. The unit was established because some of the senior aids to Secretary Rumsfeld believed that these agencies were too dismissive of reports from Iraqi exiles and others that suggested that Saddam Hussein had programs to develop weapons of mass destruction and that he had ties with al Qaeda.[76] CIA analysts pointed out that the unit was staffed by ideological conservatives eager to offer the Bush administration an alternative view to the one provided by the CIA.

The notion that Iraq had ties to al Qaeda has come to be viewed as another example of the "politicization of intelligence". This was a prominent finding of a special intelligence group set up by the Undersecretary of Defense for policy, Douglas Feith, after the 9/11 attacks. The purpose of the group, as stated by Feith, was to search for terrorist links around the world that Washington intelligence agencies had overlooked.[77] He denied that its purpose was solely to find terrorist links with Iraq. Other defense officials argued that very soon after its founding the group did concentrate upon these later links. Intelligence analysts elsewhere in the government complained that this group provided a hardline interpretation of Iraq's behavior that Secretary Rumsfeld used in meetings with President Bush and national security officials. The charge by the special intelligence group of the links between al Qaeda were contested both by the CIA and the Defense Intelligence Agency. Defense officials also claimed that this intelligence group had a special relationship with the Office of Special Plans, a unit established in October 2002 responsible for preparing for a possible war with Iraq. Abram Shulsky, a neo-conservative, was appointed to head it.

In his State of the Union address in January 2003, President Bush asserted that Iraq had purchased uranium in Africa. This he offered as a way of buttressing his argument that Saddam Hussein had an active nuclear development program and was a threat to the United States. In making this assertion, Bush left his administration open to the charge that he was politicizing intelligence, or in the words of *Le Monde* and the *Financial Times,* lying. Now widely recognized to have no basis in fact, this assertion has been seized upon by the Democratic candidates at the expense of the Bush administration.

Postwar Plans: Postwar Chaos

Before the war started, the Bush administration drew up plans for the postwar period that were almost as meticulous as the war plan itself. The plans for the postwar period anticipated that Baghdad's police officers would be quickly returned to duty and that Iraqi soldiers would build roads and clean up the rubble. There would be cheering Iraqi crowds and a swift resumption of electricity and other vital utilities. The quick creation of an interim Iraqi civilian authority would convince even skeptical Arabs that the United States was not going to act as an occupier. Three days before the invasion, Vice President Cheney assured his listeners, "We will in fact be treated as liberators."[78] The plans assumed that the war would remove Saddam Hussein and his associates from power but leave civic structures in place.[79] But these structures did not survive the war, and chaos and anarchy ensued. The Bush administration tried to put the best face on the situation. Secretary Rumsfeld offered this explanation: "Freedom's untidy. And free people are free to commit mistakes, and to commit crimes."

In late January 2002, Secretary Rumsfeld nominated General Garner to head the Office of Humanitarian and Reconstruction Assistance, an agency that was to serve as the provisional government of Iraq. A neo-conservative with impressive business credentials, the general had served in northern Iraq in 1991. He also happened to be a former president of SY Coleman, a defense contractor that helped Israel develop its Arrow missile system, and was undisputedly pro-Zionist. His job was to oversee relief, reconstruction, and civil administration, with the goal of turning over his duties in stages to the Iraqis. He was to report to General Franks who was responsible for security.

Gathering a group of 200 specialists together, Garner left Washington in mid-March. But by early April he was still cooped up in a Kuwaiti hotel, able to make only day visits to Iraq because the Central Command deemed it unsafe to do otherwise. When he did move his office to Baghdad, he had only a tiny staff that lacked telephones, email, and the minimum of security when it left the office.[80] The general arrived in Baghdad on April 21, 2003 and made a low-key address to a gathering of doctors at Yarmuk hospital that was without electricity.[81] Much of Baghdad was also without electricity and TV, making it impossible for most Iraqis to know that the general had arrived.

In the meantime, the administration in Washington decided on a new policy: to accelerate the transfer of power to an Iraqi civilian authority. The administration also decided to replace General Garner—which also indicated that Washington had decided on a quicker transfer of power to the Iraqis. The original plan, and the one still in place as late as March, 2003 called for a three-step process from American to Iraqi control: an interim authority, then a provisional government, and finally the election of an Iraqi government by popular vote after the writing of a constitution.[82] But this plan was later rejected by the National Security Council on the grounds that a power vacuum was being created in Iraq and that it was being filled by anti-American forces often sympathetic to the theocratic government in Iran. The new plan called for the creation of a transitional government, not an interim authority, to be done within a month, by the end of May. The powers of the transitional government were not spelled out, but they could be expanded as thought expedient. The acceptance of the new plan was a victory for the Pentagon which wanted to put an Iraqi face on power quickly, and a defeat for the State Department and the CIA that advocated a go slow policy. They argued that to move too quickly would allow exiles like the Pentagon-backed Ahmad Chalabi of the Iraqi National Congress undue influence at the expense of candidates within the country. With the backing of Vice President Cheney, the Pentagon prevailed.

Secretary Rumsfeld revealed in an interview that he and his deputy Wolfowitz combed a list of fifty candidates looking for a successor to Garner before settling on Lewis Paul Bremer III. Although, like the general, he was a neo-conservative, he was a former diplomat, having served as Secretary of State Kissinger's executive assistant in the 1970's and as managing director of Kissinger Associates, the global consulting firm.[83] On the day of the announcement of the firing of Garner, black smoke billowed over Baghdad. It came from the burning of the city's telephone exchange center, lit on fire by car thieves to distract attention from what they were doing. On the other side of the city, hundreds of looters poured into a former palace of Saddam Hussein as American troops left it. With no functioning police force, hundreds of looters ranged through the city every day. Criminals shot officials and other criminals, and Iraqis began taking potshots at American soldiers. The chaos that continued to reign in Baghdad and other Iraqi locales was arguably one reason why Garner was sacked, but not the only one. The Kurdish leader Massoud Barzani referred to this chaos, but also to the other reason when he added that: "We are paying the price for the political conflicts in Washington."[84].

In another abrupt reversal of policy on May 16, Mr. Bremer told the assembled Iraqi leaders that the planned transitional government would not be created by the end of the month.[85] American officials would remain in charge of the government. A British diplomat expressed a preference for reverting to the use of the term "interim authority" for whatever polity was to be created in the future, not the term "provisional government." No date was set for the creation of the interim authority, and no details about its powers and functions were revealed. One Iraqi who attended the meeting said that the Iraqis who attended expressed strong disappointment at the reversal of policy. Bremer later revealed that for the immediate present he wanted to form a "political council" of 35 Iraqis that he would appoint and consult on policy matters and appointments of Iraqis to ministry posts under the occupation authority.[86]

One of the first directives of the Bremer government will be to disarm the country, to deprive militias, other groups, and ordinary citizens of heavy weapons that the former Hussein government had distributed widely among the population to facilitate civilian resistance to the U.S. invasion. Exempt from the directive, the Kurds were to be allowed to retain heavy weapons on the grounds that they fought with U.S. forces against Saddam Hussein. The largest Shiite group, the one controlled by the Ayatollah al-Hakim, objected to this exception, arguing that all militias should be treated alike. But it is this group's militia, the Badr Brigade, which is of the most concern to the Bremer administration since it was trained and supported by Iran.

The American military forces in Iraq have discovered that they are facing an unexpected source of organized resistance and danger. It consists of groups of former Baath party members, former members of the Iraqi army, those who benefited from the Saddam Hussein regime, and a steady trickle of Arab militants who come to Iraq specifically to kill Americans.[87] There are some 140,000 American troops in Iraq, and as they fan out to secure outlying areas they become prime targets for what is slowly being recognized as a mounting guerrilla-style resistance, whose goal is to so harass American forces that Washington will finally realize that it should leave.

On June 22, 2003 Mr. Bremer promised before a meeting of the World Economic Forum in Shumeh, Jordan to dismantle Iraq's state-run economy by selling state-run companies and drafting new legislation to encourage foreign investment and foreign trade.[88] Granting that the resulting rapid change would cause pain to some, he promised before the assembled businessmen and politicians to use oil revenues to establish a "safety net" for this purpose. His plan is to convert Iraq into a Middle East model of free trade and deregulation. The plan is to start by privatizing more than 40

Mr. Bremer promised to dismantle Iraq's state-run economy by selling state-run companies and drafting new legislation to encourage foreign investment and foreign trade.

government-owned enterprises that do everything from manufacturing steel to packaging food. Surviving state-owned businesses will have to face competition and make do without government subsidies or special deals. A senior official added that work had started on the drafting of a commercial code to protect investors and property rights.

After some wrangling with other American companies, the Bush administration awarded the first major contract for the reconstruction of Iraq to the Bechtel corporation. The initial payment to the corporation was $680 million, but independent estimates put the cost of the reconstruction effort outlined in the contract that Bechtel won at $20 billion. The contract covers virtually all of the major reconstruction projects in Iraq. These include ensuring that potable water is available; rebuilding Iraq's only deep water port at Umm Qasr; repairing two international and three domestic airports; reconstructing electric power plants; and building roads, railroads, schools, hospitals, and irrigation systems. Only

American companies were allowed to make bids. British companies were upset, because of their exclusion from the bidding process. Administration officials justified this by arguing that it would demonstrate to the Iraqi people that the United States is a liberator, intent upon bringing economic prosperity and democracy to them.

With some 47,000 employees worldwide, Bechtel is a huge corporation that took in $11.6 billion in 2002. "It has deep and longstanding ties with the power centers in Washington." Its chief executive serves on President Bush's Export Council, and a Bechtel director, George Schultz, was Secretary of State in the Reagan administration. Caspar Weinberger was the general counsel for the company before becoming Defense Secretary in the same administration. A *New York Times* editorial commented: "Awarding the first major contract for reconstruction in Iraq to a politically connected American company under restricted bidding procedures sends a deplorable message to a skeptical world."[89]

Domestic Casualties of War: State and Local Government

The initial appropriation to pay for the cost of the war was some $80 billion, to be followed by more appropriations. This has come at a time of recession and in the midst of federal tax cuts favored by the Bush administration. Despite the fact that they result in an astronomical federal debt, these tax cuts have become the favorite weapon of the neo-conservatives in their war against the welfare state. The states, the main providers of welfare, are now in the worst financial shape since World War II.[90] Financially dependant on the states, the cities and counties are in bad shape as well. State and local governments have used money set aside for rainy days, raided tobacco funds that were supposed to have provided health care for children, and taxed every possible vice. They have laid off employees, closed libraries early, withdrawn health care for the poor and mentally ill, dismissed teachers and state troopers, trimmed city police forces, and other services long taken for granted. States are scrambling to cut $100 billion from budgets that by law must be balanced. The president of the National Conference of State Legislatures said: "State governments are under siege. This is the real deal, and it's only going to get worse." Half of the school districts in Kansas have cut staff. In Texas 275,000 fewer children will receive health care in a state that ranks first

> "State governments are under siege. This is the real deal, and it's only going to get worse."

in the number of children without medical coverage. President Bush made it clear in an address in February at the National Governors Association that help is not on its way. "It's because we went through a recession and we're at war."

The brunt of the cuts at the state level have been in Medicaid and education, their two largest areas of spending. These cuts are in accord with the ideology of the neo-conservatives who would cut holes in the welfare state. Ironically, the third largest area of state spending and cuts is for prisons, cuts not in accord with the neo-conservative emphasis on physical security. Nor are the cuts in local police forces. These cuts have not only reduced security against crime, but also against terrorism. Local police forces have been called the first line of defense against terrorism. Facing a budget deficit of 3.8 billion, New York City cut its police force by 4,000 and the budget of the police department by 250 million.[91] At the same time the department has assigned 1,000 of the reduced force to counterterrorism at a cost of 150 million.

COUNTERTERRORISM: THE ROOT DOCTRINE GETS A FACE-LIFT

While at this writing, the U.S. has not yet launched actions against other "axis of evil" nations, the extension of its counterterrorism activities that are already taking place—and continue to reflect the basic premises of the Root Doctrine—merit brief attention. The aid and support that Washington currently gives to states to wage the war on terrorism has features in common with the aid and support previously provided to states that practiced state terrorism during the Cold War. This parallel is scary. The record leads to the fear that Washington is still loyal to the Root doctrine and that current recipients of Washington's largesse are violating human rights or practicing state terrorism, or will do so in the future. Chapter One indicated that during the Cold War, it was the CIA and special forces that were the main agents that taught counterinsurgency warfare, which served as the major means used in committing state terrorism. Both institutions, more often U.S. special forces than the CIA, have been busy in the war on terrorism teaching what now is called counterterrorism, the re-baptized version of counterinsurgency.

Both forms of violence seek to improve the intelligence capability of the receiving states and their counterinsurgency (now called counterterrorist) capability. The newly formed army of Afghanistan is being trained by American special forces. The Philippines, a country that is to witness the largest deployment of U.S. troops since 9/11 aside from Afghanistan and Iraq, is scheduled to receive more than 600 troops, 160 of whom are special forces.[92] Their primary job is to train the local soldiers in their war against the Abu Sayyaf rebels, but they will serve on patrols in rebel areas and will be authorized to fire in self defense. A measure of the importance accorded the mission by the Pentagon is the fact that the head of special operations forces in the Pacific was put in charge of the training operation.

Aid to Uzbekistan and to the warlord General Abdul Rashid Dostom was described above.. Three other countries merit particular attention as counterterrorism proliferates.

Russia and the Chechens

Chechnya, a part of the Soviet Union whose inhabitants were subjected to Soviet terror, did not attain its independence as so many other ethnic groups succeeded in doing when the Soviet empire dissolved, and it has resorted to violence to attain this objective. The sad fate of this ethnic group provides the first example of the triangular relationship forged during the war on terrorism. Violence in the period from 1994 to 1996 resulted in Moscow's granting a large measure of independence to Chechnya, but the violence erupted again in 1999. Estimates of the number killed vary but the numbers range from 90,000 to 200,000. It was reported in the early part of October 2002 that Russia had stationed some 85,000 troops in the area.[93] They man checkpoints by day, but retreat to their bunkers at night when violence reigns.

Both sides in the war have been guilty of terrorism, and President Putin has made it a point of honor to suppress the rebellion. In early 2000 Russian jets leveled Chechnya's capital Grozny and then occupied the city. Amnesty International reported that Russian police and soldiers have committed "serious violations of international human rights and humanitarian law" in Chechnya.[94] Years of abuse by Russian soldiers have been documented by organizations such as Human Rights Watch.[95] This abuse and these violations have alienated Chechen youth and have provided a fertile field for the recruitment of more guerrillas. Early on, Putin promised support to Washington in its war on terrorism, and Washington has reciprocated by shifting its attention from Russian oppression and terrorism, and focusing on the terrorism of the Chechen rebels.

Putin promised support to Washington in its war on terrorism, and Washington reciprocated by shifting its attention from Russian oppression and terrorism, and focusing on the terrorism of the Chechen rebels.

On October 24, 2002, some 40 of these rebels seized and held as hostage over 750 in a theater in Moscow less than three miles from the Kremlin.[96] This seemed to give the lie to Putin's claim that the Chechen rebellion had been all but crushed. Wearing masks and camouflage and heavily armed, they stormed into the crowded theater and wired themselves and the music hall with explosives. They declared that the purpose of the action was to free Chechnya. Putin responded by dispatching Russian special forces, commandos from the country's elite alpha counterterrorist squad to the scene. The siege lasted for 57 hours. A few shots by the rebels were mistakenly interpreted to mean that they were killing hostages. The commandos responded by pumping a sedative gas into the theater's ventilation system, and then storming the building and methodically shooting unconscious Chechens. Russian prosecutors later declared that 128 hostages died following the siege, 5 from gunshot wounds and 123 from the gas.[97] Private sources put the number higher, giving the total number of hostages killed as high as 142. Some sources claimed that only one hostage died of gunshot wounds, the rest from the gas.

Russian officials refused to divulge the name of the gas used. They adopted a policy of silence, the adamant denial of error, and even prevarication–reminiscent of their Soviet predecessors. President Bush supported the rescue operation by the commandos, arguing that it saved hundreds of lives.[98] "The president feels very strongly that the people to blame here are the terrorists," a White House spokesman told reporters.[99] "The people who caused this tragedy to take place are terrorists who took hostages and endangered the lives of others." The British have also condemned the attack. Moreover, Washington has repudiated Mr. Maskadov, regarded as a moderate leader of the Chechens, the one with whom the Russians could negotiate, and one who condemned the attack on the theater in Moscow, as "damaged goods," until he can demonstrate that he is not allied to extremists. A spokesman for Putin declared that Russia's goal now is to "wipe out" the Chechen separatists and that talks to find a political solution are almost impossible. He added that he did not know one Chechen leader with whom Russia could negotiate.

Algeria and the Islamic Salvation Front

In 1992 the Islamic Salvation Front (FIS), dominated by militant Muslims, won the national election in Algeria. The incumbent government promptly cancelled the election and maintained its grip on the political system. In a ten-year period a civil war between the FIS and the government cost the lives of some

100,000 victims. Human rights groups accused the government of brutality in its campaigns against its antagonists. Until December 2002, military training was the only type of military involvement that Washington had with Algeria. This training started in 2001 and was scheduled to increase more than fourfold in the following two years. On December 9, 2002 the Bush administration announced that it would sell weapons to the Algerian government to help combat Islamic militants.[100] No weapons had been given or sold to the Algerian government since it cancelled the elections in 1992, and the amount to be sold after December 2002 was not determined. But an American official declared that the Algerians had proved to be helpful in general and that America wanted to be helpful to them. Algeria has indicated that in its fight against the FIS, more modern equipment such as attack helicopters would be useful.

Colombia

Washington has been providing military assistance to Colombia for over half a century. Over time, U.S. assistance has been categorized as in support of varying policy directives: the war against communism, next the war on drugs, and now the war on drugs as well as against terrorism. On a one-day visit to Bogota on December 4, 2002, Secretary of State Powell stated that the government's battle there against the drug trafficking of the leftist guerrillas and the rightwing paramilitary groups was part of the Bush administration's war on terrorism.[101] The secretary said it no longer made sense to separate the war on terrorism from the battle against narcotics, because they were linked as threats to democracy. Left unsaid was the fact that once again, the greatest number of casualties of the civil war has been inflicted by the army and the rightwing paramilitary groups, not by the leftist guerrilla groups. This general statement is found in several sources, one source charging the rightwing paramilitaries with over 70 percent of the politically motivated deaths. [102] It has been left to the National Union of Public and General Employees in Canada to give a more complete numerical breakdown. The union estimated that about 85 percent of the deaths have been caused by the rightwing paramilitary forces, 10 percent by the army, and 5 percent by the leftwing guerrillas. As incredible as this breakdown seems, it is substantially the same as found by truth commissions for Guatemala and El Salvador. Moreover, most of the fatalities in Colombia, some 80 percent, are civilians, and they are disproportionately union leaders.

Between 1986 and 1995, the war resulted in the deaths of 45,000, including 36,000 civilians. Amnesty International estimates that 3,700 were killed in 2001 alone, " mostly at the hands of the paramilitary groups."[103] In 2001 as many as 347,000 were displaced within Colombia, and more than 3,000 were kidnapped by guerrillas or paramilitary groups.

Washington gave $1.8 billion in aid to Colombia in the period from 2000 to 2003 earmarked for fighting narcotics and for the military and law enforcement. The Bush administration is asking for $537 million for fiscal 2003, up from $411 million for fiscal 2002. Colombia has become the number three beneficiary of U.S. aid (after Israel and Egypt).[104] Nearly $100 million of the money asked for fiscal 2003 is earmarked to safeguard the 500-mile oil pipeline in Eastern Colombia owned by Occidental Petroleum of Los Angeles. Next year 60 special operations forces and intelligence operatives will be sent to train Columbian forces to guard the pipeline.

Amnesty International charged that rightwing paramilitary forces operate in extensive collusion with the Colombian military. The former operate in highly militarized areas where they are allowed to travel freely and to pass through military roadblocks. "Frequently, serious human rights violations are committed against civilians in joint military-paramilitary operations."[105] In 1995 the rightwing paramilitary groups united to form a federation called the Self-Defense Units of Colombia, the AUC.[106] It is led by Carlos Castano and financed by his drug-trafficking activities and by wealthy and middle-class Colombians who lack faith that the army can protect their lives and their fortunes. Violence and the displacement of civilians in the countryside increased sharply. By 1998 AUC had tripled in size to 11,000.

On May 24, 2002 the Colombian voters elected the hardline candidate Alyaro Uribe Velez as president of the country. He received 53 percent of the vote in a field of four candidates. He appointed General Carlos Ospina as head of the army. Human Rights Watch charged that just four years before, the general, then lieutenant-colonel in charge of the Fourth Brigade, worked closely with the death squads of Carlos Castano to kill and to "disappear" some 42 members of the village of El Aro.[107] The village was considered to be sympathetic to the guerrillas. The soldiers surrounded the village to prevent anyone from escaping; after that the death squads went about their business. They captured a shopkeeper, tied him to a tree, gouged out his eyes, cut off his tongue, and castrated him. Next they mutilated and killed eleven villagers, including three children; burned the church, the pharmacy, and most of the houses; and smashed the water pipes. When they left, they took 30 people with them who were never seen again. This attack was only one of dozens of atrocities that Human Rights Watch charges were helped by the Fourth Brigade. The latter has been equipped with helicopters by the U.S. army. One of the first acts of President Uribe on assuming office was to promote General Ospina to his present position as head of the army and to instruct him to develop more death squads in the contested areas of the country.

CHAPTER 10

Conclusions and Recommendations

This, the concluding chapter, finds that the evidence of the preceding chapters indicates that Washington was an accessory to state terrorism during the Cold War through its counterinsurgency and other support programs, and promises to continue to be so in its newly launched war on terrorism, albeit with one striking difference: the willingness of Washington to take the U.S. itself to war against governments it deems enemies.

THE MAJOR FINDINGS OF THE STUDY

The charge leveled by Archbishop Tutu that Washington supported "some of the world's worst dictators" has been proved to be true in the six detailed country studies and in other evidence presented in the preceding chapters. These dictatorships followed policies of wholesale state terrorism, organized campaigns of deliberate acts of a physical and psychological nature designed to intimidate or coerce their victims by causing them intense fear, anxiety, apprehension, panic, dread, and horror. A mark of this terror in South America was the forceful disappearance of the victim. He or she was not only tortured before being killed, but the body was "disappeared" so that a proper burial would be impossible and the family would be denied closure. In Chile victims' bodies were burned or thrown from helicopters into the sea. The truth commission for Argentina was able to identify 8,960 such victims, "*desaparecidos*," whose mortal remains could not be found. The vast majority of the victims of state terrorism were not only innocent of acts of terrorism, but even of belonging to guerrilla organizations. The truth commission appointed by the United Nations for Guatemala charged the governments of that country with committing genocide, while the truth commission appointed by the Archdiocese of Guatemala City accused these governments of "genocidal activities," and left it to future research to determine if genocide actually had been committed. The Vatican's Foreign Minister charged the Indonesian forces that invaded East Timor in 1999 with genocide that did not spare the Catholic Church.

The vast majority of the victims of state terrorism were not only innocent of acts of terrorism, but even of belonging to guerrilla organizations.

The first sentence of the report of the truth commission for Argentina probably expressed what must have been a common reaction of many of the readers of this study. "Many of the events described in this report will be hard to believe." These readers by now are probably convinced that the truth commission reports were indeed "encyclopedias of horror," accounts of grisly, inhuman actions committed in great part by terrorist governments. Some 80,000 South Africans were arrested by apartheid governments and detained without habeas corpus or a trial. Many of these, especially African youth, were tortured. According to a United Nations task force, the invasion and subsequent atrocities committed by "the evangelical racists" in surrounding countries resulted in the deaths of an estimated 1.5 million people, half of them children. The estimate is that the three campaigns of terror waged by the Indonesian government resulted in a like number of deaths. The truth commission reports for Guatemala and El Salvador agree that some 95 percent of the atrocities committed during what were touted as "guerrilla wars" were committed by the governments of these countries. The American chairperson of the truth commission for El Salvador was so startled by this finding that he said that he wished that the guerrillas had committed more atrocities—in order to have made the findings of the commission more credible!

The comparison of the brutality of the terrorist states with that of their guerrilla enemies throws some light on the thesis of Professor Kirkpatrick who hypothesized that the brutality of communist regimes far exceeded that of authoritarian regimes. The comparison in this volume is not between the brutality of governments, but between that of authoritarian governments and guerrillas. The latter were sometimes communist, sometimes not. But the brutality of the authoritarian governments examined in this study greatly exceeded that of the guerrillas. The African National Congress even signed the Geneva Convention on the conduct of wars of national liberation and made a conscious effort to conduct its armed struggle within the framework of international humanitarian law.

The crimes of the state terrorists were the more egregious in that their perpetrators with precious few exceptions enjoyed immunity from prosecution. Even General Pinochet who during the height of the repression in Chile met every morning with General Contreras, the architect of Chilean terrorism, to go over what was planned for the day, was not extradited by England as requested to stand trial in Spain for having killed Spanish citizens during the repression. The reason given was the general's ailing health.

The findings of five truth commission reports were the major sources used for convicting the governments of El Salvador, Guatemala, Chile, Argentina, and South Africa of state terrorism and of having committed many more atrocities than the guerrillas. These reports in turn were based on thousands of interviews, mostly with the victims of terrorism. Twenty-eight thousand interviews provided the evidentiary base for the report on South Africa. Eight thousand of the interviewees were applying for amnesty, the other 20,000 were victims or witnesses to the atrocities. The United Nations commission for Guatemala stressed the same theme as this study, arguing that the response of the governments of that country to the guerrillas was totally disproportionate to any threat they posed. The governments indicted in the current study knew of the military inferiority of the insurgents, but exaggerated their capabilities in order to scare the middle and upper classes into accepting state terrorism.

The governments knew of the military inferiority of the insurgents, but exaggerated their capabilities in order to scare the middle and upper classes into accepting state terrorism.

As this study demonstrates, the countries which perpetrated the terrorism upon their own citizens were supported by Washington. Father Bourgeois is correct that it is at the School of the Americas "that the killing starts," that soldiers from Latin America learned counterinsurgency warfare there. Thousands of its graduates and those from other similar schools supported by Washington learned the techniques of state terrorism or techniques which, when slightly modified , could be so used. Two of the three dictators who ruled Argentina during the dirty war were educated at the School of the Americas.

True, the typical military government practicing terrorism did not receive the huge subsidy received by El Salvador, which received six billion dollars in aid from Washington in the period 1979 to 1992. But U.S. aid was often military, and often dispensed when by all estimates, Washington knew that the terrorism was taking place. In the case of Chile, the CIA has verified this fact, reporting that: "US military assistance and sales grew significantly during the years of greatest human rights abuses." In the case of Indonesia, Washington was afraid that General Suharto lacked the "courage to go forward" against the communist party and its allies and sympathizers. The bright prospect of witnessing the physical destruction of the Communist Party of Indonesia led Washington to encourage the slaughter that followed. U.S. support of Israel, which practices state terrorism against the Palestinians, has been massive, to the current tune of some three billion per year. Support for the former Shah of Iran took the form of the sale of the latest weapons to this oil rich country. Aid from Washington in the case of South Africa reached the extravagant level of help in producing weapons of mass destruction. These efforts were successful, and South Africa produced some chemical weapons and six atomic bombs. France, Britain, and Germany also aided, as did Israel. The latter cooperated with Pretoria, a strange case of nuclear cooperation between the survivors of the holocaust and the racists of Pretoria. Equally strange were the Israeli sales of munitions to Argentina during the dirty war, a repression that had an anti-Semitic edge to it. Washington and its Western allies helped Saddam Hussein develop WMD, and Washington maintains a stony silence in the face of Israeli possession of nuclear weapons.

Washington's support for rightwing dictators was bipartisan, but with the Republicans being more supportive than the Democrats. Schmitz traced the policy of support back to 1922, named it the Root Doctrine, and alleged that observance of it during the Cold War was a continuation of such observance in an earlier period. Chapter Seven demonstrated the bipartisanship of this policy by presenting instances of support from administrations from Harding to Clinton. Support was even extended to Saddam Hussein and the Khmer Rouge. The good neighbor policy and the Root doctrine were not only compatible with each other, but the adherence to the latter became a part of the strategy to accomplish the former insofar as it permitted foregoing the need to invade to change unwanted regimes. The Truman doctrine divided the world into the part that was free and the communist part that was totalitarian. The Truman administration then put rightwing dictatorships, if anti-communist, in the free world camp. President Kennedy befriended Mobutu, a dictator who ruled and plundered the Congo for 32 years. President Johnson invaded the Dominican Republic, overturned a regime that had been democratically elected, and helped install a dictator who ruled there for decades. President Carter supported the Shah of Iran.

A major theme that runs through the study is anti-communism, the ideology that supposedly fueled Washington as well as the rightwing dictatorships it supported. Also significant was Washington's concern to maintain stability in the countries given support so as to promote trade and investment opportunities for American business. The president of the Coca Cola company expressed his enthusiasm for expanding sales to Indonesia in this way. "When I think of Indonesia—a country on the equator with 180 million people, a median age of 18, and a Muslim ban on alcohol—I feel I know what heaven looks like." This remark gains salience in the context of America's new global enemy—resurgent Islam—and the fact that some 52 countries of the world have predominantly Muslim populations.

Most often during the Cold War period, the opposition to the dictatorships was not really communist, but activists struggling for some form of lesser social change. While resurgent Islam has replaced communism as the targeted ideology in the new war on terrorism, the struggle for social change in order to ameliorate well being remains a constant factor. The struggles could better be denominated as the ins versus the outs, or the haves versus the have-nots. Certainly an analysis of the victims of the rightwing dictatorships would lead to that conclusion. The Catholic Church, particularly its progressive wing, those who favored the theology of liberation, stood up to the dictatorships in Latin America, and often suffered the consequences. This church can hardly be accused of being communist. I accept class as the major motive that runs through the study, opposite movements struggling to change or to preserve the basic structure of society. Insofar as the individual societies themselves are not isolated from global society, with its existing socio-economic relations and attendant relative benefits for the dominant countries, and the U.S. in particular, it is hard to escape the implications of classic notions of imperialism and local resistance to it.

Even though class is a common theme that runs through the volume, subsidiary issues arise, and they do have impact. On this point I agree with Father Falla who accepted class as the central motive for state action in Guatemala, but recognized the ancillary role of the mestizos' prejudice against the Mayas. Similarly the domination of one people or peoples by another people or peoples also occurred in South Africa and was manifest in the struggle for self-determination in East Timor. But the racial divisions in South African society follow class divisions as well, and the struggle over East Timor had a class side to it as well as the more obvious nationalist side. "The dirty war" in Argentina had a more obvious subsidiary side, namely anti-Semitism. With the war on terrorism directed primarily at Islamic populations, it is to be expected that defense of Islam will play a further role in marshalling local resistance to negative socio-economic conditions and domination from outside, as will Islamic ideology in guiding it.

The preceding chapters indicate that the CIA actually planned the coup in Guatemala that brought down the democratic government bent on reform. In Chile it was in communication with three groups that were planning coups against the Allende government. It aided one such group, but claimed that it did not aid the one that succeeded. In Iran, the CIA was responsible for the toppling of the secular Mossadegh government, ushering in the rule of the Shah, which led in turn to the Iranian Islamic revolution. It set out to assassinate President Lumumba of the Congo, but someone else evidently beat the agency to it. It organized the Contras and carried out a series of attacks on Nicaragua's ports. It aided Saddam Hussein when he came to power in 1963 by providing him with a list of his opponents so that he could assassinate them. It launched a disinformation campaign in Indonesia in 1965 intended to induce the communist party to assassinate General Yani and to encourage the rightwing military to slaughter the communists and their sympathizers.

Washington as the Supplier of Arms to the World and Aid to the Violators of Human Rights

The reader might object that the detailed case studies and the other lesser ones chosen for the study do not represent Washington's typical behavior. However, Amnesty International found Washington to be the premier exporter of armaments that are often imported by nations that violate human rights Between 1989 and 1996, Washington sold over $117 billion worth of arms, 45 percent of world sales.[1] In the year 2000, Washington again was first in sales, and its share of the world market stood firm at 45.8 percent of the total.[2] In that year, Russia ranked second and France third. Israel ranked first in the year 2000 as the premier importer of weapons of those countries ranked as developing countries. Washington's sales are often lubricated and supported by financial assistance and military training. Since 1990 the hegemon has given away an additional $8 billion in "surplus" equipment from American stocks. These gifts included 4,000 heavy tanks, 500 bombers, and 200,000 light arms.

In September 1997 Washington released figures on exports of rifles, small arms, and riot control weapons—the dual use materials that can be used for police protection or for the violation of human rights including the practice of state terrorism. The figures showed that these exports were increasing rapidly. In the opinion of Amnesty International, they were exported to countries where human rights violations by governments were persistent and severe—Bahrain, Bolivia, Colombia, Egypt, Israel, Mexico, Pakistan, Saudi Arabia, and Turkey. From September 1991 to December 1993 the U.S. Commerce Department issued over 350 licenses for the export of such items as thumb cuffs, thumbscrews, leg irons, and shackles. The exports were to 57 countries, many of which had poor human rights records.[3] Over 2,000 licenses were issued to 105 countries under another program for the sale of electro-shock batons, cattle prods, shotguns, and shotgun shells. In addition, thousands of military personnel are trained by Washington either in the homeland or overseas. Over 100,000 from more than 100 countries have been trained under the International Military and Education Training program since its establishment in 1976. A larger number receive training under the auspices of the Foreign Military Sales program. More than 150 facilities in the United States and overseas are maintained for this purpose such as the infamous School of the Americas, mentioned above, whose graduates have become notorious for their gross violations of human rights.

Quantifying the Relation of Military Aid to Human Rights Violations

Three quantitative studies statistically verify the relationship between aid from Washington and the observance or non-observance of human rights by many receiving governments. The first tests this relationship for the twenty-three nations of Latin America for the fiscal years 1962 to 1977. The other two add countries from other regions, periods, and administrations. The second adds the Carter administration; the third compares the Carter and Reagan administrations. The human rights tested for in the first study were torture and other forms of cruel, inhuman, and degrading treatment, including prolonged detention without trial. These violations include some forms of state terrorism. The problem of determining the level of observance or non-observance of human rights was left in this study to the composite judgment of 38 experts from Western noncommunist countries who had published widely on the subject or who had occupied key positions in non-governmental or governmental human rights organizations. The experts' mean evaluation of human rights violations for the 23 Latin American countries served as the dependent variable. Chile was judged to be the greatest violator, Costa Rica the least. The independent variable was aid from Washington.

Aid has tended to flow disproportionately to Latin American governments that torture their citizens.

The correlations between the level of human rights violations and aid in the first study were found to be "uniformly positive," indicating that aid has tended to flow disproportionately to Latin American governments that torture their citizens.

In addition, the correlations are relatively strong: 8 of the 18 coefficients in Table 2 are +.40 or greater.[4] The seven countries that received little aid from Washington maintained a relatively high level of support for human rights, while the 16 that received comparatively large amounts of aid had a low level of respect for these rights. Colombia was the only major deviant from this pattern. The positive correlations persisted when account was taken of the marked differences in populations that characterize the countries in the region. When account was taken of these differences, "the findings suggest that the United States has directed its foreign assistance to governments which torture their citizens."[5] The positive correlations re-occurred when poverty was controlled for. Of the poorer countries, those that placed at the higher level of human rights violations received more aid. The positive correlations were even higher if military aid was related to human rights violations rather than total aid. This was the case because Washington favored with lethal aid the very repressive governments of Argentina, Brazil, and Uruguay, but also because the non-repressive governments received almost no military aid.

The findings of the second study re-enforce those of the first study, but add to them. For its field of inquiry, it used ten Latin American countries plus ten other countries from outside the region: eight from Asia plus Egypt and Israel. It extended its period of coverage to include the Carter administration. It faced the same dilemma as the first study in that, as it stated, there existed no reliable quantitative data on state violations of human rights and state terrorists' activities.[6] Governments have not been eager to advertise their infractions. As shown above, they minimize their infractions, while exaggerating those of their opponents. This study did not depend on the composite judgment of experts to estimate the observance of human rights by the states examined. Rather it used the ratings of three organizations: the U.S. State Department, Amnesty International, and Freedom House.

The second study found again that during the Nixon and Ford administrations U.S. foreign assistance was directly related to human rights violations. The more violations, the more aid received.[7] This was found to be the case if the ratings of the 20 countries were subjected to Schoultz's statistical technique, which was designed for testing interval data, or if a technique designed for ordinal data was used. Moreover, no great changes were found from the end of the Nixon-Ford period to the time of the Carter administration. Under this latter administration some positive correlations between amount of aid given and respect for human rights did occur, but they were so small as to lack much significance.[8]

The third study used the same three scales as the second one, but expanded its research arena to include 59 countries. Its time frame included the years from 1978 to 1983, thus allowing conclusions to be drawn about the Carter and the Reagan administrations and a comparison of the two. It found that no matter which scale was used for human rights violations no significant negative correlations with aid from Washington could be found for any year tested.[9] Furthermore, some of the correlations were positive, suggesting that the more violations that occurred, the more aid was forthcoming. This was found to be the case both for economic and for military aid. During the Carter administration military aid was terminated for only eight countries, all of them in Latin America. But five of these countries did this on their own, refusing the aid because of criticism of their human rights records by the State Department. Moreover, economic assistance continued, as did military spare parts and support equipment.[10] The article concluded that the best way to predict U.S. foreign aid disbursements for a given year is to use as a basis for prediction the foreign aid pattern of the previous year, indicating the consistency of aid patterns over time, whether in the hands of Democratic or Republican administrations. The article made two major points. The first was that the Reagan human rights policy regarding aid distribution did not differ significantly from that of the Carter administration. The second was that the human rights policy of neither the Carter nor the Reagan administrations appeared to significantly to influence "the distribution of United States foreign assistance, whether it be military or economic aid."[11] The authors charged that Carter's policies did not match the standard set by his rhetoric, but they added that his rhetoric might have mitigated the loneliness felt by the victims of human rights abuses. A more cynical view, of course, would be that the initiative was simply another of many efforts to provide a more pleasing façade to the brutal realities of U.S. foreign policy, in this instance specifically tailored to compete with the allure of communist rhetoric. The similarity between the aid patterns of the Carter and Regan administrations would probably come as a surprise to the general American public, as would the Carter administration's financial support for dictators that violated human rights.

WASHINGTON'S POLICY TOWARD THE INTERNATIONAL CRIMINAL COURT

By April 11, 2002, sixty-six nations had ratified the treaty establishing the International Criminal Court (ICC), thus assuring that the court would become a reality.[12] This is the first permanent tribunal established by the international community with the power to try individuals no matter their nationality or the scene of their crime for genocide, crimes against humanity, and war crimes. Following the terms of its constitutive treaty, its jurisdiction went into effect on July 1, 2002. The ICC is a great improvement over the long established World Court that can try cases only among states and cannot try the culprits, the individuals, who actually commit the crimes. The new court also represents a great improvement over the international criminal courts established for the former Yugoslavia and Rwanda. Washington played a leading role in the establishment of the International Tribunal for the Former Yugoslavia and the International Criminal Tribunal for Rwanda, and these tribunals' jurisdictions were restricted solely to their specific situations. The new court is the appropriate court for trying those accused of terrorism, including those accused by Washington of this crime. As indicated below, however, in all likelihood, this is not to be.

The International Criminal Court has been broadly welcomed by democratic nations, human rights organizations, and American lawyers associations. Most democratic nations have ratified the treaty that established it, including all members of the European Union. The Secretary General of the United Nations welcomed its establishment, exclaiming: "The long held dream of the International Criminal Court will now be realized. Impunity has been dealt a decisive blow." He added that its establishment constituted "a giant step forward in the march towards universal human rights and the rule of law." Richard J. Goldstone, the former chief prosecutor of the United Nations International Criminal Tribunals for the former Yugoslavia and Rwanda, declared that: "It will also be necessary to visit pariah status upon any nations that persistently refuse to become parties to the [ICC Rome] treaty"[13]

"It will be necessary to visit pariah status upon any nations that persistently refuse to become parties to the International Criminal Court." Richard J. Goldstone

that established the court. His statement, if taken seriously, would require that "pariah status" be visited upon Washington.

Washington's seat at the birthday celebration of the court was empty. This was symbolic not merely of the Bush administration's refusal to become a member of the court, but also of its hostility to the court. The *New York Times* remarked in an editorial: "But it (the court) has an implacable foe in the Bush administration, which argues that the court will open American officials and military personnel in operations abroad to unjustified, frivolous, or politically motivated suits." The main initial reason Washington gave for its opposition is that members of the American armed forces might be called before it for prosecution. This book has demonstrated why Washington might well be afraid of this possibility. Later the Bush administration added the specter of high civilian officials being tried before it as well. Administration officials informed Washington's allies in Europe that a major reason for seeking exemption was "to protect the country's top leaders from being indicted, arrested, or hauled before the court on war crimes charges."[14] To make their point, these officials referred to the pending trials of Henry Kissinger before American and Peruvian courts. The former Secretary of State is accused of aiding the coup that brought Pinochet to power and of supporting the ensuing dictatorship. Information presented in Chapter Three suggests that he is guilty of the latter charge. The officials said that at the heart of their concern was the fate of President Bush and Secretaries Rumsfeld and Powell.

Congress demonstrated that it is a foe of the court by passing a law forbidding Americans at all levels of government from cooperating with it—even as Washington seeks to have Americans exempted from its jurisdiction. The administration informed the Security Council that Washington would not take part in any peacekeeping operations unless its personnel are exempted from the jurisdiction of the court.[15] Some two weeks later on June 30, 2002, Washington's delegate vetoed the extension of the peacekeeping force in Bosnia, giving as its reason the danger faced by American soldiers of frivolous and politically motivated suits from the International Criminal Court.[16] Kofi Annan argued that the action of the American government put the entire peacekeeping system of the United Nations at risk.[17] The problem was temporarily solved, or at least put off, when it was discovered that in the Rome treaty there was provision for immunity from its jurisdiction for one year for peacekeeping personnel from those countries that do not accept the court.

Then Washington opened the war against the court on another front. It concluded pacts with Rumania and Israel whereby these countries agreed not to send American personnel to the court for prosecution.[18] Later Tajikistan and East Timor signed on as well. The agreement with Israel was a two-way instrument. Washington also agreed that it would not send Israeli personnel to the court for prosecution. The deputy chief of mission at the Israeli embassy in Washington claimed that **A new anti-terrorism law permits Washington to terminate all military aid to those countries that, upon becoming members of the ICC, do not pledge not to deliver Americans for trial by the court.** Israel shared America's concerns. It fears that its troops could be tried for actions taken against the Palestinians. An anti-terrorism law passed in early August 2002 provided Washington with teeth in negotiating such bilateral agreements. By its terms the administration can terminate all military aid to those countries that upon becoming members of the court do not pledge not to deliver

Americans for trial by the court.[19] Members of NATO and other very close allies of the United States are exempt from this provision, but many more countries are included. As a Pentagon spokeswoman declared, practically every other country except those referred to above and those on the list of countries accused of aiding terrorists receive some type of military aid from the United States. Pursuant to this act, aid to thirty-five countries has been suspended.[20] Another provision of the anti-terrorism law allows the president to free any American who is in the custody of the court by "any necessary and appropriate means," including the use of the military. The European Union reacted to this policy by warning those nations wishing to join the organization to resist signing such agreements.[21] This in turn resulted in a strong response from Washington. At the time of this writing, it appears that those nations that wish to join NATO might be caught between the conflicting policies of Washington and Europe.

The Bush administration also "unsigned" the Rome treaty, a most unusual procedure. In its last days, the Clinton administration signed the treaty with no intention of presenting it to the Senate for ratification. On May 6, 2002 the Bush administration sent a letter to the Secretary General of the United Nations declaring that the Clinton administration's signing of the treaty establishing the court was no longer legally binding on the United States.[22] Ironically on the same day that the Bush administration sent the letter, Slobodan Milosevic, the former President of Yugoslavia, was being tried at The Hague by the International Tribunal for the Former Yugoslavia. He was indicted by this tribunal on May 27, 1999, charged with having planned and engaged in a campaign of terror and violence against civilians of Albanian origin in Kosovo. The former president was being tried on 60 counts of genocide, crimes against humanity, and war crimes—the very crimes for which the International Criminal Court has jurisdiction.[23]

Goldstone refuted Washington's stated excuse for not supporting the establishment of the new court, the allegation "that some renegade or malicious prosecutor might some day initiate unfounded political prosecutions against United States citizens" as "virtually impossible" because of the safeguards already set forth in the Rome treaty.[24] These include the requirement that a panel of three judges approve of each prosecution and the exemption from the court's jurisdiction of cases in which the country of the accused person has conducted a good-faith investigation of the alleged crime.

Washington's preference for situation-specific international criminal courts should be viewed in the broader context of its policy of exposing and calling for the punishment of those states regarded as its enemies that violate human rights and practice terrorism, while covering over and excusing from punishment its allies and friends for committing the same offenses or worse. Washington's policy with respect to these courts is generically the same as that illustrated in the previous chapters—exposing and calling for punishment for the communists and their allies that violate human rights and practice terrorism while covering over, supporting, and excusing from punishment friendly rightwing dictatorships. This policy violates the principle of universality, a norm that Goldstone argues is the "essence of justice." He put it this way: "A decent and rational person is offended that criminal laws should apply only to some people and not to others in similar situations."[25] He went on to say that he felt distinctly uncomfortable when in October 1994 in Belgrade, he was asked by the Serbian minister of justice why the United Nations had established a tribunal for the former Yugoslavia while it had not done so for Cambodia and Iraq. Why were the Serbs being treated differently? Was this an act of discrimination? The only answer Goldstone could think of was that the international community had to begin somewhere. However, "if there were no follow-through and if other equivalent situations in the future were not treated comparably, then the people of the former Yugoslavia could justifiably claim discrimination."[26]

Obviously, the Bush administration has no intention of using the International Criminal Court to prosecute suspected terrorists. It intends to establish special military tribunals for this purpose, an announcement that has sparked considerable controversy. Human rights advocates argued that the special courts would not only violate the civil liberties guaranteed under American law, but that they would breach international law guaranteeing fair treatment for prisoners of war, such as the Geneva Conventions.[27]

IN SEARCH OF AN APPROPRIATE RESPONSE TO TERRORISM

A general conclusion to draw from the past history illustrated in this book is that the war on terrorism should be modified and recast so that it does not result in the creation of more terrorists as a response to practices by states themselves that overshadow in magnitude and cruelty the very actions they purport to prevent or forestall. Nor should it be waged in such a way that it violates international law, moral principles, or human rights. Washington has the right, indeed the duty, to defend the United States against terrorism. The question arises as to how it should do this.

Ironically, the way the Bush administration has chosen to fight what it calls "the war on terrorism" is immoral, illegal, overly belligerent, and in many ways counterproductive. The irony arises in part because what the administration declares to be a war against terrorism is a partial war against the retail, lesser variety of the phenomenon. The much more lethal and horrible state terrorism is not only exempt from being targeted in the conflict, but it is given support as witnessed by the administration's aid programs for state terrorism in Colombia and Algeria. It is also ironic that the enemies in the two wars that the Bush administration has chosen to fight so far have been the past beneficiaries if not the past co-belligerents of previous administrations. The Mujahideen from which both al Qaeda and the Taliban originated received billions in aid from the Carter and especially the Reagan administrations. Washington and its Western allies aided the Saddam Hussein regime in the first Persian Gulf war against Iran, a war of aggression by a regime practicing state terrorism, to the point of helping that regime produce WMD. This possession was later used as a principal reason/excuse for invading Iraq, starting yet a third Persian Gulf war. The Reagan administration joined Saddam as a co-belligerent in his oil war against Iran by sinking half the Iranian navy and by putting the American flag on Kuwaiti vessels to protect them so that Kuwait could help Saddam finance his war against Iran.

The following are a few suggestions on the way Washington should defend itself against terrorism. Washington should convert its partial war against private terrorism to a program of opposition to terrorism in general by including state terrorism. This expanded program would require Washington to reverse its own historic policy of aiding those countries that practice state terrorism or repress human rights. It would punish those states that practice state terrorism or that support terrorists mainly by criticism or in extreme cases by treating them as pariah states..

The part of the new program designed to protect the United States against the immediate threat of private terrorism should be renamed, perhaps given the name "the defense against terrorism," rather than "the war on terrorism," because this new label better describes not only what should be done, but also what should not be done. The defense of the United States against terrorism should be carried on without resort to war. The two military adventures in Afghanistan and Iraq are proving to be counterproductive. They drag on and on after we are told that the major hostilities have ended, with enormous initial and continuing costs in wealth and American and foreign lives. Many civilians have been killed in these wars, thus stoking the anger of Arabs and Muslims, and helping to recruit more of them as terrorists. These adventures have stretched U.S. military forces thin, with the result that the Bush administration is considering increasing the size of the armed forces even more.[28] As indicated in the previous chapter, Washington's war against Iraq has strained its relations with its most important allies, increased the alienation of Arabs and Muslims, and soured relations with the world in general. The wars have wasted resources that could better be used for local defense against terrorism, education, Medicare, and aid to the poor both in this country and abroad. This has happened at a time when the Bush administration is successfully implementing its neo-conservative program of crippling the welfare state by implementing federal tax cuts that favor the rich but impoverish state and local government, undermining their ability to protect their citizens against terrorism.

The defense of the United States from terrorism without recourse to war has been called the "criminalization," of the conflict, *i.e.*, treating the terrorists like criminals.[29] Their actions "should be conceptualized as crimes, not acts of war, to which the proper response is criminal investigation and prosecution within a rule of law and legally mandated measures for preventing and deterring similar crimes."[30] This approach has appeal in that it would require that Washington adopt a defense against terrorism that does not involve the waging of war. But the downside is that it could demean the position of those who are fighting for a just cause and who do not target civilians. They would be treated as ordinary criminals. To treat them as prisoners of war would be more just. The Geneva Conventions provide a number of important protections for prisoners of war, among them the prohibition of psychological torture and the limiting of the information that prisoners need give to their captors to only their name, rank, and serial number. Washington has violated these standards. Secretary Rumsfeld has declared that the prisoners of war on Guantanamo Bay are being kept there mainly for the information that can be obtained from them. On the other hand, these conventions allow the keeping of the prisoners until the end of the war. We are told that "the war on terrorism" could last many years. The prisoners on Guantanamo are not given the protection afforded ordinary criminals by the criminal law code of the United States. They are not allowed the right of habeas corpus, and they are held without charges being made against them. This is the typical behavior of dictatorships. A scrupulously just system for these prisoners and others in like situation should be established. Washington should realize that the world is watching, including terrorists and those thinking of becoming terrorists.

The terrorists that Washington is hunting for are not ordinary criminals; typically they are highly motivated, religious people. The defense program adopted by Washington should include the willingness, when possible, to negotiate with these people. The refusal to negotiate, the demand for unconditional surrender, not only prolongs struggles, but it is based on the false premise that one side is all right, the other all wrong. To the bold affirmation by the Bush administration that "we do not negotiate with terrorists," the response is that "you already have." During the hostilities in Iraq, the Central Command negotiated with the People's Mujahideen, a group designated as terrorist by the State Department. An issue that could be negotiated is Washington's relationship with Israel, a close relationship that has fueled much of the hatred that the terrorists hold toward the United States. The military aid to Israel would certainly have to be stopped in any event if a policy of not aiding state terrorism were to be adopted.

The defense against terrorism advocated here would adopt many of the programs adopted by the Bush administration, but it would cast them in an international mold, with scrupulous regard for human rights, and with opposition to, not support for, state terrorists. Those adopted would include such measures as expanding and reforming intelligence agencies, creating and strengthening federal and local anti-terrorism agencies and programs, improving the security of airports and seaports, increasing the regulations on the transfer of money from country to country, cooperating in the sharing of intelligence about terrorists with other countries. To strengthen and to legitimize the defense, international institutions would be used, especially the International Atomic Energy Commission and the rest of the United Nations system. Terrorists would be tried by the International Criminal Court or similar international courts to be established. Convictions by such courts would lessen the hatred that will follow convictions by American courts, especially if they are military courts and especially if they use the death penalty. The Bush administration should join the International Criminal Court and stop the campaign it is waging against it. This campaign is prima facie evidence that the members of the administration believe that they themselves and some of their subordinates could be convicted in legitimate legal proceedings of war crimes, crimes against humanity, or genocide. A serious

> **Washington's campaign against the ICC is prima facie evidence that the members of the administration believe that they themselves and some of their subordinates could be convicted in legitimate legal proceedings of war crimes, crimes against humanity, or genocide.**

attempt should be made to raise the standard of living of the world's poor, including the providing of alternate education facilities for the poor Muslim boys who attend those madrasas that teach hatred of non-Muslims. The hatred referred to here must not be confused with the legitimate opposition to Western policies implemented at the expense of the Muslim and Arab worlds. The reference is rather to commands like those of Osama bin Laden: "kill Jews and Americans."

Preemption and Counter-proliferation: The Open Espousal of Aggression

Containment, deterrence, and nonproliferation served the country well during the Cold War. Their declared purpose was not to attack the Soviet Union or those seeking to produce WMD, but to deter the Soviets from attacking, contain their expansion, and prevent the spread of WMD peacefully by persuasion and pressure. True, Washington's behavior did not live up to the standards set by these declarations, but the invasions that did occur were accompanied by a list of excuses and rationalizations that did not include the assertion that we have the right in principle to invade. This Cold War policy contrasts in several significant ways with the strategic policy of the Bush administration as spelled out in the new National Security Strategy of the United States.

Completed in September, 2002, this document sets forth a "robust" policy in the struggle against "terrorism with a global reach," those states that support it, the proliferation of weapons of mass destruction, and the systems that would deliver these weapons to their chosen targets. Absent from the new National Security Strategy are the time honored strategies of deterrence, containment, and non-proliferation. In their place, the document substitutes preemption and counter-proliferation.[31] Both are, or certainly can be, aggressive policies that would put the initiation of hostilities in the hands of Washington. Counter-proliferation allows the use of force to dismantle weapons and their component parts. Preemption allows the initiation of war, what is traditionally called "aggression", by Washington. Some scholars refer to it as "preventive war." Professor Graham Allison of Harvard characterized it as being "illegitimate." Archbishop Renato Martino, the prefect of the Pontifical Council for Justice and Peace of the Vatican, told reporters that a preventive war is a "war of aggression" and therefore not a "just war."[32] Allison gave as an example of preventive war the Japanese attack on Pearl Harbor. The Japanese defendants before the International Military Tribunal for the Far East pleaded that their attack was in response to the American embargoes against Japan that were ruining the Japanese economy The tribunal rejected their argument and found 18 of the defendants guilty of aggression because of their complicity in the attack on Pearl Harbor.[33]

International law does accept self-defense as a legitimate reason for using force, but none of the reasons given by the Bush administration for attacking Iraq satisfy this requirement. The administration argued that the United States was in danger because Iraq possessed weapons of mass destruction and because the Iraqi regime had ties to al Qaeda. The third reason given by the administration, regime change, is not recognized by international law as a legitimate reason for initiating hostilities. Until now no WMD have been found in Iraq, and the evidence indicates that Iraq had no links to al Qaeda. But even if the WMD had been found and the links to al Qaeda had been discovered, the attack against Iraq would not have been legally justified. For such an attack to be justified, the initiator of the attack must show that there is an instant and overwhelming necessity for self-defense, leaving no other choice of the means of protection and no time for deliberation.[34] Certainly, the administration has not shown that there was an overwhelming necessity for the attack. It rushed to war, without attempting to initiate, much less exhaust, other ways of protecting the nation. The United Nations Charter (Article 33) seems to require that the parties to a dispute that could endanger peace first refer their problem to such processes as mediation even before they refer it to the Security Council. Moreover, the Charter (Article 51) suggests that the right of self-defense is justified only after "an armed attack has occurred."

Preemption and counter-proliferation are violations of international law and of the principles of morality as well. History offers numerous cases of invasions of Latin American countries by Washington. But the Bush administration has now made preemption a declared policy of the United States, a standard way of fighting the war on terrorism. Obviously, this is no way to carry on a project of defense—the policy raises questions as to whether the war on terrorism is intended in actuality to serve as an umbrella for the expansion of U.S. imperial presence abroad and to deepen the funding trough for the military industrial complex.

The adoption by the world's sole remaining superpower of the doctrines of preemption and counter-proliferation represents a severe setback for the development of international law. Reacting to the enormous amount of bloodshed and destruction caused by two world wars, the international community has been attempting to outlaw aggression and punish those responsible for it. The reaction has seen the establishment of the World Court, the Nuremberg War Crimes Tribunal, the International Military Tribunal for the Far East, and the International Criminal Court. International lawyers have even incorporated some of the principles of just war theory into their legal lexicon.[35]

If its motive is truly self-defense, Washington should not seek self-defense by means that would provide seeds which, when planted and cultivated, would produce a new crop of terrorists. This was the way the Cold War was fought. In pursuing its goal of defending against terrorism, Washington should not support a host of dictators who wage terrorist campaigns against or trample on the rights of their own citizens. And in particular, in relation to the populations most concerned in the present war on terrorism, Washington should not duplicate its activities in the Arab-Israeli conflict by supporting a democratic government that wages terror against the Palestinian Arabs. The war on terrorism is intimately connected with the Arab-Israeli struggle. Arab and Muslim terrorists have forged this connection by blaming the United States for its support of Israel, a country that practices state terrorism against an Arab people.

Washington must discover whether the bitterness that has resulted among Arabs and Muslims from Washington's support for state terrorism by Israel has been replicated both within and outside the Muslim world, due to its support for state terrorists elsewhere during the Cold War and more recently during the war on terrorism. If so, new policies that would decrease this bitterness should be adopted and old policies that increase it should be discontinued. Every effort should be made to prevent the creation of new crops of terrorists. Washington's policy toward Israel should be changed. Hamas' popularity can only be increased as the Palestinians see that the airplanes that bomb them are made in America, as are the bombs and missiles that kill them.

Other victims of Washington-aided terrorism are still conscious of the terror that was committed against them, and they could refocus the hatred produced by it to the United States. That the politico-moral climate that permitted atrocities to occur in Latin America during America's counterinsurgency wars is far from having dissipated is indicated by the fact that the perpetrators themselves—rather than seeking refuge from retribution for their crimes—feel free not only to proclaim them, but to demand belated payment for their outrages. In Guatemala, Nicaragua, and El Salvador, the "civil patrollers" and the Contras are demanding payment for the terrorism that they committed during the repression. President Alfonso Portillo of Guatemala is considering paying the civil patrollers in that country $2,600 apiece.[36] They have maintained their structures, and assassinations and death threats continue in this unfortunate country. Meanwhile, the victims of state terrorism in Guatemala have received essentially nothing as compensation for the terrorism inflicted on them. The peace agreements promised land and education for the majority Mayan peasants, the chief victims of the repression. This has not been done; even pilot projects that would improve their lot are behind schedule.

The American public should lend every effort to force Washington to adopt policies to ameliorate the suffering and to soothe the anger and bitterness of these victims.

Washington should try in every way to blunt the bitterness of the victims of the state terrorism that it has supported in the past. The American public should lend every effort to force Washington to adopt policies to ameliorate the suffering and to soothe the anger and bitterness of these victims. Washington's

actions overall to forestall or eliminate movements and even democratic governments committed to ameliorating the poverty of their citizens has raised the
question whether it owes the poor some compensation for supporting military
governments that prevented social change. Certainly Washington's culpability
exceeds that required for conviction under the Torture Victim Protection Act of
1992. As indicated in Chapter One, the law allows victims or their surviving
relatives to sue those who knew of crimes of torture or the probability of their
occurring, and who could have stopped them, but took no action to do so. Two
retired generals were tried and convicted in Florida under the act for state terrorism that occurred during their dictatorship in El Salvador. Undoubtedly, at minimum,
many more could be similarly tried.

    Washington seems to be oblivious to addressing the injustices gener-
ated by past U.S. policy, absorbed as it is with its own "war on terrorism" directed
at the Middle East. President Bush's resolve to capture the terrorists and bring
them to justice is compartmentalized and exclusive. It does not include the members of the death squads in Guatemala, nor Generals Pinochet and Suharto and
the other military officers, former state terrorists, who are enjoying their retirement
with their families in their own countries or in the sunshine of Southern Florida.
They will not be hunted down to be caught dead or alive, or even brought to justice.
In fact, their terrorist activities will not be exposed by Washington unless its policy
changes. This exemption from justice could reasonably be presumed to increase
the resentment and bitterness of the surviving victims of state terrorism against
their former rulers and also against the United States in the many cases in which
Washington served as an accomplice to the state terrorists. This exemption by
definition is ironic, but more importantly, it is unjust, and it could be the source of
future terrorism against the United States. I would target, at least for purposes of
investigation, exposure, and possible trial, the wholesale state terrorists for the
purpose of attaining justice and so as to prevent the possible creation of more
retail terrorists who would terrorize the United States.

A TRUTH COMMISSION FOR WASHINGTON

    The American public is generally unaware that Washington aids state
terrorists, an ignorance somewhat similar to that of the publics in countries where
rightwing dictators practiced state terrorism. Usually, state terrorism took place in
secret, and often what the state did was blamed on the guerrillas. This ignorance
of what happened was nowhere more evident than in South Africa. As Archbishop
Tutu pointed out, the townships that housed the blacks were usually out of sight
of the whites who lived in their affluent suburbs.[37] It was inconvenient for whites to
visit a black township. Some did, but the great majority preferred to remain in their
privileged, segregated suburbs. The geographic distance that separated these
whites from the black victims of state terrorism is nothing like that which sepa-
rates the American public from the victims of the state terrorism supported by
Washington. Nonetheless, the levels of ignorance of these whites and the American public were similar until the publication of the truth commission report for
South Africa. The existence of "the free press" in the United States has not made
up for the lack of a truth commission nor obviated the need for the establishment
of such a commission. The ignorance of the American public is fed by
Washington's narrow, self-serving definition of terrorism that excludes state terrorism from coverage. This definition is picked up by the media, applied to the
news, and distributed to the American public.

Another factor is the widespread belief in the myth of American "exceptionalism," a central feature of the socialization process in the United States: that the U.S. acts in the world not out of selfish interests, but as a force for good. During the Cold War this myth was used to find a congruence between Washington's interests and human rights observance, or as usually put, with "democracy."[38] Those regimes that promoted the interests of Washington's elites, the anti-communists, were by definition, "democratic," or at least, purported not to be tyrannical. Firm believers in the myth find it hard to believe, as an instance, that the elites in Washington tried to initiate the massacre of the Indonesian Communist Party and its sympathizers—that these elites did everything in their power to encourage Suharto to commit this barbaric act. Not a single one of the officials in Washington or Djakarta questioned the policy on either ethical or political grounds. Quite the contrary.

Some twenty-one truth commissions have been established in different parts of the world.[39] In these cases post-terrorist governments, the United Nations, the Catholic Church, or some other institution has sided with the ideologues of memory, who would have us remember the crimes committed by terrorist governments. Those who established these commissions disagree with the partisans of oblivion who, on the contrary, bid us to forget. Their logo is "forgive and forget." The logo of the partisans of memory is "remember so as not to repeat."

A preliminary step, they remind us, is to find out what happened. The truth commissions have been established to find out the truth, to find new truth, to lift the veil of denial about widely known but unspoken truths, or, more cynically, to narrow the range of permissible lies.[40] I am suggesting the establishment of yet another truth commission, because the American public needs to know what has been done in its name. The proposed truth commission should include a number of academicians with a knowledge of the subject matter. But public hearings should be held and other means employed so as to publicize the activities of the commission and its findings. The commission's work should not become an essentially academic exercise, as seems to have been the case with Germany's commission. It should have access to the relevant documents and the needed resources, necessary for the extensive research it would be required to undertake. Its findings should be well publicized. The public should be educated as to what its governments have done. What is needed is full disclosure with adequate ventilation of the bleaker side of Washington's policies and actions since 1945, exposed and repeated so that the American people will realize what has been done in their name.

Knowledge is the first step toward contrition and the determination not to repeat and to prevent others from repeating. It is the first step in deciding to change directions for one's self and thereby providing greater legitimacy for one's insistence that others do so as well.

Endnotes

INTRODUCTION

[1] These words were first written by Cardinal Arns, Archbishop of Sao Paulo (Joan Dassin, *Torture in Brazil: A Report by the Archdiocese of Sau Paulo*. Vintage, New York,1986 : XXVIII), and I echo them here with great love for my country.

[2] *New York Times*, January 7, 2002, p. A8.

[3] Frederick H. Gareau, *The United Nations and Other International Institutions: A Critical Analysis*. Chicago, Burnham, 2002, pp. 244-250.

[4] *New York Times*, January 12, 2002, p. A7.

[5] *New York Times*, July 17, 2002, p. A5.

[6] *New York Times*, August 27 2002, p. A3.

[7] *New York Times*, September 13, 2002, p. A6.

[8] *New York Times*, October 18, 2001, p. B3.

[9] *New York Times,* January 22, 2002, p .A11.

[10] *New York Times*, June 14, 2002, p. A10.

[11] *Truth and Reconciliation Commission of South Africa Report*. Volume 2. London, Macmillan, 1999, p.189.

[12] Michael McClintock, *Instruments of Statescraft: U.S. Guerilla Warfare, Counter Insurgency, and Counter-terrorism, 1940-1990*. New York. Pantheon Books, 1992, p. 309.

[13] Alex P. Schmid and Albert J. Jongman, *Political Terrorism: A New Guide to Actors, Authors, Concepts, Data Bases, Theories, and Literature*. Amsterdam. North Holland Publishing Co. 1988.

[14] Martin Meredith, *Coming to Terms: South Africa's Search for Truth*, New York, Public Affairs, 1999, p. 293.

[15] *New York Times*, November 13, 2001, p. B5.

[16] *New York Times*, January 15, 2002, p. A9.

[17] *New York Times*, September 25, 2001, p. A6.

[18] *The New Encyclopedia Britanica*. Vol 20, *Macropedia*. p. 524.

[19] Martin Caidin, *The Night Hamburg Died*. New York. Ballantine Books, 1960 p.65.

[20] *New York Times*, January 18, 2003, p. A17.

CHAPTER 1: The School of the Americas and Terrorism in El Salvador

[1] Michael McClintock, *The American Connection:* Vol. II. *State Terror and Popular Resistance in Guatemala*. London. Zed Books, 1985, p. 30.

[2] Michael McClintock, *Instruments of Statescraft: U.S. Guerrilla Warfare, Counter Insurgency, and Counter-terrorism, 1940-1990*. New York. Pantheon Books, 1992, p. 175.

[3] McClintock, 1992:236.

[4] McClintock, 1992:445.

[5] McClintock, 1992:232.

[6] McClintock, 1992:234.

[7] McClintock, 1985:210.

[8] McClintock, 1985:214.

[9] *New York Times*, March 16, 1993, p. A7.

[10] McClintock, 1985:382.

[11] *A Global Agenda, Issues before the 47th General Assembly of the United Nations*. University Press of America. New York. 1992, p.68.

[12] *The United Nations and El Salvador 1990-1995*. The United Nations Blue Book Series, Vol. IV. Department of Public Information. United Nations, New York, p. 38

[13] Thomas Buergenthal, "The United Nations Truth Commission for El Salvador," *Vanderbuilt Journal of Transnational Law*, Vol. 27, No. 3, October, 1994, p. 517.

[14] *The Peace Process in El Salvador*. Hearing before the Subcommittee on Western Hemisphere Affairs of the Committee on Foreign Affairs. House of Representatives. One Hundred Third Congress. First Session. U.S. Government Printing Office. Washington. 1993, pp.1-2.

[15] *The Peace Process in El Salvador*, pp. 25-26.

[16] *The Peace Process in El Salvador*, p. 29.

[17] *United Nations Chronicle*, Vol. 24, No. 4, December 1992, p. 35.

[18] Buergenthal, 1994:543.

[19] *From Madness to Hope: the Twelve Year War in El Salvador. Report of the Commission on the Truth for El Salvador*. New York. United Nations, 1993, p. 43.

[20] Buergenthal, 1994:528.

[21] Jack Nelson-Pallmeyer, *School of Assassins*. Maryknoll. Orbis Books, 1997, p. 7.

[22] *From Madness to Hope*, pp. 115-116.

[23] *From Madness to Hope*, p.29.

[24] McClintock, 1992:385.

[25] McClintock, Vol.1,1985:206.

[26] *From Madness to Hope*, p.137.

[27] Nelson-Pallmeyer, 1997:7.

[28] McClintock, 1985, Vol.1, pp. 262-263.

[29] *From Madness to Hope*, p.128.

[30] McClintock, 1985:355, footnote 54.

[31] McClintock, 1985:264.

[32] *From Madness to Hope*, p. 66.

[33] *From Madness to Hope*, p. 218.

[34] *From Madness to Hope*, p. 218.

[35] *From Madness to Hope,* p. 218.

[36] *The Peace Process in El Salvador,* p.11.

[37] *New York Times*, Nov. 4, 2000, p. A4.

[38] *New York Times*, November 4, 2000, p.1.

[39] *New York Times*, July 24, 2002, p. A8.

[40] *National Catholic Reporter*, August 2, 2002, p.14.

[41] *New York Times*, June 26, 2002, p. A6.

[42] McClintock, 1992:303. The latter type of operation has discrete and unmistakable boundaries, usually well-defined objectives and time limits, and is thus much easier to oversee. An example would be if U.S. special forces would plan, implement, and supervise their own operation, or even if they would teach their own forces counterinsurgency.

[43] *New York Times*, March 16, 1993, p. A7.

[44] *New York Times*, March 9, 1999, p. A10.

CHAPTER 2: Guatemala: A Country Incommunicado

[1] Philip S. Taylor, Jr., "The Guatemalan Affair; A Critique of United States Foreign Policy," *The American Political Science Review*, Vol. L, No.3. Sept., 1956, p. 793.

[2] McClintock, 1992, p. 139.

[3] Ronald M. Schneider, *Communism in Guatemala 1944-1954*. New York. Praeger, 1959:311.

[4] McClintock, 1985, p. 29.

[5] *REMHI. Recovery of Historical Memory Project*. Maryknoll. Orbis, 1999. Since this publication was not available to the author, use was made of a summary of it, entitled *Guatemala Never Again*.

[6] *Guatemala: Memory of Silence. Report of the Commission for Historical Clarification: Conclusions and Recommendations*. Science and Human Rights Program of the American Association for the Advancement of Sciences. Washington, D.C. 1999. Conclusions, paragraph 1. References to this report are hereafter denominated *Guatemala: Memory of Silence*.

[7] *Guatemala: Never Again*, p. 290.

[8] *Guatemala: Memory of Silence*, para. 21.

[9] *Guatemala: Never Again*, p. 296.

[10] *Guatemala: Memory of Silence*, para. 134.

[11] *Guatemala, Memory of Silence*, para..134.

[12] *Guatemala: Memory of Silence,* para. 87.

[13] Ricardo Falla, *Massacres in the Jungle: Ixcan, Guatemala 1975-1982*, Boulder, Westview,1994, p.180.

[14] *Guatemala: Memory of Silence,* para. 61.

[15] *Guatemala: Memory of Silence*, para. 88.

[16] *Guatemala: Never Again*, pp. 48-49.

[17] *Guatemala: Memory of Silence*, para. 65.

[18] *Guatemala: Never Again*, p. 56.

[19] *Guatemala: Memory of Silence*, para. 67.

[20] *Guatemala: Never Again*, p. 30.

[21] *Guatemala: Never Again*, p. 30.

[22] *Guatemala: Never Again*, p. 33.

[23] *Guatemala: Never Again*, p. 80.

[24] *Guatemala: Never Again*, pp. 73-74.

[25] *Guatemala: Never Again*, p. 298.

[26] Guatemala: Never Again, p. 79.

[27] *Guatemala Never Again*, pp. 152-153.

[28] *Guatemala: Never Again*, p. 128.

[29] *Guatemala: Never Again*, p. 130.

[30] *Guatemala: Never Again*, p.131.

[31] *Guatemala: Memory of Silence*, para. 42.

[32] *Guatemala: Never Again*, pp.127-128.

[33] *Guatemala Never Again*, p. 289.

[34] *Guatemala: Never Again*, p. 299.

[35] *Options for United States Policy toward Guatemala*. Hearings before the Subcommittee on Western Hemisphere Affairs of the Committee of Foreign Affairs. House of Representatives. One Hundred First Congress, second session July 17, 1990. Washington D.C. 199, p. 4.

[36] *Options for United States Policy toward Guatemala*, pp.116-117.

[37] Hector Gros Espiell, the expert on Guatemala of the United Nations Commission on Human Rights, in a 1990 report to that commission presented a very pessimistic picture of the situation in Guatemala at that time and during the immediately preceding years, during the time that Gramajo held high position in the army. Espiell saw this situation in the same light as Professor Heymann. He complained of the "insupportable gulf between law and reality." The United Nations Human Rights Commission in its report on Guatemala in the same year deplored the many human rights violations that had occurred in the country, expressed profound concern at the reappearance of death squads, and called upon the Guatemalan government to initiate or to intensify investigations so as to bring to justice those responsible for disappearances, torture, murder, and extra-legal executions (*Issues before the 46th General Assembly of the United Nations.* D.C. Heath, Lexington, 1991. pp.195-196.)

[38] *Options for United States Policy toward Guatemala*, pp.112-113.

[39] *Options for United States Policy toward Guatemala*, pp.108-109.

[40] *Options for United States Policy toward Guatemala*, p.108.

[41] *Guatemala: Memory of Silence*, para.121.

[42] *Guatemala: Memory of Silence*, para.113.

[43] *Guatemala: Memory of Silence*, para.122.

[44] *Guatemala: Never Again*, p. 80.

[45] *Guatemala: Never Again*, p. 292.

[46] This reticence and the caveat raise the issue of intentions, a difficult aspect of the genocide debate. Those interested in pursuing this issue are directed to examine them in *Genocide: Conceptual and Historical Dimensions*, edited by George J. Andreopolous (Philadelphia, University of Pennsylvania. 1994).

[47] Michael McClintock, 1985, p. 257.

[48] *Guatemala: Never Again*, pp. 46-47.

[49] *Guatemala: Memory of Silence*, para. 36.

[50] *Guatemala: Memory of Silence*, para.13.

[51] *Guatemala: Never Again*, p.198.

[52] *Guatemala: Never Again*, p.111.

[53] *Options for United States Policy toward Guatemala*, p.155.

[54] *Guatemala: Never Again*, p. 211.

[55] Pietro Gleijeses, "Grappling with Guatemala's Horror," *Latin American Research Review*. Vol.32, No.1, 1997, p. 233.

[56] *Guatemala: Memory of Silence*, para. 122.

[57] *Political Killings by Governments.* Amnesty International Report. 1983, p.32.

[58] *Political Killings by Governments.* Amnesty International Report. 1983, p. 33.

[59] *New York Times*, March 11, 1999, p. A26.

[60] *New York Times*, March 11, 1999, p. 1.

[61] Kathy Ogle, "Guatemala's REMHI Project: Memory from Below," *NACLA Report on the Americas*, Vol. XXX11, No. 2, Sept, Oct 1998, p. 33.

[62] *New York Times*, October 23,1998, p. A3.

[63] *New York Times*, March 26, 1999, p. A6.

[64] *New York Times*, May 9, 1998, p. A3.

[65] *New York Times*, October 9, 2002, p. A10.

[66] *New York Times*, July 19, 2002, p . A20.

[67] *New York Times*, November 9, 2002, p. A6.

[68] *New York Times*, February 25, 2003, p. A3.

[69] *New York Times*, February 27, 2003, p. A8.

[70] *New York Times,* August 19, 2002, p. A7.

[71] *New York Times,* August 19, 2002, p. A7.

[72] *New York Times*, May 3, 2002, p. A5.

[73] *New York Times*, January 18, 2003, p. A5

CHAPTER 3: Chile: The Forgotten Past Is Full of Memory

[1] Mark Ensalaco, *Chile Under Pinochet: Recovering the Truth.* Philadelphia, University of Pennsylvania, 2000, p. 203.

[2] *CIA Activities in Chile*, September 18, 2000. http:/www.cia/publications/chile/index.html.

[3] *CIA Activities*, p. 3

[4] Edy Kaufman, *Crisis in Allende's Chile: New Perspectives.* New York. Praeger. 1988, p.141.

[5] *CIA Activities*, p. 2.

[6] *CIA Activities*, p. 7.

[7] *CIA Activities*, pp. 3-4.

[8] *CIA Activities*, p6.

[9] *New York Times*, February 25, 2003, p. A6.

[10] *CIA Activities*, p.12.

[11] Kaufman, 1988:12.

[12] Kaufman, 1988:11.

[13] Kaufman, 1988:118

[14] Kaufman, 1988:117.

[15] Mary Helen Spooner, *Soldiers in a Narrow Land: the Pinochet Regime in Chile.* Berkeley, University of California Press, 1994, p. 23.

[16] Ensalaco, 2000:3.

[17] *Report of the Chilean National Commission on Truth and Reconciliation.* Notre Dame University, 1993. Translated by Phillip E. Berryman, p. 147. References below will be to the translator's name.

[18] Jorge Correa revealed that his fellow countrymen took pride in the long history of their dedication to democratic institutions and contrasted this dedication to the history of the "banana republics" in the region (Jorge Correa, "Dealing with Past Human Rights Violations: The Chilean Case After Dictatorship," *The Notre Dame Law Review*, Vol. 67, 1992, Issue 5, pp.1457-1464, as found in Neil J. Kritz, editor, *Transitional Justice: How Emerging Democracies Reckon with Former Regimes.* Washington D.C. United States Institute of Peace. 1995. Vol. 2, p.494.

[19] Berryman, 1993:64.

[20] Berryman, 1993:57.

[21] Berryman, 1993:79-80.

[22] Berryman, 1993:67.

[23] Berryman, 1993:453.

[24] Correa, 1995:456.

[25] Correa, 1995:463.

[26] Ensalaco, 2000: 204.

[27] Berryman, 1993:632.

[28] Luis Roniger and Mario Sznajder, *The Legacy of Human Rights Violations in the Southern Cone: Argentina, Chile, and Uruguay.* Oxford, Oxford University Press, 1999, p. 214.

[29] Ensalaco, 2000:226-227.

30 Berryman, 1993, Tables 1 to 9, pp. 899-904.
31 Berryman, 1993:679.
32 Berryman, 1993:679.
33 Berryman, 1993:453.
34 Berryman, 1993:621
35 Berryman, 1993, Table7, p. 902.
36 Berryman, 1993:778
37 Berryman, 1993, Table 9, p. 904.
38 Berryman, 1993:497.
39 Berryman, 1993:59.
40 Berryman, 1993:472.
41 Berryman, 1993:472.
42 Spooner, 1994:115.
43 *CIA Activities*, p. 5.
44 Edy Kaufman, 1998:118.
45 *CIA Activities*, pp.11-12.
46 Spooner, 1994:114.
47 Berryman, 1993:60.
48 Berryman, 1993:637.
49 Berryman, 1993:499.
50 Berryman, 1993:637.
51 Berryman, 1993:501.
52 Berryman, 1993:486.
53 Marc Cooper, *Pinochet and Me: A Chilean Anti-Memoir*. London, Verso. 2001, p.137.
54 Berryman, 1993:504.
55 Berryman, 1993:465.
56 Berryman, 1993:629
57 Berryman, 1993:762.
58 Berryman, 1993:461.
59 Berryman, 1993:756-757.
60 Berryman, 1993:461
61 Berryman, 1993:628.
62 *CIA Activities*, p.12.
63 *CIA Activities*, p.13.
64 *CIA Activities*, pp. 13-14.
65 *CIA Activities*, p. 14.
66 *CIA Activities*, p. 5.
67 Berryman, 1993:632.
68 Hugo Fruhling, "Determinants of Gross Human Rights Violations by State and State-sponsored Actors in Chile 1960-1990," pp. 391 ff. of Wolfgang S Heinz and Hugo Fruhling, *Determinants of Gross Human Rights Violations by State and State-sponsored Actors in Brazil, Uruguay, Chile, and Argentina*. The Hague, Martinus Nijhoff, 1999, p. 496.
69 Berryman, 1993:632.
70 Ensalaco, 2000:157.
71 Spooner, pp.111-112.
72 Jack Donnelly, *International Human Rights*. Boulder. Westview Press, 1993:126-131.
73 *New York Times*, May 8, 2002, p. A7.
74 Hugh O'Shaughnessy, *Pinochet: the Politics of Torture*. Washington Square,

New York University, 2000, p.1
75 *NACLA: Report of the Americas*, Vol.XXX11, No.6, May-June, 1999, p.19.
76 *New York Times*, December 10, 2001, p. A3.

CHAPTER 4: Argentine's Dirty War

1 Mark Falcoff, "Argentina Under the Junta, 1976-1982," chapter 8 of *Friendly Tyrants: An American Dilemma*, edited by Daniel Pipes and Adam Garfinkle. New York, St. Martin's Press, 1991, p. 169.

2 Iain Guest, *Behind the Disappearances: Argentina's Dirty War Against Human Rights and the United Nations*. Philadelphia. University of Pennsylvania, 1990, p. 298.

3 Guest, 1990:354.

4 Guest, 1990:336.

5 *A Report by Argentina's National Commission on Disappeared Persons*. London, Faber and Faber, 1986. This is the English translation of *Nunca Mas* written by CONADEP. It is hereafter referred to as *Nunca Mas* (Never Again).

6 Alison Brysk, *The Politics of Human Rights in Argentina: Protest, Change, and Democratization*. Stanford. Stanford University. 1994, p.69.

7 *Nunca Mas*, 1986:445.

8 *Nunca Mas*, 1986:436.

9 *Nunca Mas: Informe de la Comission Nacional Sobre la Desaparicion de Personas*. Buenos Aires, Editorial Universitaria de Buenos Aires. 1986, p.481. Hereafter referred to as *Nunca Mas*.

10 Wolfgang S Heinz, "Determinants of Gross Human Rights Violations by State and State-sponsored Actors in Argentina 1976-1983," in Heinz and Fruhling, pp. 595 ff.

11 *Nunca Mas*, 1986:7.

12 Heinz, 1999:600.

13 *Nunca Mas*, 1986:26.

14 *Nunca Mas*, 1986:11.

15 *Nunca Mas*, 1986:347.

16 *Nunca Mas*, 1986:480.

17 *Nunca Mas* (Never Again), 1986: 67.

18 *Nunca Mas* (Never Again), 1986:72.

19 Heinz, 1999:648-649.

20 *Nunca Mas*, 1986:259.

21 Heinz, 1999:662.

22 Heinz, 1999:663.

23 *Nunca Mas*, 1986: 7.

24 *Nunca Mas*, p. 248.

25 *Nunca Mas*, p. 15.

26 *Nunca Mas* (Never Again), 1986:221.

27 *Nunca Mas* (Never Again), 1986:221-222.

28 *Nunca Mas* (Never Again), 1986:228-229.

29 Joseph S. Tulchin, *Argentina and the United States: A Conflicted Relationship*. Boston. Twayne Publishers, 1990, p.112.

30 Guest, 1990:278.

31 Heinz, 1999:697.

32 Tulchin, 1990:116.

33 *Nunca Mas* (Never Again), 1986:442.

[34] Heinz, 1999:689.
[35] Heinz, 1999:614.
[36] Tulchin, 1990:112.
[37] *Nunca Mas* (Never Again), 1986:443.
[38] Heinz, 1999:694.
[39] Heinz, 1999:699.
[40] Guest, 1990:350.
[41] Guest, 1990:351.
[42] Guest, 1990:352.
[43] Guest, 1990:389.
[44] Guest, 1990:278.
[45] *The Guardian*, December 6, 2003.

CHAPTER 5: South Africa, Apartheid and Terror

[1] Gwendolen M. Carter, "South Africa: Background of Rival Nationalisms." Chapter 3 of in Gwendolen M. Carter and Patrick O'Meara, eds., *Southern Africa in Crisis.* Bloomington. Indiana University, 1977, p.101.
[2] Carter, p. 117.
[3] *Truth and Reconciliation Commission of South Africa Report*. London, Macmillan, 1999, Volume 5, p. 228. It is hereafter referred to as TRCR, with respective volumes.
[4] Desmond Mpilo Tutu, *No Future without Forgiveness*. New York. Doubleday. 1999, p. 222.
[5] TRCR, Vol. 2, p. 325.
[6] TRCR, Vol.1, p. 54.
[7] TRCR, Vol.1, p. 12.
[8] TRCR, Vol.1, p. 168.
[9] TRCR, Vol. 5, pp.196-197.
[10] TRCR, Vol.3, p. 3.
[11] TRCR, Vol. 5, p. 212.
[12] TRCR, Vol. 5, p. 215.
[13] Martin Meredith, *Coming to Terms: South Africa's Search for Truth.* New York, Public Affairs, 1999, p. 183.
[14] Meredith, 1999:48.
[15] Meredith, 1999:48.
[16] TRCR, Vol. 5, p. 264.
[17] TRCR, Vol. 5, p. 264.
[18] TRCR, Vol. 5, p. 222.
[19] TRCR, Vol. 5, p. 278
[20] Meredith, p. :292.
[21] TRCR, Vol. 5, p. 230.
[22] TRCR, Vol. 5, p. 239.
[23] TRCR, Vol. 5, p. 244.
[24] Meredith, 1999:274-275.
[25] Meredith, 1999:277.
[26] Meredith, 1999:277.
[27] Meredith, 1999:278.
[28] TRCR, Vol. 2, p. 696.
[29] TRCR, Vol. 5, p. 249.
[30] TRCR, Vol. 5, p. 253.

[31] TRCR, Vol. 5, pp. 232-233.

[32] TRCR, Vol.2, pp. 326-327.

[33] TRCR, Vol. 3, p. 7.

[34] TRCR, Vol. 2, p.187.

[35] Don Foster, *Detention and Torture in South Africa: Psychological, Legal, and Historical Studies*. New York, St. Martin's Press, 1987, p.103.

[36] TRCR, Vol. 2, p.190.

[37] Foster, p. 104.

[38] Meredith, p. 119.

[39] Foster, 1987:105.

[40] TRCR, Vol. 2, p. 330.

[41] TRCR, Vol. 2, p. 188.

[42] TRCR, Vol. 2, p. 194.

[43] Meredith, 1999:119.

[44] TRCR, Vol. 2, p. 192

[45] Meredith, 1999:122.

[46] TRCR, Vol. 2, pp. 192-3.

[47] Meredith, 1999:123.

[48] William Minter, "Destructive Engagement, the United States and South Africa in the Reagan Era", Chapter 10 of *Frontline Southern Africa*, edited by Phyllis Johnson and David Martin. Peterborough, Ryan,1989, p. 390.

[49] William Minter, *King Solomon's Mines: Western Interests and the Burdened History of Southern Africa*. New York, Basic Books, 1986, p.3 44.

[50] Minter,1986:132.

[51] David F. Schmitz, *Thank God They're On Our Side: The United States and Right-Wing Dictatorships, 1921-1965*. Chapel Hill University of North Carolina, 1999, p. 148.

[52] Minter 1986:135.

[53] Abdul S. Minty, "South Africa's Nuclear Capability, the Apartheid Bomb," chapter 7 of *Frontline Southern Africa*, edited by Phyllis Johnson and David Martin. Peterborough, Ryan,1989, p. 284.

[54] Thomas Borstelmann, *Apartheid's Reluctant Uncle: the United States and Southern Africa in the Early Cold War*. New York, Oxford University, 1993, p.197.

[55] Borstelmann, 1993:204.

[56] Minter, 1986:135.

[57] Christopher Coker, *The United States and South Africa, 1968-1985: Constructive Engagement and Its Critics*. Durham, Duke University, 1986, p. 4.

[58] Minter, 1986:190.

[59] Minter, 1986:138.

[60] Minter, 1986:159.

[61] Minter, 1986:160.

[62] Minter, 1986:161.

[63] Minter,1986:188.

[64] Minter, 1986:162.

[65] Minter, 1986:199.

[66] Minter, 1986:196.

[67] Coker, 1986:14.

[68] Minter, 1986:223.

[69] Minter, 1986:242.

[70] Coker, 1983:133.

[71] Minter, 1986:291.

[72] Coker, 1986:105.

[73] Minter, 1986:315.

[74] Minter, 1986:314.

[75] Desmond Mpilo Tutu, *No Future without Forgiveness*. New York. Doubleday. 1999, p. 237.

[76] Phyllis Johnson and David Martin, "Introduction" to *Frontline Southern Africa*, edited by Phyllis Johnson and David Martin. Peterborough, Ryan,1989, p xxv.

[77] *South African Destabilization: The Economic Cost of the Frontline Resistance to Apartheid.* United Nations. Economic Commission for Africa. United Nations. New York. October, 1989, p.15.

[78] TRCR, Vol. 2, p. 9.

[79] TRCR, Vol. 2, p. 16.

[80] Abdul S. Minty, "South Africa's Military Build-up: the Region at War," chapter 6 of Johnson and Martin., p 239.

[81] Coker, 1986:205.

[82] Minter, 1986:315.

[83] Minter, "Destructive Engagement," 1989:400.

[84] Pauline Baker, *The United States and South Africa: the Reagan Years.* Ford Foundation, 1989, p.25.

[85] Baker, 1989:45.

[86] Baker, 1989:63.

[87] TRCR, Vol. 5, p. 257.

[88] TRCR, Vol. 5, p. 222.

[89] TRCR, Vol. 2, p. 43.

[90] TRCR, Vol. 2, p. 43.

[91] TRCR, Vol. 2, p. 73.

[92] TRCR, Vol. 2, p. 77.

[93] Economic Commission for Africa. United Nations. New York. October, 1989.

[94] United Nations Children's Fund. New York. January, 1987.

[95] *Children on the Frontline: the Impact of Apartheid, Destabilization and Warfare on the Children of Southern Africa.* United Nations Children's Fund. New York. January, 1987, p.1:

[96] *Children on the Front Line*, 1987, p. 9.

[97] Tom Brennan, *Refugees from Mozambique: Shattered Land, Fragile Asylum.* American Council for Refugee Nationalities, 1986, p. 2.

[98] *Children on the Front Line,* 1987, p. 1.

[99] *Children on the Front Line,* 1987, p. 2.

[100] *Children on the Front Line*, 1987, p. 1.

[101] *Children on the Front Line*, 1987, p. 10.

[102] The United Nations Interagency Task Force. Economic Commission for Africa. United Nations. New York. 1989.

[103] *South African Destabilization,* 1989:13.

[104] *South African Destabilization,* 1989:15.

[105] Baker,1989:58.

[106] *South African Destabilization*, 1989:15.

[107] Tom Brennan,1986:15.

[108] TRCR, Vol. 2, p. 510.

[109] TRCR, Vol. 2, p. 517.

[110] TRCR, Vol. 2, p. 517.

[111] Minty, "South Africa's Nuclear Capability, the Apartheid Bomb," p 283.

[112] Coker, 1986:212-213.

[113] Minty, "South Africa's Nuclear Capability, the Apartheid Bomb," pp.300-302.

[114] Fred Marte, *Political Cycles in International Relations: The Cold War and Africa 1945-1990.* Amsterdam, VU University Press, 1994, p. 278.

[115] Minty, "South Africa's Nuclear Capability, the Apartheid Bomb," 1989:302.

[116] TRCR, Vol. 2, p. 367.

CHAPTER 6: Indonesia: Three Series of Massacres

[1] Audrey R. and George McT. Kahin, *Subversion as Foreign Policy: The Secret Eisenhower and Dulles Debacle in Indonesia.* New York. The New Press, 1995, pp. 120, 128, 132.

[2] Kahin and Kahin, 1995:177.

[3] Kahin and Kahin, 1995:207.

[4] Kahin and Kahin, 1995:210.

[5] Kahin and Kahin, 1995:210.

[6] Peter Dale Scott, "The United States and the Overthrow of Sukarno, 1965-1967," *Pacific Affairs*, 58, Summer 1985, pp. 239-264.

[7] Gabriel Kolko, *Confronting the Third World: United States Foreign Policy 1945-1980.* New York. Pantheon, 1988, p.180.

[8] Harold Crouch, *The Army and Politics in Indonesia.* Ithaca, Cornell, 1978, p. 139.

[9] Damien Kingsbury, *The Politics of Indonesia.* Melbourne, Oxford, 1998, p. 57.

[10] Kolko, 1988:180-181.

[11] Kolko, 1988:181.

[12] Kahin and Kahin, p. 230.

[13] Kolko, 1988:181.

[14] Kolko, 1988:182.

[15] Matthew Jardine, *East Timor: Genocide in Paradise.*Tucson. Odonian Press, 1995, pp. 37-38.

[16] Justus M. van der Kroef, *Indonesia after Sukarno.* Vancouver. University of British Columbia, 1971, pp. 165-168.

[17] Crouch,1978:338.

[18] Kingsbury, 1998:3.

[19] Crouch, 1978:346.

[20] Crouch, 1978:224.

[21] Kingsbury, 1998:190.

[22] Kingsbury, 1998:71.

[23] Kingsbury, 1998:202.

[24] Schwartz, 2000:204.

[25] Robert Pringle, *Indonesia and the Philippines: American Interests in Island Southeast Asia.* New York. Columbia University, 1980, p.107.

[26] Allan Nairn, Foreword, pp.xxiv-xxv of Constando Pinto and Matthew Jardine, *East Timor's Unfinished Struggle: Inside the Timorese Resistance.* Boston. South End Press, 1997.

[27] Nairn, 1997: xxix-xxv.

[28] Pringle,1980:106.

[29] Pringle, 1980:106-107.

[30] Jardine, 1995:42.

[31] *Yearbook of the United Nations.* 1975, Vol. 29, p. 866.

[32] *Yearbook of the United Nations.* 1976, vol. 30, p. 754.

[33] *Yearbook of the United Nations.* 1978, vol. 32, p. 869.

[34] *Yearbook of the United Nations.* 1982. vol. 36, p. 1349.

[35] *Yearbook of the United Nations.* 1982. vol. 36, p. 1348.

[36] Schwartz, 2000:205.

[37] Nairn,1997: xiv.

[38] Jardine, 1995:74.

[39] Pinto and Jardine,1997:189.

[40] Nairn, 1997: xviii.

[41] Schwartz, 2000:213.

[42] Schwartz, 2000:223.

[43] Schwartz, 2000:224.

[44] Schwartz,2000,326.

[45] *New York Times*, August 30,1999, p. A3.

[46] *New York Times*, September 8, 1999, p. 1.

[47] *New York Times*, September 23, 1999, p. A21.

[48] *New York Times*, September 9, 1999, p. A8.

[49] *New York Times*, September 7, 1999, p. A8.

[50] *New York Times,* September 7, 1999, p. A8.

[51] *New York Times*, September 7,1999, p. A8.

[52] *New York Times,* September 19, 1999, p.12.

[53] *New York Times,* September 10, 1999, p. A10.

[54] *New York Times*, September 13, 1999, p. A6.

[55] *New York Times*, September 14, 1999, p. A14.

[56] *New York Times*, December 28, 2002, p. A7.

[57] *New York Times*, September 14, 1999, p. A14.

[58] *New York Times,* September 21, 1999, p. 1.

[59] *New York Times*, October 9, 1999, p. 1

[60] *New York Times*, August 3, 2002, p. A3.

[61] *New York Times*, May 2, 2002, p. A5.

[62] *New York Times*, January 24, 2002, p. A12.

CHAPTER 7: The Root Doctrine and Some Notorious Instances of U.S. Support for Dictators

[1] David F. Schmitz, *Thank God They're On Our Side: The United States and Right-Wing Dictatorships, 1921-1965.* Chapel Hill University of North Carolina, 1999.

[2] Schmitz, 1999:305.

[3] Ruth Wedgewood, Op. Ed., *Wall Street Journal*, December 16th, 2002.

[4] Schmitz, 1999:45.

[5] Id. Wedgewood refers to it in fact as the "Bush and Root" doctrine.

[6] Valdas Anelauskas, *Discovering America As It Is.* Atlanta. Clarity Press, Inc. 1999, pp.406-407.

[7] William R. Keylor, *The Twentieth Century World: An International History.* New York. Oxford, 1996, pp. 210-211.

[8] Schmitz, 1999:74.

[9] Schmitz, 1999:142.

[10] Schmitz, 1999:148.

[11] Audrey R. and George McT. Kahin, *Subversion as Foreign Policy: The Secret Eisenhower and Dulles Debacle in Indonesia.* New York. The New Press, 1995, p. 6.

[12] Peter Kornbluh, "Nicaragua", chapter 16, of Peter J. Schraeder, ed., *Intervention in the 1990's: U.S. Foreign Policy in the Third World*. Boulder. Lynne Rienner, 1992, p. 288.

[13] Kornbluh, 1992:289.

[14] Kornbluh, 1992:292.

[15] Kornbluh, 1992:296.

[16] *Everyone's United Nations*. United Nations. New York. 1986. p. 371.

[17] *Yearbook of the United Nations 1986*, Vol 40, United Nations. New York. 1986, p.982.

[18] *Yearbook of the United Nations 1986*, Vol 40, p.194.

[19] Sean Kelly, *America's Tyrant: The CIA and Mobutu of Zaire*. Washington, American University, 1993, p. 60.

[20] Kelly, 1993:71.

[21] Kelly, 1993:52.

[22] Kelly, 1993:2.

[23] Kelly, 1993:244.

[24] Kelly, 1993:17.

[25] Fred Marte, *Political Cycles in International Relations: The Cold War in Africa 1945-1990*. Amsterdam, VU University Press, 1994, p.178.

[26] Ben Kiernan, "The Cambodian Genocide: Issues and Responses," pp.191ff. of George J. Andreopolos, *Genocide: Conceptual and Historical Dimensions*. Philadelphia, University of Pennsylvania, 1994, p.191.

[27] Kiernan, 1994:207.

[28] *New York Times*, April 17,1998, p.13.

[29] Kiernan,1994:217.

[30] Michael Haas, *Cambodia, Pol Pot, and the United States: the Faustian Pact*. New York, Praeger, 1991, p. X11.

[31] Haas, 1991:15.

[32] Haas, 1991:30.

[33] Haas, 1991:98.

[34] *New York Times*, April 30,1998, p. A16.

[35] *New York Times*, April 19,1998, p.13.

[36] *New York Times*, April 20,1998, p. A1.

[37] *New York Times*, November 11, 2002, p. A6.

[38] *New York Times*, December 24, 2002, p. A11.

[39] *New York Times*, December 21, 2002, p. A35.

CHAPTER 8: The Historic Roots of the War on Terrorism

[1] Abdullah Samardar, *A Preliminary Mathematical Test for Dependency Theory*. A Dissertation submitted to the Political Science Department. Florida State University. December, 1985, p. 64.

[2] Eric Hoogland, "Iran", Chapter 17, in Schraeder, 1992:306.

[3] James A. Bill and Robert Springborg, *Politics in the Middle East*. New York. Harper, 1994, p.198.

[4] Hooglund, 1992:308.

[5] Samardar, 1985:125.

[6] Samardar, 1985:176.

[7] Hooglund, 1992:310.

[8] Samardar, 1985:172.

[9] Bill and Springborg, 1994:381.

[10] Bruce W. Jentleson, *With Friends Like These: Reagan, Bush, and Saddam 1982-1990.* New York. Norton, 1994, p. 39.

[11] Judith Miller and Laurie Mylroie, *Saddam Hussein and the Crisis in the Gulf.* New York. Times Books, 1990, p. 85.

[12] Miller and Mylroie, 1990:142.

[13] Miller and Mylroie, 1990:252.

[14] Miller and Mylroie, 1990:246.

[15] Miller and Mylroie, 1990:252-253.

[16] Miller and Mylroie, 1990:143.

[17] Gareau, 2002:215.

[18] Jentleson,1994:62-63.

[19] Jentleson,1994:69.

[20] Jentleson,1994:92.

[21] Bill and Springborg, 1994:387.

[22] Miller and Mylroie, 1990:74.

[23] *New York Times*, December 21, 2002, p. A10.

[24] Patrick L. Sloyan, "Undisclosed Connection / Scientist On Gulf War Syndrome Linked to Supplier of Iraqi Anthrax", *Newsday*, November 27, 1996.

[25] *New York Times*, January 28, 2003, p. A10

[26] Miller and Mylroie, 1990:75

[27] Miller and Mylroie, 1990:79.

[28] Jentleson, 1994:388

[29] Bill and Springborg, 1994:388.

[30] Martin Van Bruinessen, "Genocide in Kurdistan?: The Suppression of the Dersim Rebellion in Turkey (1937-1938) and the Chemical War Against the Iraqi Kurds (1998)," pp. 141 ff. of George J. Andreopolos, ed., *Genocide: Conceptual and Historical Dimensions.* Philadelphia, University of Pennsylvania, 1994, p.161.

[31] Van Bruinessen, 1994:161.

[32] Van Bruinessen, 1994:164.

[33] *New York Times*, December 11, 2002, p. A22.

[34] Gareau, 2002:216.

[35] Bill and Springborg, 1994:391.

[36] Cited in Ramsey Clark *et al.*, *War Crimes: A Report on the United States War Crimes Against Iraq.* Washington, D.C. Maisonneuve Press, 1997, p. 51.

[37] Gareau, 2002:219.

[38] *New York Times*, October 30, 2002, p. A12.

[39] L. Larry Leonard, "The United Nations and Palestine," International Conciliation, No. 454, October, 1949, pp. 627-628.

[40] Leonard, 1949: 738, 740.

[41] Chaim Herzog, *The Arab-Israeli Wars: War and Peace in the Middle East,* New York. Vintage, 1984, p.13.

[42] Bill and Springborg, 1994:309.

[43] Leonard, 1949:754.

[44] Deborah Gerner, *One Land, Two Peoples: The Conflict over Palestine,* Boulder. Westview,1991, p. 59.

[45] The former term refers to a group of people so categorized because of their distinctive religion, culture, ethnicity, and/or race. The state of Israel bases the distinctiveness of Jews on their religion, and Israel is a sectarian state. A Zionist is a Jew who is convinced that Jews have the "right to return" to Palestine and to establish a state there. Not all Jews are Zionists, although many of them are. One can be anti-Zionist or critical of Israel without being anti-Semitic.

[46] Benny Morris, *The Birth of the Palestinian Refugee Problem 1947-1949*, New York. Cambridge,1987 as quoted in Gerner, p. 53.

[47] Amnesty International, USA, *United States of America. Rights for All.* New York. 1998, p.128.

[48] *Everyone's United Nations*, United Nations, New York, 1986, p. 76.

[49] *Everyone's United Nations*, 1986, p. 76.

[50] *A Global Agenda, Issues before the 47th General Assembly*, p. 361.

[51] *A Global Agenda, Issues before the 45th General Assembly*, p. 23.

[52] *A Global Agenda, Issues before the 38th General Assembly*, p. 19.

[53] *New York Times,* September 16, 1982, quoting Dr. Witsoe, Gaza hospital.

[54] *Newsweek*, October 4, 1982, Ray Wilkinson; *The Guardian*, September 20, 1982; and *The New York Times*, September 26, 1982.

[55] *Jerusalem Post*, September 21, 1982.

[56] See the Israeli Ministry of Foreign Affairs website, http://www.mfa.gov.il/mfa/go.asp?MFAH0ign0.

[57] Edward W. Said, *The Question of Palestine*, New York. Vintage, 1992, p. 240.

[58] *United States of America. Rights for All.* 1998:128.

[59] Francis A. Boyle, *Palestine, Palestinians and International Law,* Clarity Press, Inc., Atlanta, 2003, pp. 178-200.

[60] Mark Gaffney, *Dimona the Third Temple? The Story Behind the Vanunu Revelation.* Brattleboro, Amana, 1989, p. 5.

[61] Leonard S. Spector, *Nuclear Ambition: The Spread of Weapons.* Boulder, Westview, 1990, pp. 160-161.

[62] Bill and Springborg, 1994:365.

[63] A Global Agenda, Issues before the 47th General Assembly, p. 44.

[64] A Global Agenda, Issues before the 48th General Assembly, p. 48.

[65] *New York Times*, April 6, 1998, p. A13.

[66] *New York Times*, March 22, 2000, p. A6.

[67] *New York Times,* March 6, 2003, p. A10.

[68] *New York Times,* February 4, 2003, p.A8.

[69] *New York Times*, May 1, 2003, p. A7.

[70] *New York Times*, May 14, 2003, p. A16.

[71] *New York Times*, May 27, 2003, p. A12.

[72] *New York Times,* September 11, 2002, p. A23.

[73] *New York Times,* October 12, 2002, p. A9.

[52] Limitations of space prevent any further discussions on the tangled relations between Washington and Arab client governments in the region, or governments related to other Muslim populations.

CHAPTER 9: The War on Terrorism

[1] *New York Times*, January 15, 2003, p. A10.

[2] Douglas Kellner, *From 9/11 to Terror War: the Dangers of the Bush Legacy.* Lanham. Rowman and Littlefield, 2003, p. 263.

[3] *New York Times*, February 2, 2002, p. A1

[4] *New York Times*, November 27, 2002, p. A12.

[5] *New York Times*, May 23, 2003, p. A19.

[6] *New York Times*, June 2, 2003, p. A20.

[7] *New York Times*, November 20, 2002, p. A1.

[8] *New York Times.* September 14, 2001, p. A17.

[9] *New York Times,* October 6, 2001, p. B5.

[10] *New York Times,* June 17, 2003, p. 27.

[11] *New York Times,* January 30, 2002, p. A1.

[12] Ibid. Whether this policy initiative was generated in response to September 11th, or in fact had been in existence earlier, in documents such as the White Paper produced in September of 2000 entitled "Rebuilding America's Defenses: Strategy, Forces and Resources for a New Century" by the Project for the New American Century, or PNAC, which has been claimed to be an ideological match, is a matter of current speculation.

[13] Angelo Rasanayagam, *Afghanistan, A Modern History: Monarchy, Despotism or Democracy. The Problems of Governance in the Muslim Tradition.* London. Tauris, 2003, p.105.

[14] Richard W. Miller, "Terrorism, War, and Empire," p.196 of James P. Sterba, *Terrorism and International Justice.* New York, Oxford University Press, 2003.

[15] Rasanayagam, 2003:222.

[16] Rasanayagam, 2003:141.

[17] Rasanayagam, 2003:171.

[18] Rasanayagam, 2003:170-171.

[19] Rasanayagam, 2003:143.

[20] James P. Sterba, "Terrorism and International Justice," chapter 11 of James P. Sterba, ed., *Terrorism and International Justice.* New York. Oxford University Press, 2003, pp.215-216.

[21] Richard W. Miller, "Terrorism, War, and Empire," chapter 10 of Sterba, 2003, p. 190.

[22] *New York Times,* April 25, 2003, p. A1.

[23] *New York Times,* May 28, 2003, p. A7.

[24] *New York Times,* June 4, 2003, p. A21.

[25] *New York Times* July 1, 2003, p. A23.

[26] *New York Times,* May 6, 2003, p. A14.

[27] *New York Times,* February 22, 2002, p. A12.

[28] *New York Times,* December 26, 2001, p. B1.

[29] *New York Times,* April 8, 2003, p. A11.

[30] Wesley L.Gould, *An Introduction to International Law.* New York, Harper and Brothers, 1957,. p. 638.

[31] *New York Times,* January 23, 2002, p. A1.

[32] *New York Times* April 23, 2003, p. A19.

[33] *New York Times,* June 17, 2003, p. A1.

[34] *New York Times,* March 4, 2003, p. A13.

[35] *New York Times,* November 13, 2001, p. B4.

[36] *New York* Times, October 27, 2001, p. B4.

[37] *New York Times,* June 24, 2003, p. A6.

[38] *New York Times,* July 2, 2003, p. C11.

[39] *New York Times,* October 29, 2001, p. A1.

[40] Gareau, 2002:203.

[41] *New York Times,* October 30, 2001, p. B4.

[42] *New York Times,* October 19, 2001, p. B3.

[43] *New York Times,* September 29, 2001, p. B6.

[44] Babak Dehghanpisheh, John Barry, and Roy Gutman, "The Death Convoy of Afghanistan," *Newsweek* , August 26, 2002, p. 22.

[45] *New York Times,* August 29, 2002, p. A12

[46] Dehghanpisheh, Barry, and Gutman, 2002, p. 24.

[47] *New York Times*, August 29, 2002, p. A12.
[48] *New York Times*, August 29, 2002, p. A12.
[49] *New York Times*, June 3, 2003, p. A14.
[50] *New York Times*, June 6, 2003, p. A1.
[51] *New York Times*, June 7, 2003, p. A9.
[52] *New York Times*, September 20, 2002, p. A1.
[53] *New York Times*, October 12, 2002, p. A1.
[54] *New York Times*, November 9, 2002, p. A9.
[55] http://www.wwws.org/articles/2003/mar2003/lawy-m22.shtml.
[56] http://www.wwws.org/articles/2003/mar2003/ilaw-m26.shtml
[57] http://www.wwws.org/articles/2003/feb2003/law-mf27.shtml.
[58] *The Florida Catholic,* September 19, 2002, p. 2.
[59] *New York Times*, November 14, 2002, p. A31.
[60] *New York Times*, October 9, 2002, p. A12.
[61] *New York Times*, January 29, 2003, p. A11.
[62] *New York Times*, October 5, 2002, p. A10.
[63] *New York Times*, March 6, 2003, p. A12.
[64] *New York Times*, February 21, 2003, p. A14.
[65] *The Florida Catholic*, February 27, 2003, p. A15.
[66] *New York Times*, January 14, 2003, p. A11.

CHAPTER 10: Conclusions and Recommendations

[1] Amnesty International USA, *United States of America. Rights for All.* New York. 1998, p. 135.
[2] *New York Times,* August 8, 2002, p. A8.
[3] *United States of America. Rights for All*: 1998:138-139.
[4] Lars Schoultz, "U.S. Foreign Policy and Human Rights Violations in Latin America: A Comparative Analysis of Foreign Aid Distributions." *Comparative Politics*. Vol 13, No. 2, January, 1981, p. 155.
[5] Schoultz, 1981:162.
[6] Michael Stohl, David Carleton, and Steven E. Johnson, "Human Rights and U.S. Foreign Assistance from Nixon to Carter," *Journal of Peace Research*. Vol. 21, No. 3, 1984, p. 217.
[7] Stohl, Carleton, and Johnson, 1984:215.
[8] No clear statistical pattern emerged for this administration. "Mr. Carter was not consistent in his application of principle." See Stohl, Carleton, and Johnson, 1984:224. This conclusion was reached whether Schoultz's statistical approach was employed or whether an approach designed for ordinal data was substituted. The same result was obtained no matter which of the three organizations' ratings was used.
[9] David Carleton and Michael Stohl, "The Foreign Policy of Human Rights: Rhetoric and Reality from Jimmy Carter to Ronald Reagan," *Human Rights Quarterly*, Vol. 7 #2, May, 1985, p. 215.
[10] Carleton and Stohl, 1985:216.
[11] Carleton and Stohl, 1985:218
[12] *New York Times*, April 12, 2002, p. A3.
[13] Richard J. Goldstone, *For Humanity: Reflections of a War Crimes Investigator.* New Haven, Yale University, 2000, p.133.
[14] *New York Times*, September 7, 2002, p. A4.

[15] *New York Times*, June 19, 2002, p. A3.

[16] *New York Times*, July 1, 2002, p. A3.

[17] *New York Times*, July 4, 2002, p. A1.

[18] *New York Times*, July 7, 2002, p. A1.

[19] *New York Times*, August 10, 2002, p. A1.

[20] *New York Times*, July 2, 2003, p. A8.

[21] *New York Times*, August 14, 2002, p. A11.

[22] *New York Times,* May 7, 2002, p. A9.

[23] *New York Times*, May 7, 2002, p. A5.

[24] Goldstone, 2000:129.

[25] Goldstone, 2000:122.

[26] Goldstone, 2000:123.

[27] *New York Times,* December 26, 2001, p. B1.

[28] *New York Times*, July 21,2003, p. A1.

[29] Douglas Kellner, *From 9/11 to Terror War: The Dangers of the Bush Legacy.* Lanham: Rowman and Littlefield, 2003, p. 3.

[30] Danielle Archibughi and Iris Marion Young, "Envisioning a Global Rule of Law," Chapter 8 of Sterba, 2003:161.

[31] *New York Times*, September 20, 2002, p. A1.

[32] *New York Times*, December 26, 2002, p. A12.

[33] Solis Horowitz, "The Tokyo Trial," *International Conciliation*, November, 1950, No. 465, p. 584.

[34] William W. Bishop, Jr., *International Law: Cases and Materials.* Boston, Little Brown, 1962, p. 778.

[35] Gould, 1957:606.

[36] *New York Times,* August 19, 2002, p. A7.

[37] Desmond Mpilo Tutu, *No Future without Forgiveness*, New York. Doubleday, 1999, p. 217.

[38] Jack Donnelly, *International Human Rights.* Boulder, Westview, 1993. p.101.

[39] Priscilla B Hayner, *Unspeakable Truths: Confronting State Terror and Atrocity.* New York, Routledge, 2001, p. 32.

[40] Hayner, 2001:25.

Index